THE CELL BLOCK PRESENTS...

THE BEST RESOURCE DIRECTORY FOR PRISONERS

TABLE OF CONTENTS

General Resources	1
Pro Bono Attorneys	134
Book Publishers	148
Literary Agents	153
Literary Pubs/Reviews	157
The Cell Block Book Shop	175
Behind The Wall	201
Free & Low-Cost Magazines	205
The Millionaire Prisoner Penpal Attraction System	220
A Case for Relapse Prevention	225
Free Money	228
Prisoner Success Story	231
Social Networking	233
OG Able Spread	256
The Mike Enemigo Story	270
Kim Kardashian: Attorney	278
The BEST Girls Spread	286

Published by: The Cell Block™

The Cell Block
P.O. Box 1025
Rancho Cordova, CA 95741

Website: thecellblock.net
Email: info@thecellblock.net
Instagram: @mikeenemigo
Facebook.com/thecellblock.net
Corrlinks: info@thecellblock.net

Copyright © 2022 by Mike Enemigo
Last Updated 06/17/2022

Cover Design: Mike Enemigo

Send comments, reviews, interview and business inquiries to:
info@thecellblock.net

A Letter From The Cell Block:

Despite being sentenced to life in prison in 2002, I stay trying to make something happen; whatever it may be. I've never been one to let things – even prison walls, steel bars and razor wire – stop me from doing what I set out to do. And in order to be successful, I've had to build up a network of relationships and resources. After all, especially when trying to accomplish something from inside a prison cell, where you're forced to rely on assistance from other people on the outside, it is *all* about networking, relationships, and resources.

During the time I've spent doing the various things that I do and gathering up the much-needed resources, I learned that there are actually a lot of things prisoners have available to them and can do, that most just don't know about. But with the proper information, some creativity (you *must* learn to think outside of the box when you live in one) and determination, there are many, *many* things that can be done. And yes, right from the inside of *your* prison cell, too….

This realization is what inspired me to create this book. Whether it's a lawyer to help you with your case, either for a fee or pro bono, or a place for artists to sell their art so they can make better money than a fellow prisoner can often pay; whether it's a typist, agent, or self-publishing service to help authors get their books or poetry published, or a pen pal service or club that can help one make friends from all over the country – all over the world, even – right from their cell; whether it's a place that will sell prisoners books and magazines or send them for free, or an advocacy/organization to assist with an injustice; whether it's a school that offers correspondence courses, or a company that offers a personal assistant service, sells sexy pictures, or gifts we can buy and send to our loved ones, and much, much more; I have done all I can to think of what a prisoner could possibly want to do from their cell, and provide the necessary resources in order to do so. Again, be creative, determined and willing to work hard, and you may be surprised of just what you can do.

Now, it should be noted that The Cell Block does not cosign any of the companies in this directory. We are only notifying you of them and what resources they promote to offer. And though we've done our best to weed them out, some of these companies may no longer be in business anymore or have changed their mailing address. Some may even be scams looking to take advantage of us – kick us while we're down. One can never be certain. However, whatever experiences you have with any of these businesses, we want to know about it. If they're scams, write and tell us. We'll put them on blast in our next edition – let our fellow prisoners know they're bad business and shut 'em down. If their business is 100, we want to know that, too. We'll notify everybody of who is solid in the next edition and encourage them to deal with those companies. Companies that treat us well deserve to be rewarded by getting our business, companies that are foul deserve to get shut down; our fellow prisoners deserve to be made aware of who's who. This is all a part of the network.

For this latest edition of *The Best Resource Directory For Prisoners*, I've cut out a lot of the nonsense; filler other companies -- freeworld companies who wish to exploit our struggle for their profit, as this is the *only* directory created entirely by inmates – use to bulk up their books in order to make them seem more than what they are. I've sent over 400+ letters, myself, just this year to make sure the information is current, and that's not including the 500-plus sent by my teammates and a few other helpful friends from around the country. I've compacted the text as much as possible and made everything nice and clean. It's pure, useful information. Remember, this directory is a living entity; it is constantly evolving. We are constantly making adjustments that improves its quality, and I thank those of you who have participated in letting me know where weaknesses are, and how we improve them. So, if you have any suggestions or requests for resources that would assist you with your objectives, I welcome them gladly.

Sincerely,

Mike
The Cell Block

Resource 1: a source of supply or support **2:** available funds **3:** a possibility of relief or recovery **4:** a means of spending leisure time **5:** ability to meet and handle situations **6:** something to which one has recourse in difficulty

INDEX OF RESOURCES

ADVOCACIES & COALITIONS

ACLU of Idaho
ACLU GLBT Rights / AIDS Project
ACLU National Prison Proj…
ACLU Reproductive Free…
ACLU of Montana
ACLU of Northern California
ACLU NPP
ACLU of San Diego …
ACLU of Texas
ACLU of Texas Prison and …
The Action Committee For…
AFSC Prison Watch Project
Alba Morales
All Of Us or None
Alliance of Incarcerated Ameri…
American Civil Liberties Union Cap
American Civil Liberties Union
Amnesty International, USA
Amnesty Mid-Atlantic …
An End to Silence
Arab American Anti Discriminat…
Barrios Unidos
California Families to Abolish …
California NORML
Campaign to End the Death…
Center for Constitutional Rights
Center on Wrongful Conviction…
Citizens Against Recidivism
Citizens United for Alternat …
Citizens United for Rehabil…
Coalition for Jewish Prisoners
Colorado Criminal Justice…
Columbia Legal Services, Instit…
Community Alliance on Prisons
Compassion Works for All …
Convicts for Christ
CorrectHelp
Correctional Association of …
Corrections Accountability Project
Critical Resistance
Death Penalty Focus
Dharma Friends Prison Out…
Disability Rights Education and Defense Fund
Dishonorable Courts

D.R.I.V.E. Movement
Drug Policy Alliance
End Violence Project
ETC Campaign
The Exoneration Project
FACTS: Families to Amen…
Fair Chance Project
Families Against Mandatory…
Family and Corrections…
Fight for Lifers West
Florida Justice Institute
Friends and Family of …
Friend Committee on …
Friends Outside
Human Rights Coalition
Human Rights Watch
Innocence Project
International Prison Watch …
Just Detention International
Justice Now
Justice Watch
Justice Works!
JustLeaderShipUSA
Juvenile Lifers
Lawyers Committee for Civil …
Legal Aid Society Prisoner's…
Lewisburg Prison Project
Malcom X Grassroots Movement …
Middle Ground Prison Reform
NAACP National Prison Project
National Action Network
National AIDS Treatment Advoca…
National Center on Institution…
The National Coalition to Abolish
National Lawyers Guild Prison …
National Native American Prison…
National Network for Immig…
The Network/La RED Ending Abu …
New York State Prisoner Justice Co
Northern Arizona Justice Project
The November Coalition
NW Immigrant Rights Project
NY Campaign for Telephone …
NYC Jericho Movement
Oregon CURE …
Oregonians for Alternatives …
Pennsylvania Prison Society

People's Law Office
Power Inside
Prison Activist Resource Center
Prisoner Express
Prisoners' Rights Office
Prisoner Visitation and Sup…
Prison Legal News
Prison Letters For Our Struggling
Real Cost of Prison Projects
Safe Streets Arts Foundation
Sagewriters
Santa Cruz Barrios Undios
Solitary Watch
Special Litigation Section
Stanley Tookie Williams …
Stopmax Campaign
Texas Civil Rights Project
The Campaign for Youth …
Un-Common Law
Women's Prison Association
Wisconsin Innocence Proje…

ART/ARTIST

American Indian Art Magazine
Art with Conviction
Ashley Rice Collection
Bead and Button
Bud Plant Comic Art
Celebrity Tattoo
Cell Block Art
Con-Art
Contexts Art Project
Deviantart.com
Oatmeal Studios
Game Informer Reader Art Contest
NFC
Occasion Gallerie
Prison Creative Arts Project
Real Artist Tattoo Gallery
Safe Streets Arts Foundation
Skin&Ink Letters
Sunshine Artist
Tattoo Flash

BOOK DONATORS

Appalachian Prison Book …
ARE Prison Program
Ashville Prison Book Program
Athens Books to Prisoners

Book'em
Books for Prisoners San Deigo
Books Through Bars
Books to Prisoners
Chicago Books to Prisoners
DC Prison Book Project
Inside Books Project
Internationalist Prison Books…
Midwest Books to Prisoners
NYC Books Through Bars
Portland Books to Prisoners
Prison Book Program
Prison Library Project
Prisoners Literature Project
Providence Books Through …
Spring Grass Book 'Em
Urbana- Champagne Books …
Wisconsin Books to Prison…
Women's Prison Book Project

BOOK PUBLISHERS

Beginning on page 144   `.

BOOK SELLERS

A Book You Want
Acclaimed Books
American Correctional…
BBPD
The Cell Block
Direct Access
Groundwork Books Collective
L33t Gaming
Left Bank Books
The Osborne Association
Pathfinder Press
PM Press
Prison Professor
SEC.MEMPS
South End Press
Sureshot Books
Wall Periodicals

CHRISTIAN

Amazing Facts
American Bible Academy
American Bible Society
American Rehabilitation
Ministries
Ben & Ima Prayen
Berean Prison Ministry
Bible Helps

Calvary Chapel of Philadelphia
Christian Pen Pals
Christianpenpals.org
Crossroads Bible Institute
Grace Ministries Bible College…
Global University
In Perfect Peace Ministries
International Bible Society
International Christian College...
Joyce Meyers Ministries
Message of the Cross Ministries
Mike Barber Ministries
Mount Hope Prison Ministry
The Missing Link
Moody Bible Institute
Mt. Hope Prison Ministry
Our Daily Bread
Pan American Literature Mission
PMI Center for Biblical Studies
Prisoner Fellowship Ministry
Prisoners for Christ Outreach ...
Rock of Aged Prison Ministry
St. Dismas Guild
United Prison Ministries
International

CLEAR PLASTIC PRODUCTS

See package companies.

CLOTHES/SHOES

See package companies.

CUSTOM CDs

See package companies.

DISCOUNT CALLS

3 Amigos Communications
Affordable Inmate Calling
Services
Cons Call Home
Corrio SPC
Freedom Line
FREE JAIL CALLS
Get Connected
Inmate Toll Busters
Jail Calls
JailCallsUSA.com
Local123.net
Ocslocal.com
Save on Prison Calls

SP Telecom
Tim's Inmate Mail Service
VFC

EDUCATION

Adams State College
American Rehabilitation …
Arts in Criminal Justice
The Asian Classics Institute…
Bard College
bestgedtutor.com
Blackstone Career Institute
Boston University Prison
Education
College in Prison
Complete GED Preparation
Cornell Prison Education Program
Distance Ed. Accrediting Comm.
Education Behind Bars
Education Justice Project
Global University
Grace College Prison Extension…
Graduate School USA
Hudson Link for Higher Edu…
Indiana University
International Christian &...
International Sports Sciences...
Lansing Correctional Facility
Maine State Prison College
Programs
NCJRS – The National Instit…
New Freedom Collage
Oakland City University Prison…
Ohio University College Prog…
Operation Outward Reach, Inc.
The Paralegal Institute
PASS Program
Penn Foster Career School
Prisoners' Guerilla Handbook
Prison University Project
Project Rebound
Purdue University Northern …
SJM Family Foundation, Inc.
Spanish for Prisoners
St. Mark's School of Legal
Studies
Stratford Career Institute
University Beyond Bars
University of North Carolina
Upper Iowa University
Windham School District

ELECTRONICS

See package companies.

E-MAIL SERVICES

Conpals
Inmate Classified

FAMILY-BASED SERVICES

Amachi Program
Casa Frontera Visitor Center
Center for the Children of
Incarcera
Children of Incarcerated Parents
Edwin Gould Services for
Children
Families of Parchman Prison …
Family and Corrections Network
Families United
FamliySupportAmerica.org
Forever Family, Inc
Friends outside
Hour Children
Legal Services for Prisoners with
…
Matthew House
Middle Ground Prison Reform
National Center for Youth Law
National Fatherhood Initiative
National Incarcerated Parents …
National Institute of Corrections
PB&J Family Services, Inc.
Pelipost.com
PictureDoney.com
Prison Information Network
Prison Place
San Francisco Children of …
South Dakota Prisoner Support …
Spletter
Support for Kids with Incarc…
United Shuttle

FAMILY/FRIEND LOCATORS

U.S. Mint Green

GIFT SHOPS

Bottled Thoughts
Brilliance Audio, Inc.
Cell Shop
From Inside Out

Harvest 21 Gifts
infoLINKS
Jaden Moore of New York
Julie's Gifts
Loving a Convict
Millennial Masterpieces

FOOD

See package companies.

GREETING CARDS

Acclaimed Books
Ajemm Brothers Greeting Cards
Ashley Rice Collection
Diversified Press
Freebird Publishers
Millennial Masterpieces
Occasion Gallerie

HEALTH

AIDS in Prison Project
AIDS Law Project of
Pennsylvania
Aids Treatment News
Alianza
Allegheny County Depart.of …
American Diabetes Association
AMFAR Aid Research
Cell Workout
Centerforce
Center for Disease Control's
Natio…
Center for Health Justice
Correct Help
Disability Rights Texas
Drug Policy Alliance
Hepatitis and Liver Dis...
Hepatitis C Awareness Project
Hepatitis C Support Project
Hepatitis Prison Coalition
HIV/Hepatitis C Prison
Committee
Hepatitis, AIDS, Research
Trust…
Institute For Criminals Justice
Healt
International Sports Sciences...
Latino Commission on AIDS
Lesbian AIDS project
Medical Malpractice Experts

National AIDS Treatment
Advoc…
National Health Prison Project
The National Hepatitis C Prison...
Our Bodies, Ourselves
Positively Aware; National
Magaz…
Prison AIDS Resource Center
Prison Diabetes Handbook...
Prison Health News
Prisoners with AIDS Rights
Advoc…
San Francisco AIDS Foundation
Services to Elder Prisoners, PA
The Vitamin Outlet
The Wrongful Death Institute

INMATE SERVICES

Affordable Inmate Services
Help From Beyond the Walls

INTERNET RESEARCHERS

4 The Pack Ent.
A Book You Want
Affordable Inmate Services
Help From Beyond the Walls
One Stop Services
Package Trust

ISLAMIC/MUSLIM

Alavi foundation
Assisting Incarcerated Muslims
Conveying Islamic Message
Society
Council on American Islamic...
Diamma Akhewel
Islamic Ahlulbayt Association
Islamic Center
Islamic Center of Springfield
Missouri
Islamic Circle of North America
Muslims for Humanity
Why Islam

LATINO

Barrios Unidos
Centro Legal de la Raza
Chican@ Power & Struggle…
La Raza Centro Legal, Inc
La Voz de Esperanza
Latino Commission on AIDS

Latino on Wheels
Legal Publications in Spanish, Inc

LEGAL BOOKS/ SELLERS

A Jailhouse Lawyers Manual
Actual Innocence
Advanced Criminal Procedure...
Arrested: What to do...
Arrest-Proof Yourself
Center for Constitutional Rights
Columbia Human Rights Law
Rev..
Criminal Injustice...
The Criminal Law Handbook...
Criminal Law In a Nutshell...
Criminal Procedure...
Deposition Handbook
A Dictionary of Criminal...
Fast Law Publishing
Flipping Your Habe
Flipping your Conviction...
The Habeas Citebook...
How To Win Your Personal…
Jailhouse Lawyers...
Journal Broadcasting and
Commu..
Law Dictionary
Legal Action Center Services
Legal Publications in Spanish
Legal Research: How to Find...
Levin, Michael R, ESQ.
Lewisburg Prison Project
Looking for a Way Out
Marijuana Law
Minkah's Official Cite Book
No Equal Justice: Race...
Nolo Press
Nolo's Plain-English Law Dic...
Oceana Press
Oxford University Press, Inc
Prison Grievances
Prison Nation...
Prison Profiteers
Prisoners' Rights Union
Prisoners' Self-help Litigation
Ma..
Prisoners' Union
Protecting Your Health & Safety
PSI Publishing
Raw Law
Representing Yourself In Court
Robert's Company
Smith's Guide to Habeas Corpus

Sue the Doctor & Win...
Ten Men Dead
Thomson Rueters
West
Winning Habeas Corpus & Post...
With Liberty for Some...
Writing to Win...

LEGAL HELP/SERVICES

Ahrony, Graham, & Zucker
Alba Morales
American Academy of Paralegals
Angres, Robert L, ESQ
Another Chance for Legal, LLC
Appeals Law Group
Banks, Jeffery S. ESQ
Battered Women's Justice Project
Bee Smith
Benjamin Ramos, Attorney at
Law
Butler Legal Group
Carbone, Charles
CaseSearch
Centro Legal de la Raza
Center on Wrongful Convictions
Centurion Ministries, INC
Chicago Innocence Project
Colorado Innocence Project
Committee for Public Counsel
Pr…
Connecticut Innocence Project
Correct Help
Cox, Harvey
David Rushing
Defense Investigation Group
Disability Rights Education and
De…
Elmer Robert Keach
Equal Justice Initiative
Executive Prison Consultants
The Exoneration Initiative
The Exoneration Project
Expert Witness
Fast Law Research
Feria and Corona
Florida Institutional Legal
Services
Georgia Innocence Project
Georgia Justice Project
Harvey Cox, MS
Hawaii Innocence Project
Hopkins Law Offices
Hoy, Marion

Idaho Innocence Project
Illinois Innocence Project
Inmatenavigator.org
Innocence and Justice Project
Innocence Project for Justice
Innocence Project of Florida
Innocence Project of Minnesota
Innocence Project New Orleans
Innocence Project NW Clinic
Innocence Project of Texas
Innovative Sentencing Solutions
Innocence Project (National)
Jailhouse Lawyers Guild
Jackson & Reed
Justice Brandeis Law Project
The Last Resort Innocence Project
Law Offices of C.W. Baylock
Law Office of David Rushing
The Law Office of William
Savoie
Legal Action Center
Legal Liability Protection
Legal Move Logistics
Lewisburg Prison Project
Litigation Support
Maloof, Michael W.
Marilee Marshall & Assoc...
Medical Malpractice Experts
Metropolitan Prison Consulting…
Michigan Innocence Clinic
Mid-Atlantic Innocence Project
Mississippi Innocence Project
MNN, Inc
Montana Innocence Project
NAACP Legal Defense & Ed…
National Center for Youth Law
National Center on Institutions
&...
National Clemency Project
National Innocence Network
National Lawyers Guild
Nebraska Innocence Project
New England Innocence Project
Nicole M. Verville
NJ Office of the Corrections
Omb…
North Carolina Center on Actual
…
Northern California Innocence
Proj..
Oklahoma Innocence Project
Office of the Public Defender....
Palmetto Innocence Project
Penal Law Project

Pennsylvania Innocence Project
The Portia Project
Prison Law Clinic
Prison Law Office
Prisoner Legal Services
Prisoners' Legal Services of Masa..
Prisoners' Legal Services of NY
Prisonology
Prison Web
Project for Older Prisoners
Public Interest Law Firm
Reinvestigation Project
Resentencing Project
Rodriquez, Stephen G. and…
Ruis De Law Torre Law Firm
Schatkin, Andrew Esq
Schmidt, William Esq
The Sentencing Project
Southern Poverty Law Center
Stanford 3 Strikes Project
State Public Defender – San…
Susan L. Burke
Sylvia Rivera Law Project
Texas Center for Actual Innocence
Texas Innocence Network
Timberwolf Litigation & Research
Timothy C. Chiang-Lin
Thurgood Marshall School of Inn..
Transformative Justice Law Project
TR&R
United Consulting Services
University of Baltimore Innocen…
University of Miami Law Innoc…
University of Texas Center for…
Wesleyan Innocence Project
West Virginia Innocence Project
William L. Schmidt
Winning Writ Writers

Note: For more legal help resources see our list of over 130 pro bono attorneys starting on page 132

LEGAL INFORMATION

American Bar Association
Battered Women's Justice Project

Carolina Case Law
Center for Constitutional Rights
Central Texas ABC
Columbia Human Rights Law Rev
Criminal Legal News
Georgetown ARCP
Legal Information Services Assoc…
National Criminal Justice Refere…
National Legal Aid and Defend…
PLN Accumulative Index
Prisonlawblog.com
Prisoner Rights Information Sys…
Prisoners' Rights Research Project
The Sentencing Project
Set My Way Free Ministries, Inc
TR&R
W. Barron

LEGAL WEB PAGES

Conpals
Friends Beyond the Wall

LGTB

Black and Pink
Gay and Lesbian Advocates and…
Gay Identity Center of Colorado
Gender Muting Collective
Lesbian AIDS Project
Lesbian and Gay Insurrection
Midwest Pages to Prisoners Project
Midwest Trans Prisoner Penpal …
National Center for Lesbian Rig…
National Gay and Lesbian Task…
The Network/La RED Ending…
Out of Control Lesbian Commit…
Pace Post Conviction Project
Prisoner Correspondence Project
Sinister Wisdom, Inc.
Sylvia Rivera Law Project
The Transformative Justice Law…
T.I.P. Journal
Transformative Justice Law Proj…
Transgender, Gender Variant,…
Tranzmission Prison Books

Wisconsin Books to Prisoners…
Women's Prison Book Project

LIFERS/DEATH PENALTY

American Civil Liberties Union…
California Lifer Newsletter
Campaign to End the Death Penalty
The Center for LWOP…
Citizens United for Alternati…
Death Penalty Focus
Death Penalty Information Center
D.R.I.V.E. Movement
Fair Chance Project
Fight for Lifers West
Incarcerated Citizens Council
Juvenile Lifers
L.I.F.E. Association
Lifeline
Lifers to be Free
Lifers United
The Moratorium Campaign
Muncy Inmate Coordinator
The National Coalition to Abolish…
National Death Row Assistance…
Oregonians for Alternatives to the…
PA Lifers Association
The Other Death Penalty Project
The Voices.Con Newsletter

LITERARY AGENTS
Beginning on page 149

Alive Communications, Inc.
Betsy Amster Literary Enterprises
B.J. Robbins Literary Agency
Bookends, LLC
Briar Cliff Review
Browne & Miller Literary…
Castiglia Literary Agancy
Concho River Review
Curtis Brown, LTD
Defiore & Co.
Diana Finch Literary Agency
Dunham Literary, Inc.
Dystel & Godrich Literary…
The Evan Marshall Agency
Fineprint Literary Management
Jeany Naggar Literary Agency. Inc.
Jodie Rhodes Literary Agency

The Joy Harris Literary Agency...
Loretta Barrett Books, Inc.
Lowenstein Associates, Inc.
Mendel Media Group, LLC
Michael Larsen/Elizabeth
Pomada,
Philip G. Spitzer Literary
Agency...
Richard Henshaw Group
RLR Associates, LTD
Robin Straus Agency, Inc.
Rosalie Siegel
Russell & Volkening
Sandra Dijkstra Literary Agency
Sanford J. Greenburger
Associates...
Sheree Bykofsky Associates, Inc.
Trident Media Group
Veritas Literary Agency
Victoria Sanders & Associates
The Wendy Weil Agency, Inc.
WM Clark Associates
Writers House

LITERARY
PUBS/REVIEWERS
Beginning on page 153

African American Review
AGNI Magazine
Alaska Quarterly Review
Alligator juniper
American Literary Review
The American Scholar
The Antioch Review
Apalachee Review
ARC Poetry Magazine
Arion
Arkansas Review
Ascent; English Dept.
The Awakening Review
Baffler
The Bayou Review
Bellevue Literary Review
Bellingham Review
Bellowing Ark
Beloit Poetry Journal
The Bitter Oleander
Blackbird
Blue Mesa Review
Boston Review
Briar Cliff Review
Brilliance Corners
Callaloo

Calyx
Capilano Review
The Caribbean Writer
Carolina Quarterly
The Chattahoochee
Chicago Review
Cimarron Review
College Literature
Colorado Review
Columbia
Commentary Magazine
The Comstock Review
Conjunctions
Connecticut Review
Court Green
Crab Orchard Review
Crazyhorse
Daedalus
Denver Quarterly
Descant
Eclipse; A Literary Journal
Ecotone
Epoch
Eureka Literary Magazine
Event
Fantasy & Science Fiction
Faultline
Fiction; Mark J Mirksy, Editor
Fiction International
Fiddlehead; Campus House
Field
The First Line
Florida Review
Folio
Fourteen Hills
Fourth Genre
Georgia Review
Gettysburg Review
Grain
Green Hill Literary Lantern
Greensboro review
Gulf Coast
Harper's Magazine
Harpur Palate
Harvard Review
Hawaii Pacific Review
Hayden's Ferry Review
The Healing Muse
Hiram Poetry Review
Hotel Amerika
Hudson Review
Hunger Mountain
Idaho Review
Iris, UVA Women's Center

Iron Horse Literary Review
Isotope; Utah State University
Italiana Americana, University of
Rhode Island
Jabberwock Reviews
Jewish Currents
The Journal
Karanu
Kenyon review
Land Grant College Review
The Laurel Review; Dept. of
English
Literal Latte
The Long Story
Louisiana Literature
Louisville Review
Malahat Review
Massachusetts review
McSweeney's
Meridian, University of Virginia
Michigan Quarterly Review
Mid-American Review
Midstream
Missouri Review
Natural Bridge
New Delta Review
New England Review
New Letter, University of
Missouri
New Ohio Review; English Dept.
New Orleans Review
The New York Quarterly
Nimrod International Journal
Ninth Letter
North Carolina Literary Review
North Dakota Quarterly
Northwest Review; The Editor,
NWR
Notre Dame Review
Nylon
Oklahoma Today
Oxford American
Painted Bride Quarterly
Pearl
Phoebe; George Mason University
MSN 206
The Pinch, Dept. of English
Pleiades
Ploughshares, Emerson College
Poet Lore
Potomac Review
Pottersfield Portfolio
Prairie Fire
Prairie Schooner

Prism International
Quarterly West
Raritan, Rutgers University
Rattle
Rattapallax
Redivider, Emerson College
RHINO
Room
The Saint Ann's Review
Salmagundi; Skidmore College
Salt Hill; English Dept.
Santa Monica Review
Seattle Review
Seneca Review
Seven Days
Sewanee Review; Univers…
Shenandoah
Sonora Review
So-To-Speak
The South Carolina Review
South Dakota Review
Southeast Review, English Dept.
Southern Humanities Review
The Southern Review
Southwest review
Speakeasy; The Loft Literary
Center
The Spoon River Poetry Review
St. Anthony Messenger
Sun
Swivel
Sycamore Review
Talking River Review
Tampa Review; The University …
The Texas Review; English Dept.
Thema
Threepenny Review
Tikkun
Tin House
Transition Magazine
Turnrow; English Dept.
War, Literature, and the Arts;
Engl..
Wascana Review
Washington Square Creative
Writ…
Watchword
Witness
Xavier University
Yale Review
Zahir; Sheryl Tempchin
Zoetrope

MAGAZINES

American Indian Art Magazine
Auto Restore
Auto Week
Baseball America
Bead and Button
Blade Magazine
Don Diva Magazine
The Editorial Eye
ESPN
Esquire
Forbes
Friction Zone
Hollywood Scriptwriter
In the Wind
Indian Life Magazine
In-Touch Ministries
Kite
Latino on Wheels
Live From Da Trap
LLG
Lowrider Magazine
National Geographic
The Order of the Earth
Outlaw Bikers
QOC
Slingshot Magazine
SMOOTH
Sports Weekly
State V. Us
Streetsweepers Ent.
Sub 0 Ent.
Sunshine Artist
Time Magazine
Writer's Digest

MAGAZINE SELLERS

Alice S. Grant Publications
American Magazine Service
Direct Access
Discount Magazine Subscriptions
Inmatemags.com
Loved Ones Needs
The Magazine Wizard
Magazine City
Tightwad Magazines
Wall Periodical

MAIL FORWARDING

Help From Beyond the Walls

MEDITATION

Amitabha Buddhist Society of
USA
Association for Research and
En…
Baus Book Circulation
Bridge Project
Buddhist Association of the
Unite…
Chuang Yen Monastery
Buddhist Churches of America
Dallas Buddhist Association
Gassho Newsletter/Atlanta Soto
Inside Dharma
Insight Meditation Society
International Buddhist Meditation
Liberation Prison Project
National Buddhist Prison
Sangha/Zen
Prison Dharma Network
PSSC/Parallax Press
Sravasti Abbey/Ven Thubten
Chodron
Strawberry Dragon Zendo
The Sutra Translation Committee
Syda Foundation Prison Project
Tricycle Magazine: The Buddhist
Upaya Prison Outreach Project

MISC.

60 Minutes
Allan Davis
American Motorcyclist
Association
Anti-Repression Music
Bigshot Productions
Caged Kingdom
Camelback Group
Catalogchoice.org
CDCR, office of Ombudsman
Celito Lino Properties
Cheaters
Death Before Dishonor
Exotic Fragrances
Fox Broadcasting
Genealogical Research, Refere…
Getgrrandpasfbifile
Gold Star Fragrances
In Scan Document Service
InsightCrew
Internal Affairs, CDCR
L33t Gaming
Library of Congress

Military Records; National Person...
National Directory of Catalogs
Trump, President Donald
PETA
Prism Optical, Inc
Prison Mindfulness Institute
Prisonnewsnetwork.us
Thomas Merton Centre
U.S. Dept. of Justice
U.S. Small Business Association

MISC.
RELIGIOUS/SPIRITUAL

Anthroposophical Prison Outreach
Association of Happiness for …
BTP
Greenman Ministry
Human Kindness Foundation
Inner Traditions
In-Touch Ministries
Jewish Prisoners Assistance Foundation
Jewish Prisoners Services …
Miracles Prisoner Ministry
Prison Ashram Project
Prison Fellowship
Prison Library Project
Rising Sun Publications
Susman, Eli
Watchtower

MUSIC SELLERS

Music By Mail
Walkenhorst's

NATIVE AMERICAN

American Indian Art …
Bayou La Rosa
Indian Life Magazine
Mettanokit Outreach
National Native American Prison…
Native American Pride Committee
Native American Prisoners' …
Navajo Nation Corrections Project

PACKAGE COMPANIES

Access Securepak California

Union Supply Direct California
Walkenhorst's

PARALEGAL SERVICES

A&K Paralegal Services
Angres, Robert L., Esq.
Butler Legal Group
Inmatenavigator.org
Miller Paralegal

PAROLEE/EX-OFFENDER

Better People
Catholic Charities USA
Cleveland Career Center
Conquest Offender
Correctional Library Services
D&D Worldwide Services
Dress for Success
Energy Committed to Offenders
Evolve
Exodus Transitional Commun…
Ex-offender Re-entry Website
Fair Chance Project
From Jail to a Job
Homeboy Industries
Impact Publications
Justice Watch
Justice Works!
Legal Action Center Services
LWPP
Making Career Connections
The Missing Link
Open, Inc.
Prison Fellowship Ministry
Project Return
Salvation Army
Second Chance Act
SJM Family Foundation, Inc.
St. Patrick Friary
Support Housing & Innovative …
Task Force on Prisoner Re-entry
Transitional Housing for Georgia

PEN PAL CLUBS

Bhandari, Suresh
Christian Pen Pals
Lifeline
Nubian Princess Ent...
Reaching Beyond the Walls
SoUnique Magazine
Sylvian Clarke

PEN PAL LISTS

Co-Sign Pro
ESCTS

PEN PAL MAGAZINES

The Fog Corporation

PEN PAL WEBSITES

Blackface Productions
Christianpenpals.org
Con Pals
Conpals
Convict Mailbag
Diversified Press
DRL
Friends Beyond the Wall
Friends 4 Prisoners
Inmate Alliance
Inmate Classified
Inmate Connections
Inmateconnection.com
InmateNHouseLove.Com
Inmate LoveLink
Inmate Mingle
Inmate Pen Pal Connection
Inmates in Waiting
JailBabes.com
LostVault.com
Loveaprisoner.com
Meet-An-Mate
Nubian Princess Ent.
Outlaws Online, Inc.
Penacon.com
Pen-A-Con
Pen Pal Connection
Prison Connection
Prison Pen Pals
Prison Inmates Online
Prisonpenpalmingle.com
Prisoner Promotions
Prisonvoice.com
South Beach Singles, Inc
Tele-pal.com
TIC Interests
Waitingpenpals.com
Wire of Hope
Writeaprisoner.com
Writesomeoneinprison.com
Writetoinmates.com
Write to Prisoners

PERSONAL ASSISTANTS

Eli Solutions
Escape Mate
Inmates Little Helpers
Level 4 Secure Services
One Stop Services

PHOTO DUPLICATION / MANIPULATION

Con Pics
Flikshop.com
Inmate Photo Provider
Package Trust
Pelipost.com
PhotoSweep.com
PictureDonkey.com
WeShipPics.com

PHOTOCOPIES

IPP

PRISON(ER)-BASED PUBS

AFCS
Alabama Prison Project
Angolite
The Beat Within
The Best 500 Non-Profit...
California Lifer Newsletter
California Prison Focus
The Cell Block
The Cell Door
The Celling of America
Coalition for Prisoners'...
Criminal Legal News
Fanorama Society...
The Fire Inside
The Fortune News
Freebird Publishers
Graterfriends
Inmate Shopper
Internationalist Prison...
Journal of Prisoners on Prisons
Justice Denied
Kite Magazine
La Voz de Esperanza
Mennonite Central ...
MIM Distributors
The New Abolitionist
Prison Focus

The Prison Journal
Prison Legal news
The Prison Mirror
Prisonworld Magazine
Prisoner's Right Union
San Quentin News
State V. Us
Southland Prison News
The Voices.con Newsletter
Union supply Turning the Tide:
Journal...

PRO BONO ATTORNEYS

See our listing on page 132

SEX ABUSE

An End to Silence
Association for the Treatment....
Prison Rape Elimination…
The Safer Society Foundation
Sex Abuse Treatment…
Stop Prisoner Rape

SEXY PHOTOS

4 the Pack
Akin
Babe's Emporium
Branlettes Beauties
Butterwater, LLC
Cellmate & Convict Services
Chronos Masterpieces
CNA Entertainment
Co-Sign Pro
Curbfeelers
FIYA Girls
Flix 4 You
F.O.S.
Ghost Photos
Grab Bag
High Caliber Latina
Hot Pics
Inmate-Connection.com
Kill Shot King
Krasnya, LLC
MartysMillions
Meshell Baldwin Publications
Moonlite Productions
Nickels and Dimez
Nubian Princess Ent.
Package Trust
Pantee Publishing

Photo Tryst
Photoworld
Picmate.net
The Senza Collection
Sexy Girl Parade
SoUnique Magazine
South Beach Singles, Inc.
Summerbunnies.com
Suthern Cumfort
UVP
Villa Entertainment
Who Want What?

SOCIAL NETWORK SITES

See website builders.

SONGWRITER RESOURCES

International Acoustic Music
Awards
USA Songwriting Contest

SPORTS

African America Golf Digest
Baseball America
ESPN
San Francisco Forty …
Sports Weekly

STAMP BUYERS

Cash For Your Stamps
The Greenback Exchange
Help From Beyond …
Prison/Inmate Family Service
Prison Stamps Exchange

STATIONARY

H. Avery

SUPPORT GROUPS (NA/AA)

Alcoholics Anonymous General...
Association for the Treatment …
Atkins House
Baitil Salaam Network
Baker Industries
Bayou La Rosa
Catholic charities USA
Georgia Justice Project
ISO World Services, Inc

Narcotics Anonymous
Project Blanket

TYPING SERVICES

Ambler Document Processing
Gillins Typing Service
Jeff Vincent
Liz's Paper Jungle
The Office
Sanders, Louise S.
Sandra Z. Thomas
TJL

URBAN BOOKS/
PUBLISHERS

A Million Thoughts…
Anatomy of Hip-Hop...
Badland Publishing
The Cell Block
DC Book Diva
Envisions Publishing
Final Round
Gorilla Convict …
King Poe Publishing
LC Devine Media, LLC
RJ Publications
Sisyphen Tasks, LLC
Wahida Clark Presents…

VIRTUAL ASSISTANTS

See personal assistants.

WEBSITE BUILDERS

Affordable Inmate Services
Help From Beyond the …
Inmate Pen Pal Connection
Inmate Web Sites
Wow Me Web Design

WOMEN ONLY

The Action committee…
Battered Women's Justice..
California Coalition for…
Chicago Books to Wo…
Hasting Women's Law…
Justice Now
Keeping the Faith: The …
Ms. Magazine
NASW Women's Council..
National Clearinghouse…
Off Our Backs
Our Bodies, Ourselves
Women and Prison: A Site
women.

WRITER/AUTHOR

APWA
Ashley Rice Collection
Association for Authors…
The Blue Book of Grammar...
The Blumer Literary…
Children's Book Insider
Cimarron Review
Damamli Publishing…
Defiore and Company
The Editorial Eye
Freebird Publishers
Freelance Success
Get Your Poetry Pub…
Hawkeye Editing
Hollywood Scriptwriter
Info
INKWELL Magazine
K. Carter
LeNoir Publications
Locus
Manning Document Publishing
Manuscripts To Go
The Marshall Project
Minutes Before Six
Occasion Gallerie

Outlook on Justice
Pen American Center
The Poetry Wall…
Poete Maudit
Poets and Writers, Inc
The Poet Workshop
Poetry Society of America
The Prison Journal
Prison Foundations
Professional Press
Randy Radic
Rolling Stone – Letters
Sagewriters
Sanders, Louise S.
Sentinel Writing Competitions…
Sinister Wisdom, Inc
Skin&Ink Letters
Slipstream Poetry contest
SMOOTH Fiction
SMOOTH Talk
Teachers and Writers
Corroborative
The ThreePenny Review
Thousands Kites
Walk In Those Shoes
Women and Prison: A Site.
Word Out Books
Writer's Digest
Writer's Guild of America
Writer's Market Companion
Writing To Win

Writers/Authors: Also see
Literary Pubs/Reviews, Literary
Agents and Book Publishers for
more information!

ZINES

Bernard Library Zine…
East Bay Prisoner Support
Fanorma Society Pub…
Worker's Vanguard

WANT MONEY?

MONEY IZ THE MOTIVE: Like most kids growing up in the hood, Kano has a dream of going from rags to riches. But when his plan to get fast money by robbing the local "mom and pop" shop goes wrong, he quickly finds himself sentenced to serious prison time. Follow Kano as he is schooled to the ways of the game by some of the most respected OGs who ever did it; then is set free and given the resources to put his schooling into action and build the ultimate hood empire...

MONEY IZ THE MOTIVE 2: After the murder of a narcotics agent, Kano is forced to shut down his D&C crew and leave Dayton, OH. With no one left to turn to, he calls Candy's West Coast Cuban connection who agrees to relocate him and a few of his goons to the "City of Kings" -- Sacramento, CA, aka Mackramento, Killafornia! Once there, Kano is offered a new set of money-making opportunities and he takes his operation to a whole new level. It doesn't take long, however, for Kano to learn the game is grimy no matter where you go, as he soon experiences a fury of jealousy, hate, deception and greed. In a game where loyalty is scarce and one never truly knows who is friend and who is foe, Kano is faced with the ultimate life or death decisions. Of course, one should expect nothing less when...Money iz the Motive!

BLOCK MONEY: Beast, a young thug from the grimy streets of central Stockton, California lives The Block; breathes The Block; and has committed himself to bleed The Block for all it's worth until his very last breath. Then, one day, he meets Nadia; a stripper at the local club who piques his curiosity with her beauty, quick-witted intellect and rider qualities. The problem? She has a man -- Esco -- a local kingpin with money and power. It doesn't take long, however, before a devious plot is hatched to pull off a heist worth an indeterminable amount of money. Following the acts of treachery, deception and betrayal are twists and turns and a bloody war that will leave you speechless!

MOB$TAR MONEY: After Trey's mother is sent to prison for 75 years to life, he and his little brother are moved from their home in Sacramento, California, to his grandmother's house in Stockton, California where he is forced to find his way in life and become a man on his own in the city's grimy streets. One day, on his way home from the local corner store, Trey has a rough encounter with the neighborhood bully. Luckily, that's when Tyson, a member of the MOBTAR, a local "get money" gang comes to his aid. The two kids quickly become friends, and it doesn't take long before Trey is embraced into the notorious MOB$TAR money gang, which opens the door to an adventure full of sex, money, murder and mayhem that will change his life forever... You will never guess how this story ends!

Get ALL The Money!

Each book is only $12.00 + $4.00 S/H!

"The new standard of urban crime lit."

THE CELL BLOCK; PO BOX 1025; RANCHO CORDOVA, CA 95741

GENERAL RESOURCES

3 Amigos Communications
850 S. Boulder Hwy, Ste. 225
Henderson, NV 89015

• Use our service to make international phone calls from any city, county, state or federal facility!

• Stop paying the $1 per minute to call your family and friends. Using our service your calls will be billed at the local rate for your facility (subject to local number availability).

• With our service your only need one local number. Our scheduling option lets your number connect with as many international numbers you want based on day of the week.

• We don't make you sign up for a "plan" and pay for blocks of minutes that you don't need or want. With our service you only pay for what you use.

• Arrange payment from your trust account, by phone or online.

• We guarantee our service is the easiest, lowest cost way to make international calls or your money back.

For more information and order form to get started, send SASE.

Website: 3amigoscommunications.com
Email: info@3amigoscommunications.com

4 The Pack Ent.
POB 4057
Windsor Locks, CT 06096

These guys sell sexy pics, erotic stories, and do internet searches and online shopping. Send SASE for **FREE** flier.

60 Minutes
51 West 52nd Street
New York, NY 10019

News show.

A Book You Want
PO Box 16141
Rumford, RI 02916

Barbara runs this company. She does all kinds of services for a fee; search for hard- to-find books, internet searches, etc. Write/Send SASE for **FREE** information.

ACCESS SECUREPAK
P.O. Box 50028
Sparks, NV 89435

Package company that sells food, CDs, shoes, clothes, appliances and more. Write for a **FREE** catalog.

Comment: Since the last comment (above), I ordered a package from Access because I wanted some of the Pro Club clothes I can't get anywhere else. I also ordered food, including 8 bags of Doritos (the $4.95 bags). These fools charged me for all 8 bags, but only sent 4. So they got me for about $20. - - Mike

Acclaimed Books
Box 180399
Dallas, TX 75218-0399

Can provide full color scripture greeting cards, Mother's Day cards, Father's Day cards, general assorted cards and holiday cards for as low as 5¢ per card.

ACLU of Idaho
P.O. Box 1897
Boise, Idaho 83701

The ACLU of Idaho is a non-partisan organization dedicated to the preservation and enhancement of civil liberties and civil rights. They believe that the freedom of press, speech, assembly, and religion, and the rights to due process, equal protection and privacy, are fundamental to a free people.

Phone Number: 208.344.9750
Fax: 208.344.7201

ACLU LGBT Rights / AIDS Project
125 Broad St, 18th Floor,
New York, NY 10004

Experts in constitutional law and civil rights, specializing in sexual orientation, gender identity, and HIV/AIDS.

ACLU of Montana
PO Box 1317
Helena, MT 59624

Phone Number: (406) 443-8590

ACLU NPP
915 15th St. NW, 7th Fl.
Washington, DC 20005

The National Prison Project seeks to create constitutional conditions of confinement and strengthen prisoners' rights through class action litigation and public education. Their policy priorities include reducing prison overcrowding, improving prisoner medical care, and eliminating violence and maltreatment in prisons and jails, and minimizing the reliance on incarceration as a criminal justice sanction. The Project also publishes a quarterly journal, coordinates a nationwide network of litigators, conducts training and public education conferences, and provides expert advice and technical assistance to local community groups and lawyers throughout the country. The NPP is a tax-exempt foundation funded project of the ACLU Foundation.

ACLU of Northern California
39 Drumm Street
San Francisco, California 94111

The ACLU of Northern California works to preserve and guarantee the protection of the Constitution's Bill of Rights.

Phone Number: 415-621-2493

ACLU of San Diego & Imperial Counties
P.O. Box 87131
San Diego, CA 92138-7131

The ACLU of San Diego and Imperial Counties fights for individual rights and fundamental freedoms for all through education, litigation, and policy advocacy.

Phone Number: 619-232-2121

ACLU of Texas
Executive Director: Terri Burke
P.O. Box 8306
Houston, TX 77288

Phone Number: (713) 942-8146
Web: http://www.aclutx.org

ACLU of Texas Prison and Jail Accountability Project
P.O. Box 12905
Austin, TX 78711-2905

Phone Number: (512) 478-7300

ACLU Reproductive Freedom Project
Reproductive Freedom Project
American Civil Liberties Union
125 Broad Street 18th Fl
New York, NY 10004-2400

Phone Number: 212-549-2633
Website: aclu.org/reproductive-freedom

ACLU of Washington
901 Fifth Avenue, Suite 630
Seattle, WA 98164

Actual innocence: When Justice Goes Wrong and How to Make it Right

This book describes how criminal defendants are wrongly convicted, DNA testing and how it works to free the innocent, devastating critique of police and prosecutorial misconduct. The book is 403 pages, $16.00, and can be bought from Prison Legal News.

Adams State University
208 Edgemont Boulevard
Alamosa, CO 81102

They offer associates, bachelors, and master's degrees via correspondence. Since they are regional accredited, their credits should transfer to most colleges and universities in the United States. Three credit hour courses cost around $500 plus books.

Advanced Criminal Procedure in a Nutshell

This book is designed for supplemental reading in an advanced criminal procedure course on the post-investigation processing of a criminal case, including prosecution and adjudication. It's 505 pages, $43.95, and can be bought from Prison Legal News.

AFCS
2161 Massachusetts Ave
Cambridge, MA 02140

They have a 24-page quarterly magazine titled "Outlook on Justice." It's $2 per year.

Affordable Inmate Calling Services

Keeping you connected while saving you money! No hidden fees. One flat monthly rate. **FREE** setup with referral information. No charges to add/remove numbers. No transfer fees. 100% BOP compliant! Currently only available for federal prisoners. 450 minutes, 2 numbers; $15 + tax a month. Additional numbers for $1.50 each. Get $5.00 for each referral you send to them. Additional minute plans available.

Inmates Contact: inmates@alcsllc.net or 303-214-0097

Families Contact: www.aicsllc.net, bllling@aicsllc.net, or 866-645-9593

AFSC Prison Watch Project
89 Market Street, 6th Floor
Newark, NJ 07102

American Friends Service Committee Prison Watch Project has published the Fifth Edition of the Survivors Manual: Surviving in Solitary, by Bonnie Kerness,
(June 2012, 94 pages), which is **FREE** to prisoners and $3 for all others. This book is a powerful collection of voices from solitary, as people currently or formerly held in isolation vividly describe their conditions and their daily lives.

Phone Number: 973-643-3192
Website: afsc.org/story/survivors-manual-those-suffering-solitary

Ahrony, Graham, & Zucker, LLP
401 Wilshire Blvd., 12th Floor PH
Santa Monica, CA 90401

This is an appellate and post-conviction law firm. They specialize in appeals, Habeas Corpus Writs (Factual Innocence), parole hearings, SB 260 hearings, MDO hearings, re-sentencing, probation violations, rap sheet correction, prison and parole issues, 115 discipline issues, for California and federal courts. California cases only.

Unsolicited documents will NOT be returned.

Phone: 310-979-6400 or 310-288-0319
Website: AhronyGraham.com

AIDS Law Project of Pennsylvania
1211 Chestnut Street, Suite 600
Philadelphia, PA 19107

Phone 215-587-9377
Website: http://www.aidslawpa.org

AIDS Project of L.A.
1313 N. Vine Street,
Los Angeles, CA 90028

Resource guide for inmates living with AIDS called "Be Good to Yourself" that discusses nutrition, exercise and self-massage for people incarcerated. **FREE** to inmates.

Aid to Inmate Mothers

PO Box 986
Montgomery, AL 36101-0986
AIM provides services to Alabama's incarcerated women with emphasis on enhancing personal growth and strengthening the bonds between inmate mothers and their children.

Phone Number: 334-262-2245
Website: inmatemoms.org

AIDS ARMS Network, Inc
351 West Jefferson Blvd., Suite 300
Dallas, Texas 75208-7860

Supports victims.

Phone Number: (214) 521-5191

AIDS in Prison Project
The Osborne Association
809 Westchester Ave.
Bronx, NY 10455

Brochures for HIV-positive people. Info hotline in English and Spanish. Also provides transitional housing with case management for recently released and ex-prisoners.

Phone Number: (718) 707-2600
Email Address: info@osborneny.org

AIDS Treatment News
AIDS.ORG
PO Box 69491
Los Angeles, CA 90069

AIM
765 McDaniel Street
Atlanta, GA 30310

An advocacy group for incarcerated mothers. AIM can provide helpful information for all women in prison who have children but can only provide social services in the Atlanta area.

Phone Number: (404) 658-9606

A Jailhouse Lawyer's Manual
435 West 116th Street
New York, NY 10027

A Jailhouse Lawyer's Manual publishes three books designed to explain your rights and help you navigate the justice system.

The JLM 10th Edition (2014) ($30 for prisoners) is the main volume of the JLM. It is a 1288-page book that can help you learn about: Researching the law; Appealing your conviction or sentence; Receiving medical care; Protecting your civil liberties; and more.

The Immigration Supplement (2011) ($5 for prisoners) is a 116-page supplement to the main JLM containing information about immigration and the rights of non-citizens.

The Texas Supplement (2014) ($20 for prisoners) is a 408-page supplement to the main JLM containing information specific to Texas state prisoners.

To order the JLM, send a check or money order (no credit cards or stamps accepted) and your shipping information. For institutional prices or questions, contact jlm.board.mail@gmail.com.

Ajemm Brothers Greeting Cards
PO Box 10354
Albany, NY 12201

They sell greeting cards for all occasions and circumstances. Write/Send SASE for **FREE** information.

Akin
POB 164701
Fort Worth, TX 76161

Send SASE for **FREE** catalog of hot girls.

A&K Paralegal Service
13017 Westeria Dr. Suite 382
Germantown, MD 20879

15 years' experience, specializing in prison litigation – single cell negotiation, ICC transfer, internet research, copies, sentence reduction/modification, parole biography and more. "We have the winning strategies because we research each and every case effectively and efficiently." Any state, reasonable fees. Send SASE for brochure.

Phone Number: (240) 246-7857
Website: andkparalegal.com

Alabama Prison Project
215 Clayton St
Montgomery, AL 36104

They sell a newsletter for $4 a year and will accept stamps for payment. Write/Send SASE for **FREE** information.

Alaska Innocence Project
PO Box 201656
Anchorage, AK 99520-1656

Provides legal, educational, and charitable services to identify and exonerate individuals who have been wrongfully convicted in Alaska. AIP suggests and implements policies, practices and reforms that will prevent wrongful convictions and hasten the identification and release of innocent persons.

Phone Number: 907-279-0454
Website: alaskainnocence.org

Alavi Foundation
500 Fifth Avenue, Suite 2320
New York, NY 10110

Write for more information to get **FREE** Qurans and Islamic Literature.

Phone Number: 212-944-8333.

Alba Morales
Florida Direct File Project
Human Rights Watch
350 5th Ave., 33rd Floor
New York, NY 10118

Were you under 18 at the time of your offense? Were you prosecuted in adult court in Florida? Human Rights Watch is conducting an investigation on how Florida prosecutors use direct file and how this process affects juveniles. If your case got to adult court in Florida via direct file, contact this person.

Alcoholics Anonymous General Service Office
PO Box 459 Grand Central Station
New York, NY 10163

FREE information, local phone lines, meetings in most communities.

Phone Number: (212) 870-3400

Alianza
PO Box 63396
Washington, DC 20009

They provide information on AIDS in Spanish.

Allegheny County Department of Aging
441 Smithfield Street Building
Pittsburgh, PA 15222

They provide a broad range of human services for persons over age 60, the handicapped and the needy. Information and referral, care management, senior center-based services, senior employment program, home help, congregate/home delivered meals and emergency housing assistance. *Former* **inmates**, victims and families living in Allegheny County may obtain additional program information and assistance in accessing services by contacting the Department of Aging.

Allan Davis
2084 Creighton Dr.
Golden, CO 80401

"It's now possible to sell your intellectual knowledge on the internet using Facebook. Our average client makes just over $80,000 in the first year (gross sales). Our goal, within 30 days of release, to set up a 'package' of intellectual knowledge and offer it. If you do not have specialized knowledge then we can train you in 3-4 categories.

The Process: We send you an application. You send us the completed application and we determine if we have a fit. We only work with people who A) Have a burning desire to succeed, and B) Are able to create and package cutting edge ideas -- useful to business owners." Send SASE for more information.

Comment: All I do is read business books and work on my various business endeavors. I have a lot of "intellectual knowledge" that can be useful to business owners. 80 stacks a year? I'm with that! So I wrote this company thinking it was just a matter of time before I made it big. I explained that I have "Life", so I wanted to know if there was a way I could participate from my cell - - I pointed them to a bunch of shit I'm already doing from my cell. They responded that I could but would not make as much. OK, it's all good. Even 40 stacks a year from my cell is big shit. They sent me their application. I filled it out. They responded tellin me I was a fantastic candidate for their company and what they were doing. At this point in their letter, I was already spendin' my millions. Then I kept reading and got to the point where they were asking me for money -- to start? WTF? This immediately made me think of one of them Dateline episodes where some Nigerian hoodwinks some American schmuck into sending money in order to "free" tied-up monies in exchange for a cut. Maybe they're legit, I can't call it. I just know they were asking for a lot of money; more than most inmates have; and as much as I love you, more than what I'ma spend to see if it's legit or not. Sorry. If any of you have any info, please let me know. -- Mike

Alice S Grant Publications, INC
PO Box 28812
Greenfield, WI 53228

Comment: "My go-to source for low-cost magazine subscriptions. Order 5 mags, get 1 FREE for certain magazines. Great, fast customer service. I've used Alice for years. Send a SASE for her current rates! The Millionaire Prisoner endorsed and recommended!" -- Josh Kruger, author of The Millionaire Prisoner

All Of Us or None
C/O Legal Services for prisoners with children
1540 Market St. 490
San Francisco, CA 94102

Organizes to build political power and restore the civil and human rights of people who have been in prison or who have past convictions. Write for more information.

Phone number: 415-255-7036 X337
Website: allofusornone.org.

Alliance of Incarcerated Canadians/Foreigners in American Prisons (AICAP)
C/O NMB INC
131 Bloor St. W. Ste 200
Toronto, M5R 2E3 Canada

Phone Number: (416) 968-9417

Amachi Program

Big Brothers and Big Sisters of Greater Charlotte
3801 E Independence Boulevard, Suite 101
Charlotte, NC 28205

Phone Number: 704-910-1301

Amazing Facts
PO Box 909
Roseville, CA 95678

Write for a **FREE** sample magazine and **FREE** bible studies.

Ambler Document Processing
Jane Eichwald
P.O. Box 938
Norwalk, CT 06852

They type manuscripts and screenplays (only) with prices starting at $2 per page. Write/Send SASE for **FREE** information.

Phone Number: (203) 849-0708
Website: jane@protypeexpress.com

Comment: "Jane is the person who typed up my first book when the prisoncrats confiscated all our typewriters. Great, professional service. She put my manuscript on CD-ROM and sent it to my mom, plus sent me a hard copy. If I needed another typesetter for a book, I'd use her in a heartbeat. TMP endorsed!" -- Josh Kruger, author of The Millionaire Prisoner

American Academy of Paralegals
PO Box 1541
Houston, TX 77251

A membership organization providing Continuing Legal Education (CLE) courses and Paralegal Certification in all areas of law to those persons pursuing that profession nationwide. Send SASE for more info.

American Bar Association
321 N. Clark St.
Chicago, IL 60610

Allows site-users to search for a list of resources available in their state, including pro bono or inexpensive lawyers, help in dealing with lawyers, legal information, and self-help materials.

Phone Number: (800) 285-2221

American Bible Academy
P.O. Box 1627,
Joplin, MO 64802 – 1627

FREE English and Spanish Bible Correspondent Courses for prisoners. All courses are 120 pages in length.

American Bible Socicty
1865 Broadway,
New York, NY 10023 – 7505

Works directly with correctional chaplains. If your chaplain needs **FREE** Scriptures (**FREE** Bibles in English and Spanish) for your facility, please contact.

American Civil Liberties Union
Capital Punishment Project
201 West Main Street, Suite 402
Durham, N.C. 27701

Partnering with ACLU affiliates in death penalty states, and with coalition partners nationally, CPP promotes both abolition and systemic reform of the death penalty.

Phone Number: 919-682-5659

American Civil Liberties Union
125 Broad Street, 18th Fl.
New York, NY 10004

Helps prisoners who are facing discrimination because they are transgender, lesbian, gay, bisexual or have HIV.

American Correctional Association
206 N. Washington Street
Alexandria, VA 22314

Sells publications, including self-help books.

Phone: (703) 224-0000
Website: aca.org

American Diabetes Association
ATTN: Center for Information
1701 North Beauregard Street
Alexandria, VA 22311

You can also call their Center for Information and Community Support at 1-800-DIABETES (1-800-342-2383). Their hours of operation are Monday - Friday, 8:30 a.m. - 8:00 p.m. EST.

Website: diabetes.org

American Indian Art Magazine
7314 East Osborn Drive
Scottsdale, AZ 85251

For more than 35 years, American Indian Art Magazine has been the premier magazine devoted exclusively to the great variety of American Indian art. This beautifully illustrated quarterly features articles by leading experts, the latest information on current auction results, publications, legal issues, museum and gallery exhibitions and events.

Phone (480) 994-5445
Website: aiamagazine.com

American Magazine Service
1042 Fort Union Blvd. #387
Midvale, UT 84047

Phone Number: (800) 428-6242

American Motorcyclist Association
13515 Yarmouth Dr
Pickerington, OH 43147

American Rehabilitation Ministries
P.O. Box 1490
Joplin, Missouri 64802-1490

They offer bible correspondence courses **FREE**.

AMFAR AIDS Research
120 Wall Street, 13th Floor
New York, NY 10005-3908

Amitabha Buddhist Society of USA
650 S. Bernardo Ave.
Sunnyvale, CA 94087

Phone Number: 408-736-3386

Amnesty International, USA
5 Penn Plaza
New York, NY 10001

Phone Number: 212-807-8400
Email: aimember@aiusa.org

Amnesty Mid-Atlantic Regional Office
600 Penn. Ave., SE 5th Floor

Washington, DC 20003

Phone Number: (202) 544-0200

Anatomy of Hip-Hop Volume 1

This book is by Erskine Harden and Anthony Booth, AKA "The Hip-Hop Connoisseurs", and available from Lavish Life 88 Entertainment.

Synopsis: Enough of the ungratifying fables, and bold face lies about the movement called Hip-Hop! This book takes the reader on an in depth history lesson from the mid-70s to the present, including every element of the genre, giving the much deserved respect to the founding fathers (Kool Herc, Grandmaster Caz and Busy Bee to name a few), in a secure effort to educate the youth and misinformed. This book shines a light on aspects of hip-hop that unfortunately aren't usually mentioned; breakdancing, graffiti and fashion were just as important in the foundation, along with rap music. We, the Hip-Hop Connoisseurs, decided to tell the whole story from conception, growth, and dominate existence of the global phenomenon we love and respect.

Comment: As a Hip-Hop connoisseur myself, reading this book was like going on a fun ride down Hip-Hop Memory Lane. Things I haven't thought about in years were mentioned; as were a few things I didn't know about -- both events and artists. There are a few things I think could and should have been included, but it's probably due to where I'm from verses where they're from -- our respective underground scenes, etc. For example, Brothe Lynch Hung and C-BO were not mentioned at all. Both Bo and Lynch were fuckin' with Master P at his hottest, and Bo was on two songs on Pac's "All Eyes On Me". There probably could have been more on Mac Dre, too, being he's had such a huge impact on the culture where he's from and beyond.

Any fan of hip-hop will appreciate the ride this book takes you on; any upcoming hip-hop artist should be obligated to read it as a history lesson. I don't know everything, but it's at least 95% accurate. Good read. -- Mike

An End to Silence
College of Law
4801 Massachusetts Ave NW
50th Street Building
Washington, DC 20016

The Project on Addressing Prison Rape is committed to eliminating sexual abuse for individuals in custodial settings. The Project on Addressing Prison Rape is a leader in addressing the implications and implementation of the Prison Rape Elimination Act of 2003 (PREA) and its forthcoming standards. Since 2000, the Project on Addressing Prison Rape has provided training; technical assistance and legal guidance for correctional agencies, advocates and survivors who want to effectively prevent, respond and eliminate sexual abuse in custodial settings.

Phone Number: 202-274-4385

Angel Tree; IDSI
510 SE Delaware Ave
Bartlesville, OK 74003

Through Angel Tree, a program of prison fellowship, your child(ren) can receive gifts at Christmas, with love, from you. To share the love of Jesus Christ, church volunteers buy gifts and give them to your child(ren) with age-appropriate presentation of the gospel. Contact your prison's chaplain to request a participation form, or write to them directly.

The Angolite
Louisiana State Penitentiary
Angola, LA 70712

To subscribe, send your name and address to:
The Angolite
C/O Cashier's Office Louisiana State Prison
Angola, LA 70712 USA

The Angolite is the inmate published and edited magazine of the Louisiana State Penitentiary (Angola) in West Feliciana Parish, Louisiana. Each year, six issues are published. Subscriptions are $20 per year.

Phone Number: (504) 655-4411

Comment: This is an award winning magazine of interest to Louisiana State Prisoners. It's a very high quality publication, even if its target demographic is limited. - - Mike

Angres, Robert, L. Esq.
4781 E. Gettysburg Ave., Suite 14
Fresno, CA 93726

Personalized service at reasonable rates with office conveniently located in the Central Valley near seven California State Prisons. 14 years of experience in criminal law. Contact for post-conviction remedies – CA cases only.

Phone Number: (559) 348-1918

Anthroposophical Prison Outreach
1923 Geddes Ave.
Ann Arbor, MI 48104

Do you, as a prisoner, feel that there must be some meaning in your prison experience that is still to be discovered? Or that you can give it meaning? If so, you might be interested in Anthroposophy -- the path from the spirit in man to the spirit in the universe. Anthroposophy embraces a spiritual view of the human being cosmos, but its emphasis is on knowing, not faith. It is a path in which the human heart and hand, and especially our capacity for thinking, are essential.

Comment: Write these guys and ask them to send you their Anthroposophical Prison Outreach Library Book List. It contains over 200 books you can borrow for FREE. Subjects include Inner Development; Family Life; Esoteric Studies; Ancient Myth, Evolution, and History; Social Questions; Arts and Literature; Science and Nature; Spiritual Fiction; Meditations, Verses, Prayers; and more. - - Mike

Anti-Repression Music (ARM)
PO Box 421188
San Francisco, CA 94142

ATTENTION LYRICISTS, POETS, & PROSE WRITERS!

"Inmates and political prisoners: We need lyrics about injustice for our punk rock band A.R.M. Let us spit your words out here!"

Comment: I don't write this kind of music or poetry, but I have some old raps that might work for them. Might be worth trying. Never know what could come it. — Mike

Another Chance 4 Legal, LLC
PO Box 78
Mullins, SC 29574

"AC4L is the only **FREE** interactive post conviction web site! Ask us any question you have about post-conviction or prison issues for **FREE** at: ANOTHERCHANCE4LEGAL@GMAIL.COM.

Trust in AC4L to solve your legal query. AC4L has been doing effective, affordable and credible post-conviction litigation with over 25 years of experience."

Phone Number: 843-879-8361

Anti-Recidivism Coalition
1320 E. 7th St., Suite 260
Los Angeles, CA 90021

This company goes hard for California lifers and are working hard on things like getting our family visits back, getting better good time credits for all Cali inmates and supporting things like SB260, SB261 and SB9. They are always in need of signatures for their
Petitions. Please write and ask how you can assist, and/or have your family go to safetyandrehabilitation.com. This organization is supported by actors Jake Gyllenhaal and Jonah Hill, and rappers like Nas and Common, plus many other people.

Raising Awareness Through Art...

"Our team at ARC has been looking for ways to bring new supporters into this movement, to help us fund reentry programs, housing, mentoring, job training and support for people coming home. Having seen the incredible artists behind the walls, we are proposing doing a huge and high-profile art auction to raise funds and awareness for this movement. It would not be your traditional art auction, it would be at a major museum, with celebrity art auctioneers, and the ability to raise tremendous awareness, bring in massive press and a considerable amount of funding, all to benefit a nonprofit organization and also the artist inside (50/50). We have many board members with powerful connections in the art world, and believe art from inside could sell for 5x or 10x what it traditionally would get.

So, if you are interested in having us sell your pieces to benefit a nonprofit organization as well as support your rehabilitation and reentry, please send a photograph of your piece. (if you're able) or contact us to receive your piece and figure a starting amount for the auction."

Phone: 213-955-5885

Comment: This is a great organization /movement. They cannot be supported enough. By the time this is published, the Raising Awareness Through Art auction written about will probably have taken place. HOWEVER, if you are interested in participating, I suggest you write them and ask about it anyway. They may do more than one, especially if the one they do is successful. In addition, if enough people ask about it, they may do something more consistent to help us prison artists, like start a great website that is supported by their celebrity contacts and board of Directors. We can "petition" them to do something like this for us, just like they petition for law/policy changes. Think outside the box! —Mike

Appalachian Prison Book Project
P.O. Box 601
Morgantown, WV 26507

Sends **FREE** books to: KY, MD, OH, TN, VA, and WV only.

Website: aprisonbookproject.wordpress.com.

Appeals Law Group
33 E. Robinson Street, Suite 220
Orlando, FL 32801

"Aggressive appellate and post-conviction relief attorneys. We specialize in U.S. Supreme Court Appeals, Direct Federal and State Appeals, post-Conviction Relief Motions, Writs of Habeas Corpus, Writs of Error Coram Nobis, Motions for Certificate of Appealability, Pardon and Commutation Petitions, Clemency Petitions, Sentencing Petitions, 2254 and 3355 Petitions, 3582 Petitions, Federal Drugs -2 Motions, Rules

60(b)Motions, Actual Innocence Claims. Call today for a **FREE** consultation!

Due to high volume, unsolicited documents will not be returned. Serious financial inquiries only. Payment plans available on a case-by-case basis. This is an advertisement for legal services. Offices located in FL, NC and MN."

Phone Number: 1-800-411-6898

APWA
198 College Hill Road
Clinton, NY 13323-1218

The American Prison Writing Archive is an Internet-based, non-profit archive of first-hand testimony to the living and working conditions experienced by incarcerated people, prison employees and prison volunteers. Anyone who lives, works or volunteers inside American prisons or jails can contribute non-fiction essays, based on first-hand experience: 5,000-word limit (15 double-spaced pages); a signed APWA permission-questionnaire must be included in order to post on the APWA. All posted work will be accessible to anyone in the world with Internet access. For more info and to download the permissions-questionnaire, go to www.dhinitiative.org/projects/apwa, or write to the address above.

Archipelago
13017 Wisteria Dr. #310
Germantown, MD 20874

This company offers affordable gifts inmates can buy and have sent to loved-ones. Send a first-class stamp for their catalog.

ARE Prison Program; Assn
215 67th St
Virginia Beach, VA 23451

They send religious books to prisoners. Write/Send SASE for more information.

Arab-American Anti-Discrimination Committee
1732 Wisconsin Ave, NW
Washington, D.C. 20007

Provides advice, referrals, and full-time staff attorneys to help defend interest of the community. Also serves as a vital clearing house of accurate information on Arab culture and history for education and school systems.

Phone Number: 202-244-2990

Arizona Justice Project; Arizona State University

MC 4420
411 N. Central Avenue, Suite 600
Phoenix, AZ. 85004-2139

The Arizona Justice Project is primarily a volunteer-based organization that reviews and assists in cases of actual innocence, or cases in which a manifest injustice has occurred. Accepts both DNA and non-DNA cases and represents indigent Arizona inmates whose claims of innocence have gone unheeded. Conducts post-conviction DNA testing in cases of forcible rape, murder, and non-negligent homicide cases, shaken baby syndrome and arson and other cases where the testing might demonstrate actual innocence.

Phone Number: 602-496-0286
Website: azjusticeproject.org

Arrested: What to Do When Your Loved One's in Jail

Whether a defendant is charged with misdemeanor disorderly conduct or first-degree murder, this is an indispensable guide for those who want to support family members, partners or friends facing criminal charges. It's 240 pages, $16.95, and can be bought from Prison Legal News.

Arrest-Proof Yourself

This essential "how not to" guide written by an ex-cop explains how to act and what to say when confronted by the police to minimize the chances of being arrested and avoid additional charges. Includes information on basic tricks that police use to get people to incriminate themselves. It's 288 pages, $14.95, and can be bought from Prison Legal News.

Arts in Criminal Justice

Phone Number: (215) 685-0759
info@www.artsincriminaljustice.org
www.artsincriminaljustice.org

Art With Conviction
PO Box 12255

Tucson, AZ 85732

"We are a not-for-profit organization that is out to promote the artistic talents and creativity of individuals who have been convicted of felony crimes. This organization is dedicated to transforming the way the phrase 'convicted fell is heard in our society, to stripping the phrase of all of the meaning added to it beyond designating someone who has received a felony conviction. To that end, we create a forum for convicted felon artists to showcase through their art, creativity, talent, imagination, hopes, and dreams. This way, our community can see that these men and women are a contribution to us and the artists can see that the community is interested in what they have to offer.

We have not yet selected the date for our next show, but we are always accepting submissions for consideration.

Send SASE for submission form. We need one form per piece submitted. I understand you may not be able to make copies of the form, but all we really need is the information that would go on the form. So if you can write down that information for us on a blank piece of paper for each piece, which works too. Please make sure you sign and put the copyright before your name.

I cannot say which subject matter or theme works best, but what I can say is you should submit the pieces you are proud of and want to be featured in a gallery show.

We will then forward the submissions to the selection committee and they will select the pieces that will be displayed in the next show. All forms of art are welcome, from paintings to crafts.

We do sell the pieces that we show if that is what the artist wishes, but our focus is not on making the sales. Not every piece submitted is shown at every show. We are working on getting an online store up to sell pieces, but we are not there yet. More information about the sale of submissions is in the submission form, so please read it carefully and fill it out, so we know what you want done with your art. To be perfectly candid, if your primary objective is to sell as much of your work as possible, you may want to find a different avenue.

However, if you are interested in helping us pursue our mission of transforming the way the community views convicted felons, then please, by all means, we look forward to receiving your submissions.

We have no problem displaying and selling prints of pieces. In fact, prints are quite popular as they tend to be priced a little more affordable than originals. We also have experienced artists from the commercial and fine art fields helping us price the art, in case you don't know how to price it.

If you have any questions, concerns, comments, or suggestions, please feel free to write us at our mailing address."

Asheville Prison Books Programs
67 N. Lexington Ave.
Asheville, NC 28801

Sends **FREE** reading material to indigent inmates in facilities in North Carolina, South Carolina, Georgia and Tennessee. Can sometimes provide books in Spanish. Donations gladly accepted!

Email Address: prisonbooks31@hotmail.com

Ashley Burleson
Attorney and Counselor at Law
1001 Texas Ave., Suite 1400
Houston, TX 77002

Post-conviction State and Federal Habeas Corpus, Parole Representation, and Family Law for Texas inmates.

The Asian Classics Institute (ACI)
PO Box 144,
New York, NY 10276, USA

Phone Number: (212) 475-7752
Website: www.acidharma.org
E-mail: aci@world-view.org

Ashley Rice Collection
Blue Mountain Arts, Dept. WHIM
P.O. Box 4549
Boulder, CO 80306

This is a greeting card company. Send card material that is light, lively and very original with SASE.

Assisting Incarcerated Muslims (AIM)
PO Box 460
Clayton, LA 71326

Phone Number: (318)757-0557

Association For Research & Enlightenment
c/o Prison Outreach,
215 67th St,
Virginia Beach, VA 23451

Books about the life and work of Edgar Cayce, meditation, and reincarnation. Prisoners are limited to one book every two months.

Association of Happiness for All Mankind
4368 NC Highway 134,
Asheboro, NC 27205

Spiritual books and newsletter.

Association for the Treatment of Sexual Abusers
4900 S.W. Griffith Drive, Suite 274
Beaverton, Oregon 97005, USA

Phone Number: (503) 643-1023
E-mail: atsa@atsa.com

Athens Books to Prisoners
30 1st Street
Athens, OH 45701

Email:athensbooks2prisoners@gmail.com
Website: athensbookstoprisoners

Atkins House
313 E. King Street
York, PA 17403

Atkins House, located in York, PA, is a residential and outpatient treatment center for women offenders providing counseling for drug, alcohol and sexual abuse as well as victim awareness, life skills and mother-child transition after incarceration. Atkins House is a non-profit service organization.

Phone Number: (717) 848-5454
Website: www.atkinshouse.org

ATS HENDERSON
544 Parkson Rd, STE F
Henderson, NV 89011

Inmate services. Great prices. Photos of models, pen pals, copy service, VIP services, gifts to friends and family, internet searches, etc. Send SASE for complete info.

Attorney Ivy McCray

Civil Litigation, Family Law, Probate, Appeals. "If you don't see it here, let's talk."

Phone Number: (415) 306-0888

AudioGiftsRUs
P.O. Box 147
Swansea, MA 02777

AudioGiftsRUs is an inmate-base company that uses innovative technology to allow incarcerated individuals to easily send audio recorded gifts to their love ones.

Phone: 978-816-0039
Email: AudioGiftsRUs@gmail.com

Auto Restore
3 Burroughs
Irvine, CA 92618

Auto Restorer is a monthly how-to newsletter with in-depth articles and step-by-step photos on auto and truck restoration, written by people experienced and knowledgeable on the subject. It serves as a forum for readers to interact with experts and other restoration enthusiasts. 12 issues for only $20.

Phone Number: (949) 855-8822
Website: autorestoreermagazine.com

Auto Week
1155 Gratiot Avenue
Detroit, Michigan 48207-2997

This is the #1 auto magazine in the USA. Its $29.95 for a 1-year subscription; 26 issues per year.

Phone Number: (313) 446.6000
Website: http://www.autoweek.com

Badland Publishing
POB 11623
Riviera Beach, FL 33419

They sell urban books. Write for a catalog.

Phone Number: (561) 842-4746
Website: badlandpub.com.

Baitil Salaam Network

675 Village Square Dr. LL1,
Stone Mountain, GA 30021.

If you are a woman needing transitional housing or a place to parole, call or write.

Phone Number: 770-255-8500
Email:haleem1@aol.com

Baker Industries
184 Pennsylvania Avenue
Malvern, PA 19355

Baker Industries is a unique 501(c) (3) nonprofit organization that promotes a work rehabilitation program employing an overlooked and underutilized workforce population. "We focus specifically on four groups of vulnerable adults: people with disabilities, recovering substance abusers, individuals on parole, and homeless persons, and give them all the opportunity to learn the importance of a solid work ethic in a real work environment."

Phone Number: 610-296-9795
Website: http://bakerindustries.org.

Ball State University Correctional Education Program
Online and Distance Education
Carmichael Hall Room 200
Muncie, IN 47306

Offers degree programs for men incarcerated at Pendleton Correctional Facility.

Phone Number: 765-285-1593

Banks, Jeffery S., Esq.
485 West 5th St.
Reno, NV 89503

Post-conviction filings, appeals, writs, petitions, placement, immigration removal and more.

Phone Number: (775) 324-6640

Bard Prison Initiative
Bard College
PO Box 5000
Annandale-on-Hudson, NY 12504-5000

Phone Number: 845-758-7308
Website: bpi@bard.edu

Comment: This is a terrific in-prison college program. They offer a select group of New York state prisoners the opportunity to earn college degrees for FREE -- Mike

Barrios Unidos
1817 Soquel Avenue
Santa Cruz, CA 95062

Baseball America
4319 South Alston Avenue, Suite 103
Durham, NC 27713

Since 1981, Baseball America has been finding the prospects and tracking them from high school to the big leagues. That means you get comprehensive coverage every step of the way, from high school and colleges to the minors and the majors. 26 issue subscription for $92.95.

Battered Women's Justice Project
1801 Nicollet Ave South, Suite 102
Minneapolis, MN 55403

Provides assistance/info to battered women charged with crimes and to their defense teams. **FREE** newsletter. No direct legal representation.

Phone Number: 800-903-0111 x1
Website: bwjp.org

Battling The Administration

This book, by David Meister, is an "inmate's guide to a successful lawsuit." Written from a prisoner's perspective, this book is excellent for both the first-time litigant and the old hand when it comes to navigating the strange world of prisoner's rights. Its 555 pages, $34.95, and available from Wynword Press.

Comment: "Great book for prisoners litigating their own lawsuit in federal court. I used this book to settle a lawsuit over one book they confiscated, so it was worth it. TMP endorsed!" -- Josh Kruger, author of The Millionaire Prisoner

BAUS Books Circulation
2020 Route 301
Carmel, NY 10512

Buddhist books, only $1-2 postage fees. Write for list of books.

Bayou La Rosa
302 NJ St. #13
Tacoma, WA 98403

Native American Indian support.

B.B.P.D.
PO Box 248
Compton, MD 20627

This company offers over 1,000 books. From the look of their list it seems as if they offer all the most popular genres and titles amongst prisoners: Classical African Civilizations; Antebellum/General History; Civil Rights/ Black Liberation; African/Indigenous Religions; Modern Black Religious Thought; Islam Related; Religious "Anthropology"; Spiritual Philosophy; Political Issues; Masonry/Secret, Societies/Conspiracies; Sociology/Family/Love; Psychology/Education; General Health and Nutrition; Business/Economics/Motivational; Law/Reference; Street Life/ General Literature; Prison Life; Languages; Books in Spanish; and even some specials/used and out-of-print titles. The prices are typical. They also offer a few urban style magazines. Send them a SASE for a **FREE** catalog

Website: bookstoinmates.com

Bead and Button
Kalmbach Publishing Co.
21027 Crossroads Circle
P.O. Box 1612
Waukesha, WI 53187-1612

This magazine is full of materials, ideas, supplies, and accessories. 6 issues for $26.95.

Phone Number: 1-800-533-6644
Website: beadandbutton.com

The Beat Within
PO Box 34310
San Francisco, CA 94134

"We're a nonprofit organization that publishes the writing and artwork of incarcerated youth throughout the country. The Beat Within's mission is to provide incarcerated youth with consistent opportunity to share their ideas and life experiences in a safe space that encourages literacy, self-expression, critical thinking skills, and healthy, supportive relationships with adults and their community. Outside of the juvenile justice system, The Beat Within partners with community organizations and individuals to bring resource to youth both inside and outside of detention. We are committed to being an effective bridge between youth who are locked up and the community that aims to support their progress towards a healthy, non-violent, and productive life.

The last few pages of our publication are dedicated to writing from incarcerated individuals outside of juvenile hall, which includes writing from jails, camps, ranches, prisons, etc., which is where your writing can be published.

We understand that in the past, subscriptions have been free. We regret to inform you that with such high demand, the cost of publication and postage, and the nature of our business (non-profit supported by a limited number of grants), we can no longer provide free subscriptions. Should you desire a specific copy or a subscription, please inquire and send a SASE. You can receive a **FREE** issue, however, if you are published. If published, we will send you the issue your writing appears in.

We look forward to reading your work and passing along your words to the youth and all Beat readers!"

Behive Books Behind Bars
c/o Weller Book Works
607 Trolley Square
Salt Lake City, UT 84102

Sends books to prisoners in these western states only: AZ, CA, CO, ID, MT, NM, NV, OR, UT, WA, and WY.

Bee Smith
PO Box 60156
San Diego, CA 92166

Copies law and does web searches.

Benjamin Ramos, Attorney at Law
705 E Bidwell, Suite 2-359
Folsom, CA 95630

Experienced Habeas Corpus practitioner admitted in all California state and Federal courts. Gives parole representation, challenges bogus gang validation and more.

Phone: 916-358-9842

Berean Prison Ministry
PO Box 761
Peoria, IL 61652

They provide **FREE** bible study material and KJV bibles.

Barnard Library Zine Collection
3009 Broadway
New York, NY 10027

They provide photocopies of zines written by women with an emphasis on zines by women of color. The more specific your question or request the better the assistance they will be able to provide.

BESTGEDTUTOR.COM

Expert online tutoring, has coached over 1200 students to successfully pass the GED, and specializes in biggest challenges on GED tests -- math and essay writing. Personalized training for about $1.00 a day. Contact Janice Chamberlin.

Better People
3711 NE Martin Luther King, Jr. Blvd.
Portland, Oregon 97212

Better People is an established employment and counseling program solely dedicated to helping individuals who have legal histories find, keep and excel in well-paying jobs with fair, decent employers. Servicing the Portland metropolitan area.

Phone Number: (503)281-2663
Website: betterpeople.org

Bhandari, Suresh
Top Floor Udar Guest House
Malvi 313203
Udaipur, India

This company can hook you up with a woman in India who wants to get married. Send them a photo, a full matrimonial bio and $5.

Bible Helps
PO Box 391
Hanover, PA 17331

They provide **FREE** bible tracts.

Bigshots Products
POB 741176

Boynton Beach, FL 33474

Adult novels, hundreds of titles. Send SASE for a **FREE** list!

Black and Pink

Community Church of Boston
Black & Pink
614 Columbia Rd
Dorchester, MA 02125

A volunteer organization that lists queer and transgender prisoners on a pen-pal website, distributes a monthly newsletter of primarily queer/trans prisoner writing, and advocates for specific prisoner needs when possible while also working to abolish the Prison Industrial Complex as a whole.

Phone Number: 617-942-0217

Blackface Productions

I DO NOT RECOMMEND DOING BUSINESS WITH THIS COMPANY!

Comment: These fools claim to be the first adult dating and pen pal website that includes help sections for legal requests. They want you to send a SASE and a book of stamps for their brochure. I see they're advertising in PLN again. It's not the first time. They advertised this same thing a few years back, too. I sent them a book of stamps and got a letter apologizing that they were having complications with their website that they needed to work out. Of course, they didn't send my stamps back. If anyone has a positive experience with these guys, tap in and let me know. -- Mike

Blackstone Career Institute

1011 Brookside Rd, Ste 300,
P.O. Box 3717
Allentown, PA 18106 – 3717

Low-cost paralegal course by mail.

"Blackstone Career Institute's distance learning program enables students to learn about the law and the paralegal field by studying at their own pace and at their facility. No computer, proctors, or facility institutors are required. Upon completion, graduates will have obtained a paralegal certificate and gained knowledge they can use now and in the future.

Here are five reasons why Blackstone is the best choice for paralegal training:

1. Students learn from the best.

2. Blackstone is nationally accredited by the Accrediting Commission of the Distance Education Accrediting Commission (DEAC), regionally accredited by the Middle States Commission on Secondary Schools, and has been privately licensed since 1984. Our 915-clock hour program meets the educational requirements to sit for the Certified Paralegal/Certified Legal Assistant (CP/CLA) Exam sponsored by the National Association of Legal Assistants and administered at testing centers across the country. As BCI Graduate A. Vasquez says, "I have gained knowledge and practical skills that will help me far into the future. BCI sets the standard for excellence in paralegal education."

3. Students start their own library.

4. As part of the tuition, students receive ten volumes of our Modern American Law series as well as four more exclusive Blackstone study units to guide them through their studies. But that's not all; students will also receive two additional reference resources to assist them throughout the program -- the Blackstone Law Glossary and Merriam-Webster's Dictionary of Law — as well as the book Writing to Win: The Legal Writer upon graduation.

5. Students get everything they need -- for less.

6. Blackstone's Paralegal Studies Certificate Program remains one of the most reasonably priced in the country. Everything students need to graduate is included with their tuition -- textbooks, study guides, exam services, and student support delivered through the mail. We also offer a BCI Interest-free payment plan, and our career program is approved for GI Bill Education Benefits.

7. Students decide when and where to study.

8. Students set their own schedule and progress at their own pace. They can finish as quickly as they wish or take the full two years they are permitted.

9. Students prepare to follow their dream!

10. Our paralegal program will give students the opportunity to enhance their knowledge, help others, or acquire new skills they can use in the future. In addition to our Modern American Law series, we have included research, ethics, and Job search skills in our 915-clock hour program.

With BCI, incarcerated individuals will be taking an important step towards a better future. Send for full information now!"

Phone Number: 800-826-9228
Website: blackstone.edu

Comment: While not very challenging casework, they are a quality, dependable and affordable company that offers correspondence courses to prisoners. -- Mike

BLADE Magazine
700 E State St.
Iola, WI 54990

BLADE Magazine – The World's Number One Knife Publication.

Phone Number: (715)445-2214
Website: www.blademag.com

The Blue Book of Grammar and Punctuation

A guide to grammar and punctuation by an educator with experience teaching English to prisoners. It's 110 pages, $14.95, and can be bought from Prison Legal News.

Book'em
P.O. Box 71357
Pittsburgh, PA 15213

FREE books to PA prisoners only. Focuses on educational and non-fiction books.

Books Between Bars
1117 Peach Street
Abilene, Texas 79602

Books Between Bars can provide one book every 60 days to Texas prisoners who write to request it. Each request takes 7-14 days to process. The requests can be fiction, nonfiction, biography, self-help, parenting religious, etc. Write for a copy of an application form, which needs to be filled out and sent back to Books Between Bars.

Book to Prisoners
c/o Left Bank Books
92 Pike St., Box A
Seattle, WA 98101

Request by subject. Very limited legal and religious material available. Cannot pay postage to prisons in CA, or to prisoners requiring "New Books."

Phone Number: (206) 442-2013
Website: bookstoprisoners.@live.com

Books To Prisoners
c/o Groundwork Books,
0323 Student Center
La Jolla, CA 92037

FREE books. Serves all states

Books Through Bars
4722 Baltimore Ave
Philadelphia, PA 19143

Provides books to prisoners in PA, NY, NJ, DE, MD, WV, and VA. Please request books by subject or topic rather than by specific titles. They generally have little to no legal materials.

Phone Number: (215) 727-8170
Website: booksthroughbars.org

Books Through Bars – NYC
c/o Bluestockings Bookstore
 172 Allen St
New York, NY 10002

Ships to prisoners nationwide. Specializes in political and history books. Occasionally sends fiction and educational books. No religious literature. Donations of stamps and cash are appreciated.

Books Through Bars / Providence
c/o Paper Nautilus Books
5 Anqell St.
Providence, RI 02906

Nationwide. Write with a list of subjects you're interested in.

Boston University Prison Education Program
808 Commonwealth Avenue
Boston, MA 02215

Phone: (617) 353-3025
website: prisoned@bu.edu

Comment: This is another terrific in-prison college program that's allows Massachusetts state prisoners to earn associates, bachelors, and master's degrees for FREE. This is a terrific organization. — Mike

Bottled Thoughts
P.O. Box 596
Wills Point, Texas 75169

Bottled Thoughts is committed to providing unique gifts to express your love for that special someone. "Our customer service department aims to achieve the highest possible standard in all that we do. Our number one priority is helping our customers execute a heartfelt reaction with creativity and flair."

Your message will be beautifully printed on themed paper and placed in a glass bottle with sand and sea shells, tied with a ribbon. They also have a few gifts you can order, as well as gift packages for children. Write/Send SASE for more information.

Phone Number: 1-877-705-0425

Branlettes Beauties
PO Box 5765
Baltimore, MD 21282

Our prices are simple:

1-4999 photos = 0.45 cents each
5000+ photos = 20% discount
1-9 catalogs: $3.00 each (+SASE)
10 catalogs: $25.00 + SASE (4 stamps)

Select your favorite:

White catalogs (60 volumes), Black catalogs (60 volumes), Asian and Latino catalogs (60 volumes). Please state what style photos -- provocative poses or nude.

FREE catalog? Yes! Just send us 2 US Forever stamps and a SASE and we will send to you one nude or BOP-friendly sample catalog (1 per customer) with 84 gorgeous girls in full color. Act now as this offer will not be around long!!

Branlettes Breathless Beauties Bag: A random selection of 50 of the rare and exotic. Yes, 50 beauties all posing just for you! Plus 2 of our finest color catalogs! Only $19.99! Did you read that right? Yes, only $19.95 for 50 of Branlettes breathless beauties (please specify nude of BOP-friendly)! Plus two of our finest color catalogs **FREE**! (You pick the volumes) Our regular shipping/handling policies apply.

All sales are final! Each catalog has 84 gorgeous ladies to choose from. High quality prints on 4X6 glossy photo paper.

Shipping and handling:

Due to various prison policies regarding how many pictures can be sent in one envelope, our policy is as follows:

01-5 photos - $1.00 per envelope
06-15 photos - $1.50 per envelope
16-25 photos - $2.00 per envelope

Our simple policies: Special requests are not permitted and all models are of legal age. Due to tremendous time and cost answering letters, unless you are placing an order or a question regarding your order, we will not reply to any other questions. A SASE is required for any inquiries or concerns!

You and you alone are responsible for your selections being allowed into your facility! Know your institution's policies as to what image content is allowed. Returned orders are non-refundable. They will be held for 14 calendar days in order for you to send self-addressed stamped envelopes (3 first-class stamps per envelope), with a street address for every 20 pictures. All returned images held after 2 weeks will be resold and we will return to our stock.

All payments are by institutional checks or US postal service or Western Union money orders! These payments are processed immediately and shipped in less than 3-4 weeks. Any other company money orders delay shipment 8-10 weeks or until that money clears our bank. Yes, we deal with people that are, while in prison, still trying nickel and dime scams.

Bridge Project
Center For Community Service and Justice
4501 N. Charles St
Baltimore, MD 21210

FREE brochure of contemplative meditation.

Brilliance Audio, INC
1704 Eaton Dr.
Grand Haven, MI 49417

These guys sell gifts. Write/Send SASE for more information.

Brothers Against Banging Youths
632 Harden Dr. #2
Inglewood, CA 90302

"We are an alternatives option program for 'Youth at Risk. The mission of Brothers Against Banging Youths (B.A.B.Y.) is to prevent and deter young people in the South Los Angeles area from joining gangs by educating them and their parents on the recruitment strategies of gangs, as well as provide counseling services to those 'At Risk' youth whom are prime targets of gang recruitment. Additionally, we will provide before and after school activities for youth, thus keeping them engaged in positive activities and programs decreasing the likelihood of them turning to gangs to participating in other negative activities."

Books To Prisoners
c/o Left Bank Books
92 Pike Street Box A
Seattle, WA 98101

Books on spiritual growth and Edgar Cayce. Prisoners may receive 2 **FREE** books per month. Request books by topics not titles.

Email Address: bookstoprisoners@cs.com

Bud Plant Comic Art
PO Box 1689
Grass Valley, CA 95945

The Bud Plant Incredible Catalog is published 3 times a year. These 248-page monsters cover everything from the upper levels of the underground to mainstream comic art. The first copy is three bucks (redeemable on your first order) and then continuously as long as you keep ordering from them. They also send smaller update catalogs every couple of months. Many of the comics included in Beyond Cyberpunk! are available through *Bud Plant*. The service is prompt, the calls are toll-free, and your comics come tightly wrapped in protective paper. *Bud Plant* also carries lots of adult comics and how-to art books.

Phone Number: 1-800-242-6642

Buddhist Association of the United States
Chuang Yen Monastery
2020, Route 301
Carmel, NY 10512

FREE books.

Phone: 845-228-4287
Email:book@baus.org

Buddhist Churches of America
1710 Octavia Street
San Francisco, CA 94109

Phone Number: (415) 776-5600 x11
Website: buddhistbookstore.com

Butler Legal Group
818 18th St. NW, Suite 630
Washington, DC 20006

These guys will type your briefs or help you write a motion. Write/Send SASE for more information.

Phone Number: (202)223-6767

Butterwater, LLC
PO Box 669
Mathews, NC 28106

Catalogs:
The Butterwaters 1&2: $2.50 or 5 stamps (with SASE). **FREE** online!
The Butterwaters 3&4: $2.50 or 5 stamps (with SASE). **FREE** online!
The Butterwaters 5: $2.50 or 5 stamps (with SASE). **FREE** online!
The Butterwaters 6: $2.50 or 5 stamps (with SASE).
The Butterwaters 7: $2.50 or 5 stamps (with SASE).
White Pages 1: $2.50 or 5 stamps (with SASE).
White Pages 2: $2.50 or 5 stamps (with SASE).
Pink 11 (nude): $5.00 or 10 stamps.
Pink 12 (nude): $5.00 or 10 stamps.
The "B" side: **FREE** online.

Send SASE today for a **FREE** catalog!

4X6 color photos. One dollar ($1.00) per photo. Minimum order is ten (10) photos for ten dollars ($10.00), plus $2.50 shipping and handling. Orders can be shipped as per facility rules (5 per envelope, etc...). We do not accept cash. Please send money order or Corr. facility check. Use order form or create your own list.

Website: thebutterwaters.com

The Buzz Report

Subscribe today and get all of your sports scores and lines delivered conveniently to your email inbox, every day! Add infosportzzbuzz.com to your Corrilinks email subscription list for info on how to get The Buzz!

Caged Kingdom
4023 Banbury Way
Antioch, CA 94531

"Caged Kingdom serves with compassion! No high prices! You can actually earn money by becoming a member of Caged Kingdom. It's ridiculous to pay 50, 40, or even 30 dollars for a profile that may or may not find you a compatible penpal. Know your worth and

get what you deserve! Do you have an untapped talent? Let's not let it go to waste. Artists, get paid for your art, keep rights to your work and get paid continuously. Writers, you have the same opportunity as artists. You must be a member to be eligible. $7 gets you a full membership, your profile displayed on cagedkingdorn.net for people to contact you, access to resources and a chance to participate in regular contest for real cash. At Caged Kingdom you get more for less! We're here to assist. Affordable for everybody! Have your relatives outside sign you up at cagedkingdom.net or request an application. Send your request with an SASE. We also accept Forever stamps!

Email: cagedkingdom@gmail.com

California Coalition for Women Prisoners
1540 Market St. Suite 490
San Francisco, CA 94102

Runs action center and produces newsletter "The Fire Inside."

California Families to Abolish Solitary Confinement

Website: http://www.abolishsolitary.com/

California Innocence Project
California Western School of Law Institute for Criminal Defense Advocacy
225 Cedar Street
San Diego, CA 92101

Cases Accepted:
DNA and non-DNA cases from Southern California: Imperial Co., Kern Co., Los Angeles Co., Orange Co., Riverside Co., San Bernardino Co., San Diego Co., San Luis Obispo Co., Santa Barbara Co., and Ventura Co., sentence of more than 3 years will consult.

Phone Number: 619-525-1485

California Lifer Newsletter
PO Box 277
Rancho Cordova, CA 95741

CLN is a newsletter published six times per year, with reviews of the latest published and unpublished state and federal cases concerning parole issues and many more topics of interest to prisoners. CLN for prisoners is $30 or (60 First Class Forever Stamps) per year.

Phone Number: (916) 402-3750
Website: lifesupportalliance.org

California NORML
2215 R Market St. #278
San Francisco, CA 94114

This is a national organization working to change laws that criminalize marijuana sales, possession, and use. Write/Send SASE for more information.

Phone number: (415)563-5858
Website: canorml.org

California Prison Focus
1904 Franklin Street, Suite 507
Oakland, CA 94612

"Our newsletter magazine is primarily by prisoners and for prisoners, their friends and families. The current and past issues are available **FREE** for download. You can also receive a paper copy at your home (or send one to your relative or friend in prison). We request a donation of $20 or more for four issues to help cover editing, printing, and mailing costs. Write/Send SASE for more information."

Phone Number: (510) 836-7222
Website: www.prisons.org

Calvary Chapel of Philadelphia
13500 Philmont Ave.
Philadelphia, PA 19116

FREE Bible correspondence course.

The Camelback Group
1220 South Almar Circle
Mesa, AZ 85204

Phone number: (602) 535-1298
thecamelbackgroup .com

This is an internet public relations group that will
help remove unwanted, negative postings for when
you are
Googled, etc.

Campaign to End the Death Penalty
P.O. Box 25730
Chicago, IL 60625

A national grassroots abolitionist organization that
works with prisoners, family members and
organizers. CEDP publishes a newsletter called The
New Abolitionist (**FREE** to prisoners).

Phone Number: (773) 955-4841.

Carbone, Charles
PMB 212
3128 16th St.
San Francisco, CA 94103

This is an attorney that specializes in prison rights.
CA only.

Website: prisonerattorney.com

Carolina Caselaw
5401 A South Blvd #281
Charlotte, NC 28217

Write/Send SASE for more information.

Casa Frontera Visitor Center
PO Box 70407
Riverside, CA 92513

These guys provide transportation (by reservation)
from Ontario Airport to the CA Institution for
Women, as well as provide visiting families with
proper visiting attire, information, light
refreshments, and a place to rest.

Phone Number: (909)597-7845.

CaseSearch
2611 Canfield St.
Houston, TX 77004

An established paralegal firm providing factual
investigation and legal research into state and federal
post-conviction habeas corpus. Referrals to attorneys
upon completion.

Phone: 346-276-7288

Cash for your Stamps
P.O. Box 687
Walnut, CA 91788

Get the highest return for all your stamps. Send
SASE for brochure.

Catalogchoice.org
They list thousands of catalogs on their website.
Some cost money but others are **FREE**.

Catholic Charities USA
P.O. Box 17066
Baltimore, MD 21297-1066

They provide a host of services including emergency
services, food banks, soup kitchens, home delivery
meals, clothing assistance, disaster response,
transitional housing, temporary shelter, counseling
and mental health services, substance abuse
treatment and recovery services and adoption
services.

Phone: 703-549-1390
Website: www.catholiccharitiesusa.org

**Caught: The Prison State and the Lockdown of
American Politics**

This book is by Marie Gottschalk. Its $35.00 and
available from Princeton University Press at
press.princeton.edu. Here are a few blurbs…

"Caught may well be the best book on this subject to
appear in decades." -- Glen C. Altschuler, Huffington
Post

"Devastatingly persuasive." -- Stephen Lurie, Los Angeles Review of Books

"A searing critique of current Incarceration policies and prevailing approaches to prison reform... Caught is brilliantly argued, breathtakingly capacious In Its Informational reach, and intellectually bold. A stunning achievement." -- Mary Falnsod Katzenstein, Cornell University

CDCR, Office of the Ombudsman
1515 S. St. Room 540 North
Sacramento, CA 95811

Celebrity Tattoo
Attn: Brian
11730 West Colfax Ave.
Lakewood, CO 80215

These guys buy and sell tattoo line art. Write for more information.

Phone Number: (720)436-2912
Website: findthattattoo.com

Celito Lindo Properties, LLC
9201 Warren Pkway
Frisco, TX 75035

Inmate real estate services. Buy, sell, exchange. Any type of real estate; any location; and condition.

Phone: 214-702-5500

The Cell Block
PO Box 1025
Rancho Cordova, CA 95741

The Cell Block is an independent multimedia company with the objective of accurately conveying the "street/prison" experience with the credibility and honesty that only one who has lived it can deliver, through literature and other arts, and to entertain and enlighten while doing so.

Available titles:

- The Best Resource Directory For Prisoners, by Mike Enemigo
- The Art & Power of Letter Writing for Prisoners, by Mike Enemigo
- Thee Enemy of the State, by Mike Enemigo
- Conspiracy Theory, by Mike Enemigo
- Black Dynasty, by Mike Enemigo, Dutch & Assa Reigns
- BMF, by Mike Enemigo, Dutch, & King Guru
- BASic Fundamentals of The Game, by Maurice "Mac BA$" Vasquez
- Loyalty & Betrayal, by Mike Enemigo & Armando Ibarra
- Jailhouse Publishing, by Mike Enemigo
- The Millionaire Prisoner 2-in-1 by Mike Enemigo & Josh Kruger
- The Millionaire Prisoner Part 1, by Mike Enemigo & Josh Kruger
- The Millionaire Prisoner Part 2, by Mike Enemigo & Josh Kruger
- The Millionaire Prisoner 3: Success University by Mike Enemigo & Josh Kruger
- A Guide to Relapse Prevention for Prisoners, by Charles Hottinger Jr.
- A.O.B., by Mike Enemigo, Dutch & Manny Fresh
- Pimpology: The 7isms of the Game, by Mike Enemigo & Manny Fresh
- Money iz the Motive, By Mike Enemigo & Ca$ciou$ Green
- Money iz the Motive 2, By Mike Enemigo & Ca$ciou$ Green
- Mob$tar Money, By Mike Enemigo & Ca$ciou$ Green
- Block Money, By Mike Enemigo & Ca$ciou$ Green
- Devils & Demons, by Mike Enemigo, Dutch & King Guru
- Devils & Demons 2, by Mike Enemigo, Dutch & King Guru
- Devils & Demons 3, by Mike Enemigo, Dutch & King Guru
- Devils & Demons 4, by Mike Enemigo, Dutch & King Guru
- How to Hustle & Win: Sex, Money, Murder Edition; by Mike Enemigo & King Guru
- How To Write Urban Books For Money & Fame: Prisoner Edition, by Mike Enemigo & King Guru
- Pretty Girls Love Bad Boys: The Prisoner's Guide To Getting Girls, By Mike Enemigo & King Guru
- Raw Law: Your Rights, And How To SUE When They Are Violated, By Mike Enemigo & King Guru
- The Prison Manual: The Complete Guide To Surviving The American Prison System, by Mike Enemigo
- The Ladies Who Love Prisoners: Secrets Exposed!, by Mike Enemigo

- Get Out, Stay Out: The Secrets To Getting Out of Prison Early, And Staying Prison For Good!, by Mike Enemigo & Shane Bowen
- The Mob, by Mike Enemigo, Dutch & Boss Mafi
- OJ's Life Behind Bars: The Real Story!, by Mike Enemigo & Vernon Nelson

Website: thecellblock.net
Instagram: mikeenemigo
Facebook: facebook.com/thecellblock.net
E-mail: info@cellblock.net
CorrLink: thecellblock.net@mail.com

The Cell Door Magazine
149850 Road 40.2
Mancos, CO 81328

Mission Statement: Articles are written by prisoners or people who are closely associated with the prison experience. Our goal is to acquire readers who choose Cell Door for its quality and educational/entertainment value, learning in the process that prisoners are intelligent, personable, talented human beings.

Comment: This mag is a 5.5 x 8.5 color booklet with articles and art by prisoners. It's nice and it's FREE. You can also submit writings and art of your own, too. - - Mike

CELLBLOCKART.COM

Email: frank@mesaart.net

Comment: These guys are not connected to my company, The Cell Block. I'ma have to check them out, though. They offer fine art prints, digital prints, posters (12" X 18"), and t-shirts. - - Mike

The Cellings of America

This is PLN's first anthology and it presents a detailed "inside" look at the workings of the American criminal justice system. It's 264 pages, $22.95, and can be bought from Prison Legal News.

Cellmate & Convict Services
PO 653
Venus, TX 76084

This company sells sexy non-nude photos. They have over 150 catalogs, featuring Camel Toe, Next Door Nikki, Vida Guerra, Blac Chyna, Amber Rose, Butt Shots, Jennifer Lopez, Sasha Gray, Kardashians, Jenna Shea, Nicki Minaj, Brazil Women, Ariana Grande, and much, much more.

4x6 photos are $.50; 5x7 photos are $1.50; 8x10 photos are $3. They do have some bulk deals. Send SASE for more info.

Website: cellmates2015.com

Comment: I reached out to them to do business, proceeding with their guidelines precisely. Boss Lady is only occasionally responsive. Maybe overwhelmed, I don't know. I completed my VERY expensive end of the bargain months ago. Despite my due diligence in follow-up, I have received NOTHING. - - Paul Keller, Washington

Cell Workout

This book, written by a former prisoner (L.J. Flanders), is a bodyweight training guide designed for use in a prison cell without the need for actual weights. This program is suitable for any age, ability and fitness level and promises results for everyone who tries it. There are step-by-step instructions of how to do the exercises, photographs and sample workouts to follow. The aim of this book is to benefit the physical and mental health of people in prison and outside. Get the body you want -- inside and out!

CellPals!
PO Box 296
Leonville, LA 70551

Cell Shop
PO Box 1487
Bloomfield, NJ 07003

This company sells gifts that prisoners can buy for their loved-ones. Write/Send SASE for more information.

Phone Number: (973)770-8100
Website: cellshopgiftshop.com

Centerforce
PO Box 415
San Quentin, CA 94964

Community-based organization providing HIV-related education for inmates.

Center for the Children of Incarcerated Parents

P.O. Box 41-286
Eagle Rock, CA 90041

Provides **FREE** educational material for incarcerated parents and their children, as well as therapeutic services, family reunification services, and related information. Many services are **FREE**.

Center for Constitutional Rights

666 Broadway, 7th Fl.
New York, NY 10012

CCR is a non-profit legal and educational organization committed to the creative use of law as a positive force for social change and dedicated to advancing and protecting rights guaranteed by the US Constitution.

Phone Number: 212-614-6481
Website: ccrjustice.org

Center for Disease Control's National Prevention Information Network

P.O. Box 6003
Rockville, MD 20849-6003

Provides info, publications, and technical assistance on HIV/AIDS, STDs, and TB M-F 9am-6pm (Eastern Time.) Se habla espanol. General medical info hotline on ALL medical questions is 1-800-CDC-INFO.

Center for Health Justice

900 Avila Street, Suite 301
Los Angeles, CA 90012

This is a hotline for prisoners with HIV and Hep; collect calls accepted.

Phone Number: 213-229-0985
Website: centerforhealthjustice.org

The Center For LWOP Studies

2851 West Ave. L #302
Lancaster, CA 93536

ATTENTION VERMONT LWOP PRISONERS!

"The Center for Life Without Parole Studies wants to work in partnership with you to end LWOP sentences for adults in Vermont. It is the Centers position that LWOP sentences are, in fact, the death penalty and should be abolished for everyone, not just for juveniles.

The Center believes LWOP prisoners are the source of vitally important experiential knowledge and wisdom, and without you we cannot accomplish our goal of ending this cruel, inhumane, and degrading sentence. If you are interested in participating, please send to the address above any information you have about LWOP in Vermont, other materials you think may be helpful, and any ideas you have about pursuing this work. We look forward to hearing from you."

Center on Wrongful Convictions

Northwestern University School of Law
375 East Chicago Avenue
Chicago, Illinois 60611-3069

Phone Number: (312) 503-2391
Website: law.northwestern.edu

Central Texas ABC

PO Box 7187
Austin, Texas 78713

They have D.I.Y. legal booklets and some anarchist literature. Write/Send SASE for more information.

Centro Legal De La Raza

3022 International Blvd, Suite 410
Oakland, CA 94601

Provides many services for immigrants and helps with detention cases.

Centurion Ministries, INC

221 Witherspoon
Princeton, New Jersey 08542-3215

A private non-profit organization that will ONLY consider cases of wrongful conviction in the U.S. and Canada that involve a sentence of life in prison or death. CM does NOT consider self-defense or accidental death cases. Do not call or email, ONLY submit a written summary of the facts of a case and the facts supporting your innocence. All letters are responded to. Submit a case for consideration to the address listed. For submission procedures and guidelines:

http://www.centurionministries.org/criteria.html

Phone Number: (609) 921-0334

Chandra Yoga Resources

1400 Cherry St

Denver, CO 80220

FREE books on devotional yoga and mantra meditation.

Channel Guide Magazine
PO Box 8501
Big Sandy, TX 75755

This TV guide offers daily schedules for over 120 channels, weekly TV best bets, over 3,000 movie listings, TV crossword, Sudoku, celebrity interviews and more. For one year (12 Issues), send $30.00 check or money order.

Phone Number: 866-323-9385

"I have a subscription and use it to plan my TV watching for the weekend. Definitely worth it if you like moves like I do. TMP endorse and recommended! - - Josh Kruger, author of The Millionaire Prisoner

Cheaters
4516 Lovers Lane, Suite 104
Dallas, TX 75225

Comment: *You know she's cheating, bruh. You might wanna write these fools. - - Mike*

Chicago Books to Women in Prison
4511 N. Hermitage Ave
Chicago, IL 60640

FREE books to women prisoners in AZ, CA, CT, FL, IL, IN, KY, MO, & OH.

Chicago Innocence Project
205 West Monroe Street, Suite 315
Chicago, IL 60606

The Chicago Innocence Project investigates cases in which prisoners may have been convicted of crimes they did not commit, with priority to murder cases that resulted in sentences of death or life without parole.

Phone: 312.263.6213

Chican@ Power and the Struggle for Aztlan

This book is by a MIM (Prisons) Study Group. It costs $20 + s/h ($10 for prisoners), and the production costs are huge. Chican@ Power is an invaluable resource for anyone struggling for liberation of the internal semi-colonies of the United States. They don't want anyone to be prevented to read the book for lack of funds, so they're asking anyone who can contribute $10 for their copy, or more to cover for others, to please step up and send in your donations today! If your facility allows, you can send them stamps. To send a check, they need to send you their instructions so write and tell them first. Send to Under Lock & Key.

Chicken Soup for the Prisoner's Soul
P.O. Box 7816
Wilmington, DE 19803

Inspirational seminars and books. Seminar: "A Winning Recipe for Success Behind Bars." Books include: "Chicken Soup for the Prisoner's Soul," "Serving Productive Time," Serving Time, Serving Others" and "Chicken Soup for the Volunteer's Soul."

Phone Number: 302-475-4825
Website: www.tomlagana.com

Children of Incarcerated Parents
PO Box 41-286
Eagle Rock, CA 90041

Works to stop intergenerational incarceration. Provides resources in three areas: education, family reunification, and services for incarcerated parents and their children.

Children's Book Insider, LLC
901 Columbia Road
Fort Collins, CO 80525

Questions & Information: 970-495-0056

Christian Pen Pals
PO Box 11296
Hickory, NC 28603

ChristianPrisonPenPals.org

Post your profile immediately, just like any dating website, and edit it any time of day or night. Friends and family can register, pay for your ad with PayPal, and upload your photos, address, description and bio.

Chronos Masterpiece
509 Laurel #1111
La Marque, TX 77568

100-4x6-photo grab bags for $35. You choose the style: Hispanic, Butts, Blondes, Selfies, White, Young, Flat-Chested, Amateur, Asian, Redheads. Send SASE for more info.

Email: chronosmasterpieces@outlook.com

Citizens Against Recidivism
P.O. Box 9 - Lincolnton Station,
New York, NY 10037.

They work to achieve the restoration of all the rights of citizens among people in prison or jail, as well as those who've been released, in collaboration with other community and faith-based organizations.

Phone Number: (212)252-2235
Website: www.citizensinc.org

Citizens United for Alternatives to the Death Penalty
PMB 335
2603 Dr. Martin Luther King Jr. Hwy
Gainesville, FL 32609

The Religious Organizing Against the Death Penalty Project seeks to build a powerful coalition of faith-based activists. Nationally, it works with official religious bodies to develop strategies and to promote anti-death penalty activism within each faith tradition. At the grassroots level, the Project links with individuals and faith communities, establishing "covenant" relationships to foster local abolition efforts.

Phone Number: (800) 973-6548

Citizens United for Rehabilitation of Errants National CURE
PO Box 2310
Washington, DC 20013-2310

CURE is a membership organization. "We work hard to provide our members with the information and tools necessary to help them understand the criminal justice system and to advocate for changes."

Phone Number: 202-789-2126
http://www.curenational.org

The Classroom and the Cell: Conversations on Black Life in America

This book is written by Mumia Abu-Jamal and co-authored by Columbia University professor Marc Lamont Hill. It's available from Third World Press -

- TWPBooks.com. For Mumia's commentaries, visit www.prisonradio.org. Keep updated on him at freemumia.com. Encourage the media to publish and broadcast Mumia's commentaries and interviews.

Cleveland Career Center
C/O Edward Little
1701 E 13th St.
Cleveland, OH 44114

These guys have a project called PROES – providing real opportunities for ex-offenders to succeed. PROES focuses on immediate employment, augmented with support services, and they work in conjunction with employment solutions programs of Alternatives Agency, Inc., a halfway house for formally incarcerated individuals.

Phone number: (212) 664-4673

CNA Entertainment, LLC
PO Box 185
Hitchcock, TX 77563

"Hey there! We are a visual media entertainment mail order LLC that distributes photos of a large variety of models to the prison population across the country. We currently have over 180 non-nude catalogs with a variety of different themes. We also offer custom printing and personal photo reproduction. For more information about any of our services or products, please drop us a line and we will fill you in. Hope to hear from you soon and have a great day."

Website: CNAEntertainment.com
Email: CNATexas@live.com

Comment: This company has a lot going on -- pictures, custom calendars, bookmarks, 20-photo "proof" sets, and more, all with bad bitches on them. This is one of the biggest, most serious non-nude photo companies I've seen and they are well organized. - Mike

Coalition for Jewish Prisoners
1640 Rhode Island Avenue NM
Washington, DC 20036

Coalition For Prisoner's Rights Newsletter
Box 1911
Sante Fe, NM 87504-1911

Prisoners' Rights - Prison Project of Santa Fe.

Monthly newsletter **FREE** to currently and formally incarcerated individual and family members. Stamps and donations needed.

Phone Number: (505) 982-9520

College In Prison

Written by Bruce Michaels, this book is $14.95 and can be purchased at barnsandnoble.com.

Colorado Innocence Project
Wolf Law Building | 401 UCB
2450 Kittredge Loop Drive
Boulder, Colorado 80309

Phone Number: 303-492-8047
Website:
colorado.edu/law/academics/clinics/colorado-innocence-project

Colorado Criminal Justice Reform Coalition
1212 Mariposa St., #6
Denver, CO 80204

The mission of the Colorado Criminal Justice Reform Coalition is to reverse the trend of mass incarceration in Colorado. They also strongly oppose the for-profit, private prison industry and its presence in Colorado.

Phone Number: (303) 825-0122
Email: info@ccjrc.org

Colossal Book of Criminal Citations
c/o Barkan Research
PO Box 352
Rapod River, MI 49878

3700+ citation references for Supreme, Circuit, District and State courts; Sample Federal and State; Jury instructions; District court addresses; 100+ topics; 500+ legal definitions. Prisoner price is $54.95. You can also order the PDF file online at Barkanresearch.com for $19.95.

Columbia Human Rights Law Review
Attn: JLM Order
435 West 116th Street
New York, NY 10027

The *JLM* Eighth Edition main volume is $30. The *Immigration & Consular Access Supplement* is $5. The books may be ordered together, or either book may be ordered separately. First-class shipping is included in both prices. **They do not accept postage stamps as payment.**

Phone Number: (212) 854-1601

Columbia Legal Services, Institutions Projects
101 Yesler Way, Suite 300
Seattle, WA 98104

Phone Number: 206-382-3399
Website:www.columbialegal.org

Commentary Magazine
165 East 56th St.
New York, NY 10022

Committee for Public Counsel Services Innocence Program
Lisa Kavanaugh, Program Director
CPCS Innocence Program
21 McGrath Highway, 2nd floor
Somerville, MA 02143

Phone Number: 617-623-0591
Website: lkavanaugh@publiccounsel.net

Community Alliance on Prisons
PO Box 37185
Honolulu, HI 96837

A coalition that focuses on alternatives to incarceration, prison reform legislative issues, community education, and effective interventions for Hawaii's non-violent offenders.

Compassion Works for All and Dharma Friends Prison Outreach Project by mail:
Compassion Works for All
Attn: Anna Cox
PO Box 7708
Little Rock, Ar. 72217-7708

Website: JUSTUSFRIENDS.org

Complete GED Preparation

This useful handbook contains over 2000-GED-style questions to thoroughly prepare students for taking the GED test. It offers complete coverage of the revised GED test with re- testing information, instructions and a practice test, its 922 pages, $24.99, and can be bought from Prison Legal News.

Con-Art
PO Box 61

Lankin, ND 58250

Want to see your arts and crafts? These guys specialize in selling work by incarcerated people. They accept all art, from any institution. Contact Colten Pede or Kellie Warner.

Phone: 701-331-2518

CONPALS / InmateConnections.com
465 NE 181st Ave, 308
Portland, OR 97230

"92% response rate! 75,000 hits daily! A+ rating with the BBB!

Ready to go online? Sign up now! Choose the basic webpage for $45 and get your first-contact emails all year long! Or, choose the Deluxe Webpage for $65 and got ALL your emails from everyone, including friends and family, all yearlong!

We offer personal, Legal, and Art & Business webpages.

Basic webpages are $45. Deluxe webpages are $65. Add another $10 to either page option and receive our brochure, 'How to Write a Better Pen Pal Ad'. You may submit your statement after you've had a chance to review our brochure. Brochure only available with purchase of web page and cannot be purchased separately.

Our service includes: Maximum 150-word statement and 2 scanned images displayed on your page; OR, Maximum 250 words statement on your page a 1 scanned image displayed on your page. Your professionally-designed web page on the inmateconnections.com website for a full year. Photo re-touching and enhancement. Personal web pages for male prisoners: Your linked photo placed in directories for state or federal prisoners; in age directory, alpha directory, photo gallery and in directory of newly-listed prisoners for the first 30 days. Your linked photo placed in directories for lifer, gay/bisexual, and death row prisoners, if applicable. Personal web pages for female prisoners: Your linked photo placed in directories for female prisoners and in our directory of newly-listed prisoners for the first 30 days. Legal web pages for male and female prisoners placed in our directory of legal web pages and newly-listed prisoners for the first 30 days. Art & Business web pages placed in directory of Art & Business web pages and newly-listed prisoners for the first 30 days. If you purchase

a Legal or Art & Business web page it is recommended that you also purchase a personal web page. You will get more exposure to your Legal or Art & Business web page this way. With any of these options you will also get a printout of your page mailed to you, as well as Email messages (if any) mailed to you each week.

EXTRA EXPOSURE & MORE...

Front Page Placement: 4 weeks, $20; 12 week, $50; 1 year, $150. This gets your photo on the first page visitors see after entering the site.

Landing Page Placement: 4 weeks, $30; 12 weeks, $75; 1 year, $225. This gets your photo on the Home page.

Pen Pal Express: 4 weeks, $60; 12 weeks, $150; 1 year, $450. This gets your photo on the left-hand side of every page on the site.

Triple Exposure: 4 weeks, $75; 12 weeks, $175; 1 year, $525. This gets your photo in all three of the above areas!

Hit Counter: $20 per year. This is so you know how many visits your page has received.

URL Submission: $10 per year per URL. This is a hand submission of your URL to Google, Yahoo and MSN.

Language Translation: $15 per language. You get an auto-translation of your page into any major language so your page is in English AND other languages.

Linked Photo Rotation: $25 per year. Rotates 2 photos of you in the directories. Each additional photo added to rotation is $10.

Extra Words: $5 per 50 words.

Extra Photos: $10 per photo.

Personal Email Address: $60 per year. You get your own personal email address at yourconpals.com. Your family and friends can contact you without having to go to your web page. Email messages downloaded and mailed to you each week.

Payment Options: We accept personal checks, institution checks and money orders. We accept all major credit cards as well as PayPal. To pay these methods, you will need to have someone on the outside go to our web site to pay online. STAMPS: We accept new, unused stamps. When paying with stamps, please send as many books and whole sheets, and as few loose stamps as possible. Do not put tape on stamps. The easy formula for calculating payment for stamps; DOLLARS X 3 = NUMBER OF STAMPS. For example, a payment of $10 would be 30 stamps."

Comment: Seems like a loss. My family can't even send me emails, and they're having problems navigating the website without promotions constantly popping up on their screen. - - Peter Sierra, CA

Connecticut Innocence Project
c/o McCarter & English
Cityplace I
185 Asylum Street, 36th Floor
Hartford, CT 06103

Phone: 860-275-6140

Conquest Offender Reintegration
PO Box 73873
Washington, DC 20056-3873

Federal prisoners, who want to be released to DC, write for an application for transitional housing.

Phone Number: (202)723-2014

Cons Call Home
12748 University Drive
Fort Myers, FL 33907

They provide discount calls.

Toll Free 888-524-6151
Website:ConsCallHome.com
ConsCallHome.com®
A Millicorp™ Division

Contemporary Verse 2
502-100 Arthur St.
Winnipeg, Manitoba R3B 1H3 Canada

Contexts Art Project
4722 Baltimore Ave.
Philadelphia, PA 19143

The Contexts Collective hopes to represent to the public through the artwork of prisoners some of the realities of prison life; instill in the artist the sense of accomplishment and pride evoked by an exhibit of their own art; and raise money for Books Through Bars.

Phone Number: 215-727-8170 #5.
contexts@booksthroughbars.org

Conveying Islamic Message Society
PO Box 834
Alexandria, Egypt

Convictmailbag.com
Po Box 661
Redondo Beach, CA 90277

This is a pen pal website. They accept stamps for payment. Write/Send SASE for more information.

Convicts for Christ
3651 N.W. 2nd Street
Fort Lauderdale, FL 33301

Inmate/prison advocacy. Individual & group counseling. Mail prison counseling, Christian & otherwise. Housing & job referrals.

Phone Number: 954-931-3292

Cornell Prison Education Program
Cornell University
115 Day Hall
Ithaca, NY 14853

Phone Number (607)255-4338
Website: http://cpep.cornell.edu/

CorrectHelp
1223 Wilshire Boulevard, #905
Santa Monica, CA 90403

Phone Number: (310)399.8324

Correctional Library Services
The New York Public Library
455 Fifth Avenue, 6th floor
New York, NY 10016

Phone Number: 212-592-7553

Corrections Accountability Project
40 Rector Street, 9th FL
New York, NY 10006

Send us your testimonial!

Have you or your loved ones been exploited by the high costs and poor quality of prison service companies like Securus, Keefe, JPay, and others? We want to hear from you.

Note: Upon receipt of your testimonial, we will send a release form, on which you will have the option to specify how you would like to be identified, including anonymously.

Corrio SPC
2620 Bellevue Way NE, Ste. 175
Bellevue, WA 98004

Stop worrying about busy schedules, and start leaving messages with Corrio.

Note: Corrio is formerly known as Voice Freedom Calls. Corrio is not available in Texas or Arizona state facilities.

Website: corriospc.org

Council on American Islamic Relations
453 New Jersey Avenue, S.E.
Washington, DC 20003

Phone Number: 202.488.8787
Website: www.cair.com

Cox, Harvey
PO Box 1551
Weatherford, TX 76086

This guy specializes in helping prisoners with transfers, grievances, and parole. Write for details.

Phone Number: (817) 596-8457
Website: prisonconsultant.com.

CPCS Innocence Program
ATTN: Lisa Kavanaugh, Program Director
21 McGrath Highway, 2nd floor
Somerville, MA 02143

The purpose of the CPCS Innocence Program is to obtain exonerations for indigent Massachusetts state defendants who are actually innocent of the crimes of which they have been convicted. Defendants are actually innocent if no crime was committed or if someone else committed the crime in question.

Phone Number: 617-623-0591
Website: publiccounsel.net

Criminal Injustice: Confronting the Prison Crisis

This remarkable anthology exposes our increasingly conservative and punitive justice system and uncovers the economic and political realities behind the imprisonment of large numbers of the working class, working poor and people of color. It's 374 pages, $19.00, and can be bought from Prison Legal New.

The Criminal Law Handbook: Know Your Rights, Survive the System

This book was written by attorneys Paul Bergman and Sara J. Berman-Barrett. It breaks down the civil trial process in easy-to-understand steps so you can effectively represent yourself in court. The authors explain what to say in court, how to say it, etc. It's 528 pages, $39.99, and can be bought from Prison Legal News.

Criminal-Law in a Nutshell, 5th Edition

Provides an overview of criminal law, including punishment, specific crimes, defenses and burden of proof. It's 387 pages, $43.95, and can be bought from Prison Legal News.

Criminal Legal News
PO Box 1151
Lake Worth, FL 33460

The people who bring you Prison Legal News proudly announce the introduction of its companion publication, Criminal Legal News. Same timely, relevant, and practical legal news as PLN, BUT CLN provides legal news you can use about the criminal justice system prior to confinement and post-conviction relief. Stop resisting and subscribe today!

"Criminal Legal News is a 40-page monthly print publication published by the Human Rights Defense Center, a 501(c)(3) nonprofit human rights organization that zealously advocates, educates, and litigates on issues pertaining to prisoners' rights as well as individuals going through the criminal justice system.

CLN and its well-known companion publication Prison Legal News serve as vital links for prisoners who otherwise don't have access to current legal and prison-related news and information.

CLN's coverage of criminal justice issues includes, but is not limited to, criminal law and procedure, police brutality, prosecutorial misconduct, habeas corpus relief, ineffective counsel, sentencing errors, militarization of police, surveillance state, junk science, wrongful convictions, false confessions, witness misidentification, paid/incentivized informants, search and seizure, right to remain silent, right to counsel, right to speedy trial, due process rights, and much more.

$48.00 a year for prisoners. Sample issue or back issue, $5.00 each. Inmates can pay with brand-new books of Forever stamps.

Criminal Procedure: Constitutional Limitations, 7th Edition

Intended for use by law students, this is a succinct analysis of constitutional standards of major significance in the area of criminal procedure. It's 603 pages, $43.95, and can be bought from Prison Legal News.

Critical Resistance - National
1904 Franklin St., Suite 504
Oakland, CA 94612

Critical Resistance works to build an international movement to end the Prison Industrial Complex by challenging the belief that caging and controlling people makes us safe. If you are not already familiar with this group, you should check 'em out. Please do not contact CR for legal help.

Phone Number: (510)444-0484

Critical Resistance - NYC
451 West Street
New York, NY 10014

Phone Number: (212)462-4382
Website: criticalresistance.org/crnyc

Critical Resistance – Southern Regional Office (reopened)
P.O. Box 71553
New Orleans, LA 70172

Phone Number 504-304-3784
Website: crsouth@criticalresistace.org

Crossroads Bible Institute
PO Box 900
Grand Rapids, MI 49509-0900

FREE bible correspondence courses.

Crusade 4 Hope
PO Box 27231
Raleigh, NC 27811

"Diamonds Beyond the Wall" by Miss Veronica. Poems and essays on prison life from a woman's view. Positive and uplifting. Send SASE for more information.

Curbfeelers
PO 421175
Houston, TX 77242

"We are your premier, top-tier Kill Shot picture provider. Curbfeelers catalogs offer a selection of voer 40,000 pictures for you to choose from. No other company offers this kind of selection! Curbfeelers works harder for you, too. We search through hundreds of thousands of pictures each year and work with each shot so that they look better. Curbfeelers also processes orders fastest.

Your order will ship within 24 hours of us receiving it because we own our own commercial FujiFilm photo processing equipment. This allows us to get your orders out immediately and produces a higher quality photo.

Black and white catalogs are 12 stamps each or cash equivalent. Pictures are $.75 each, or 3 stamps. There is a 15-picture minimum order.

Send SASE for more info!"

Comment: Seems expensive. Been waiting 2 weeks to get info from company. Heard good things, though. We'll see.... -- Troy Shaw, Indiana

DC Book Diva Publications
#245 4401 – A Connecticut Ave, NW
Washington, DC 20008

This is an urban book publishing company that sells books for $15 plus $3.99 for S/H, but she will sell them to prisoners for $11.25 + $3.99 S/H.

DC Prison Book Project

PO Box 34190
Washington, DC 20043-4190

Sends donated reading material to prisoners and educates the public about issues surrounding prisoner education and literacy. Give about a 3-month turnaround time.

DC Prisoners' Project

Washington Lawyers' Committee for Civil Rights and Urban Affairs
11 Dupont Circle NW, #400
Washington, DC 20036

Advocates for humane treatment and dignity of people charged under Washington, DC law -- even if you're being held anywhere in the federal system. They focus on health and medical issues, abuse, religious rights, mental Health, deaf issues and some parole matters. Letters should provide as much detail and chronology of the situation as possible. They sometimes accept collect calls, but .mail is better

D&D Worldwide Services, L.L.C.

P.O. Box 40081
Houston, TX 77240

Need help with your parole review? This company has 14 years of helping those in prison obtain another chance. Their parole plan shows you as a favorable candidate for parole!

Phone Number: (281)580-8844
Website: myparol.info

Damamli Publishing CO

11 Greyfell Place
Pleasant Hill, CA 94523-1713

Phone Number: (925) 705-1612

David Rushing

723 Main St. Ste. 816
Houston, TX 77002

This law office does federal writs, Texas parole and Texas writs.

Death Before Dishonor

Nkosi Shake Zulu -- El 369182
Washington Corrections Center
PO Box 900
Shelton, WA 98584

This is DC street legend Wayne Perry. He gives only Eyone Williams permission to speak on his behalf.

Instagram: Wayne_silk_perry

Death Penalty Focus

5 Third Street, Suite 725
San Francisco, CA 94103

Phone Number: 415-243-0143
Website: deathpenalty.org

Death Penalty Information Center

1015 18th Street NW, Suite 704
Washington, DC 20036

DPIC focuses on disseminating studies and reports related to the death penalty to the news media and general public covering subjects such as race, innocence, politicization, costs, of the death penalty, and more. Most of their publications are freely downloadable from their website, Or available for a small fee in printed format. Request a copy of their "Resource Order Form," and also a current list of their publications concerning individual state death penalty issues.

Phone Number: 202-289-2275
Website: deathpenaltyinfo.org

Defense Investigation Group

PO Box 86923
L.A., CA 90086

$500 post-conviction investigations, locates up to three people in Los Angeles/Orange counties.

Deposition Handbook

How-to handbook for anyone who conducts a deposition or is going to be deposed. It's 352 pages, $34.99, and can be bought from Prison Legal News.

deviantart.com

They sell and post art for artists. At 14 million members, they attract all kinds of businesses looking for various styles of art. If you are an artist and looking to make some real money, have your people contact them for details.

Dharma Companions

PO Box 762
Cotati, CA 94931

Dharma Friends Prison Outreach Project
Compassion Works for All
PO Box 7708
Little Rock, AR 72217-7708

Dharma Publishing
35788 Hauser Bridge Rd.
Cazadero, CA 95421

Phone Number: 1-800-873-4276

Dharma Seed Archival Center
P.O. Box 66,
Wendell Depot, MA 01380

A Dictionary of Criminal Law Terms

This handbook contains police terms such as preventive detention and protective sweep, and phrases from judicial-created law such as independent-source rule and open-fields doctrine. A good resource to help navigate your way through the maze of legal language in criminal cases. It's 768 pages, $33.95, and can be bought from Prison Legal News.

Disability Rights Education and Defense Fund Inc.
3075 Adeline St, Suite 210
Berkeley, CA 94703

CA Prisoners Only. DREDF takes on very few cases each year. "We receive far more requests for assistance than our resources allow us to take on. If we cannot take your case we can provide you with referrals to other organizations. Please do not send original supporting materials. Please note, we do not provide assistance with disability benefits such as denial of Social Security Disability benefits."

Disability Rights Texas
2222 West Braker Lane
Austin, Texas 78758

Phone Number: (512) 454-4816(Voice)

Discount Magazine Subscription Service, INC.
PO Box 60114
Fort Myers, FL 33906

If a publisher authorized agency offers a lower current price on any magazine this company offers, they will match the price, guaranteed. Write/Send SASE for a **FREE** catalog.

Distance Education Accrediting Commission
1101 17th Street, Suite 808
Washington, DC 20036

Phone Number: (202) 234-5100

Diversified Press
PO Box 135005
Clermont, FL 34713

This company offers a pen pal page, customized greeting cards and more. They are willing to accept stamps as payment. Write/Send SASE for more information.

Don Diva Magazine
603 W. 115th Street, #313
NY, NY 10025

Don Diva is an urban magazine – "the original street bible." A yearly subscription is $20.00; 4 issues a year. Single issues are $5.99 each. Send SASE for order form and info.

Website: dondivamag.com

Dress for Success
3820 Walnut St. Suite 2
Harrisburg, PA 17109

Provides professional attire and career support services to disadvantaged women.

Phone Number: (717) 657-3333

D.R.I.V.E. Movement

Founded by Death Row prisoners, the DRIVE movement seeks to unite the Death Row community to push forward and initiate change in the conditions. Through a group of passionate prisoner activists who have put aside all barriers of ethnicity, creed, color and beliefs, to focus on the injustices forced upon us by this system. Resists by means of inner-resistance, outer-petition drives, direct actions, and hunger strikes.

Email Address: drivemovement@yahoo.com

DRL
PMB 154
3298 N. Glassford Hill Rd, Suite 104
Prescott Valley, AZ 86314

This company offers a pen pal service with a lifetime membership for $40. Write/Send SASE for more information.

Drug Policy Alliance
131 West 33rd Street, 15th Floor
NY, NY 10018

DPA is the nation's leading organization promoting drug policies that are grounded in science, compassion, health and human rights. DPA is putting out a call for drug war stories. If you would like to be profiled in the media, your story would be entered in a data base for possible use. They want you to send your name, current prison, ethnicity, kind of drug involved, whether or not a weapon was involved, contact information for outside representative, if possible (phone number and/or e-mail), and a short story of your case to "Drug War Stories! DPA" at the address above.

Drug Policy Alliance
131 10th Street
San Francisco, CA 94103

One of the leading U.S. organizations promoting alternatives to the war on drugs, with extensive on-line library, reports on drug policy reform by state, public health alternatives to criminalization, and more.

Durham Law Office
Craig H. Durham
910 W. Main Suite 328
Boise, ID 18370

Appeals, post- conviction, habeas, and parole services for Idaho inmates.

East Bay Prisoner Support
PO Box 22449
Oakland, CA 94609

"We disseminate fiery ideas. We want this fire to spread from the pages of our zines to the architecture of their system. We hope these ideas can foment rebellions across the walls that divide us. Coordinated, these rebellions can shake the foundations of law and order that keep us down. This

is our propaganda. This is our project. We share it with our comrades inside. We reach out to places they don't want us to find and contact people they don't want us to meet. We no longer wish to obey laws, punch clocks, pay rent, compete against each other, follow orders, bow to authority, appeal to moralities, ask for permission, always knowing that to resist is to end up in cages, like all those inside."

This is an anarchist zine publisher that will send zines once a month to prisoners in CA, AZ, NM, TX, UT, and NV. They will send to queer, trans, and women prisoners in any state. The zines are **FREE** and they will fill orders once a month. Each order is any one zine or a combination of zines up to 30 sheets. Send SASE for **FREE** catalog.

The Editorial Eye
66 Canal Center Plazas, Suite 200
Alexandra, VA 22314

This is a magazine that covers standards and practices for writers and editors.

Education Justice Project
University of Illinois at Urbana-Champaign
805 W. Pennsylvania Ave. M.C. 058
Urbana, IL 61801

They demonstrate the positive impacts of college-in-prison programs and organize educational programming at Danville Correctional Center through the University of Illinois.

Phone Number: 217.300.5150
Website: educationjustice.net

Edwin Gould Services for Children

Phone Number: 212-437-3500
Website: info@egscf.org

Eli Solutions
PO Box 88
Mullins, SC 29574

Comment: The first time I heard of these guys was when I saw an ad in December, 2016, in PLN, for a book titled "The X-Drug Dealer's Guide To: Prisoner's Independent Financial Survival." The ad said we can get it FREE as long as we pay the tax and shipping and handling fee of $6.95. I wrote these fools about the book but never got a response back. Being that I'm an ex drug dealer and current self-made millionaire prisoner, I was looking forward to the book and was disappointed I didn't get it. Since then I've seen this same address used for several (4-5) different company names. These guys advertise all kinds of services under different names. Send a SASE for their info. I'm unsure about these guys. Let me know if you've had a good or bad experience with them. -- Mike

Elmer Robert Keach, III, PC
1040 Riverfront Center
P.O. Box 70
Amsterdam, NY 12010

This experienced civil rights attorney is dedicated to seeking justice for those who are incarcerated; reasonable hourly rates for criminal defense, appeals, post-conviction relief and habeas corpus. Send SASE and request inquiry guideline for whatever it is you wish to hire him for.

Phone Number: 518-434-1718
Website: keachlawfirm.com

End Violence Project,
P.O. Box 1395,
Bryn Mawr, PA 19010

Committed to ending violence without violence (This group has worked with PA Lifers in the past).

Phone Number: (610)-527-2821

Energy Committed to Offenders
P.O. Box 33533
Charlotte, NC 28233-3533

Provides services to inmates, ex-offenders and their families. INMATES: pre-release planning, ECO presentations about ECO services and pre-release planning, correspondence support, half-way house for female offenders completing their prison sentence -referrals from NC Department of Correction only. Will accept collect calls from inmates.

Phone Number: (704) 374-0762.
Website: ecocharlotte.org

Equal Justice Initiative
122 Commerce St.
Montgomery, AL 36104

Legal representation for indigent defendants and those denied fair treatment in the legal system (such as trials marked by blatant racial bias or prosecutorial misconduct). They mostly help death-row prisoners and children prosecuted as adults. They usually don't answer unless they are interested in the case.

Escape Mate

This is an online concierge service for those of you who have Corrlink accounts. They have plans as low as $29.99 for 3 months.

Website: escapemate.com

ESPN
935 Middle St.
Bristol, CT 06010

This is a sports news magazine.

Website: espn.com.

The Essential Supreme Court Cases: The 200 Most Important Cases for State Prisoners

This 2015, 330 page "indispensable reference book" is by Ivan Denison and costs $19.95.

ETC Campaign
C/O Michigan CURE
PO Box 2736
Kalamazoo, MI 49003

ETC campaign is a national effort to reduce the high cost of prison phone calls.

Website: ectcampaign.com

Evolve
1971 Stella Lake Dr.
Las Vegas, NV 89106

Evolve offers motivational counseling, case management, vocational education, and job placement to individuals with criminal histories.

Phone Number: (702) 638-6371

Executive Prison Consultants
2384 Oaktrail Drive, Suite 2

Idaho Falls, ID 83404

Executive Prison Consultants is the nation's leading prison preparation and survival consultancy. Specializing in the needs of federal prisoners, Executive Prison Consultants regularly assists clients with disciplinary appeals, transfer requests, RDAP eligibility, medical care, and other specialized, individualized client concerns.

Website: executiveprisonconsultants.com

E-mail: info@executiveprisonconsultants.com

Expert Witness

Coercive Interrogation and Interview Techniques

Brian Leslie is a court qualified expert in coercive interrogation and interview techniques and former Chief of Police. He has testified in and worked on many high-profile criminal cases including as a contracting expert on several criminal cases for the United States Army JAG core and State Public Defenders.

- False confessions resulting from coercive questioning
- Improper witness interviews conducted by law enforcement
- Inductive and Deductive investigative techniques used
- Complete Forensic Reports
- Expert witness testimony

Find out how our expert services may provide assistance in your upcoming motion, hearing or trial. Have your attorney or family member contact us at: 1-888-400-1309.

Website: criminalcaseconsultants.com

Exodus Transitional Community, Inc.
2271 3rd Avenue
New York, NY 10035-2231

Fellowship of formerly incarcerated individuals that helps people coming out of prison build stable lives and fully reintegrate back into society.

Phone Number: 917-492-0990
Website: www.etcny.org

Ex-Offender Reentry Website

This site has lots of books and resources for ex-offenders, how to search for a job, write resumes, etc., all geared to ex-offenders. All info must be bought in the form of books.

Website: exoffenderreentry.com

The Exoneration Initiative
233 Broadway
Suite 2370
New York, NY 10279

Phone: 212.965.9335
Website: http://exonerationinitiative.org

The Exoneration Project
312 North May Street, Suite 100
Chicago, IL 60607

The Exoneration Project is a non-profit organization dedicated to working to **FREE** prisoners who were wrongfully convicted. The project represents innocent individuals in post-conviction proceedings; typical cases involve DNA testing, coerced confessions, police misconduct, the use of faulty evidence, junk science and faulty eyewitness testimony, and effective assistance of council claims.

Exotic Fragrances
1645 Lexington Ave
New York, NY 10029

Write to receive **FREE** 30-page catalog. No SASE needed.

Comment: One of the biggest catalogs I've seen. You name it, they've got it, and they respond freebirdpretty fast. - - Robert Bennett

FACTS: Families to Amend California's Three Strikes.
3982 S. Figueroa Street #209
Los Angeles, CA 90037

A coalition working to change the "three strike" rules. Membership is $10 per year, and includes a subscription to the quarterly newsletter – The Striker. Ask for prisoner membership options, FACTS Works to amend California's Three Strikes law to target violent felonies only. Quarterly newsletter (by donation). Print return address exactly if you want a response. Flyers printed in English and Spanish.

Phone Number: (213) 746-4844.

Fair Chance Project
1137 E Redondo Blvd
Inglewood, CA 90302

Fair Chance Project represents a movement led by liberated lifers, their families and concerned community members advocating for just sentencing laws and fair parole practices. The group seeks to integrate newly liberated lifers back into their communities enabling them to become valuable resources towards the development of self-sustaining communities. Send $5 or $5 worth of stamps for your prisoner membership, which includes a newsletter titled Fair Chance News.

Families Against Mandatory Minimum
1100 H Street NW, Suite 1000
Washington, DC 20005

FAMM is a national advocacy group that focuses on mandatory minimums and offers a quarterly newsletter –FAMMgram. $10 per year for prisoners.

Website:famm.org

Families of Parchman Prison Inmates
P.O. Box 2174
Starkville, MS 39760

"We serve as a support center to anyone who has a family member incarcerated or recently released from Parchman and any other prison in Mississippi."

Phone Number: (662) 323-5878.

Family and Corrections Network
93 Old York Road Suite 1 #510
Jenkintown, PA 19046

The mission of Family and Corrections Network (FCN) is to uphold families of prisoners as a valued resource to themselves and their communities in order that the criminal justice system, other institutions and society become supportive of family empowerment, integrity, and self-determination. FCN works alongside families of prisoners, program providers, policy makers, researchers, educators, correctional personnel and the public by: convening national meetings for mutually respectful learning,

interaction and dialogue; distributing information through FCN's publications, web site, and speakers' bureau; designing and supplying technical materials, tools and services; advocating criminal justice policy reform that upholds the value of families; encouraging networking among families of prisoners for mutual support and cooperative action; and creating opportunities for linking with and learning from families of prisoners.

Phone Number: (215) 576-1110

Families United
P.O. Box 9476
Philadelphia, PA 19139

For children with a loved one incarcerated. After-school and other programs for kids.

Phone Number: 215-604-1759.

Fanorama Society Publisher and Prisoner Zine Distro
109 Arnold Ave.
Cranston, RI 02905

Publishes zines created by people in prison and provides these zines to other prisoners. Several are queer/trans. Payments may be made in cash, state money orders, or postage. Write for list.

Fast Law Publishing
PO Box 577
Upland, CA 91785

They publish how-to legal books. Write/Send SASE for more information.

Fast Law Research
POB 2315
Port Orchard, WA 98366

Services by Fast Law. Rates you can afford. Send SASE.

FCPS
74 Garilee Ln
Elizabethtown, PA 17022

Forensic Clemency and Parole Services. They can assist you in preparing petitions for filing by collecting needed information for you. For more info, contact them.

Federal Receiver, J. Clark Kelso

California Prison Receivership
PO Box 588500
Elk Grove, CA 95758

In 2002, California settled a class-action lawsuit by agreeing to reform their medical care system, and the federal court appointed a federal Receiver to oversee the reform process. The receiver's job is to bring the level of medical care in California prisons to a standard which no longer violates the U.S. Constitution. Prisoner patients under the control of the CDCR and their families may write to the above address with concerns about health care issues (except for mental health, dental, or substance abuse and treatment). Some patient-care issues brought to the Receiver's attention may prompt clinical investigation and action. All information provided to the Receiver is considered in implementing systemic improvements.

Phone Number: 916-691-3000
Website: cphcs.ca.gov
Felonism: Hating In Plain Sight

What's the real cause of the oppression you experience? What are some real solutions? Felonism: Hating in Plain Sight has the answers. Available on Amazon, or send $15 to Linda Polk, Book; PO Box 128071; Nashville, TN 37212.

Feria & Corona
10 Universal City Plazas, Suite 2000
Universal City, CA 91608

This is a law firm; it accepts California cases only.

Phone Number: (818)905-0903.

Fight for Lifers West
P.O. Box 4683
Pittsburgh, PA 15206

Dedicated to supporting people sentenced to life without parole and their loved ones, while striving to improve the criminal justice system and building positive community relationships.

Phone Number: 412-361-3066
Website: fightforliferswest.mysite.com

The Fire Inside
1540 Market St. #490
San Francisco, CA 94102

This is a quarterly newsletter of the California Coalition for Women Prisoners; **FREE** to women.

FIYA GIRLS
PO Box 192
Dequincy, LA 70633

"Check us out! We are the best in the game! Here we have the sexiest and hottest babes. We have plenty of nail-biting catalogs, with different types of breath-taking women of all races to choose from. Fiya girls catalog has the biggest selections to choose from.

1.Send $2.00 or 5 stamps to receive hi gloss color catalog #19. It has over 450 white girls, coeds and Spanish girls. All hot poses in bras, G strings and panties. It also comes with 1 **FREE** pic.

2. Send $2.00 or 5 stamps to receive hi gloss color catalog #18. It comes with 1 **FREE** pic. It has over 440 new black, white and Spanish girls. All have super big apple bottoms! You don't want to miss out on catalog 18 and 19. ALWAYS SEND AN ALTERNATE ADDRESS WITH YOUR ORDER IN CASE YOUR ORDER IS REJECTED. WE WILL SEND IT TO THE STREET ADDRESS THAT YOU PROVIDED US WITH.

3. If your jail or prison is strict on sexy photos, send $3.00 along with SASE for the get-in cat #1. They will let it in and the photos too.

4. Send $13.00 to get non-nude 10 pic get-in set. Make sure to say if you want black or white girls when you want a get-in 10 pic set.

5. Send $20.00 to get the 30 pic get-in set and a **FREE** get-in #1 cat. It contains all races wearing bikinis on beaches and beside pools. Get the all NEW supervised high gloss color VIP catalog #4. Over thousands to choose from. All races! Non-nude strippers, porn stars and all!!! Only $15.00 (**FREE** s/h). Includes 2 **FREE** pics. Price on all pics in VIP cat #4 is now only $1.00 each. Must choose at least 15 pics. And send a SASE for each envelope. We ship up to 22 pics per envelope. You need to put 2 postage stamps on each envelope.

6. ALL NUDE BIG BUNDLE CATALOG PACKAGE ONLY $15.00. Comes with **FREE** pics.

7. Get mail get paid book is still only $10.00.

8. We have over 100 10-pic sets of black, white and Asian women in sets of 10 different poses. They are

very hot 10-pic sets. Only $13.00 a set or you can choose 3 sets for $23.00.

9. VIP yearly membership is only $45.00.

10. Send $5.00 to get one of the hottest all white girls coed catalogs on the market --cat #11. It has over 450 to choose from.

11. Cat #20 has over 400 sexy white girls to choose from. Send $3.00 to get it.

12. The 5 pack has a large selection of ebony women with apple bottoms mixed with Asian and white women. It's hot!! Send only $7.00. It comes with 2 **FREE** pics. It has hundreds to choose from.

13. 50 PICS OF HOT NON-NUDE WITH THE BEST QUALITY ASIANS WEARING LINGERIE AND BIKINIS FOR ONLY $25.00 **FREE** SHIPPING.

14. VOL #1. 50 PICS OF HOT NON-NUDE BEST QUALITY MIXED SET OF WHITE, BLACK AND SPANISH GIRLS AND PORN STARS WEARING STRIPPER OUTFITS ONLY $25.00. **FREE** SHIPPING.

15. VOL #2, 3, 4 AND 5 HAVE 50 PIC SETS OF WHITE, BLACK, AND LATIN GIRLS! EACH 50 PIC SET IS ONLY $25.00. **FREE** SHIPPING.

16. BUY ALL 5 GRAB BAG SETS. EACH SET HAS A MIX OF RACES. THEY ARE ONLY $25.00 A SET. **FREE** SHIPPING! THERE ARE A TOTAL OF 10 SETS. VOL #1-10. BUY ALL 10 NUDE SETS AND GET 50 **FREE** SHOTS!

VIP cat 5 has over a couple thousand choices. Only $15.00. **FREE** s/h. Cats 27-32. VIP cat 6 has over a couple thousand choices only $15.00. **FREE** s/h 33-cat 38). VIP cat 5 and 6 consist of white camel toe shots, bikini shots, curvy models, petite models, Latino models, beach shots, bedroom shots, G string shots, mini skirts, latex, spandex, fitness models, armature porn stars, micro thongs, booty shorts, tight jeans, blondes, redheads, brunettes, big breast, slim waist, big booties, erotic poses, college coeds, huge camel toes. New anmie sluts. They are super hot! VIP cat #5 and #6 are non-nude catalogs."

Comment: I wrote their ad they way they wrote it so you can judge for yourself. In addition, though I have seen guys get their

orders from them, I ordered some pics and the "Get Mail Get Paid" book and never got it. - Mike

flikshop.com
1-855-flikshop

Your family can download their **FREE** app, then send you pictures of friends, family, etc., in the form of a postcard for as low as 79 cents each.

Comment: "Started by a former prisoner, Marcus Bullock, and profiled in Forbes magazine. Definitely legit. Have your family and friends check them out if they send photos or cards." - - Josh Kruger, author of The Millionaire Prisoner

Flipping Your Conviction: Post-Conviction Relief for State Prisoners

This 2013, 449 page book by Ivan Denison has instructions, rules, forms and examples and costs $49.95.

Flipping Your Habe: Overturning Your State Conviction in Federal Court

This 2014, 336 page book by Ivan Denison has instructions, rules, forms and examples and costs $34.95.

Flipping Your Conviction: State Post-Conviction Relief for the Pro Se Prisoner

Step-by-step instructions on how to successfully challenge a state conviction. Analysis and framing of legal issues; sub claims under ineffective assistance; state appeals; 33 forms and more! This book, by Ivan Denison, is 500 pages, $49.99.

Flix 4 You
PO Box 290249
Sandhills, SC 29229

"Get them cuz they're hot! Flix 4 You is often imitated, but can't be duplicated! We offer the best quality photos and fastest service in the game! Only .75 per photo! New Deal: order 10-14 photos, get 1 photo **FREE**; 15-19 photos, get 3 photos **FREE**; order 20-24 photos, get 5 photos **FREE**; order 25 or more, get 10 photos **FREE**. Over 100 catalogs to choose from, all just $5.00 each or 20 stamps! Black,

Latin, Asian, White, celebrity, pornstars, club scenes, bikini shots, iPhone cuties, selfies and more! From fully clothed to fully nude! We otter photos that will satisfy everyone's needs!!

Overstock special: 20 photos for $7.50. You choose race, front shot or back shot, and we will choose from our overstock collection. You cannot choose from any specific catalog.

Shipping and handling is $2.20 per envelope. Each envelope only hold 25 photos, if you need more than 1 envelope, you must send additional shipping and handling. New policy as of January 1, 2015: we will no longer be responsible for rejected catalogs or photos! Be sure to order according to your facility's mailroom policy."

Comment: Flix 4 You sent me a couple of their catalogs - - 'Insta-grammy 2' and 'Legs, Tights, Assets 2'. The catalogs are printed in color and offer several choices each. Their images are some of the best I've seen. The baddest bitches on the planet. - Mike

Florida Institutional Legal Services
14260 West Newberry Road #412
Newberry, FL 32669

Florida Institutional Legal Services, Inc. (FILS) is the only statewide legal services program in Florida dedicated to serving people who are institutionalized.

Phone Number: 352-375-2494
Website: floridalegal.org/newberry.htm

Florida Justice Institute
3750 Miami Tower
100 S.E. Second Street
Miami, FL 33131-2309

They are a nonprofit public interest law firm that conducts civil rights litigation and advocacy in the areas of prisoners' rights, housing discrimination, disability discrimination, and other areas that impact the lives of Florida's poor and disenfranchised.

Phone: 305-358-2081; 888-358-2081
Website: info@floridajusticeinstitute.org

The F.O.G. Corporation
PO Box 17733
Honolulu, HI 96817

This is a Vietnam friendship magazine. Send SASE for details.

Forbes Magazine
PO Box 5471
Harlan, IA 51593

Note: This address is for subscription services only. This is a financial information magazine.

Comment: "Real bailer shit. Jay-Z, Donald Trump-type money. Read it and be inspired to make legit money. TMP endorsed and recommended. Cheaper to order through a magazine discount subscription service though." - - Josh Kruger, The Millionaire Prisoner

Forever Family, Inc.
387 Joseph Lowery Blvd.
2nd Floor, Suite A
Atlanta, GA 30310

Forever family works to ensure that, no matter what the circumstances, all children have the opportunity to be surrounded by the love of family.

Phone Number: 404-223-1200
Website: http://foreverfam.org/

The Fortune News
53 West 23rd Street, 8th Floor
New York, NY 10010

Phone Number: (212) 691-7554

The Fortune Society
29-76 Northern Blvd,
Long Island City, NY 11101 – 2822

Helps ex-prisoners break the cycle of crime and incarceration, and educates the public about prison and the causes of crime. **FREE** newsletter for prisoners.

F.O.S.
PO Box 42922
Phoenix, AZ 85080

"Hey guys, I'm back!!!! We finally relocated to Phoenix, AZ. I've missed you all!!! In case you haven't figured it out, it's me again. I've been gone for a while now and I feel it's time to make you guys REALLY happy. While I was gone, I was bust doing photo shoots! For you guys who don't know me, you can call me MOMS. I'm the one who is always wanting to do something "nice", a "little extra"; just my soft heart, I guess. I've been around the block a couple of times and I know just about every scam there is, so don't even start with me. Just remember, I want your money, not your nonsense, and we'll get along fine. You do your part and I'll do my part to deliver a professional, satisfactory product. Deal? Now for the BEST part; we have produced a NEW LINE OF FLIERS which will feature EXCLUSIVE photos. They're originals, NOT computer copies. This line of photos will be introduced by our company only. These photos absolutely cannot be purchased anywhere else.

The new flier series feature 59 flyers of assorted photos each. There are 40 photos to a page. Each flyer costs $1.50 or 5 stamps a flyer and are in color. Request the flyer you want by number.

The semi-nude flyers are as follows...

Hispanic girl flyers: 1, 2, 19, 20, 21, 32, 36, 46, 47, 52, 53, 54, 55. Same girl (Cuba, who is from Cuba) flyers: 22, 23, 24, 25, 26, 27. Hispanic and white girl photos are: 3, 4, 6, 7, 9, 12, 13, 14, 15, 17, 35, 38, 48, 49. Hispanic and Black girl flyers are: 8, 10, 11, 16, 18, 28, 30, 31, 45, 50, 51. Mixture of ladies: 5, 29, 37, 41. Chubby Chaser's girl flyers: White 39, 40, 42. White only flyer: 49. American Indian Flyers: 33, 34, 43, 44 (in flyer 33 she is wearing a see-through top so don't order if you can't get flyer). Flyer 56 is the flyer for guys who love feet. Flyer 57 is a big butt flyer. Flyer 58 is camel toe and Flyer 59 is a very tame flyer for guys who have a hard time getting photos and/or flyers in.

There are 33 nude flyers. The flyers and photos are the same price as the semi-nude. Nude flyers 1, 3, 4, 5, 7, 8, 9, 10, 11, 12, 13, 14, 17, 18, 21, 22, 23, 24, 25, 26, 27, 28, 29, 30, 31, 32, 33, 34 are mixed Hispanic and White girls. Nude flyer 2, 15, and 16 are Black girls and nude flyers 6, 19, and 20 are mixed Hispanic and Black. Sample nude flyer 40 is mixed girls.

Please notify us to whether or not you can have front shots only. This way we will delete the images not allowed from the print process before sending it to you. However, you are agreeing to receive less than 40 images per catalog by doing so. Remember, it's up to you to keep us informed of your institution's rules and regulations!

Photo and flyer prices are $1.00 each or 2 Forever stamps. Any checks $50.00 and over, photos are $.75 each which would be 67 photos. A stamp worth $1.15 gives you one photo. If you can receive 10-25 photos per envelope, 2 stamps must be included for each envelope. For 3-5 photos per envelope, 1 stamp per envelope.

We now have an email address for your family to contact us if they need to: Freedomofspeech@gmail.com

Hugs and Kisses,
Moms"

Fox Broadcasting
PO Box 900
Beverly Hills, CA 90213

Free Battered Women
1540 Market Street suite 490
San Francisco, CA 94102

"In California, the majority of women prisoners are survivors of domestic violence; some are doing time for defending themselves and their children, or were forced to confess to crimes. Join the movement to **FREE** battered women from prison."

Phone Number: (415) 255-7036 x320

Freebird Publishers
Box 541
North Dighton, MA 02764

They offer a bunch of services, products and publications. They "Service All Your Outside Needs With Inside Knowledge". Send SASE for more information.

Email: Diane@FreebirdPublishers.com
Web: FreebirdPublishers.com

Comment: "Diane used to be one of us − − a prisoner, and has made it legit. Has many things going on out there. Check them out. They have published 3 of my books." − − Josh Kruger, author of The Millionaire Prisoner

Freedom Line
Box 7 − WCB
Connersville, IN 47331

Local phone numbers for $2.50 a month, anywhere in the USA, only 50¢ a minute. 15¢ a minute to Mexico. No sign-up or hidden fees. Send SASE.

WebSite:freedomline.net

FREE Jail Calls

Get a **FREE** guaranteed ConsCallHome number and 20 minutes of **FREE** talk time every month.

Phone: 855-232-2012
Website: freejailcalls.com

Freelance Success
32391 Dunford St.
Farmington Hills, MI 48334

This is an e-letter. It's $99 for a year subscription. 52 issues per year.

Phone Number: 1-877-731-5411
Website: freelancesuccess.com.

Friction Zone
60166 Hop patch Springs Rd.
Mountain Center, CA 92561

This magazine costs $30 for a 1-year subscription; 12 issues per year.

Phone Number: (909) 659-9500
Website: frictionzone.com.

Friends 4 Prisoners
20770 Hwy. 28 N. Ste. 108-178
San Antonio, TX 78258

Ready to meet new people on the outside? Join friends4prisoners.com and start making connections with new friends!

• Owned and operated by a former inmate

• Profiles start at $30 for 1 year

• Different membership levels available

• Various payment options available

• Professionally designed website

• Advertised on Google and Social Media

• Web traffic from over 140 countries!

Have a friend or family member create your profile today at: friends4prisoners/profiles/create

Send SASE to receive a full brochure.

Friends and Family of Louisiana's Incarcerated Children

1600 Oretha C. Haley Blvd.
New Orleans, LA 20005

FFLIC is fighting for the closure of Swanson and Jetson Centers for Youth and for an increase in community-based services that help our children grow and thrive in their own homes and communities.

Phone Number: (337) 562-8503.

Friends Beyond the Wall, Inc.
55 Mansion St., #1030
Poughkeepsie, NY 12602

"Since 1999, Friends Beyond the Wall has been connecting our members with the outside world through our Friendship, Romance and Legal Connection Service. Our talented New York Graphic and Web Designers create your beautiful, full-color web site ad profile, using the photo and message you provide. Your web site is available on the Internet to a worldwide audience of millions, and web site visitors may simple 'click' to send you a response!"

The ads range from $29.95 - $59.95. They have a guarantee that, if you follow ALL their tips and suggestions and do not receive a response to your ad in six months of publication, your ad will be extended by a full six months, and your photo link will be displayed **FREE** in their special sections Headline Ads, New and Featured Ads, and the No Response Sections for specified times to be of further assistance.

For a **FREE** brochure/application listing all of their ad options, prices and suggested tips, send them a SASE.

Website: friendsbeyondthewall.com

Friend Committee on Legislation of California
926 J St. #707
Sacramento, CA 95814

This is a Quaker founded group that advocates and lobbies for CA state laws that are just, compassionate, and respectful of the inherent worth of every person. It's $12 for a 1-year membership, which includes their newsletter. However, no direct services to prisoners.

Phone Number: (916) 443-3734

Friends Outside

42

Po Box 4085
Stockton, CA 95204

They provide services to prisoners and their families. They also provide pre-release and parenting programs at all California State Prisons (through case management). They operate visitor centers at all California State Prisons too. Write for a **FREE** publication – "Children of Incarcerated parents," "The Bill of Rights," and "How to Tell Children about Jail and Prisons."

From Jail to a Job

This is said to be the best ex-offenders job search manual available.

Website: jailtojob.com

GainPeace
1S270 Summit Ave, Suite 204
OakBrook Terrace, IL 60181

Questions about Islam? Islam is a religion of inclusion. Muslims believe in all the profits in both testaments. Read Quran, the original and unchanged word of God, the last and final testament. Watch Peacetv.tv.

Website: Gainpeace.com

Game Informer Reader Art Contest
724 First Street North, 3rd Floor
Minneapolis, MN 55401

Game Informer is a video game magazine. They run an art contest. Most of it is video game related, but I've seen pieces that aren't. "Submit your art to win our monthly prize. Please include your name and return address. Entries become the property of Game Informer and cannot be returned."

Gassho Newsletter/Atlanta Soto Zen Center
1404 McClendon Ave
Atlanta, GA 30307

Website: www.aszc.org

Gay and Lesbian Advocates and Defenders

Gay & Lesbian Advocates & Defenders
30 Winter Street, STE 800
Boston, MA 02108

Phone Number: (617) 426-1350

Gay Identity Center of Colorado
1151 South Huron Street
Denver, CO 80223

Phone Number: (303) 202-6466
Website: www.gicofcolo.org.

Genealogical Research, Reference Service Branch
National Achieves & Records Admin
8th and Pennsylvania Ave. RM 205
Washington, DC 20408

If you are interested in researching your family history, this is a good place to start. Write and request their **FREE** 20-page booklet.

Phone Number: (202) 523-3218

Gender Mutiny Collective
P.O. Box 0494
Chapel Hill, NC 26514

Georgetown ARCP
600 New Jersey Ave. NW
Washington, DC 20001

The Georgetown Law Journal Annual Review of Criminal procedures is a topic-by-topic summary of criminal procedures in the United States Supreme Court and each of the twelve Federal Circuit Courts of Appeals. The publication costs $15.

Georgia Innocence Project
2645 North Decatur Road
Decatur, GA 30033

Phone Number: 404-373-4433
Website: ga-innocenceproject.org/Alabama

Georgia Justice Project
438 Edgewood Ave.
Atlanta, GA 30312

GJP combines legal and social services. Staff attorneys and social workers develop long-term relationships with clients who must make a commitment to rehabilitation before being accepted as clients.

Get Connected
2127 Olympic Parkway; Suite 1006-248
Chula Vista, CA 91915

This is a discount call service. Write/send SASE for more information.

Phone Number: (866) 514-9972
Website: getconnectedus.com.

getgrandpasfbifile.com
This is an online FBI-file service.

Website: getmyfbifile.com

Get Your Poetry Published

"Be Published Now. Our Services Can Help. Request **FREE** Publishing Kit!"

Website: be-published.com

Gillins Typing Service
229-19 Merrick Blvd. Suite 228
Laurelton, NY 11413

They offer reliable and prompt service typing manuscripts and legal material for $1.75 per page w/ line editing. Send SASE for brochure.

Phone Number (718) 607-9688

Girls and Mags
BOX 533
Rehoboth, MA 02769

Comment: Girls and Mags is a new company by George Kayer. George is the founder of Inmate Shopper. He's now retired from Inmate Shopper and has sold it to Freebird Publishers. -- Mike

Global University
Beren School of the Bible
1211 South Glenstone Avenue
Springfield, MO 65804

Highly recommended career school offering religious studies.

Gold Star Fragrances
100 West 37th St.
New York, NY 10018

This company carries over 1,000 imported perfume oils; as well as soaps, massage oils, body lotion, shower gels and more. Write/send SASE for **FREE** catalog.

Gorilla Convict Publications
1019 Willott Rd.
St. Peters, MO 63376

Gorilla Convict is the publishing company operated and owned by incarcerated author Seth Ferranti. He's written such books as Prison Stories, Street Legends volume 1 and 2, and The Supreme Team, among others. His books are $15 each, plus $5.25 for s/h for the first book, and $2.25 for each additional book.

Comment: When I first decided books are what I'ma do I ordered two from Seth -- Prison Stories and Street Legends (the first one). He wrote and published them from his prison cell so they inspired me and let me know it can be done. He's out now and runs the website gorillaconvict.com. Seth is one of my big homies in this game, he's lended me an enormous amount of support, and for that I'm forever grateful. -- Mike

Grab Bag Hot Pics

20 sexy photos for $10. **FREE** s/h, but add $3 for tracking. You choose the category, they choose the photos. All pics are 4x6 glossy, non-nude. No duplicates in entire order. Choose from Asian, White, Latino, Black, Straight Stuntin, Football Babes and Western Chicks.

This deal is available from Freebird Publishers. Send $10 per set ordered with info on paper. They are not responsible for mailroom refusals and they will give no refunds, only credit vouchers.

Grace College Prison Extension Program
200 Seminary Dr
Winona Lake, IN 46590

Grace College and the Indiana Dept. of Corrections Offer Associate of Science and Bachelor of Science degrees to individuals who are incarcerated in maximum security units in the following facilities: Indiana State Prison, Miami Correctional Facility, Wabash Valley Correctional, Facility, and Pendleton Correctional Facility.

Phone Number: 800-544-7223
Website: grace.edu

Grace Ministries Bible College & Institute
PO Box 291962
Dayton, OH 45429

This study is highly recommended for the serious student. Diplomas and certificates offered for various Christian Theological Studies. Must be able to receive cassettes and/or CDs. **FREE** tuition available. Donations are accepted to help off-set costs.

Graduate School USA
600 Maryland Avenue, S.W.
Washington, DC 20024-2520

Website: customersupport@graduateschool.edu.

Graterfriends
Pennsylvania Prison Society
245 N Broad St., Suite 300
Philadelphia, PA 19107

This is a newsletter relating to prisons and prisoners' issues. Subscriptions are $3 (for prisoners).

Website: prisonsociety.org.

Comment: This is a terrific newsletter which publishes prisoners' writing in each and every issue. - - Mike

The Greenback Exchange
PO Box 11228, Dept. NLN 5
Costa Mesa, CA 92627

They buy unused stamps. Send SASE for details.

Greenman Ministry
310 Morton St Ste. 390
Richmond, TX 77469-3119

Promotes Wiccan, Heathen and other Pagan religious practices, with emphasis on serving TX-based prisoners. Write for a sample newsletter, catalog of books, pamphlets & religious items, and a list of TX prisons where they hold rituals. Does not have the resources to give **FREE** books.

Greeting Cards by Freebird Publishers

"We provide a hassle-free way of sending greeting cards to your loved ones. We create and mail custom cards printed with your loved one's name, your closure and name. We also offer signature and custom message services. Choose from 100's of cards by name brands.

General Card Catalog: Includes romance, missing you, birthday and anniversary. Holiday Card and Gift Catalog: Includes everything from Halloween to New Years. Valentine Day Card and Gift Catalog: filled with love, romance, affections and more. Easter Card and Gilt Catalog: Includes cards for everyone on your list and gifts too. Mother's Day Brochure: beautiful, heartfelt cards that is sure to please her.

Send $2 or 6 f/c stamps for each catalog, and $1 or 3 f/c stamps for each brochure to Freebird Publishers."

Groundwork Books Collective
0323 UCSD Student Center
La Jolla, CA 92037

They carry books on the following subjects: Africa, African-Americans, Asia, Asian-Pacific Islander, Chicano/a, China, CIA, FBI, Police, Cultural Criticism, Ecology, Education, Feminist Theory, Labor, Latin American/Caribbean, Native American, Political Theory, Racism, United State history, Political Economy and Imperialism and much, much, more. Books are 40% off for those who can afford to pay. 2 **FREE** books will be given per person for those who are indigent.

Phone Number: 858-452-9625.

The Habeas Citebook: Ineffective Assistance of counsel.

This is PLN'S second published book, which exclusively covers ineffective assistance of counsel-related issues in federal habeas petitions. Great resource for habeas litigation with hundreds of case citations. It's 200 pages, $49.95, and can be purchased from Prison Legal News.

Hamden Consulting
1612 Homestead Rd.
Chapel Hill, NC 27516

Their objective is to end abusive prisoner phone service.

Harvest Time Books
Altamont, TN 37301

Address it exactly like that. Ask for their catalog and they'll send you a list of **FREE** books.

Comment: I sent for a lot of their books when I was doing a SHU and they sent 'em, but they were just way too religious for me. - - GURU

Hasting Women's Law Journal
100 McAllister, Suite 2207
San Francisco, CA 94102

HWLJ seeks submissions from women in prison about their experiences for publication. Write/Send SASE for more information.

H. Avery
8280 SW 24th St., Apt. 7111
Pompano Beach, FL 33068

H. Avery sells address labels. It's $7 for 500, and $12 for 1,000; 3 lines of text.

Hawaii Innocence Project
Attention: Prof. Hench
University of Hawai`i School of Law
2515 Dole Street
Honolulu HI 96822

The Hawaii Innocence Project (HIP) provides **FREE** legal assistance to Hawaii prisoners with substantiated claims of actual innocence in seeking exoneration, including investigating and obtaining DNA testing.

Phone Number: (808) 956-6547
Website: http://www.innocenceprojecthawaii.org

Hawkeye Editing
PO Box 16406
St. Paul, MN 55116

Editing and typing services. Reasonable rates and rapid response. **FREE** evaluation of and manuscript, plus **FREE** proofreading and corrections on a single-page personal letter. Just enclose a SASE for return of your document. For quickest response, their service is also available through CorrLinks.

Help From Beyond Walls
POB 318
Palmyra, ME 04965

This is a prisoner services company that does it all: pen pals ads, stamp reimbursement, photo editing, gift ordering, internet reach, letter forwarding, website creation and much more. Write/Send SASE for more information.

Comment: Sent $50 for an order 17 months ago and never got it. I was able to cancel the check, though, because it was never cashed. - - Troy Shaw, Indiana

Help From Outside
2620 Bellevue Way NE #200
Bellevue, WA 98004

Phone Number: 206-486-6042
Website: helpfromoutside.com

This company will help you accomplish the things you need to get done on the outside but can't -- finance and business, social networking, phone calls, information, administrative work and more. Send SASE for a brochure and application.

Comment: "When Prisoner Assistant went out of business, I moved my operations to HFO and used them until my twin brother got out the feds. I was very pleased. If I needed another executive assistant to take care of my needs, I'd use HFO again in a heartbeat. TMP endorsed and recommended!" - - Josh Kruger, author of The Millionaire Prisoner

Helping Educate to Advance the Rights of the Deaf (HEARD)
PO Box 1160
Washington, D.C. 20013

HEARD is an all-volunteer nonprofit organization that provides advocacy services for deaf, hard of hearing and deaf-blind inmates across the nation. HEARD's mission is to promote equal access to the justice and legal system for deaf defendants, detainees, prisoners, and returned citizens. HEARD can train and correspond with wardens, corrections officers and directors of departments of corrections; and can refer cases to our network of attorneys.

Phone Number: 202-455-8076
Website: behearddc.orp

Hepatitis C Awareness Project
PO Box 41803
Eugene, OR 97404

FREE information, treatment options.

Hepatitis and Liver Disease: What You Need to Know

Describes symptoms and treatments of hepatitis B & C and other liver diseases. Includes medications to avoid, what diet to follow, exercises to perform and a bibliography. It's 457 pages, $17.95, and can be bought from Prison Legal News.

Hepatitis C Support Project
PO BOX 15144
Sacramento, CA 95813

The Hepatitis C Support Project (HCSP) is a registered nonprofit organization founded in 1997 to address the lack of education, support, and services available at that time for the HCV population.

Website: www.hcvadvocate.org

Hepatitis Prison Coalition
Hepatitis Education Project
911 Western Avenue, Suite 302
Seattle, WA 98104

Provides hepatitis and blood born infection classes in all WA state prisons. Links prisoners with medical care upon release. Their newsletter, HEP News, is **FREE** to prisoners subject to available funding. Send SASE for more details.

Phone Number: (206) 732-0311

High Caliber Latina
PO 749
Blythewood, SC 29016

This is a non-nude photo company. It's the sister company of Flix 4 You. The prices are the same. See our Flix 4 You listing for more details.

Website: highcaliberlatina.com

HIV/Hepatitis –C Prison Committee
California Prison Focus
1904 Franklin Street, Suite 507
Oakland, CA 94612

Phone Number: (510) 836-7222

Website: www.prisons.org

Hepatitis, AIDS Research Trust
513 E. 2nd St
Florence, CO 81226

Write for a monthly newsletter.

Hollywood Scriptwriter
PO Box 10277
Burbank, CA 91510

If you want to start writing movie scripts, order this magazine. It's $36 for a 1-year subscription, 6 issues.

Homeboy Industries
130 West Bruno Street
Los Angeles, CA 90012

"Homeboy Industries is a re-entry and rehabilitation program for formerly gang involved and previously incarcerated men and women. We offer **FREE** services, including: tattoo removal, employment services, twelve step meetings (AA/NA/CGA), educational classes, case management, mental health counseling, legal services, solar panel installation training etc.

These post release services will aid you in your transition to life on the outside. For instance, you can receive assistance with: 1) obtaining your Social Security card, Driver's License or California ID; 2) creating a resume, searching for employment, learning interview techniques, building job skills; 3) obtaining your GED through prep classes and one on one tutoring; 4) learning life skills, anger management, parenting, building healthy relationships, interpersonal communication, leadership, alternative to violence, etc.
All of our services and classes are offered in-house at our headquarters in downtown Los Angeles. We cannot put you on a waiting list, since you have to come in person to participate.

It is my sincerest hope that you will consider us in your plans to get on the right track upon your release, and that you come become a part of the Homeboy family."

Phone: 323-526-1254
Website: HomeboyIndustries.org

Hopkins Law Office
140 B Street, #5-240
Davis, CA 95616

Licensed attorney for California and Arizona, 9th Circuit & Supreme Court. Reasonable flat-fees. 13 years fighting post-conviction cases. Focuses on appeals and PCR cases.

Phone: 520-465-2658
Email: objectionyourhonor@hotmail.com
Website: thehopkinslawoffice.com

Hour Children
36-11 12th St.
Long Island City, NY 11106

Phone Number: (718)-433-4724

How to Win Your Personal Injury Claim, 7th edition

While not specifically for prison-related personal injury cases, this book provides comprehensive information on how to handle personal injury and property damage claims arising from accidents -- including dealing with doctors, attorneys and insurance companies. It's 304 pages, $34.99, and can be bought from Prison Legal News.

Hoy, Marion
PO Box 833
Marble Falls, TX 78654

This is a legal consultant that specializes in whether or not you have a case against your arresting officer.

Hudson Link For Higher Education
PO Box 862
Ossining, New York 10562

Phone Number: 914-941-0794

They offer **FREE** college courses to prisoners in select New York state prisons.

Human Kindness Foundation
P.O. Box 61619
Durham, NC 27715

Two **FREE** books or catalogs of other hard to find spiritual books. Sends spiritual books **FREE** to prisoners.

Human Rights Coalition
4134 Lancaster Ave
Philadelphia PA 19104

Phone Number: 267.293.9169

Human Rights Watch
1630 Connecticut Avenue N.W. Suite 500
Washington, D.C. 20009

Stands with victims and activist to prevent discrimination, to uphold political freedom, to protect people from inhumane conduct in wartime, and to bring offenders to justice. Investigates and exposes human rights violations and hold abusers accountable, challenges governments and those who hold power to end abusive practices and respect to International Human Rights Law. They work on a variety of prison issues.

Phone Number:202-612-4321.

Hungry Robot

"There are 1.7 million children who have a parent In prison In the U.S. (Bureau of Justice Statistics). If you are one of the 357,300 parents held in state or" federal prison, then stop and consider the importance of gilding your child's growth. Hungry Robot displays the destructive habits of materialism, selfishness, and more, with a simple message -- 'find a purpose'. It's a perfect bed-time story, easy to read, fully illustrated with colorful action … and something worth thinking about!"

This book is by author Anthony Tinsman. It's only $2.99 and it's available on Kindle only. ASIN: B001P1CAK4, 30 pages.

Comment: Anthony is a personal friend of mine who genuinely cares about working for and contributing to 'the greater good'. If you have a child, it is your duty as a parent to spend the low $2.99 price to provide your child(ren) with this invaluable lesson. - - Mike

Idaho Innocence Project
Boise State University
1910 University Dr
Boise, ID 83725

Focuses on cases where DNA evidence would change the outcome. Write for more criteria. Do not send transcripts or legal documents. Idaho only.

Illinois Innocence Project
University of Illinois Springfield
One University Plaza
Springfield, Illinois 62703-5407

Phone Number: 217-206-6600

I'm Not Crying

This book is by Michael Norwood aka Minkah Abubakar. It's $15.00 plus $3.95 for shipping and can be ordered from Don Diva Magazine.

"A story by an African-American ex-professional bank robber, now jailed for life, for a robbery he did not commit."

Image; Center for Religious Humanism
3307 Third Ave West
Seattle, WA 98119'

Literary publication.

Immigration Service
105 East Grant Rd
Tucson, AZ 85705

Phone Number: (520)620-9950.

Impact Publications
9104 N Manassas Dr.
Manassas Park, VA 20111

They publish the "Ex-Offender's Job Hunting Guide"; it's $17.95.

Incarcerated Citizens Council
Richard Carter 310 Morea Road
Frackville, PA 17932

Indiana University
Owen Hall 001
790 E. Kirkwood Avenue
Bloomington, IN 47405

Highly recommended career college.

Indian Life Magazine
PO Box 32
Pembina, ND 58271

This magazine has a lot of Native American resources. Send $1.50 or 4 stamps and they'll send you a sample.

Phone Number: (204) 661.9333
Website: indianlife.org.

Infectious Diseases In Corrections Report
146 Clifford St
Providence, RI 02903

Publication edited and written by prison health care providers discussing HIV/AIDS and hepatitis care for incarcerated people.

Info
PO Box 64
Darien, CT 06820

Looking for a writing coach to help you with your literary works? Write/Send SASE for more information.

InfoLINKS, L.L.C.

Offers daily sports info and updates, photo forwarding from your family to you, gifts and flowers sent to your family from you, **FREE** horoscopes and quotes and **FREE** legal news. Sign up now at info@infolincs.com.

INKWELL Magazine
Manhattanville College
2900 Purchase Street
Purchase, NY 10577

Mail Entry Guidelines: Entry fee: $5 for the first poem, $3 for each additional poem. Include your name, address and email in a cover letter or on each poem.

Phone Number: (914) 323-5239
Email: inkwell@mville.edu

Inmate Alliance, LLC
POB 241
Lebanon, Oregon 97355

Inmate Alliance is more than your pen pal connection to the world, it is your way of reaching out to the world. Now remember, your personal membership listing acts like a personal ad, only much larger, and far less expensive. Your listing runs all day and night worldwide for millions to see.

PACKAGES

Foundation Listings...

One photo with your name, and application information (Bio information not included) is along with membership information page is places on our Inmate Alliance sites for one FULL year. $9.95 per year.

Copper Listings...

You can submit up to a 200-word bio, 2 photos, your name, application information and bio information included. Your photo along with membership information page is placed on all our Inmate Alliance LLC sites for one FULL year, $19.95 per year.

Silver Listings...

You can submit up to a 300-word bio, 5 photos or artwork, your name, application information and bio information included. Your name will appear as LARGE BOLD TEXT. Your photo along with membership information page is placed on all our Inmate Alliance LLC sites for one FULL year. $39.95 per year.

Gold Listings...

You can submit up to a 500-word bio, and 10 photos or artwork, your name, application information and bio information included. Your name will appear as LARGE BOLD TEXT. Your photo along with membership information page is placed on all our Inmate Alliance LLC site for one FULL year. $79.95 per year

Platinum Listings...

You can submit up to a 500-word bio, and 20 photos or artwork, 10 personalized words captioned under each photo. Your name, application information and bio information included. Your name will appear as LARGE BOLD TEXT. Your photos along with membership information page is placed on all our Inmate Alliance LLC sites for one FULL year. $99.95 per year.

You can customize your ad package to get exactly what you need. Add $5 to your ad package for each additional photo, and $5 for each additional 50 words. Please note that in

order to receive information or have items returned from Inmate Alliance LLC you will have to include a SASE.

Comment: I don't understand what they mean by "placed on all our Inmate Alliance LLC sites." "All" implies more than one, and nowhere in their info do they mention their "various" sites. Not sure about these guys. - - Mike

InmateLoveLink
4001 Inglewood Ave., Suite 101-144
Redondo Beach, CA 90278

Pen-pal site.

Comment: This is some new shit I'ma have to investigate. - - Mike

Inmate Classified
PO Box 3311
Granada Hills, CA 91394

This is a pen pal website. They also offer email forwarding. Write/Send SASE for more information.

Inmateconnections.com
465 NE 181st Ave. #308
Portland, OR 97230-6660

Pan pal hookups for prisoners! 92% response rate in 20141 75,000+ hits daily! A+ rating with the BBB! Accepts checks, credit cards, stamps, MoneyGram and Trugram. Write for a **FREE** brochure/application. Send SASE or stamp for fast reply.

Inmate-Connection.com
PO Box 83897
Los Angeles, CA 90083

"Only the best and hottest photos! We have the newest, most sensational and exclusive photos on the planet! To order our **FREE** catalog, send SASE or $1.20. All photos are prison friendly. All photos are 4X6, high quality and glossy!

Photo prices:

12 photos for $10
16 photos for $15
22 photos for $20
28 photos for $25

35 photos for $30
45 photos for $35

Minimum order is $10. Additional pics with any set are $.80 each. Add a flat rate of $2.20 for shipping on all orders. We will not ship your order without payment for postage. We do not accept stamps for payment. We have been in business since July 2002."

Comment: Good images. – Mike

Inmate Mingle
PO Box 23207
Columbia, SC 29224

"Inmate Mingle is a new, 21st Century pen pal service.

We provide a forum to connect inmates with people who are looking to correspond, speak and possibly connect with an inmate like you.

Inmate Mingle is new in the way that we approach this service. There are many others that offer this service, but none with the innovation and dedication that Inmate Mingle provides.

We have a website that is user friendly and not confusing for people to use. We offer no outside advertising to the persons that view the site; we do not let them get distracted; their main focus is to look at profiles and maybe choose to correspond with you! we also have an app for smart phones to make sure that our services are available to people on the go.

Unlike other pen pal services, Inmate Mingle promotes the site to people in the free world through search engines such as Google and Bing. We also do print ads, and soon we will do TV commercials! We promote the Inmate Mingle brand which creates more traffic to our site, which in turn means more people to view your profile. The more people that view your profile, the more possibilities of mail for you!

Platinum Ads are $50 per year and you can send 500 words or less, 4 pictures, and one song of your choice. The renewal fee is $40.

Gold Ads are $40 per year and you can send 250 words or less, 2 pictures, and one song of your choice.

Gallery Ads are $30 per year and you can send 250 words or less, 1 picture, and you can include a song for an additional $5. The renewal fee is $20.

Send SASE for application today!"

InmateNavigator.Org
827 Missouri St., Suite
Fairfield, CA 94533

Community services, E-mentorship, Legal document assistance.

Phone: 707-877-6060

InmateNHouse love .com
4001 Inglewood Ave. Suite 10 Dept. 144
Redondo Beach, CA 90278

Pen pal Company. Send SASE for details.

Inmate Pen Pal Connection
Attn: Ralph Landi
49 Crown St. 20B
Brooklyn, NY 11225

Pen pal ads, personal webpage, MySpace, Facebook and Craigslist ads. They do it all for one low price. Send 6 stamps for more information.

Inmate Photo Provider
PO Box 2451
Forrest City, AR 72336

"Don't miss another special moment or event! Stay in the loop!

Have your FAMILY/FRIENDS text you UNLIMITED photos to (870) 317-7561 or email them to you
at info@inmateprovider.com. All EMAIL/TEXT PHOTOS must include your full name, inmate number and address in the subject line in order for delivery to occur. If you ever go to the SHU, HOLE, or on LOCKDOWN at your facility, NO PROBLEM! We will continue to process your orders as long as funds are available in your prepaid account. Start your prepaid account today!) Minimum $10 deposit required.)

All photos are .50 cents per copy plus tax, shipping and handling. We also print social media photos from your Facebook page, Instagram account, Tagg, and the likes for .89 cents per copy, plus tax, shipping and handling! Our prices are based on the quality of service we provide. Photos are received and processed 24/7, seven days a week with quality service guaranteed for all local, state, federal and international inmates. Send your deposit to the above address today!

All deposits received will go toward processing your orders. For additional payment options, email us. Our representatives are standing by to assist you! We ACCEPT Money Orders, Institutional checks, JPay, MoneyGram (contact us for outside representative information to use this feature via email), family/friend debit or credit PayPal deposits are accepted. We do not accept personal checks. '

EXCLUSIVE FEATURE...

Add backgrounds, clothes and your loved ones to your photos! Starting at $15 (charges may vary according to your request and detail). Add $2.50 per additional photo used to create your photo. You must number your photo(s) and explain which features you want applied to your photo(s) on an additional sheet of paper. Based on your request, an additional 2-3 days may be needed to fulfill your order. For more information, see our Product & Service Description Pages in our catalog.

SOCIAL MEDIA...

SM Page Monitoring Packages available (prices vary). Email us at socialmedia@inmateprovider.com with questions.

NOW PROVIDING LOCAL NUMBERS ...

Affordable Inmate Calling Services, keeping you connected while saving you money! 100% Compliant! Make your everyday long distance calls into local calls today! Receive (3) local numbers for only $22. With signing up today, earn (1) **FREE** MONTH of service ($10 activation fee included). You must provide us with the" first and last name of the contact personal for each line of service requested for verification and security purposes! Once payment is received, we will contact your family/friend to activate your account. We will email or mail you your local landline number after your account is set up.

Let IPP copy, Enlarge, and Collage your Photo(s) Today! 4x6, 5x7, 8x10 and wallet size services available, color or black and white!

To learn more about our magazine subscriptions, product, services, features and rates, simply write or email us at info@inmateprovider.com. To receive information from IPP, you must provide a SASE with your request, and if you are requesting our magazine listing, please send in (3) postage stamps

Comment: I received their catalog of photo manipulation examples. The quality looks pretty decent, especially for the price. They can take your head and put it on a body wearing a suit, or some other outfit that's better than your prison clothes. They can cut the background out of your prison photo and have you standing in front of a Bently, or in your city, whatever. - - Mike

Comment: This is a good business. - - Jesse Mason

Inmates' Little Helpers
PO Box 4172
Oakland, CA 94614

"We offer many services including pics, naughty and personal; messaging services, Facebook setup, penpal, books and mags, court doc. filings, publishing, PACER. Send SASE for more info."

Email: inmateslittlehelpers@gmail.com

InmateTrivia@gmail.com

Get 3 **FREE** trivia questions once a week by adding the email above to your Corrlinks contact list. Sponsored by PhoneDonkey.com.

Inmateservices.net
13017 Wisteria Dr. #310
Germantown, MD 20874

Affordable gifts. Send a first-class stamp for catalog.

Inmate Toll Busters

Discount inmate telephone calling services for federal and state prisons, county jails and INS detention centers nationwide. **FREE** same day installation, only $1.25 per month and 6¢ per minute. They send to cell phones. International call service available.

Phone Number: (888) 966-8655
Website: inmatetollbusters.com

Innocence and Justice Project
Univ of New Mexico School of Law 1117 Stanford NE
Albuquerque, NM 87131-0001

Phone Number: 505-277-2671

Innocence Project
40 Worth St., Suite 701
New York, NY 10013

Provides advocacy for wrongly convicted prisoners whose cases Involve DNA evidence and are at the post-conviction appeal stage. Maintains an online list of state-by-state innocence projects.

Phone Number: 212-364-5340
Website: Innocenceproject.org

Innocence Project For Justice (New Jersey Cases)
Rutgers University School Of Law Constitutional Litigation Clinic
123 Washington St.
Newark, NJ 07102

INNOCENT, a Christian-based non-profit organization refers prison inmates and their families to a national network of Innocence organizations following receipt and review of claims of wrongful conviction. Utilizing expertise in the media and in community organization, INNOCENT increases public awareness of legitimate claims of innocence and problems associated with wrongful convictions. (Founded by an innocent who was released in 2004 after fighting 10 years.)

Innocence Project NW Clinic
University of Washington School of Law
William H Gates Hall, Suite 265
PO Box 85110
Seattle, WA 98145

They will only consider cases from Washington in which actual innocence is claimed. Write for questionnaire to fill out about your case.

Website: law.washington.edu/ipnw.

Innocence Project of Florida, Inc.
1100 East Park Avenue
Tallahassee, FL 32301

The Innocence Project of Florida (IPF) is an IRS-certified 501(c) (3), non-profit organization founded in January 2003 to help innocent prisoners in Florida obtain their freedom and rebuild their lives

Phone (850) 561-6767

Website:floridainnocence.org

Innocence Project of Iowa
19 South 7th Street
Estherville, IA 51334

Website: iowainnocence.org

Innocence Project of Minnesota
Hamline University School of Law
1536 Hewitt Avenue
St. Paul, MN 55104

Phone: 651-523-3152

Innocence Project of New Orleans
4051 Ulloa Street
New Orleans, LA 70119

E-mail: info@ip-no.org
Website: http://www.ip-no.org

Innovative Sentencing Solutions
78 DeepwoodDr
Avon, CT 06001

They offer a nice variety of services for federal prisoners. Write/Send SASE for details.

Phone Number; (860)922-7321
Website: innovativesentencing.com.

Innocence Project (National)
40 Worth Street, Suite 701
New York, NY 10013

Only handles cases where post-conviction DNA testing of evidence can yield conclusive evidence of innocence.

Currently not accepting new cases from California, Ohio, Washington, or Wisconsin (check state listings for those states)

Website: innocenceproject.org.

The Innocence Project of Texas 1511
Texas Ave.
Lubbock, Texas 79401

Phone: (806) 744-6525
Website: http://www.ipoftexas.org/

In Perfect Peace Ministries
POB 763

53

Rocklin, CA 95677

Christian pen-pal ministries.

In Scan Document Services
401 Wilshire Blvd, 12th Floor PH
Santa Monica, CA 90401

This is a nationwide document scanning service for inmates. "Never fear losing your documents during a search or being transferred!"

You mail them your documents. Their attorney-based service will ensure that you documents will be safely secured.

They scan the documents. The documents are scanned into a secure digital file in which you will have access to. Ask about their printing fees.

They mail you back the originals. Shipping fees will apply. They can also shred the originals per your request.

Only $59.99 -- onetime fee, permanent storage.

Scanning fees do apply: up to 500 pages is $0.30/PG; over 500 pages is $0.25/PG.

Founded and powered by attorneys who understand the value of your documents! Write today!

Phone: 800-470-5338
Website: inmatescan.com

Inside Books Project
C/O 12th St Books
827 W 12th St
Austin, TX 78701

All volunteer, non-profit organization that sends **FREE** books and educational materials to people in prison in the state of Texas.

Phone Number: (512) 647-4803

Inside Dharma
PO Box 220721
Kirkwood, MO 63122

Offers a bi-monthly Buddhist newsletter for prisoners. Write/Send SASE for details.

Inside-Out Prison Exchange Project
University of Oregon

1585 E 13th Ave
Eugene, OR 97403

Phone Number: 405-208-6161

INSIGHTCREW

Market indexes and currency prices. Includes a stock watch list (make your own watch list). List emailed to you Mon-Fri. Two **FREE** weeks when you sign up!

Email: Mkinsightcrew@gmail.com

Insight Meditation Society
1230 Pleasant St.
Barra, MA 01005

Website: www.dharma.org

The Insight Prison Project
PO Box 151642
San Rafael, CA 94915

Communication training in nonviolence in correctional facilities; expanding to include post-release training.

Phone Number: (415) 459-9800

Inspector General Hotline
State Capitol, Room 160
900 Court Street
Salem, OR 97310

Inmates who are currently being sexually assaulted are encouraged to talk to a staff member. This will allow for the quickest response. Each institution has a Sexual Assault Response Team that can respond and ensure needed services are afforded. Inmates may report in person, through an inmate communication, or through the grievance system.

The Governor's Citizen Message Line: (503) 378-4582

Institute For Criminals Justice Healthcare
1700 Diagonal Rd Ste 110
Alexandria, VA 22314

Phone Number: (703) 836-0024
Website: institute-for-criminal-justice-healthcare.

Institute of Children's Literature
93 Long Ridge Rd.

West Reddington, CT 06896

This is a writing school that will help if you are serious about writing children's books. Write and request their **FREE** catalog.

Phone Number: (800) 243-9645
Website: theinstituteofchildrensliterature.com.

Intelligent Solutions

I DO <u>NOT</u> RECOMMEND DOING BUSINESS WITH THIS COMPANY!

International Christian College & Seminary
PO Box 530212
Debary, FL 32753

Correspondence courses via mail. Tuition as little as $12.95 per month. **FREE** evaluation! Send a SASE. Associates -- Pd.D. Accredited.

Internal Affairs, CDCR
10111 Old Placerville Rd., Suite 200
Sacramento, CA 05827

International Acoustic Music Awards
2881 E. Oakland Park Blvd, Suite 414
Ft. Lauderdale, FL 3306, USA

IAMA offers a songwriting contest. Send SASE for flier with details.

Website: inacoustic.com

International Association of Sufism Prison Project
14 Commercial Blvd. Suite 101
Novato, CA 94949

A program of the IAS; also runs the Sufi Women Organization Prison Program. Correspondence opportunities and a quarterly newsletter.

Phone Number: 415-382-7834.

International Bible Society
1820 Jet Stream Dr.
Colorado Springs, CO 80921-3696

Inmates can receive **FREE** on the inside Bible (English or Spanish) and a booklet for women or men. No large print inmate bibles.

International Buddhist Meditation Center
928 South New Hampshire Ave,
Los Angeles, CA 90006

IBMC is primarily oriented toward Zen but teaches all schools of Buddhism. "We can send our quarterly newsletter c/o the prison library or chaplain. You may write to request the newsletter. We will send a maximum of 4 copies to each prison."

Phone Number: (213) 384-0850
Website: www.ibmc.info.

International Christian College and Seminary
P.O. Box 530212
Debary, FL 32753

Correspondence courses via mail, associates through PhD, credit for life experience, tuition as low as $19.95 a month. This school is not regionally credited. Send SASE for a **FREE** evaluation.

International Food Information Council Foundation
1100 Connecticut Ave., NW, Suite 430
Washington, DC 20036

IFIC, the International Food Information Council Foundation provides food safety, healthy eating and nutrition information.

Website: foodinsight.org.

International Prison Ministry
PO Box 1088
Chula Vista, CA 91912

"IPM has available **FREE** of charge to prisoners all over the US when requested and if there is time to get materials there before a release or transfer: Bibles (KJV regular print or the New KJV in regular print). The Practical Bible Dictionary/Concordance, Testimony and Devotional books. We do not send lists of our books because the inventory changes without notice. We send a list of organizations who have Bible Study Correspondence Courses, but we do not have correspondence course as such, just books which help you study the Bible. We do not send you monthly newsletters or magazines to inmates. In order to get literature, one must write and request it. We are happy to answer prisoner letters and send what we can when we can. We send New Testaments to short term facilities such as jails, reception centers, etc. No Pen Pal programs available that we know of. We are sorry we cannot fulfill the requests for different Bibles and books other than those above. "

International Prison Watch Project
PO Box 674
Las Cruces, NM 88004

An international coalition of advocates dedicated to shedding a spotlight inside our prison walls.

Internationalist Prison Books Collective
405 West Franklin Street
Chapel Hill, NC 27514

Volunteer collective that sends books to prisoners in Mississippi, Alabama, and parts of North Carolina. Has fiction as well as political and legal nonfiction. Also prints prisoners' art, writing, and news in a regular biannual publication.

Phone Number: (919) 942-1740

International Sports Sciences Association
1015 Mark Avenue
Carpentaria, LA 93013

The International Sports Sciences Association acts as a teaching institution and certification agency for fitness trainers, athletic trainers, aerobics instructors, and medical professionals in every field of health care. All seven training courses can be completed entirely through the mail. Each program costs $600

Inner Traditions, Bear & Co
One Park St.
PO Box 388
Rochester, VT 05767

They send inmates various religious publications. Write for more details.

In The Wind
PO Box 3000
Agoura Hills, CA 91376

This magazine is about custom Harleys and events. It's $16.95 for a 1-year subscription, 4 issues per year.

Phone Number: (818)889-8740
Website: easyriders.com

In-Touch Ministries
P.O. Box 7900
Atlanta, GA 30357

FREE *"In Touch"* religious magazine.

Islamic AhlulBayt Association
12460 Los Indios Trail
Austin, TX 78729

Islamic Center
2551 Massachusetts Ave, NW
Washington, DC 20008

They provide **FREE** Koran and study guides. Can send through Chaplain.

Islamic Center of Springfield Missouri
2151 East Division St.
Springfield, MO 65803

Provides **FREE** Qur'an and will write letters to prison authorities and to politicians about conditions in prisons for prisoners in Missouri and adjacent states.

Islamic Circle of North America
166-26 89th Ave
Jamaica, NY 11432

They provide Islamic material and guidance.

ISO of SAA Inc.
PO Box 70949
Houston, TX 77270 USA

Website: saa-recovery.org.

Jackson & Reed
601 Sawyer Ste. 105
Houston, TX 77007

Attorneys that offer compassionate defense, parole, and post-conviction work. Parole representation from $1500.

Phone Number: 713-429-1405
Website: jacksonandreed .com

Jaden Moore of New York
2600 south Rd., Suite 44-258
Poughkeepsie, NY 12601

This company sells tons of gifts that you can purchase and send to your loved ones. Send $2.50 or 5 stamps for a full color catalog.

Website: jadenmooreofnewyork.com.

Jailbabes.Com
c/o Arlen Bischke
PO 845
Winchester, Oregon 97495

JailBabes.com was one of the first and most popular inmate pen pal sites back in 1999. It has been absent for approximately 16 years. It is making its return under new ownership and is in no way associated with the original site. The new owner of JailBabes.com is Arlen Bischke, who also owns the top-ranked inmate pen pal site Meet-An-Inmate.cOm, which has been operating since 1998. Unlike Meet-An-Inmate.com, JailBabes.com is for women only.

An ad includes one photo and a 250-word bio. Additional photos are $3.00 (or 8 stamps) each, and you can add as many as you like.

$30.00 for 12 months

$50 for 12 months on both Jailbabes.com and Meet-An-Inmate.com

$80 for 12 months on JailBabes.com and FEATURED on Meet-An-Inmate.com

Note: With FEATURED ads, there will be an added link to your webpage via a thumbnail photo placed on the Home page of the site. Your thumbnail will also show up above all standard ads. This provides extra traffic to your page to increase your chances at obtaining pen pals. The FEATURED option is only available on the Meet-An-Inmate.com website.

Make check payable to Arlen Bischke at the above address. Send SASE for application.

Jail Calls
PO Box 271
Cedar Brook, NJ 08018

This company provides phone calls at a discount. Write/Send SASE for more information.

Phone Number: (888)892-9998
Website: jailcalls.com.

JailCallsUSA.com

$9.95 a month for unlimited calls for federal, state, and county inmates. They'll give you a local number and make it to where inmates can call your cell phone.

Phone Number: 888-776-2012

Jail House Lawyers Guild
1734 Summit
Mount Holly, VT 05785

Website: justicepersued.com.

Jailhouse Lawyers: Prisoners Defending Prisoners v. the USA

In "Jailhouse Lawyers," Prison Legal News columnist, award-winning journalist and former death-row prisoner Mumia Abu-Jamal presents the stories and reflections of fellow prisoners-turned-advocates who have learned to use the court system to represent other prisoners, and in some cases have won their freedom. A must-read for jailhouse lawyers! This book is 280 pages, $16.95, and can be bought from Prison Legal News.

Comment: "Mumia did a great job on this book. It was actually the book that got me started on the path of litigating for my rights in court. It also got me started in the writing game. Every prisoner should read this book! You can learn a lot from Mumia. TMP endorsed!" - - Josh Kruger, author of The Millionaire Prisoner

JDM
PO Box 130063
Dallas, TX 75313

Write for a **FREE** Kings James bible.

Jeff Vencent
109 Post Oak Circle
Hurst, TX 76053

This is a typing service. Write/Send SASE for more information.

Phone Number: (817) 282-1392.

Jewish Prisoners Assistance Foundation
770 Eastern Parkway
Brooklyn, NY 11213

Publishes The Scroll, **FREE** weekly newsletter for Jewish prisoners.

Phone Number: 718-735-2000

Website: www.prisonactivist.org/resources

Jewish Prisoners Services International
PO Box 85840
Seattle, WA 98145

They offer religious materials and support for Jewish prisoners and their families.

Phone Number: (206) 985-0577
Website: jewishprisonerservices.org.

John's Services
601 Mackenzie St. NE #209
Warroad, MN 56763

Send one F/C stamp for details.

Jokes
Po Box 3000
Agoura Hills, CA 91301

Easyrider magazine pays $40 for good jokes, old or new, on biker-oriented subjects.

Journal of Prisoners on Prisons
c/o Justin Piche, PhD
Department of Criminology
University of Ottawa
Ottawa, Ontario, Canada
K1N 6N5

General Information...

The JPP is a prisoner written, academically oriented and peer reviewed, non-profit journal, based on the tradition of penal press. It brings the knowledge produced by prison writers together with academic arguments to enlighten public discourse about the current state or carceral institutions. This is particularly important because with few exceptions, definitions of deviance and constructions of those participating in these defined acts are incompletely created by social scientists, media representatives, politicians and those in the legal community. These analyses most often promote self-serving interests, omit the voices of those most affected, and facilitate repressive and reactionary penal policies and practices. As a result, the JPP attempts to acknowledge the accounts, experiences, and criticism– of the criminalized by providing an educational forum that allows women and men to participate in the development of research that concerns them directly. In an age where 'crime' has become lucrative and exploitable, the JPP exists as an important alternate source of information that competes with popularly held stereotypes and misconceptions about those who are currently, or those who have in the past, faced the deprivation of liberty.

History...

The JPP grew out of presentations at the International Conference on Penal Abolition (ICOPA) III held in Montreal in 1987, where participants were concerned with the lack of prisoner representation. It subsequently emerged in 1988, and has since published over 30 issues featuring prison writers from many different countries who discuss a broad range of topics pertaining to imprisonment. Articles are used regularly in university courses, and are frequently reprinted in books and cited in academic works. Readership includes prisoners, former prisoners, activists, academics, as well as community and justice workers amongst many others. The Editorial Board that produces and manages the journal is comprised of university professors, prison justice activists, and current and former prisoners who voluntarily contribute time and effort, The JPP is funded through subscriptions and sales and is not dependent on any outside sources. It is currently published through the University of Ottawa Press in a bi-annual format. Many past contributors have received awards for their writing (e.g. PEN) and also have gone on to publish books. Writing as Resistance: The JPP Anthology 1988-2002 (Gaucher, Ed. 2002) won silver prize for book of the year in Foreword Magazine's annual awards in 2002.

Submission Guidelines...

- Prisoners and former prisoners are encouraged to submit papers, collaborative essays, discussions transcribed from tape, book reviews, and photo or graphic essays.
- The Journal will not publish any subject matter that advocates hatred, sexism, racism, violence or that supports the death penalty.
- The Journal does not publish material that usually focuses on the writer's own legal case, although the use of the writer's personal experience as an illustration of a broader topic is encouraged.

- The Journal does not usually publish fiction and does not generally publish poetry.
- Illustrations, drawings and paintings may be submitted as potential cover art.
- Articles should be no longer than 20 pages typed and double-spaced or legibly handwritten. Electronic submissions are gratefully received.
- Writers may elect to write anonymously or under pseudonym.
- For references cited in an article, writers should attempt to provide the necessary bibliographic information. Refer to the references cited in past issues for examples.
- Editors look for developed pieces that address topics substantially. Manuscripts go through a preliminary reading and then are sent to review by the Editorial Board. Those that are of suitable interest are returned to the author with comments or suggestions. Editors work with writers on composition and form, and where necessary may help the author with referencing and bibliographic information not readily available in prisons. Selected articles are returned to authors for their approval before publication. Papers not selected are returned with comments from the editor. Revised papers may be resubmitted.
- Please submit biographical and contact information, to be published alongside articles unless otherwise indicated.
- If interested in making a submission we appreciate the enclosure of a brief abstract, with clear and accurate contact details for the author.

Journal Broadcasting and Communications
PO Box 3084
Pittsburgh, PA 15230

This company sells a book titled "Writing for Lawyers," by Hollis T. Hurd, for about $6.

Joyce Meyers Ministries
PO Box 655
Fenton, MO 63026

Write to request their **FREE** monthly magazine and a **FREE** one-time-only hygiene gift.

Julie's Gifts
PO Box 1941
Buford, GA 30515

This company has a lot of nice gifts for sale. Write/Send SASE for more information.

Comment: I've never ordered gifts from Julie, but I have ordered her magazines (she runs Tightwad) and her business there was all the way straight. Fast and accurate. She gets an A+ from me for sure. - - Mike

Just Detention International
3325 Wilshire Blvd., Suite 340
Los Angeles, CA 90010

This is a human rights organization that seeks to end sexual abuse against men, women, and youth in all forms of detention.

Phone Number: 213-384-1400

Website: justdetention.org

Justice Brandeis Law Project
(formerly the Justice Brandeis Innocence Project)
Schuster Institute for Investigative Journalism
Goldfarb 69-19, MS 043
415 South Street
Waltham, MA 02453

Phone Number: (781) 736-4953

Justice Denied
P.O. Box 66291
Seattle, WA 98166

Although no longer publishing a print magazine, Justice Denied continues to provide the most comprehensive coverage of wrongful convictions and how and why they occur. Their content is available online and includes all back issues of Justice Denied magazine and a database of more than 3,000 wrongly convicted people.

Phone Number: 206-335-4254
Website: justicedenied .org

JustLeadershipUSA
1900 Lexington Avenue
New York, NY 10035

"JustLeadershipUSA is committed to cutting the US correctional population in half by 2030. To achieve this, we are relying on YOU.

JLUSA was founded by Glenn E. Martin. Six years in a New York State prisons taught him that those closest to the problem are closest to the solution, but furthest from power and resources. We want you to join our community and lend your voice to ending this country's mass incarceration crisis. Become a JLUSA Member for **FREE**! To receive a membership pack, please get in touch at the address above."

Website: justleadershipusa.org
Email: membership@justleadershipusa.org

Justice Now
1322 Webster Street Suite 210
Oakland, CA 94612

Focuses solely on the needs of women prisoners. They work on alternative sentencing, document human rights abuses in prison, and their Building a World without Prisons project (works with women prisoners to get their words and art in the media).

Phone Number: (510) 839-7654

Justice Watch
1120 Garden Street
Cincinnati, OH 45214

Works to eliminate classism and racism from prisons and opposes the death penalty. Operates Garden Street Transitional House for parolees. Publishes quarterly newsletter.

Phone Number: (513) 241-0490

Juvenile Lifers
P.O. Box 8077
Pittsburgh, PA 15216

This is a not-for-profit organization dedicated to juveniles in the state of Pennsylvania and across the country who are serving sentences of life without parole. "Our purpose is to educate the public and legislators and to reach out to juveniles and their families."

Website: juvenilelifers.org

If you have your own stories about lifers for publication email them to: lifex@prisoners.com.
http://www.prisoners.com/life.html#life

Keeping the Faith: The Prison Project

606 Maynard Ave, Suite 201
Seattle, WA 98104

Founded in 1995, "Keeping the Faith: The Prison Project" is a series of workshops with incarcerated women in WA, MA, FL, and Brazil focusing on writing, movement, and performance skills provided through lecture demonstrations, performances, and classes.

Phone Number: (206) 522-8151

K. Carter
PO Box 70092
Henrico, VA 23255

Incarcerated writer? Walkinthoseshoes.com posts inmate essays in Views From The Inside. Also mentors authors of all book genres for our 'E-Library'. Mail essays or sample chapters to the above address. Send SASE for more info.

Kentucky Innocence Project
Department of Public Advocacy
100 Fair Oaks Lane, Ste. 302
Frankfort, KY 40601

Phone Number: 502-564-3948
Website: dpa.ky.gov/kip

Kill Shot King
PO 81074
Corpus Christi, TX 78468

This guy sells "Bricks" or pre-selected photos. "Bricks" are 100 photos, and he charges $22.50 per Brick. He currently has 26 different Brick "themes" to choose from. He also sells smaller groups of photos at the following prices:

5-24 shots, $1 each
25-99 shots, $0.50 each
100-199, $0.45 each
200-299 shots, $0.35 each
300 shots and up, $0.25 each
1,000 shots and more, $0.20 each

Send SASE for FREE catalog.

Comment: I've had several complaints about this company. I recently contacted the owner and asked if he wanted to address them and here's what he said.

"Just state the facts. Inmate Shopper got out of line and I'm addressing it. I'll have a full-page ad in the next issue of Hip-Hop Weekly by the way. That shit is going to shock the nation. A lot of people don't realize I sell to each and every state and federal prison."

If you write this guy and ask him what's going on, he will send you a pre-written letter addressing everything. It seems like he's genuinely trying to get it together, but as we all know, intentions aren't enough when it comes to our money and orders, we expect results. I'ma leave this one on you to decide. — Mike

Comment: When I finally got their info, I sent $20 for catalogs and $12.50 for pics. It's been 9 months and I still haven't gotten either order. Bullshit Ripoff! — — Troy Shaw, Indiana

Email: killshotking.com

King Poe Publishing
817 Bridle Drive
Desoto, TX 75115

Floyd "Poe" Simms is the author of 'How to Became a Millionaire Buying and Renting Properties in the Hood,' and 'Lil Poe: Drug Kingpin.' Each book is $15.99 plus $4.00 for s/h. You can order them direct.

Kite Magazine
Dept: TCB
POB 100971
Brooklyn, NY 11210

Kite is a newer magazine but it definitely ain't playin' no games. It's basically like Instagram for prisoners. All the hot shit going on on IG, Kite covers. It's bi-monthly, full color, 72-page magazine. It's $24.99 for a 3-issue subscription, $49.99 for 6 issues (1 year).

Comment: Kite is one of my favorite magazines, hands down. It has all the latest goings on from IG. Kite is Mike Enemigo certified fa sho'. — — Mike

Krashna Law Firm, LLP
Omar Krashna, Attorney at Law
7700 Edgewater Drive, Suite 1030
Oakland, CA 94621

Personal injury attorney.

Phone Number: (510) 836-2999

Krasnya LLC
PO Box 32082
Baltimore, MD 21282

"Welcome to Krasnya Babes and Krasnya Studs worldwide. Tens of thousands of the hottest and most scandalous babes and dudes found on the planet. Each catalog has 120 beautiful girls or boys posing just for you! Order one catalog page for only $4.50 or 10 U.S. Forever stamps with a SASE. We will send you volume one. Each additional volume is the same price. We are more than happy to answer e-mail inquiries; however, due to mailing costs of 49¢ a letter, enclose a SASE with all inquiries sent through the mail. Otherwise, no replies! Prices and policies? Color prints on 4x6 glossy photo paper as low as 35¢ per print on orders over 500, shipped according to policy: 25 pictures shipped every 24 hours. S/h is $2.00 per envelope. Method of payment: U.S. Postal Service money orders or state and federal correctional checks made out only to Krasnya, LLC.

Send $24.95 for a grab bag of 50 photos. You specify race and main area of your interests; we will pick selection for you. We will also throw in a bonus catalog of 120 babes, nude or BOP-friendly.

Send 3 brand-new flat books of 20 U.S. Forever stamps for a grab bag of 45 photos. You specify race and main area of interest; we will pick selection. We will also throw in a bonus color catalog page of 120 babes of studs. Please include 6 forever stamps with this order for s/h.

For Krasnya clients who work the yards, have we got a great deal for you... Mr. Hustle Grab Bag Bargain Days, only 250 per babe/print. 5 grab bag minimum purchase required. $2.00 s/h per bag. 25 awesome babes per bag at only $6.25. You must buy at least 5 grab bags for this deal. You may want to sit down for this bonus bargain... Our Babes catalog special of the decade! 5 color catalogs for $6; 10 color catalogs for $12; 15 color catalogs for $18; 20 color catalogs for $24. Our catalog special is available only when you purchase the 5 grab bag minimum. The price includes **FREE** shipping on the catalogs. Because of shipping terms, all catalogs sold in multiples of 5 for $6 only. You choose male or female, nude or non-nude.

Want a **FREE** sample catalog from Krasnya? Send a BASE with 2 first class stamps. 120 babes in each catalog. You choose male or female, nude or non-nude."

E-mail: krasnyababes@hotmail.com

L33t Gaming
PO Box 30362
Midwest City, OK 73140

Comics, novels, magic, war craft gear, etc. To order full catalog, send $5.99

La Raza Centro Legal, INC.
Lawyer Referral Service and Pro Bono Project
474 Valencia Street #295
San Francisco, CA 94103-3415

This is mainly for Spanish-speaking prisoners. They handle all types of legal problems, civil and criminal. All attorneys are located in San Francisco, but no geographic requirements for clients.

La Voz de Esperanza
C/O The Esperanza Peace and Justice Center
922 San Pedro
San Antonio, TX 78212

This is a bilingual publication (English/Spanish) that's **FREE** to prisoners.

Latino Commission on AIDS
24 W 25th Street, 9th Floor
New York, NY 10010

Provides education and training for treatment for all those in need with the HIV virus. Offers written information and resources in Spanish.

Phone Number: (212) 675-3288

Latino on Wheels
585 E Larned St. Suite 100
Detroit, MI 48226

This magazine is about the latest automotive trends. 4 issues per year.

Phone Number: (313) 962-2209
Website: latinosonwheelsinc.com.

Law Dictionary

Comprehensive up-to-date law dictionary explains more than 8,500 legal terms. Covers civil, criminal, commercial and International law. This book is 525 pages, $19.95, and can be bought from Prison Legal News.

Lawyers Committee for Civil Rights Under Law
1401 New York Ave., NW, Suite 400
Washington, DC 20005

Phone Number: (202) 662-8600 or (888) 299-5227.

Law Offices of C.W. Blaylock
401 Wilshire Blvd., Floor 12
Santa Monica, CA 90401

C.W. Blaylock has been selected as a "Rising Star" by Super Lawyers. He represents inmates for Direct Appeals, Petition for Writ of Habeas Corpus, Parole Hearings, State and Federal Admission.

Phone: 310-496-4245
Website: ChrisBlaylockLaw.com

Law Office of David Rushing
PO Box 431649
Houston, TX 17243

David Rushing is the President of the National Association of Parole Attorneys, and the Chairman of the National Convention on Post-Conviction Relief.

Parole: packets, hearings, revocations, time, classification, medical, hardship, disciplinary and more!

Writs: state writs, federal writs, DNA writs, actual innocence, direct appeal and more!

Serving almost all state and federal jurisdictions -- local counsel who knows local in-and-outs, but who work for us nationally instead of for their local friends.

Great pricing options -- payment plans available.

STILL fighting endlessly for your rights – now almost everywhere.

Wrongful conviction is the worst crime of all! Contact us today, time may be running out!

Phone Number: 713-671-1300
Website: doctorhabeas.com

Law Office of Donald R. Hammond
222 W. 6th Street, Ste. 400
San Pedro, CA 90731

Attorney Don Hammond is a member of Fair Chance Project.

Phone Number: 323-529-3660
Email: don@donhammondlaw.com
Website: donhammondlaw.com

Law Office of Stanley Goff
15 Boardman Place
San Francisco, CA 94103

Police Misconduct, Criminal Defense (Prop 47 Petitions), Personal Injury, all other Civil Rights Violation.

Phone Number: (415) 571-9570
E-mail: scraiggoff@aol.com

Law Offices of Jan Karenina Jemison, MBA
A Professional Law Corporation
3738 Park Blvd. Way
Oakland, CA 94610

Advising entrepreneurs, business owners and nonprofits.

Phone Number: (510) 530-3352

The Law Office of William Savoie
909 Texas Ave, Ste. 205
Houston, TX 77002

Parole, post-conviction, pardons, prison planning (powers of attorney, probate/trusts for families).

Phone: 832-341-4802
Email: WLsavoielaw@gmail.com

LC DeVine Media, LLC
P.O. Box 4026
Flint, Ml 48504

"Welcome! The Internet has changed how we do business and have created new avenues for business owners to bring the world to their place of business, searching for new ways to keep growing and earning profits. In the 21st Century a high percentage of people in the world have access to the Internet, businesses can virtually put their products and services online and have customers come to them from all over the world, instead of just their local communities. If you are a small store front, a progressive church, a company or a sole proprietor, let us help you do business 21st Century Style! That's doing business smarter, not harder! Some of the low cost, affordable services we include: Online advertising; unique website design; logo design; brochure design; business cards; post cards; signs; editing services; self-publishing; one-of-a-kind artworks.

Services/Prices: Typing, $1 per page; general editing, $2 per page (grammar and spelling clarity only); Copying, .15 for black and white, .30 for color (per page); Facebook page, $25 set-up only (you provide pic and info); Twitter page, $25 set-up only (you provide pic and info); Websites/Blogs, $200.00 set-up only (you provide pic and info); Website (3 pages), $350.00 set-up only (you supply picture and Info); E-book publishing, $500.00 complete set-up -- copyright, ISBN, all profits yours; Printed book, $500.00 service fee, you pay all other expenses; E-book or printed paperback with company paying all costs, 50/50 contract deal. Fees are payable before work is done.

Please feel free to contact me if you desire any of the above services, or have any other services that I may assist you with. Sincerely, DeVine"

Left Bank Books
92 Pike St., Box A
Seattle, WA 98101

This company carries thousands of books.
Write/send SASE for more information.

Legal Action Center
225 Varick St. 4th Floor
New York, NY 10014

Non-profit organization providing **FREE** legal services to formerly incarcerated people, recovering alcoholics, substance abusers, and people with HIV.

Phone Number: 1-800-223-4044

Legal Action Center Services
153 Waverly Place.
New York, NY 10014

Publications about looking for work when you have a criminal record. Publication and information clearinghouse.

Legal Aid Society Prisoner's Rights Project
199 Water Street
New York, NY 10038

Priority is to address guard brutality and sexual abuse, other unsafe physical conditions, disability discrimination, lack of mental health and medical care, and lack of educational programs for young prisoners.

Phone Number: (212) 577-3300

Legal Assistance to Minnesota Prisoners
William Mitchell College of Law
875 Summit Ave., Room 254
St Paul, MN 55105

Phone Number: 651-290-6413
Website: wmitchell.edu/legal-practice-center

Legal Information Services Associates
PO Box 636
Norwalk, Ohio 44867

Attention Federal Prisoners! If it happened last week in the courts or in congress, you'll know about it first thing Monday morning. Our no-cost email newsletter focuses on what you care about -- Federal post-conviction cases, Sentencing Guidelines action and Capitol Hill sentence reform.

To receive our **FREE** newsletter, send a corrlinks invitation to newsletter@lisa-legalinfo.com.

Legal Insights Inc
25602 Alicia Parkway, Suite 323
Laguna Hills, CA 92653

Phone Number: 775-301-3588
Website: infolegalinsights.com

Professional specialists with extensive post-conviction experience. They do Just about any type of appeal and they cover all 50 states. **FREE** initial consultation.

Legal Liability Protection

Criminal arrest insurance coverage. Benefits: Immediate cash bail; criminal defense attorney coverage; expert eyewitness; reimbursement of lost wages while attending court; civil suit damage protection. Emergency Resources: 24/7 emergency hotline; local attorney referral within 24 hours; nationwide attorney network; expert witness coordination. Protect your constitutional rights!

Phone: 855-440-2245
Website: LegalLiabilityProtection.com

Legal Move Logistics
PO Box 211
Lincoln, IL 62656

"Need criminal defense paralegal help or case review? Helping to overturn wrongful convictions since 1975!
Send copies of paperwork and $35.00 to initial review. Need help understanding your case? I can help! Send SASE! All payments should be made out to Fonda Robbins."

Legal Publications in Spanish, Inc.
7 E 94th St,
New York, NY 10128

Legal Research: How to Find and Understand the Law

Comprehensive and easy to understand guide on researching the law. Explains case law, statues and digests, and much more. Includes practice exercises. This book is 568 pages, $49.99, and can be bought from Prison Legal News.

Legal Services for Prisoners with Children
1540 Market St. #490
San Francisco, CA 94102

LeNoir Publications
350 Bay St, Suite 100-361
San Francisco, CA 94133

This is a company that provides publishing services and specializes in catering to incarcerated individuals. To request a full list of their services, write/send SASE.

Lesbian AIDS Project
446 West 33rd Street c/o GMHC
New York, NY 10001

Information and support for women and lesbians living with HIV.

Lesbian and Gay Insurrection
3543 18th Street, Suite 26
San Francisco CA 94110

Phone Number: 510-434-1304
Website: lagai.org

Level 4 Secure Services, LLC
POB 7898
Moreno Valley, CA 92552

This company sells greeting cards, a pen pal service, a flower ordering service, a book ordering service, and will send videos and pics to your tablet. Send SASE for brochure.

Email: level4ss@yahoo.com

Levin, Michael R, ESQ.
1001 SW 5th Ave. Suite 1414
Portland, OR 97204

Mr. Levin is the author of "138 Mitigating Factors" and offers a newsletter. Write/Send SASE for more information.

Website: services-commerce.com.

Lewisburg Prison Project
PO Box 128
Lewisburg, PA 17837

Publishes a number of low-cost materials for prisoners, including "legal Bulletins," "Prisoner's Guide to Federal Parole," and "Due Process Standards for Administrative Detention." Provides direct legal service to all federal prisoners in Central Pennsylvania, including those at USP Allenwood and USP Lewisburg. Send SASE for publication and price list.

Phone Number: (570) 523-1104
Email Address: prisonproject@dejazzd.com.

Liberation Prison Project
P.O. Box 31527
San Francisco, CA 94131

The prison project offers **FREE** Buddhist books, prayers and practice booklets, practice items, Mandala subscriptions and video and audio tapes of teachings to individuals and Buddhist study groups in over a hundred prisons in the United States.

Website: www.liberationprisonproject.org

Library of Congress
101 Independence Ave., SE
Washington, DC 20540

Write and request copyright forms needed for books, screenplays, music, etc.

L.I.F.E. Association
Thomas Rovinski CAM
Attn: Michael Moore #AY 5139; SCI-Dallas
1000 Follies Road
Dallas, PA 18612

Lifeline
63 Forest Rd
Garston, Watford WD25 7QP, UK

International pen pal for death row prisoners only. Waiting list is 3-4 months. Postage for international is 90 cents.

Lifers to be Free
C/O NedraStribling
3982 s. Figueroa St. #210
Los Angeles, CA 90037

Families and friends of long-term lifers and liberated lifers. Current campaign to influence the Governor to not override the Board's decision to parole.

Lifers United
Dale Gardner BI
5107 Route 26, Box A
Bellefonte, PA 16823-0820

Pennsylvania has over 4,300 lifers and they want to see more of their lives profiled on this site. Friends and family of lifers need to have these stories told of what got their loved ones in prison, what have they done since their arrest to better themselves and their environment, and how would society benefit upon their release. For those who don't know, life in Pennsylvania means for the rest of their life. So push Pennsylvania's lifers to share their stories. You'd be surprised to hear what they have to say.

Ideally the profiles should not exceed 3 pages. One does not have to go into specific details of their crimes, admit guilt or identify victims. Also include a small photo. Once these are scanned they will be returned along with a printout of how it looks. This is all **FREE**. You will NEVER be charged.

Website: lifers.talkspot.com

The Lionheart Foundation
PO Box 170115
Boston, MA 02117

They send a **FREE** resource guide with books and organizations for prisoners.

Comment: I like it and have used the resources that they sent on several occasions. Send for it, you won't regret it. - - GURU

Litigation Support
PO Box 100
Myrtle Beach, SC 29578

They offer case review, motions, and more. Send F/C stamps for details.

Live From Da Trap Magazine
PO Box 7332
Newark, NJ 07107

"Live From Da Trap is the hottest urban, underground magazine to hit the streets! To purchase, send a $5.00 money order, or for more info, send SASE!"

Comment: Tory Chew sent me one of her magazines. It's 8.5 x 11, 35 pages. The pages are thicker than most mag pages and they are glossy. Tory has a radio show and she's trying to put on underground hip hop artists. $5.00 is a fair price for the magazine if you're interested in the subject. - - Mike

Local123.net

Discount phone calls.

Locus
PO Box 13305
Oakland, CA

This is a newspaper that covers the sci-fi writing field. It's $60 for a 1-year subscription; 12 issues per year.

Phone Number: (510) 339-9198

Website: locusmag.com.

Looking for a WAY OUT

This book is by Michael Norwood aka Minkah Abubakar. It's $15.00 plus $3.95 for shipping and can be ordered from Don Diva Magazine.

"An African-American legal consultant explains in easy-to-read terms how simple it is to get yourself out of prison."

LostVault.com
PO Box 242
Mascot, TN 37806

This is a pen pal website that you can have your family post your profile on for **FREE** (one ad per inmate!). If you do not have someone on the outside to do it for you, LostVault will do it for $10, or **FREE** if you are on death row. Fees are to be made payable to LostVault and need to be on a prison-issued check or money order only. Please note that we will not return your photos or send an ad copy if you do not send us a SASE! Photos without a SASE will be held for 30 days and then destroyed.

AD RULES ...

You may not update your ad for free during the 1 year on our website except for address changes, or unless we make an error on your ad. The only exception is for death row inmates, who may update their ad after each 1-year anniversary. If any inmate wants to update the
text or photo in his or her ad prior to the 1-year date, the ad will be considered new and the $10 fee will be imposed for a rewritten ad, death row included. If you do not have a photo when your ad is posted and you wish to add one later, no fee will be assessed and the
ad will run for the remainder of the 1-year cycle. Bottom line: we don't have time to redo your ad over and over. If you update your ad for any reason, even an error on our part, and wish to have a copy on your new ad, you must include a SASE.
- Your ad must be under 150 words and not contain sexually explicit or foul language.
- You may send us one photo for your ad. Note that ads with photos are viewed at least 10 times more than those without.
- If you know an inmate who wishes to send us a mail ad, they must send a SASE or stamp for application.

- Please allow 45 days before you inquire about the status of your ad or photo. Mail takes time to get back and forth and to process; ads are placed in the order they are received.

Comment: I'm not sure if you can add more words/photos if you have someone on the outside post your profile, but I plan to check soon. Also, I've seen inmates get hits off this site. - - Mike

Louisiana Books 2 Prisoners
3157 Gentilly Blvd., #141
New Orleans, LA 70122

These folks send book to prisoners for **FREE**. They serve LA, AL, AR and MS only. Please request books by genre, not title.

Loveaprisoner.com
PO Box 192
Dequincy, LA 70633

"Inmates! Get on board today! Join Loveaprisoner.com! A year is only $25 for 1 photo and a 250 word bio. Send SASE with $2 of 5 stamps for brochure."

Loved Ones Needs
PO 729
Gonzales, LA 70707

Loved Ones Needs, LLC is a prisoner sponsored company which offers the biggest and most diverse selection of magazines, books and gifts in the business to all inmates in state and federal correctional institutions. Our selection will interest the most creative mind.

We accept stamps for brochures at a rate of 5 stamps (strips only) of $1.95 each. Send a payment of $6.95 to receive all the latest brochures. Categories consist of single-issue magazines, magazine subscriptions, urban books, and gifts. New brochures are available quarterly.

Email: lovedonesneeds@gmail.com

Lowrider Magazine
PO Box 420235
Palm Coast, FL 32142

National and international coverage of Lowrider car shows. It's $35 for a 1-year subscription; 12 issues per year. (Note: look around because you can often find Lowrider for less than $35.)

Website: lowridermagazine.com.

Lycoming County Pre-Release Center
546 County Farm RD.
Montoursville, PA 17754-9208

The MacArthur Justice Center's Northwestern University School of Law
375 E. Chicago Ave
Chicago, IL 60611

Impact litigation on criminal justice issues, focused specifically on Illinois. Individual prisoner cases are rarely accepted.

Phone Number: 312-503-1271
Website: law.northwestem.edu/macarthur

The Magazine Wizard
PO Box 1846
Bloomington, IN 47402

They sell magazines at a discount.

Phone Number: (800) 936-0053
Website: magwiz.com.

Maine Books to Prisoners
c/o Norris
PO Box 12
Fairmington, ME 04938

Maine State Prison
Gary Upham, Principal
807 Cushing Road
Warren, ME 04864

Phone: 273-5300
Email: Gary.upham@maine.gov

Making Career Connections
278 Clinton Ave
Albany, NY 12210

They help individuals with criminal histories find employment.

Malcom X Grassroots Movement California Office
PO Box 3585
Oakland, CA 94609

The Malcolm X Grassroots Movement is an organization of Afrikans in America/New Afrikans whose mission is to defend the human rights of our people and promote self-determination in our community.

Phone Number: (877) 248-6095.

Maloof, Michael W.
215 N. McDonough St.
Decatur, GA 30030

Laywer.

Phone Number: (404) 373-8000

Manning Document Processing
PO Box 641
Norwalk, CT 06856

They type, design and prepare manuscripts for self-publishing. Reasonable, accurate and fast.

Manuscripts To Go
16420 Cooley Ranch Rd.
Geyderville, CA 95441

This company will help you with your manuscript(s). Write/Send SASE for more information.

Maoist International Ministry of Prisons
PO Box 40799
San Francisco, CA 94140

FREE subscriptions to "Under Lock and Key," the voice of the anti-imperialist prison movement. Offers study courses and **FREE** books on topics including; current events, revolutionary nationalism (BPP, YLP, Etc.) and Marxist classics.

Website: prisoncensorship.info.

Marijuana Law

Examines how to reduce the possibility of arrest and prosecution for people accused of the use, sale or possession of marijuana. Includes info on legal defenses, search and seizures, surveillance, asset forfeiture and drug testing. This book is 271 pages, $17.95, and can be bought from Prison Legal News.

Marilee Marshall & Associates, Attorneys at Law
523 West Sixth St., Suite 1109
Los Angeles, CA 90014

Certified criminal law and appellate law specialists for California inmates. 29 years of success.

Phone Number: 213-489-7715
Website: marileemarshallandassociates.com

The Marshall Project
156 West 56th St., Suite 701
New York, NY 10010

The background of The Marshall Project is that former New York Times Editor Bill Keller left the Times to start a new nonprofit news organization reporting solely on criminal justice, because he and many of the reporters now at The Marshall Project believed it was a pressing national issue that deserved an exclusive focus.

They launched in 2014, and the majority of their readers tend to be experts, advocates, practitioners, etc., with a direct interest in criminal justice. However, they do get a lot of readers from the general public, primarily because they co-publish many of their articles with publications like The Washington Post, The New York Times, Atlantic, Slate, Vice, etc.

ATTENTION ALL WRITERS!

Want your thoughts to be read in newspapers like The New York Times and The Washington Post? It can happen if you submit your writing to The Marshall Project. This is a call for submissions for The Marshall Project.

"The Marshall Project is a news organization that reports on the criminal justice system, including what happens inside jail and prisons. We have over 10,000 daily readers.

Part of what we do is publish first-person writing and reporting from inside jail and prisons, written by prisoners themselves. We want to give readers a sense of what life is like inside jails and prisons, and we believe that those who are actually inside are the best people to tell us.

If you are interested in writing for us – and reaching an audience of thousands of readers on the outside who want to know what life is like on the inside -- here is some information about the type of writing we are looking for.

What we are looking for: Nonfiction writing about a specific aspect of life inside. Try to focus on one specific topic and tell a story about that topic. For example, tell us a story about a friendship you've made while inside; or a story about food or going to mess hall or commissary; or about how you get exercise; or about getting an education or having a job; or how you maintain relationships with family on the outside; or a story of your relationship with staff members; or the experience of solitary confinement or other forms of punishment.

The topic could be almost anything. The most important thing is to choose a very specific part of your experience and to write us a story about it.

What we are NOT looking for: Poetry, fiction, stories about your whole life (rather than a specific topic), essays about anything outside of your direct experience."

Length: 500-2,000 words

Please include your full name, how to contact you, and the url facebook.com/thecellblock.net

Martysmillions
PO Box 513
Manville, NJ 08835

"We offer inmates exclusive nude/non-nude photos for their tablets. We also offer colored 4 x 6 nude/non-nude and hard-core photos. If interested, please send 4 Forever stamps for brochure, which will explain everything. When ordering, please know your institutional policies. We are not responsible for any rejections of photos. All catalogs are $1.50 each. All responses require an SASE.

Matthew House
PO Box 201
Monroe, WA 98272

This is a hospitality house that provides temporary housing for families visiting prisoners in Monroe, bus service to other Washington prisons, programs for children of prisoners, prison ministry, and more.

Phone Number: (360) 794-8720.

Medical Malpractice Experts
106 Mayfield Ave.
South Shore, Kentucky 41175

Negligence? Pain and suffering? Wrong diagnosis? Need treatment? Send SASE.

Email: baddocs2015@gmail.com

Mcdill Justice Project Northwestern University
1845 Sheridan Road
Evanston, IL 60208

The Medill Justice Project investigates potentially wrongful murder convictions. The case must meet all the following criteria to be considered:
- The crime took place within 250 miles of Evanston IL
- Charges include murder
- Case heard by the appellate court and sentence confirmed
- Prisoner must claim actual innocence

Phone Number: 847-491-5840
website: medilljusticeproject.org

Meet-An-Inmate.Com
c/o Arlen Bischke
PO 845
Winchester, Oregon 97495

Thank you very much for showing interest in placing a pen pal photo ad with Meet-An-Inmate.com. You decide what goes on the page, as long as all the information is true. We highly prefer a money order, but will accept stamps as an additional charge as listed. Ad includes one photo and up to a 250-word bio. Additional photos are $3.00 (8 stamps) each, and you can add as many as you like. For added exposure, you can upgrade your ad to FEATURED*. Send money order payable to Arlen Bischke at the address above.

Standard ad: $35 or 90 stamps for 12 months. $50 or 120 stamps for 24 months. Featured ad: $70 or 160 stamps for 12 months. $90 or 200 stamps for 24 months.

* With FEATURED ads there will be ab added link to your webpage via a thumbnail photo placed on the male Home page. your thumbnail will also show up above all standard ads. This provides extra traffic to your page to increase your chances of obtaining pen pals.

You must notify us of any address changes. Corrections and address changes are FREE. If you want to change or rewrite your ad there will be a $10.00 (22 stamps) additional charge. This must be done by the inmate or the person who placed the ad, not a third party. Please try to keep the ad under 250 words. A photo is highly recommended as the response of ads without photos is very poor. The original photo will be returned along with confirmation of your ad. We will send you a printout of your ad as it appears on the internet. We are a top ranked site and have been in business since 1998 and are at the top of the internet search engines for most related keywords. However, we cannot guarantee how many responses (if any) you will receive. We recommend you concentrate on "seeking friendship" instead of a serious romantic relationship.

We promote this site as a pen pal site, not a dating site. Please word your ad accordingly.

A friend or relative can submit your ad and photo for you and pay the fee online at: meet-an-inmate.com/application.htm.

We make very few changes to the wording of an ad other than correcting spelling errors; however, we reserve the right to edit, delete, reject, or change wording of any ad. Profanity or adult content is strictly prohibited. If we discover that you sent in a photo that was not of you or you gave false information on your application, we may remove your ad or correct the information. If a photo looks suspicious, we may not accept it. It's not required, but we prefer photos that were taken while in prison. Do not ask your pen pals for money.

If you experience more mail than you can handle, please advise us and we can delete your ad, or put it on hold until further notice. Putting a hold on your ad will not change the expiration date of the ad. Your name and mailing address will appear directly on the ad. There is no charge to your pen pals to write to you. We do not forward emails.

Once we go to the expense of scanning your photo and building the web page, there will be no refunds.

In New York, South Dakota, and Virginia, inmates are prohibited from using stamps as a form of payment.

Comment: I'm not sure about currently, but at least at one time, this was ranked the top pen pal website for prisoners. - - Mike

Meshell Baldwin Publications
14801 CR 438
Lindale, TX 75771

"Meshell Baldwin Publications is home to the most unique fetish pictures in the country. We cater to the man who craves more than your standard girly picture. We have older ladies, fat ladies, midgets, trannies, gay twinks, action shots, pregnant ladies, foot fetish and much more. Pictures are printed at a professional photo lab and are only 500 each plus shipping. Catalogs are black and white and are 3 Forever stamps or $1.00 each. Catalogs come in volumes of over 100 pictures. You will also get 5 **FREE** pictures when you order 10 or more pictures on your first order!

25¢ grab bag special! You tell us the type of flix and we'll pick them for you. No more than 25 flix per order. Cannot be combined with 50¢ regular f lix. Example: say you want older women, or blondes with big asses, that is what you will get. If you tell us you want gays with colored hair, we will get that for you. Keep in mind, if you order these a lot, you may get some duplications as we don't keep track of your orders. Grab bags are only from the following catalogs Fattie Action, Tranny Action, Old Lady Action, Barely Legal Action, Goth Action, Latinas Action, Asians Action, Arabs Action, or Pregnant Action.

The following catalogs are $1 each. Most have masturbation, naked butts, and lesbian/gay kissing. If this will be a problem at your institution, let us know so we can delete them before we print your catalog...

Asians vol. 1, 2
Hot Chicks 1-9, lots of camel toes and asses
Barely Legal vol. 1
Fatties vol. 1, 2
Black Babes vol. 1
Facials vol. 1, 2, 3
Older Ladies vol. 1, 2, 3, 4
Pregnant vol.1
Cigarette Smoking Gals vol. 1
Goth Gals vol. 1
Latinas vol. 1, 2
Arabians vol. 1
Foot Fetish Girls vol. 1
Cat Fight Girls vol. 1

Girl on Girl vol. 1

Single page catalogs, 250 or 1 stamp: Men Foot Fetish, Black Men, Midget Girls, Golden Showers, Hairy Muffin, Dildo Freaks, Bottle Page, Nina Hartley, Spanking, New Facials, Twink Selfies, Women Body Builders, Latino Boys, NEW Shemales.

Action Shots (Risky), 250 or 1 stamp: White 1-20, Interracial 1-12, Black 1-3, Boy On Boy 1-12, Fem Don, Bisexual, Blow Jobs 1-2, Bikini Riot Blurred, Butt Sluts Blurred.

We take institutional checks, personal checks, money orders and cash. Please make all checks out to Meshell Baldwin. S/h is as follows: 5-30 flix, $4; 31-50, $5; 51-70, $6; 71-100, $7 101-130, $8; 131-150 $9; 151-170, $10; 171-200, $11, 201-230, $12; 231-250, $13; 251-300, $14."

Message of The Cross Ministries
PO Box 9992
Colorado Springs, CO 80932

They will send you **FREE** biblical information (Christian). Write and tell them what you're interested in learning about.

Metropolitan Prison Consulting Service
554 North Fredrick Ave., Suite 225
Gaithersburg, MD 20877

Phone Number: (301) 556-7741.

Mettanokit Outreach
173 Merriam Hill Road Attn: Medicine Story
Greenville, NH 03048

Native American circles in 9 prisons in New England. Booklet describing the program and post-prison group called Ending Violent Crime.

Phone Number: (603) 878-2310

Mennonite Central Committee, US Office of Justice and Peace
PO Box 500
Akron, PA 17501

FREE publications for prisoners and their families.

Phone Number: (717) 859-1151.

Mexican American Legal Defense and Educational Fund (MALDEF) National Office
634 S. Spring St., 11th floor
Los Angeles, CA 90014

Has a regional office in GA, IL, TX, CA, and DC. Largest Latino civil rights organization. MALDEF litigates large class action cases; cannot take individual cases, nor criminal cases. Write for more info. Provides referrals. Best to use online contact form.

Phone Number: (213) 629-2512.

Miami Law Innocence Clinic
3000 Biscayne Blvd., Suite 100
Miami, FL 33137

The Innocence Clinic is dedicated to identifying and correcting wrongful convictions.

Phone: 305-284-8115

Michigan Innocence Clinic
1029 Legal Research Building
625 State Street
Ann Arbor, MI 48109

Phone: 734-763-9353

Mid-Atlantic Innocence Project
(District of Columbia, Maryland and **Virginia** Cases)
American University - Washington College of Law
2000 H Street, NW
Washington, D.C. 20052

Phone Number: 202-995-4586
Website: exonerate.org

Middle Ground Prison Reform
139 East Encanto Drive
Tempe, AZ 85281

Working for Arizona's prisoners and their families since 1983. Main areas of activity are: 1) public education about the need for criminal justice reform 2) legislative advocacy on behalf of prisoners and their visitors 3) litigation to protect and define the rights and responsibilities of prisoners and their supporters 4) referral to community resources for ex-offenders. Spanish-speaking volunteers available.

Phone Number: (480) 966-8116.

Midnight Express Books
PO Box 69
Berryville, AR 72616

"We've helped inmate author's self-publish books for over 10 years. We are the preferred service company helping inmate authors self-publish their work and the only company that publishes inmate's books full time. Helping inmate authors is all we do!

FREE standard ebook format included with every paid paperback book project!

2014 catalog of our authors' books available. To get your copy, send FIVE unused first class postage Forever stamps with your mailing address. Please print clearly.

Do you Corrlinks? We do! Sign up for our **FREE** monthly writing tips email programs. Only available via email; sorry.

Services/Prices...

Typing Services, starting at $3.50 per page: MEB is really excited to announce that we have put together a database of typists for our authors' use. Typing projects will be quoted individually and will be based on the quality of the handwriting and the documents themselves. That is to say that if the paper the project is written on is crumpled, torn or the handwriting is light, those projects will incur a higher rate. If you want you project quoted, please send in a complete copy along with any formatting requirements. We now also accept legal document typing and typing for documents other than manuscripts to be published.

Spanish Conversion, starting at $300.00: A new service we offer to authors we've already published. We'll take your book and cover and convert them to Spanish, assign them a new ISBN for a new paperback book and ebook. There are no proofs or drafts with this service.

Digital Covers, starting at $250.00: MEB will now provide access to our group of artists to prepare covers on book projects when we are not doing the entire book project. Prices will be more for just cover projects and will be quoted individually based on design concept submitted.

ISBN and Bar Codes; $200.00 with project, $250.00 without project: Authors who only need us to provide an independent ISBN registered to them or their company, with or without an entire project assignment.

Ebooks, starting at $200.00: For authors who have previously had a print bock prepared by a company other than MEB and who can provide the digital text file for the insides and pdf or indesign file for the cover, we will prepare an ebook for them and list it on Amazon for Kindle and Smashwords for distribution to other ebook retailers. Each project will be quoted independently."

Phone Number: 870-210-3772

Email: MEBooksl@yahoo.com

Midwest Books to Prisoners
1321 North Milwaukee Ave, PMB 460
Chicago, IL 60622

FREE books to Midwest prisoners.

Midwest Innocence Project
605 West 47th Street
Kansas City, MO 64113

The MIP is dedicated to the investigation, litigation and exoneration of wrongfully convicted men and women in the following states: AR, KS, MO, IA and NE. Applicant must claim actual innocence in other words, that he/she did not participate in the crime; has more than ten years left to serve on his/her sentence and/or the applicant must register as a sex offender; is not currently represented by an attorney and has NOT received the death penalty. MIP does NOT accept cases of self-defense

Phone Number: 816-221-2166
Website: themip.org.

Midwest Pages to Prisoners Project
c/o Boxcar Books
118 S. Rogers, Suite 2
Bloomington, IN 47404

Great resource for queer studies, gender and sexuality. No California prisoner requests.

Phone Number: (812) 339-8710

Midwest Trans Prisoner Penpal Project
c/o Boneshaker Books
2022 23rd Avenue South
Minneapolis, MN 55404

Mike Barber Ministries
PO Box 1086
De Soto, TX 75123

Write for information on prisoner services.

Military Records; National Personal Records Center
One, Archives Dr.
St. Louis, MO 63132

If you're interested in obtaining your military records, send a request and include your last duty station and military I.D. number.

Miller Paralegal
PO Box 687
Walnut, CA 91788

Legal research, copies, decisions, statues, and regulations, etc. Write/Send SASE for more information.

MIM Distributors
PO Box 40799
San Francisco, CA 94140

They publish "Under Lock and Key," an anti-imperialist newsletter. Write for details.

Website: prisoncensorship.info.

Minkah's Official Cite Book

This book is by Michael Norwood aka Minkah Abubakar. It's $15.00 plus $3.95 for shipping and can be ordered from Don Diva Magazine.

"Written by America's top jailhouse lawyer for prisoners, lawyers, and paralegals looking for a fast, inexpensive means of locating case citations that favor criminal defendants."

Minutes Before Six
2784 Homestead Road #301
Santa Clara, CA 95051

Your voice deserves to be included in the conversation!

Minutes Before Six is a respected online community of imprisoned writers, poets and artists whose mission is to provide contributors a worldwide forum for self-expression. In exchange for your writing or visual art, we offer the unique opportunity to be heard and have your artwork viewed. MB6 reaches on average 35,000 people per month. As a volunteer-based non-profit organization, MB6 can neither sell your work nor afford you more than first rate exposure and the online publication of select submissions. We ask that you send us your best work.

Website: MinutesBeforeSix.com

Miracles Prisoner Ministry
501 E. Adams St
Wisconsin Dells, WI 53965

FREE spiritual recovery reading materials. Chaplains may request DVDs. Send for catalogue.

The Missing Link
PO Box 40031
Cleveland, OH 44140

Life-changing, Christian residential programs.

Mission Statement of the Free Speech Society

The Free Speech Society is a movement that is dedicated towards protecting and defending the First Amendment rights of imprisoned activists. As imprisoned activists, we are embedded reporters for the people. We are the eyes and ears for the people – for the taxpayers – articulating the human atrocities that plague the prison industrial slave complex with impunity in your name.

Human atrocities compelled by racial oppression can only flourish when silence permeates the corridors of the vortex of torture, the PISC, necessitating the manifested destiny of a collective insurgence of voices of resistance forged by the rediscovery of our humanity.

Though our endeavor is just, the agents of torture and repression -- the OCS (Office of Correctional Safety), SSU (Special Services Unity), IGI (Institutional Gang investigations) and ISU (Investigations Services Unit) -- have dedicated their resources towards silencing our voices and suffocating the true spirit of free speech.

This mission statement is only a brief invite designed to both captivate and solicit free speech loving people to join our movement and assist us in mobilizing against the forces of oppression. If you are interested, please contact Steve Martinot at martinot4gmail.com

Mississippi Innocence Project
University of Mississippi School of Law
P.O. Box 1848
University, MS 38677

Phone: 662-915-5206

MNN, Inc.
Shani Bruton, ESQ
244 5th Ave., Suite B-230
New York, NY 10001

This is a non-profit legal organization.

Montana Innocence Project
P.O. Box 7607
Missoula, MT 59807

Phone: 406-243-6698

Moody Bible Institute
Moody Distance Learning
820 N. LaSalle Boulevard
Chicago, IL 60610

Religious studies.

MoonLite Productions
PO Box 1304
Miami, FL 33265

"You've seen all those videos and TV shows that show you all the beautiful girls at South Beach, partying at the hottest clubs in Miami. Now you can see for yourself, let us show you, just how hot the girls in Miami really are. We have a huge selection of hot, sexy girls showing off their beautiful bodies for you. We try our best to have something to please every taste.

Some companies sell poor quality pictures, some you can even tell they are taken from pages of magazines or posters. We offer excellent professional quality. We have girls wearing the smallest G-string bikinis, sexy outfits, lingerie or spread nude. We also have pictures with penetration, and hot XXX action. We have whatever your institution allows! Make sure you know what you are allowed to receive. If any

pictures we send you within the rules are rejected by the institution, we will exchange them when you send us a SASE and we get the originals back. If you have a question and write without an order, you MUST include a SASE or DO NOT expect a reply.

Half sets are 5 pictures for $7.49 or 25 stamps. Full sets are 10 4X6 pictures for $14.98 or 45 stamps. Get 15 pictures (a full set and a half) for $22 or 65 stamps. Get 20 pictures (2 full sets) for $29 or 85 stamps. Penetration/action sets are 8 for $14.98. Individual pictures are $1.50 each. Payment in stamps includes shipping. NO loose stamps please. Join our VIP Club and get **FREE** shipping on ALL orders while you are a member.

Sorry but we don't offer **FREE** samples. You can request a **FREE** catalog of almost 100 models when you send a $25 order or higher (not including shipping). If ordering less than add $1 to get it. To order just the catalog send $1.50 or 5 stamps. We are always looking for hot new models to add, so there are more girls which do not appear in the catalog. We can make your first order a variety set of beautiful girls. Then you could tell us who you'd like to see more of, or if you want another variety set the next time. We have a high volume of sales. Some models are so popular that it's really hard to keep their pictures in stock. You can request your favorite models, but we reserve the right to substitute if we don't have pictures that would be allowed of the girls you ask for. We suggest you give us second and third choices just in case."

Shipping/Handling for pictures:

1-5 pictures --$1.00
6-10 pictures -- $2.00
11-15 pictures -- $3.00
16-20 pictures -- $4.00, etc.
Order $100 or more and get **FREE** shipping.

Comment: Stellar, honest service and responsive feedback. - - Paul K.

Mount Hope Prison Ministry
25 Summit Ave
PO Box 1511
Hagerstown, MD 21741

They offer bible correspondence courses to inmates **FREE**.

The Moratorium Campaign

586 Harding Blvd.
Baton Rouge, LA 70807

Contact us at info@moratoriumcampaign.org

Mount Hope Prison Ministry
25 Summit Ave.
POB 1511
Hagertowm, MD 21741

FREE bible correspondence course.

MS. Magazine
ATTN: MS. In Prison Program
1600 Wislon Blvd., Suite 801
Arlington, VA 22209

Ms. is a feminist publication covering current events, politics, and culture. Women in prison can obtain a **FREE** membership by writing to the address above.

Mt. Hope Prison Ministry
PO Box 1511
Hagerstown, MO 21741

FREE bible studies.

Muncy Inmate Coordinator
Mr. Campbell Staff Liaison
ATTN: Tanya Dacri (MIO President)
PO Box 180
Muncy, PA 17756

Music By Mail
PO Box 329066
Bush Terminal
Brooklyn, NY 11232

They sell CDs. Write for a **FREE** catalog.

Muslims for Humanity
12346 McDougall St., Suite 200
Detroit, MI 48212

A resource for emergency services.

Phone Number: (313) 279-5378
Website: helpinghandonline.org.

MSU College of Law
610 Abbot Rd.
East Lansing, Ml 28823

They publish the "Disciplinary Self-Help Litigation Manual" that helps guide prisoners through the misconduct and disciplinary litigation process.

NA World Services, INC
PO Box 9999
Van Nuys, CA 91409

Quarterly recovery-oriented newsletter, **FREE** to incarcerated addicts.

Website: na.org.

NAACP Legal Defense & Educational Fund Inc.
99 Hudson Street, Suite 1600
New York, NY 10013

Non-profit law firm which deals only with cases of obvious race discrimination, handles small number of death penalty & life w/o parole cases.

Phone Number: (212) 965-2200.

NAACP National Prison Project
4805 Mt. Hope Drive
Baltimore, MD 21215

Website: naacp.org/programs/prison.

Narcotics Anonymous
World Services Main Office
PO Box 9999
Van Nuys, California 91409

Phone Number: (818) 773-9999
Website: NA.org.

NASW Women's Council Prison Project
204 Ave B
Redondo Beach, CA 90277

They provide social services for women in prison and recently released, educate social workers about prison conditions and imprisoned women's needs, advocate for prison alternatives. Write for information on special services.

Phone Number: (310) 540-3715.

National Action Network

Crisis Department
106 W. 145th St.
Harlem, NY 10039

To seek their assistance in a crisis, send them a letter 3 pages or less, printed or typed. Include your name, address, and contact information.

Phone Number: (212) 690-3070.

National AIDS Treatment Advocacy Project (NATAP)
580 Broadway #1010,
New York, NY 10012

Will mail Hepatitis C and Hepatitis C Co-Infection Handbook.

National Alliance for the Mentally Ill
3803 N. Fairfax Dr. #100
Arlington, VA 22203

Seeks equitable services for people with severe mental illnesses. Promotes treatment alternatives to criminalization of people with severe brain disorders.

Phone Number: (703) 524-7600

National Buddhist Prison Sangha/ Zen Mountain Monastery
NBPS
P.O. Box 197
Mount Tremper, NY 12457

Phone Number: (845) 688 2228
Website: nbps@mro.org.

National Center for Lesbian Rights California Office
870 Market Street suite 370
San Francisco, CA 94102

Provides legal referrals for LGBTQQI.

Phone Number: (415) 392-6257.

National Alliance of Black Panthers
339 Elm Street NW
Washington, DC 20001

Phone Number: 202-413-0255 or 202-271-0031
Website:nabp.zoomshare.com.

National Center for Youth Law
405 14th Street, 15th Floor

Oakland, CA 94612

Provides information, referrals, technical assistance, or written materials; serves as co-counsel in cases affecting a large number of children and families. Assists lawyers who are directly representing at-risk or incarcerated youth. Publishes Youth Law News.

National Center on Institutions & Alternatives (NCIA)
7222 Ambassador Road
Baltimore, MD 21244

Provides criminal justice services to defense attorneys, defendants, inmates and court systems throughout the country. "We have worked with more than 10,000 clients in all 50 states. When assisting defense attorneys or defendants facing sentencing, we provide assistance in understanding the applicable sentencing statues or guidelines and design individualized sentencing reports or memoranda, which include specific sentencing proposals. When permitted by the applicable State or Federal law, our sentencing proposals frequently include the use of creative public service that draws on the offender's strengths and background, substance abuse counseling, work-release, home confinement and community confinement. In addition to sentencing advocacy, we also provide capital case mitigation services, parole release advocacy, institutional designation and transfer and release planning."

Phone Number: 410-265-1490
Email: aboring@ncianet.org
Website: www.ncianet.org
Contact: Alice Boring.

National Clearinghouse for the Defense of Battered Women
125 South 9th St., Suite 302
Philadelphia, PA 19107

"We accept collect calls from incarcerated battered women."

Phone Number (215) 351-0010.
Website: ncdbw.org

National Clemency Project
8624 Camp Columbus Rd.
Hixon, TN 37343

35 years of clemency, parole assistance, and transfers under the International Prisoner Treaty. Write/Send SASE for more information.

Phone Number: Phone: (423) 843-2235

National Clemency Project, Inc.
3324 W. University Ave, #237
Gainsville, FL 32607

Executive Clemency for state and federal prisoners or info on sentence reduction through Executive Clemency, write the address above.

Email:nationalclemencyprojectinc.@gmail.com
Website: nationalclemencyprojectinc.com

National Clemency Project
3324 W. University Ave #237
Gainsville, FL 32607

Contact them for info on sentence reduction through executive clemency. 36 years of experience.

The National Coalition to Abolish the Death Penalty
1620 L St, NW, Suite 250
Washington, DC 20036

Phone Number: (202) 331-4090
Website:info@ncadp.org.

National Commission on Correctional Heath Care
1145 W. Diversey Pkwy
Chicago, IL 60614

Phone Number: 773-880-1460

National Criminal Justice Reference Service
P.O. Box 6000
Rockville, MD 20849-6000

Phone Number: (800) 851-3420
Website: www.ncjrs.org

National Death Row Assistance Network
Summer June - Sept
NDRAN Claudia Whitman
6 Tolman Rd
Peaks Island, ME   04108

Phone Number: (207) 766-2418

Winter Oct - May
NDRAN Claudia Whitman
12200 Rd 41.9
Mancos, CO 81328

Phone Number (970) 533-7383

National Directory of Catalogs

They list over 12,000 catalogs.

Phone Number: (612) 788-4197
Website: nmoa.org/catalogmailorder

National Fatherhood Initiative
101 Lake Forest Blvd., suite 360
Gaithersburg, MD 20877

They offer parenting education. Write/Send SASE for more information.

Phone Number: (301) 948-099
Website: fatherhood.org.

National Federal Legal Services
2392 N. Decatur Rd.
Decatur, GA 30033

- Federal Appellate Representation for all Circuits and Supreme Court.
- Member of all Federal Circuits and Supreme Court
- Over 150 appeals filed.

- Federal 2255 Habeas Petitions anywhere in the United States.
- Representation.
- Pro Se Litigation; assistance or representation.
- Over 200 Habeas represented

Experienced attorneys make the difference, winning cases throughout tne United States for over 20 years.

Website: federalappealslawyer.com

National Gay and Lesbian Task Force
2684 Lacy Street
Suite 210
Los Angeles, CA 90031

Phone Number: 323.539.2406
Website: thetaskforce.org.

National Geographic Magazine

PO Box 64116
Tampa, FL 33664

Write for information.

Phone Number: (800) 647-5463.

National Health Prison Project
32 Greenwood Ave. #4
Quincy, MA 02170 -2620

Covers wide range of topics. Will answer personal questions. **FREE** subscription to prisoners.

The National Hepatitis C Prison Coalition
Phyllis Beck, Director
PO Box 41803
Eugene, OR 97404

Offers **FREE** newsletters.

Phone Number: (541) 607-5725

National Incarcerated Parents and Families
PO Box 6745
Harrisburg, Pennsylvania 17112-6745

Website: incarceratedparents.org.

National Innocence Network

This organization responds to claims of innocence and assists prisoners in locating appropriate help. If your case is accepted by a member of the Nation Innocence Network, they will offer support services.

Website: innocencenetwork.org

National Institute of Corrections
11900 E Cornell Ave, Unit C
Aurora, CO 80014

Provides the directory of programs servicing families of adult offenders; research and publications about other prison topics. May only be available online. Write/Send SASE for more information.

Phone Number: 800.877.1461
Website:nicic.gov

National Lawyers Guild (Philadelphia)
924 Cherry St.
Philadelphia, PA 19107

Phone Number: (215) 592-7710

National Lawyers Guild Prison Law Project
132 Nassau Street, Room 922
New York, NY 10038

The National Lawyers Guild (NLG) helps publish the Jailhouse Lawyers Handbook on bringing civil rights claims alleging violation of constitutional rights in prison or jail. NLG does not provide lawyers or legal assistance, but does provide **FREE** membership for jailhouse lawyers.

Phone Number: 212-679-5100
Website: www.nlg.org

National Legal Aid and Defenders Association
1625 K St, 8th Floor, NW Ste. 800
Washington, DC 20006

They provide referral to legal programs and services in your area.

National Minority AIDS Council
1931 13th Street NW
Washington, DC 20009-4432

Develops leadership in communities of color to address the challenges of HIV/AIDS. Has a **FREE** online resource library. Helps community and faith-based organizations, correctional facilities and health departments evaluate, improve and implement effective discharge planning for HIV positive prisoners and former prisoners.

Phone Number: (202) 483-6622

National Native American Prisoners Rights/Advocacy Coalition
c/o Len Foster Navajo Nation Corrections Project
PO Drawer 709
Window Rock, AZ 86515

National Network for Immigrant and Refugee Rights
310 8th Street suite 303
Oakland, CA 94607

Helps monitor and share information to build campaigns against immigration raids, police collaboration with immigration enforcement, abuses by immigration police or other law enforcement agents, and BICE and other DHS activity in workplaces, neighborhoods, and public spaces.

Phone Number: (510) 465-1984

National Prison Hospice Association
11 S. Angell St. #303
Providence, RI 02906

NPHA helps to develop and implement hospices and better end-of-life care for terminally ill prisoners and their families. Also publishes a newsletter.

Native American Pride Committee
3256 Knight Court
Bay City, MI 48706

Native American Prisoners' Rehabilitation Research Project
2848 Paddock Lane
Villa Hills, KY 41017

Navajo Nation Corrections Project
PO Drawer 709
Window Rock, AZ 86515

They visit and provide spiritual counseling for prisoners, including death row prisoners.

Nebraska Innocence Project
P.O. Box 24183
Omaha, NE 68124-0183

The Need to Abolish the Prison System

This is a book by Steve Martinot -- a human rights activist, organizer and writer and retired machinist, truck driver and professor, most recently at San Francisco State University. He has organized labor unions in New York and Akron and helped build community associations in Akron. He was a political prisoner in New York State charged with contempt of grand jury. He has published 8 books.

Email: martinot4@gmail.com

The Network/La RED Ending Abuse in Lesbian, Bisexual Women's and Transgender Communities
PO Box 6011
Boston, MA 02114

Services include confidential hotline, emergency shelter, advocacy, and **FREE** support groups for lesbians, bisexual women, and transgender folks fleeing domestic violence.

Hotline number: 617-423-SAFE

Phone Number: (617) 695-0877

The New Abolitionist
P.O. Box 151 F
Fennimore, WI 53809

Newsletter of Prisoners Action Coalition – good contact for prison issues in Wisconsin has experience dealing with super max issues.

New Beginning
1865 Big Tree Drive
Columbus, OH 43223

New Beginning: Guidelines for Offering to Ex-Offenders Radical Hospitality in Faith Communities furnishes evidence that supports the fact that the leadership of faith communities offering radical hospitality to ex-offenders can reduce recidivism. Hope can be restored, damaged and broken relationships can be mended, forgiveness from both sides can be made, and the returning citizen remain a law-abiding member of society. Order book by calling 614-266-3387.

New England Innocence Project
160 Boylston Street
Boston, MA 02116

Phone Number: (857) 277-7858

New York State Prisoner Justice Coalition
33 Central Avenue
Albany, NY 12210

Phone Number: 518-434-4037
Website: http://www.nysprisonerjustice.org/

Nicole M. Verville
Attorney at Law
PO Box 2817
Chula Vista, CA 91912

Case Review, Writs of Habeas Corpus, Prop. 47, Transfer Request, Discrimination, Lifer Hearings. California cases only! Send SASE.

Nickels And Dimez
14173 Northwest Hwy, Suite 154
Houston, TX 77040

These guys sell non-nude photos. I've not seen the quality of the prints, but the actual images they offer are good.

Phone: 832-756-3377
Email: nicklesanddimezl@gmail.com

NJ Office of the Corrections Ombudsman
PO Box 855
Trenton, NJ 08625

Phone Number: 609-633-2596

No Equal Justice: Race and Class in the American Justice System

This book is a devastating critique that shows how the criminal justice system perpetuates race and class inequalities, creating a two-tiered system of Justice. This book is 232 pages, $19.95, and can be bought from Prison Legal News.

Nolo's Plain-English Law Dictionary

Find terms you can use to understand and access the law. Contains 3,800 easy-to-find definitions for common (and not so common) legal terms. This book is 496 pages, $29.99 and can be bought from Prison Legal News.

Nolo Press
950 Parker St.
Berkeley, CA 94710

Publishes self-help material such as "Legal Research," "The Criminal Law Handbook" and "Represent Yourself in Court." Write for a catalog.

North Carolina Center on Actual Innocence
PO Box 52446
Shannon Plaza Station
Durham, NC 27717

Phone: 919-489-3268

Northern Arizona Justice Project
Department of Criminal Justice
Northern Arizona University
P.O. Box 15005
Flagstaff, AZ 86011-5005

Working to help with the wrongfully convicted.

Phone Number: 928-523-7028
Website: http://jan.ucc.nau.edu/d-najp

Northern California Innocence Project

Santa Clara Law; Santa Clara University
500 El Camino Real
Santa Clara, California 95053

The mission of the Northern California Innocence Project (NCIP) is to promote a fair, effective and compassionate criminal justice system and protect the rights of the innocent.

Phone: (408) 554-4361
Website: lawadmissions@scu.edu

The November Coalition
282 West Astor
Colville, WA 99114

An organization of drug war prisoners and their loved ones. Their goal is to enlighten the public about unjust sentencing laws and the destructive increase in the US prison population. They publish "The Razor Wire", $6/yr. for prisoners.

Phone Number: (509) 684-1550

Nubian Princess Ent.
PO Box 37
Timmonsville, SC 29161

This company is ran by porn star Chanail. For $25 inmates can get exotic letters from her. For $27 you can get your pic and contact info on her facebook. Send SASE for details.

facebook.com/chanail.paree
Website: writesomeoneinprison.com.

NW Immigrant Rights Project
Eastern Washington Office
212 Sunnyside Ave.
PO Box 270
Granger, WA 98932

They promote justice for low-income immigrants by pursuing and defending their legal status. They also focus on direct legal services, supported by education and public policy work.

Website: nwirp.org.

Nuthing Butt Pictures

"We are strictly pictures. Catalog: send SASE and 5 stamps for 2 sample sheets with order form. Special: $6.50 for 10 naughty pics. Bonus: $55.00 for 100 naughty pics."

Email: nothingbuttpictures@gmail.com

NW Immigrant Rights Project
Western Washington Office
615 2nd Ave., Suite 400
Seattle, WA 98104

Phone Number: (206) 587-4009.

NY Campaign for Telephone Justice
666 Broadway 7th floor
New York, NY 10012

Main Office Line: 212-614-6464.

NYC Books Through Bars
C/O Bluestockings Bookstore,
172 Allen St.
New York, NY 10002

FREE nationwide, except MI. Specializes in political and history. Also literary fiction and other educational books. No religious books.

NYC Jericho Movement
PO Box 670927
Bronx, NY 10467

Phone Number: 718-325- 4407
Website: jerichony.org

Oakland City University Prison Ministries Project
Oakland City University
138 North Lucretia Street
Oakland City, Indiana 47660

Phone Number: (800) 737-5125
Website: http://www.oak.edu

Oatmeal Studios
PO Box 138
Town Rd. 35
Rochester, VT 05767

This company buys art form prisoners. Send a SASE and ask for Writer's Guidelines. They will send you instructions and samples of what they want to buy.

Occasion Gallerie

Blue Mountain Arts
P.O. Box 1007
Boulder, CO 80306

Notecard poetry is welcome. Send with SASE.

Oceana Press
75 Main St.
Dobbs Ferry, NY 10522

They sell legal manuals. Write/Send SASE for more information.

OCSlocal.com

This is a discount phone service.

Phone Number: (888) 813-0000.

The Office
PO Box 30003
Tucson, AZ 85751

This is a typing service. Write/Send SASE for more information.

Office of Correctional Education
US Dept. of Education
400 Maryland Ave. SW
Washington, DC 20202

Write for information about education grants and federal and state prisoners.

Office of the Public Defender
Carvel State Office Building
820 N. French St.
3rd Floor
Wilmington, Delaware 19801

Phone Number: (302) 577-5200

Off Our Backs Magazine
2337B 18th St NW
Washington, DC 20009

A radical feminist news journal **FREE** to women in prison.

Ohio University College Program for the Incarcerated
Haning Hall 222
Ohio University
Athens, OH 45701

They offer correspondence courses. Write for more information and cost.

Ohio University Correctional Education
102 Haning Hall
1 Ohio University
Athens, OH 45701

Provides college-level courses and certificate and degree programs acceptable in most prisons. **FREE** info packet on admission, course offerings and cost. Ask if their program is authorized in your state.

Oklahoma Innocence Project
2501 N. Blackwelder
Oklahoma City, OK 73106

Phone Number: 405-208-6161
Website: innocence@okcu.edu

One Stop Services
1271 Washington Ave., #313
San Leandro, CA 94577

One Stop Services is owned and staffed by dedicated staff members that have your best interest at heart by providing superior services at the lowest possible prices. There are similar services out there, but none can match our prices and selection.

One Stop Service Center was founded for the purpose of helping inmates with "the little things" in life when family and friends are unable to complete simple tasks. One Stop Service Center helps inmates overcome the barriers of incarceration to reach out to their family and friends and connect with them. Our mission is to provide services for inmates with particular focus on providing "hands on" services that inmates are unable to provide for themselves. From shopping for Mother's Day, Valentine's Day, etc., to locating family members, legal services, and a lot more. One Stop Service Center bridges the gap from prisons to the community. We understand the needs of inmates nationwide looking for just a little help when family members are overwhelmed with their own lives.

We provide a variety of services, publications, and forms for incarcerated people throughout the United States. A partial list of what One Stop Services offers includes: legal research and forms, editing and typing of legal and other documents, color and black and white photocopies, internet info searches, family and friend locator services, Amazon book purchases, photo reproduction and enlargement, discount magazine orders, small business info, pen pals, sexy photos, and much, much more.

If you need additional info on any services not listed, please send a SASE.

Operation Outward Reach, Inc.
227 South Sixth Street
Youngwood, PA 15697

They offer skill development and vocational training for resident offenders of five state penal institutions: Greensburg, Huntingdon, Mercer, Cresson, and Somerset. They take trainees into the community to teach carpentry and masonry by providing low-cost construction to senior citizens, other economically disadvantaged and non-profit agencies. Juvenile Day Treatment is provided in the Westmoreland County area for out-of-school young men ages 15 through 21. Purpose of this training is to provide on-the-job construction learning, G.E.D., drug & alcohol education, life skills, job skills, and adolescent fatherhood components.

Phone Number: (724) 925-2419
Website: operationoutwardreach.org

The Order of the Earth
21431 Marlin Circle
Shade Gap, PA 17255

This newspaper costs $25 for a 1-year subscription, 10-12 issues per year.

Phone Number: (814) 259-3680
Website: theorderoftheearth.com.

Oregon CURE (Citizens United for the Rehabilitation of Errands)
1631 NE Broadway #460
Portland, OR 97232

Website: oregoncure.org.

Oregonians for Alternatives to the Death Penalty
OADP
PO Box 361
Portland, OR 97207

Website: oadp.org

The Osborne Association
Attn: Keenan Pace
809 Westchester Ave.
Bronx, NY 10455

They sell publications. Write for a list and prices.

Our Bodies, Ourselves

This book about women's health and sexuality, produced by a nonprofit organization, has been called "America's best-selling book on all aspects of women's health" by the New York Times and is an essential resource for women of all ages. This book is 944 pages, $26.00, and it can be bought from Prison Legal News.

Our Daily Bread
RBC Ministries
PO Box 2222
Grand Rapids, MI 49501

They offer **FREE** monthly devotionals.

Outlaw Bikers
820 Hamilton St., #C-6
Charlotte, NC 28206

This is a biker magazine. It's $16 for l-year subscription; 4 issues per year.

OutlawsOnline.com

Post your profile immediately, just like any other dating website, and edit it any time day or night. Friends and family can register, pay for your ad with PayPal, and upload your photo, address description and bio.

Website: outlawsonline.com.

Outlook on Justice
Publication of Criminal Justice Program of the AFSC
2161 Massachusetts Ave
Cambridge, MA 02140

A newsletter of the American Friends Services Committee (Quakers). $2/year for prisoners.

Phone Number: (617) 661-6130 x120

Out of Control Lesbian Committee to Support Women Political Prisoners
3543 - 18th Street, Box 30
San Francisco, CA 94110

Website: prisonactivist.org/ooc/

Oxford University Press Inc.

198 Madison Ave.
New York, NY 10016

They publish "Prisoner's Self-Help Litigation Manual" ($35), "Brief Writing and Oral Arguments" ($40), "Introduction to the Legal system of the United States" ($25), & more.

Pace Post Conviction Project
Barbara Salken Criminal Justice Clinic
78 North Broadway
White Plains, NY 10603

Phone Number: 914-422-4230

PA Lifers Association
Attn: Gary Jones AY 7024 SCI- Huntingdon
1100 Pike Street
Huntingdon, PA 16654

PA Lifers Association
Staff Liaison Charles Bradley CAS
Attn: Tyrone Wets AF 6337 SCI Graterford
PO Box 244
Graterford, PA 19426

PA Lifers Association
Staff Liaison Attn: Gary Mobley #AM 4256 SCI Rockview
PO Box A
Bellefonte, PA 16823

PA Prison Directory Action
c/o Book 'Em
PO Box 71357
Pittsburgh, PA 15213

7 lists of PA and national resources: LGBTQI; Women and Parents; Legal, Pro Bono and Advocacy on the Inside; Prison Justice and Advocacy Groups, PA Prison, Jails and Court Info; Education on the Inside; Tips for Survivors of Abuse. Send SASE if possible.

Package Trust
370 W. Pleasantview Avenue, Suite 0303
Hackensack, NJ 07601

Package Trust is powered by Don Diva.

"Send $7.00 for our full-color catalog of services and over 500 available sexy, non-nude photos. We sell our photos for $1.00 each.

Photo Duplication: 4x6 prints are $1 each, 4x7 prints are $5 each, 8x10 prints are $10 each.

People Search! Are you looking for a person or information on a business? We can do the research for you for $5.00.

Background Search: Need a background check on someone? We will search criminal records in 43 states for $40.00.

Internet Research: For $20.00 an hour, we will provide you with thorough research from credible and relevant sources. We will research any subject you request and send you printouts of all information found.

If you would like a return response from Package Trust, you MUST send a SASE."

Phone Number: 347-815-3229
E-mail: packagetrust@dondivamag.com

Pagan Educational Network
P.O. Box 24072
Indianapolis, IN 46224

Member's eligible for *Water* after receipt of $4 (stamps okay).

Palmetto Innocence Project
P.O. Box 11623
Columbia, SC 29211

Pan American Literature Mission
5215 E. Fort Lowell Rd.
Tucson, AZ 85712

FREE Bible correspondence courses.

Pantee Publishing
POB 233
Hawthorne, NJ 07507

They sell non-nude photos. Send SASE for info.

Partnership for Safety and Justice
825 NE 20th Avenue, #250
Portland, OR 97232

Phone Number: (503) 335-8449

Pathfinders of Oregon
PO Box 3257
Gresham, OR 97030

Pathfinders are a cognitive restructuring/skill building process. It was designed to transform criminally deviant behavior into responsible conduct. FOR OREGON PRISONERS ONLY.

Phone Number: (503) 286-0600

Pathfinders Press
P.O. Box 162767
Atlanta, GA 30321-2767

50% prisoner discount. Write for a catalog. Books on the works of revolutionary and working-class leaders. There is a flat shipping and handling fee of $2.75. Books in English, Spanish, French, Farsi, Arabic, Swedish, Greek, Chinese, Russian, and Indonesian.

PB&J Family Services, Inc.
1101 Lopez SW
Albuquerque, NM 87105

Provides transportation, enhanced visiting, parent education, information, referrals, case management, child care, and more at 4 New Mexico prisons.

Phone Number: (505) 877-7060

Pelipost.com

Don't miss another special moment. Pelipost is the easiest and most convenient way to share photos from home!

How it works: 1) Upload favorite photos on Pelipost.com; 2) Enter recipient's information;
3) Photos are processed and shipped the next day! **FREE** shipping!

Tell friends and family to visit pelipost.com to join **FREE**!

Penal Law Project
Chico State University 25 Main Street, Suite 102
Chico, CA 95929

Penal Law Project assists incarcerated individuals. The program's primary purpose is to provide legal information and research for those held in California state prisons.

Phone Number: 530-898-4354

Website:aschico.com/clic/programsandadvocacy

Pen-A-Con
Box 533
North Dighton, MA 02764

This is a pen pal services owned and operated by Freebird Publishers. Profiles are $35 a year, or $95 for the duration of your incarceration. Send 2 stamps for info packet.

Email: penacon@freebirdpublishers.com Corrlinks: diane@freebirdpublishers.com

Comment: I was hit 6 times in under a month. - - Peter Sierra

PEN American Center
588 Broadway, Suite 303
New York, NY 10012

The PEN's Prison Writing Program has three basic areas of concentration:

1. The Handbook For Writers In Prison. This handbook teaches elements of writing fiction, non-fiction, and poetry. It also provides resources for inmates in terms so next steps for their completed works. The Handbook is **FREE** for all prisoners who write us a letter requesting one.

2. Our annual Prison Writing Program awards contest. PEN awards cash prizes in five categories of writing from prisoners (fiction, essay, memoir, poetry, and drama/screenplay). We receive 1500 entries a year; the contest ends September 1st. We encourage inmates of all writing levels to enter the contest. To enter, simply mail the entry to the address above. No application or form is necessary, though most inmates do send us a short letter telling us a little bit about themselves. Winners lists are available upon request.

3. Our Mentor Program. The Prison Writing Mentorship Program pairs up established writer mentors with incarcerated mentees. Our program requires at least three exchanges of writing between mentees and mentors (that is, three submissions from mentees and three observations/commentaries to the submissions from mentors). To become eligible for the program, an inmate must first enter the annual contest. Winners are offered the opportunity to participate in the mentorship program and, in some instances, writers who do not win an award but show promise are also offered a mentor.

Penn Foster Career School
925 Oak Street
Scranton, PA 18515

This is a career school with various programs of study.

Comment: They offer a ton of programs to choose from at very reasonable rates. If career training is your objective, and finances are tight, Penn Foster Career School is a great option. - - Mike

Penn Foster
14300 N. Northwest Blvd., Suite 111
Scottsdale, AZ 85260

They provide correspondence courses. Write for a **FREE** catalog.

Phone Number (800) 572-1685

Pennsylvania Innocence Project
Temple University Beasley School of Law
1719 North Broad Street
Philadelphia, PA 19122

Phone Number: 215-204-4255
Website: innocenceprojectpa@temple.edu

Pennsylvania Prison Society
245 N Broad Street suite 300
Philadelphia, PA19107-1518

Does advocacy work, including prison visits, and publishes "Graterfriends," a monthly newsletter for people in prison which is primarily inmate guided.

Phone Number: (215) 564-6005.

Pen Pal Connection
Christian Pen Pal Outreach
PO 11296
Hickory, NC 28603

We are pen pals for fellowship, friendship, encouragement and spiritual growth -- not for romantic relationships, legal assistance, or financial gain. Be open to all support and friendships. You need to have two years left on sentence because there is a wait of 12 to 18 months.

People's Law Office
1180 North Milwaukee Ave
Chicago, IL 60642-4019

Phone Number: 773-235-0070
Website: peopleslawoffice.com

Comment: "Great work on behalf of prisoners in Illinois over the years with some major class actions. If you have a serious case in Illinois, check them out. TMP endorsed!" - - Josh Kruger, author of The Millionaire Prisoner

PETA
501 Front St.
Norfolk, VA 23510

Write for a **FREE** "Animals Belong in the Jungle" coloring book.

Phone Number: (757) 622-PETA

Philadelphia FIGHT/Institute for Community Justice
1233 Locust Street, 5th Floor
Philadelphia, PA 19107

Locally, they support inmates living with HIV within the Philadelphia Prison System, providing advocacy, linkages to services, education and expedited access to their HIV primary care clinic upon release. Prison Health News is a quarterly newsletter written by and for people who have been in prison or are currently living behind the walls.

Phone Number: (215) 985-4448 x.162
Website: fight.org

The Philadelphia Trumpet
PO Box 3700
Edmond, OK 73083

Christian magazine.

Comment: This is a mag for serious Christians, but it's not a normal religious mag. This mag covers conspiracy theory-type shit. It somehow finds ways to tie in any and every single story in the bible. It's very informative. They also send inmates FREE booklets. I have a subscription and recommend it, yet every time I read an issue I get the feeling that I'm reading a mag produced by a cult. - - GURU

PhotoSweep.com
1846 E Innovation Park Drive
Oro Valley, AZ 85755

It has never been easier to receive photos today from your friends and loved ones. All they have to do is download our **FREE** PhotoSweep App to their smart phone. They select any photo on the phone, which will then be printed and mailed by PhotoSweep directly to anyone, anywhere in the USA. No more waiting in line to print or mail photos. It's all done at the touch of a button! Convenient, fast, and safe. Ask them to download the PhotoSweep App NOW. At checkout, using the discount code first10, they will receive the first 10 photos **FREE**.

Phone: 877-347-7007

Photoworld
PO Box 401016
Las Vegas, NV 89140

Celebrity photos for sale.

PictureDonkey.com

Get pictures mailed to you from friends and family on the outside! Our picture printing service is EASY. Friends and family can send us pictures from their smart phone, tablet, or a computer and we will print them on high quality photo paper and mail them to you on the next mail day! All you loved one needs is: your inmate ID; your mailing address; their email address; a smart phone tablet or computer!

As low as $0.40 each! Our prices are all flat rate! No hidden fees, shipping and handling included! Don't be fooled by low cost prints "plus shipping and handling" where a single picture can cost $2! Our service also allows you to add captions, **FREE**!

You cannot sign up directly yourself. Our service is for your loved ones on the outside. Tell them to sign up at PictureDonkey.com. There is more information on the website, including frequently asked questions and information on pricing and discounts.

Comment: They're a longtime advertiser in PLN. While VERY expensive, they're top notch in service and ethics. That gal is always gracious and up front. I thought I would mention them to

you even though I can't afford them anymore. -
- Paul Keller, Washington

Picmate.net
UVP, Dept. XA
P.O. Box 110620
Jamaica, NY 11411

Send SASE for **FREE** catalog of sexy non-nude photos of models and dancers.

PLN Cumulative Index

Provides detailed information about all PLN articles, including title, author, issue, page number, topics covered, citations, and if it is state, Jail, or BOP specific. Can be searched on over 500 subjects such as medical neglect or sexual assault. Notify them of the index(es) you are ordering: 1990495, 1996-98, 1999-01, 2002-04. $22.50 each. Order directly from Prison Legal News.

PMI Center for Biblical Studies
POB 177
Battle Creek, MI 49016-0177

Bible correspondence courses available **FREE** to inmates.

PM Press
PO Box 23912
Oakland, CA 94623

Zines, Prisoner-based pubs.

Website: http://www.pmpress.org

Poete Maudit
PO 216
Farmersville, CA 93223

Mission statement: Providing an outlet for aspiring authors to have their voices heard. At Poete Maudit Publishing we're dedicated to serving the incarcerated writing community. We offer a wide range of services including traditional publishing, self-publishing assistance, typing, and editing. For more info, send SASE to the address above.

We also run an online writers' workshop. Every month we select two essays and two poems written by our prison correspondents and post them on our website. A congratulatory letter is sent to the winners. To participate, send a short essay (250-500 words), piece of creative writing, or poem to: Larry

Coonradt; Postal Annex 40485 Murrieta; Hot Springs Rd., Suite B4; PMB 201; Murrieta, CA 92563.

Website: poetemaudit.net

The Poetry Wall; Cathedral of St. John the Divine
1047 Amsterdam Ave.
New York, NY 10025

They accept poetry of all kinds for display, and invites people to correspond with inmates whose poetry is on display.

Poets and Writers, INC
90 Broad St., Suite 2100
New York, NY 10004

An organization that publishes many books on writing, as well as a bi-monthly magazine. Write to receive a catalog.

The Poet's Workshop
C/O Sarah Lindahl
St Louis County Jail
4334 Haines Rd
Duluth, MN 55811

Publishes monthly magazine including poetry by prisoners. **FREE** to prisoners who submit poetry that is published.

Poetry Society of America
15 Gramercy Park
New York, New York 10003

Writer's competition.

Phone Number: (212) 254-9628

The Portia Project
PO Box 3567
Eugene, OR 97403

They provide legal and other assistance to women incarcerated at Coffee Creek Correctional Facility, and women who are under post-prison supervision throughout the state.

Phone Number: (541) 255-9988
Website: theportiaproject.com

Portland Books To Prisoners
P.O. Box 11222

Portland, OR 97211

Sends **FREE** books to prisoners nationwide.

Positively Aware, National Magazine On HIV/AIDS
5537 N. Broadway
Chicago, IL 60640

Covers treatment, medical, and social issues. **FREE** subscription for prisoners. Annual Drug Guide available in Spanish, not the magazine.

Power Inside
P.O. Box 4796
Baltimore, MD 21211

Provides women centered services to women including trans women and trans men. Offers support and advocacy for those who are incarcerated, homeless, addicted, or in the sex trade.

Prism Optical, Inc.
10954 N.W. 7ᵗʰ Ave.
North Miami, FL 33186

They sell a nice variety of eye glasses/frames. Write and request their **FREE** catalog.

Phone Number: (800) 637-4104
Website: prisoptical.com.

Comment: "If you can order your own glasses, you need to check out this catalog. Simply the best. They are a little expensive, though. Heck, get the catalog just to dream! TMP endorsed.' -- Josh Kruger, author of The Millionaire Prisoner.

Prison Activist Resource Center
P.O. Box 70447
Oakland, CA 94612

PARC is a prison abolitionist group committed to exposing and challenging all forms of institutionalized racism, sexism, able-ism, heterosexism and classism, specifically within the Prison Industrial Complex.

Phone Number: 510-893-4648
Website: prisonactivist.org

Prison AIDS Resources Center
926 J St. #801

Sacramento, CA 95814

They offer HIV/AIDS information.

Phone Number: (800) 221-7044

Prison AIDS Resources Center
PO Box 2155
Vacaville, CA 95696

Prison Ashram Project
Human Kindness Foundation
PO Box 61619
Durham, NC 27715

Website:http://www.humankindness.org/prison-ashram-project

Phone Number: (919) 383-5160

Prison Book Program
c/o Lucy Parsons Bookstore
1306 Hancock St Ste 100
Quincy, MA 02169

Does not send books to CA, MA, MD, MI, PA, KY, LA, NV or TX. Offers a **FREE** 40-page "We the People" legal primer. Allows two book shipments per year. Takes 3 to 6 months.

Phone Number: (617) 423-3298

Prison Book Project
Open Books Bookstore
1040 N Guillemard Street
Pensacola, FL 32501

Open Books is a non-profit, volunteer-run bookstore. Proceeds from the sale of books support the Prison Book Project, which sends thousands of books each year to indigent inmates in Florida prisons.

Phone Number: 850-453-6774
Website: openbookspcola.org

Prison Books Collective
PO Box 625
Carrboro, NC 27510

The Prison Books Collective is a North Carolina-based anti-prison group that sends books to prisoners in Southern states (primarily MS, AL and central and eastern NC) each month, and maintains an extensive radical 'zine catalog, widely distributes a monthly poster promoting political prisoner support, and publishes prisoners' art and writing.

Prison Connection
PO Box 18489
Cleveland Heights, OH 44118

This is a pen pal service. Special - $20 for 2 years. Send SASE for more information.

Prison Creative Arts Project
University of Michigan
Ann Arbor, MI 48109

This is an art exhibit that serves Michigan prisoners. Write for information.

Prison Dharma Network
11 South Angell St. #303
Providence, RI 02906

Mission is to provide prisoners, and those who work with them, with the most effective contemplative tools for self-transformation and rehabilitation. Provides books and educational materials.

Phone Number: (401) 941-0791

Prison Fellowship
PO Box 11550
Merrifield, VA 22116-1550

Prison Fellowship partners with local churches across the country to minister to prisoners, ex-prisoners, and their families. Publishes a variety of prisoner support literature including the Prison Survival Guide.

Phone Number: (877) 478-0100

Prison Fellowship Ministry
44180 Riverside Parkway
Lansdowne, VA 20176

"Prison Fellowship is a Christ-centered ministry which seeks the transformation and reconciliation of prisoners to God, family and community through Jesus Christ. We train 26 volunteers from local churches to execute their ministry. Re-entry is a focus area as well. Prison Fellowship is facilitating re-entry conferences around the United States in order to build coalitions in local communities so that each service organization, non-profit organization, church and local government agencies are able to contribute to the successful return of offenders."

Phone Number: 610-255-3926
Website: prisonfellowship.org

Prisons Foundation
2512 Virginia Ave. NW, #58043
Washington, DC 20037

Prisoner-Written Books Wanted for Publication

If you are a prisoner who has written a book, or would like to write a book, we want to publish it. All books on any subject are welcome. We do not screen or censor in any way, so you are free to write anything you wish. There is no charge to you to publish your book and no charge to anyone who wishes to read it. Plus, you retain full rights to your book if you later wish to place it with a literary agent or commercial publisher. Placing your book on our website is in fact a good way to bring it to the attention of agents and larger publishers (and protect it under common copyright law). You won't get an agent or publisher unless there is a "buzz" or following for you and your book, which our free publishing program can help secure. Even bestselling author Stephen King had to self-publish and give away his first five books, which were eventually picked up and published by commercial publishers after he was "discovered."

When we receive your book, it will be scanned in its entirety, just as you submit it to us. Do not send only a portion of your book and tell us that more will be sent later since it will be discarded. Any language is acceptable. Whether handwritten or typed, your book will be scanned and published as you submit it. Only on book per year by an author will be published free, but you can combine two or more manuscripts into an anthology to be your free book if you submit all together. If you want us to publish another separate book within 12 months, you must pay $65 per book if your book is under 125 pages or $95 if your book is 125 pages or more.

After we scan your book, it will be placed on the Internet for free worldwide distribution an reading on our popular and fully searchable website www.PrisonsFoundation.org. It will remain there indefinitely (unless you or your new publisher compensates us $75 for the cost of removal). If you want to have a family member, friend, literary agent, commercial publisher or anyone else read or download your book after it is published by us, just give that person the website address www.PrisonsFoundation.org and direct them to search for your name there. When a person clicks your name, your book(s) will appear on their computer to read, download or print without charge to them.

Here are the guidelines you must follow for us to publish your book. 1. Every page of your book should tie 8.5 by 11 unstapled loose white typing paper. If paper is lined, too light, holed, wrinkled, creased or has glue on top edges, they might not scan or will be scanned upside down; 2. Nonfiction and fiction books must be over 100 pages and not more than 600 pages; 3. Plays, screenplays, poetry books, music books, art books and comic books must be over 25 pages and not more than 150 pages; 4. A SASE or stamp must accompany your book (if you want acknowledgment and promos about your book) so we can verify that you are indeed the author (no pen name can be used); 5. The cover of your book or second page should contain your name, title of the book (unique name, not Part 2, no more than 10 words, including subtitle), date, whether the book is a novel, nonfiction. etc., a brief paragraph about it and both your prison address and your outside permanent address (if you have one); 6. Legal motions, transcripts and court records (unless they are short and part of your book) will NOT be published; 7. If your book includes photos or drawings, they must be glued or taped firmly to the pages and placed only at the beginning or end of your book unless art books or comics; 8. Use only one side of each sheet of paper (though you can use paper with one side previously used for another purpose as long as you X-out the side that is not part of your book). If you write or type your book on both sides, all odd pages will be scanned first followed by all even pages, so the reader will have to print and collate your book to read it properly. We also recommend that you number (bottom is best) and put your name on every page, print or type your book legibly and use a dictionary and thesaurus to check spelling and word usage (see reverse side for offer). Remember, once your book is published on our website, it will remain there forever. Books can be submitted electronically as Word or PDF documents to staff@PrisonsFoundation.org. No manuscript will be returned. If you want a copy for yourself, either make it before you send the book to us or wait for it to be published by us so you (or your outside contact) can download or print it from the Internet. It will be on the Internet permanently, so you can print it anytime in the near or distant future. Sorry but we cannot edit or critique your book and will only answer brief questions if you send us a SASE. Kindly allow up to 30 days for a reply and 30 days after we receive your

book for it to be published on www.PrisonsFoundation.org, though ten days are common. Please send your book to the address above.

Special Note; If you or your friends or family care to support our work with a donation, we will reward you by featuring your name and book on the front homepage of our website and a FREE link to your book. This gives you double the impact since your book will be viewable at two locations on our website. Whether you donate or not, your book will still be published and remain on our website indefinitely. But a donation gives you and your book prominent front-page publicity and a second link, which no other author receives. A $50 donation covers one year's publicity, $100 covers two years, etc. (Non-prisoners and businesses must donate twice that much for this special publicity and link.) Donations can be made online by using the donate button on our website or by sending a check or money order to the address below. Thank you for your financial support, which allows our program to grow.

Additional Paid Publishing Services Available
Publish your book on Amazon.com as an Attractive, Finished Book.

Instead of or in addition to publishing your book on our website (a free service) as a scanned and unedited manuscript, we can publish your book on Amazon.com as an attractive, finished book. It can then be sold and delivered as an appealing printed book to anyone who orders it, with you receiving a royalty for each copy sold.

To accomplish this, your manuscript must be typed, edited and formatted in a professional way. In addition, a cover must be designed for it. We are experienced in doing these things and are available to do them for you. But you must pay the costs.

The costs are as follows and include typing, editing and everything else needed for an Amazon.com book: $900 for a book up to 10,000 words (about a 40 page book), $1600 for a book from 10,000 to 25,000 words (about 40 to 100 page book), $2100 for a book from 25,000 to 50,000 words (about 100 to 200 page book). For books that exceed 50,000 words, there is an additional cost of five dollars for each 250 words.
If your book has already been typed and exists as a Word document, take 30% off the above costs. Our services will then consist of light editing of your

book, formatting your book for publishing on Amazon.com, designing your book's cover and publishing it.

The costs quoted here include a proof copy sent to you of the book before publication for your approval. Upon publication three copies of your final printed book will be sent to any three persons and addresses you wish. Additional copies may be ordered directly from Amazon.com.

From the time we receive your manuscript and payment, 30 days are required until you receive a proof copy of your book. After you approve the proof copy (you can make minor corrections but major changes will involve additional costs), an additional 15 days are required before your book is published and you receive a final copy.

Since your book will be published on Amazon.com, anyone can order a copy of it. You will receive a royalty of one dollar for each copy sold. Your book will be priced according to its size. You will receive a royalty check and a royalty statement in January of each year if 50 or more copies of your book have been sold during the year. Otherwise, no royalty and no statement will be provided. You book will remain on sale for 20 years.

If you decide that you wish to remove your book from Amazon.com because you have found another publisher or for any other reason, we will do this for you at a cost of $75. Only you can authorize this.
To have your book published on Amazon.com in accordance with the above terms, please send your manuscript and payment to the address below. If you have any questions, please write to us and include a self-addressed stamped envelope for a prompt reply. Thank you.

We Can Help With Your Grievances, Transfers, Early Release and Other Issues

The Prisons Foundation has launched a new division, Rehabilitation Foundation, which provides a VIP prisoner advocacy service called Rehabilitation Reports. When you become a member of the Rehabilitation Foundation you are entitled to use one of our advocates to help solve your problem. They will research and attempt to solve your problem as your personal advocate. This service may be what you need instead of going to the time and expense of hiring an attorney to help you.

When you become a member of Rehabilitation Foundation by filling out the form on the reverse side of this paper and paying a membership fee you provide information about the problem you are experiencing and who in the prison system you think may be able to resolve the problem. We will call the person or whoever is available and capable of resolving your problem based on your suggestion and our independent research. We will then prepare a written report which will be sent to you and also published as a Special Rehabilitation Report Regarding (Your Name) on our publication's website www.PrisonsFoundation.org.
Your report will contain your contact information and the contact information of the one or two persons we speak to capable of resolving your problem (maximum of two people are contacted). The outcome of the conversation(s) and any promises made to us on your behalf will be reported to you and posted on our website for others to see and act upon.

Here's what we will say when we call the person(s) capable of resolving your problem. 'Hello, my name is (advocate assigned to your case) and I am calling from the nonprofit Rehabilitation Foundation. We understand that inmate (Your Name) is trying to (your goal) so that he/she can become a better person and have a better chance of becoming a contributing member of society when released from prison. We are authorized to speak for this inmate and I can send you an authorization form to prove it. What is standing in the way of this request being granted and how can it be expedited? If you need help in making this happen, we have resources and political contacts that can assist you. Since we both want a safer society please do what you can to make this happen quickly. Can we count on your cooperation?"

If the person(s) we contact is not cooperative, we will argue with them by pointing out they are public servants committed to rehabilitation, not vigilante's intent on punishment. Also, if they are obstinate, we will threaten and in fact publish their name and contact information in Rehabilitation Reports with a note about their apparent opposition to rehabilitation and to the creation of a safer society and invite others to call and write them.

While we cannot guarantee success (even an attorney cannot do that), we will do the best we can. As the saying goes, "Nothing ventured, nothing gained." There is a good possibility we will be successful, but even if we are not the person(s) responsible for inflicting the injustice on you will think twice before doing it again. In addition, the Special Rehabilitation

Report that will be published about situation may create a groundswell of public and media support to resolve your problem and help avoid future ones.

Membership in the Rehabilitation Foundation expires and must be renewed at the same membership fee when a Rehabilitation Report has been researched, prepared, published, printed and sent to you. We look forward to having you as a member. If you have any questions after you become a member please know that you, we car only address them in writing and do not accept telephone calls, either collect or prepaid. If you have any questions before you become a member please include an SASE when writing to us to guarantee a response. Thank you. We look forward to assisting you in the achievement of your rehabilitation goals.

Prison Grievances

This book, written and published by Dr. Terri LeClercq, is an easy-to-understand guide on "when to write, how to write" prison grievances. Dr. LeClercq has published Expert Legal Writing, Guide to Legal Writing Style, and more than a hundred articles on rhetoric. She and her husband live in Austin, Texas where they both teach at the School of Law, University of Texas. Learn more about Dr. LeClercq and her work at prison grievances.com. Her book (ISBN 9780615739755) is $9.

Comment: Prison Grievances is an easy-to-understand, step-by-step guide on how to navigate through the very frustrating prison grievance system. It's an invaluable resource that should be read by every inmate. -- Mike

Prison Health News
1233 Locust Street, 3rd Floor
c/o Philadelphia FIGHT
Philadelphia, PA 19107

Quarterly newsletter published by former prisoners about prisoners' health.

Phone Number: 215-985-4448.

Prison Inmates Online
8033 W. Sunset Blvd. #7000
Los Angeles, CA 90046

ATTENTION INMATES! PIO WILL NO LONGER POST AND UPDATE PROFILES. THEY MUST BE PAID FOR AND POSTED ONLINE BY YOUR FAMILY. HAVE THEM CONTACT info@prisoninmates.com

"Prison Inmates Online is much more than a pen pal service. It's your link to the free world during your incarceration! A lot of inmates lose touch with family and friends after being incarcerated. With a PIO profile, friends and family can always find you, see what's going on in your life, and send you a message. Keep your profile updated and never be forgotten. If you find love, don't pull your profile down, just change your relationship status to 'In a Relationship' in your bio and keep your profile going!

Best value for your money: PIO is the best value for your online profile. Why pay more on other websites that only provide less? See how we compare to our competitors with better prices/service.

Profile price and renewals: PIO charges $40 for a profile that includes up to 300 words. Plus, every time you make a PAID update, your profile is extended for 1 year from the date of the update. Compare that to other websites who charge $40 for a profile that only contains 250 words and renewal rates up to $30 per year.

More photos than anyone else: PIO allows you to submit 5 photos with your profile. Compare that with the 1-2 photos most other services allow you to submit. Additional photos, art and tattoos are 5 for $10. Compare that to other websites that charge you $10 for EACH photo.

Featured Inmate: Our Featured Inmate panel is shown on nearly every page of PIO website and includes a courtesy in the 'ad' space section of the website. Compare that to other services who only show only show featured inmates on the homepage. Become a Featured Inmate for just $30 per month or $180 for the whole year!

Blogs and poems: List a blog or poem on PIO up to 300 words for just $10. Compare that to the $15 other websites charge. Other services like videos, tattoos and documents aren't even provided by other websites.

Documents section: Share documents (legal, stories, journals, diaries) for others to view or download. A great way to inform people who are following you or your case! It's also a rest place to store digital copies of your records in one place. Only $10 for each document title, up to 50 pages.

Tattoo section: Many men and women are drawn to people with tattoos. Why not show off yours in the tattoo section? The photos of your tattoos are linked to your profile page so it's another way to get more visitors to your page. $10 for up to 5 photos.

Videos: YouTube is the Internet's largest video sharing website and is integrated into this site. You can post any video that is listed on YouTube directly to your profile page. Your favorite music video, comedian, or even your own videos if they are posted on YouTube! Only $5 per video!"

Website: prisoninmates.com
Corrlinks: infoprisoninmates.com

Comment: This may very well be the best profile service I've seen. You can practically have everything a real, personal/company website can have. — Mike

The Prison Journal
6041 Watch Chain Way
Columbia, MD 21044

"The Journal is a publication of poems, short essays, and artwork from inmates all over the country. All works should be original. As we seek to publish items that are relevant to the prisoner community, we encourage submissions that reflect your own experiences, although we welcome inspirational work of all subjects. We receive many spiritual items.

We are particularly interested in receiving artwork/drawings. The Journal is printed in black and white, so (if you submit a color item) please keep this in mind.

We are blessed to receive so many high-quality submissions, and continued to be inspired by the voices of incarcerated men and women. We hope you will stay enthusiastic about being creative, and submit some of your own items.

God bless,
John and Ann Worley"

Prison Law Clinic
UC Davis School of Law
One Shields Avenue, TB30
Davis CA 95616

Their students provide legal services to clients incarcerated in state prison.

Phone Number: 530 752-6942

Website:.law.ucdavis.edu/Faculty/Murphy

Prison Law Office
General Delivery
San Quentin, CA 94964

Litigates and monitors class action law suits regarding medical care, mental health care, and disabled access for prisoners in CA only. Also distributes self-help legal material on a number of topics. Write with your concerns.

Phone Number: 510-280-2621
Website: prisonlaw.com.

Prison Legal News
PO Box 1151
Lake Worth, FL 33460

PLN reports on legal cases and news stories related to prisoner rights and prison conditions of confinement. PLN welcomes all news clippings, legal summaries and leads on people to contact related to those issues. Article submissions should be sent to -- The Editor -- at the above address. We cannot return submissions without an SASE. Check our website or send an SASE for writer guidelines.

PLN is a monthly publication and a one year subscription is $30 for prisoners, $35 for individuals, and $90 for lawyers and Institutions. Prisoner donations of less than $30 will be pro-rated at $3.00/issue. Do not send less than $18.00 at a time. All foreign subscriptions are $100 sent via airmail. PLN accepts Visa and MasterCard orders by phone. New subscribers please allow four to six weeks for the delivery of your first issue. Confirmation of receipt of donations cannot be made without an SASE. PIN is a section 501 (c)(3) non-profit organization. Donations are tax deductible.

IMPORTANT NOTICE!!

Are phone companies taking money from you and your loved ones?

HRDC and PLN are gathering information about the business practices of telephone companies that connect prisoners with their friends and family members on the outside. Does the phone company at a Jail or prison at which you have been incarcerated overcharge by disconnecting calls? Do they charge excessive fees to fund accounts? Do they take money left over in the account if it is not used within a certain period of time?

IMPORTANT NOTICE!!

Prison Legal News is collecting information about the ways people get cheated by the high cost of sending money into your account?

Is someone skimming money or otherwise charging you and your loved one's high fees to deposit money to fund prisoners' accounts.

Please write to PLN and/or have the person on the outside contact us to let us know specific details about the way that the system is ripping them off. We are interested in all business practices that result in money being diverted away from prisoners' accounts. Please direct all correspondence to: Ptsolkasprisonlegalnews.org or Prison Legal News;

Attn: Panagioti Tsolkas; PO Box 1151; Lake Worth, FL 33460.

We want details on the ways in which prison and jail phone companies take money from customers. Please contact us, or have the person whose money was taken contact us, by e- mail or postal mail: cwilkinsonhumanrightsdefensecenter.org or Prison Legal News; Attn: Carrie Wilkenson; PO Box 1151; Lake Worth, FL 33460.

Comment: "The publisher, Paul Wright, is a legend. He's a former prisoner who started PLN while inside Washington State Prison. PLN has grown into the Human Rights Defense Center and is a major player doing class actions on behalf of us. PLN is one of the few must-have subscriptions for me, and one of the few magazines I read cover to cover. I'll go without commissary before I go without PLN! You can order with stamps. TMP endorsed and recommended!" -- Josh Kruger, author of The Millionaire Prisoner

Prison Legal Services of Michigan
209 E Washington Ave.
Jackson, MI 49201

Phone Number: (517) 780-6639

Website: http://www.prisoneradvocacy.org/

Prison Library Project
915C W. Foothill Blvd, PMB-128
Claremont, CA 91711

FREE books: self-help, personal and spiritual growth, wellness, and metaphysical books.

Prison Literature Project
c/o Bound Together Books
1369 Haight St.
San Francisco, CA 94117

They'll send you 2 **FREE** books. You may request them every 4 months. Orders take a while to be filled, so please be patient. Do not ask for specific books. Give a subject, as well as alternative subjects, and then wait for them to arrive. Topics include: Black studies, Chicano history, basic math/writing/science, books in Spanish, novels, politics, history, and more.

Prison Mindfulness Institute
11 S. Angell St. #303
Providence, RI 02906

Website: http://www.prisonmindfulness.org/

Prison Nation: The Wherehousing of America's Poor

PLN's second anthology exposes the dark side of the 'lock-em-up' political-agenda and legal climate in the U.S. This book is 287 pages, $22.95, and can be bought from Prison Legal News.

Prison Pen Pals
PO Box 235
East Berlin, PA 17316

Connecting prisoners with pen pals since 1996.

"Our award-winning web site has been seen in 100's of newspapers, dozens of magazines and many TV shows all around the world --Cosmopolitan, The New York Times, The Ricci Lake Show, MSNBC's Homepage and more! We are the most visited, largest and longest running site of its kind on the Internet!

Economy Ad: 1 photo with your name, # and address for a FULL year on the site -- $9.95

Basic Ad: Up to 200 words and 1 photo with your name, # and address for a FULL year on the site -- $19.95

Gold Star Ad: Up to 300 words and 2 photos with your name, # and address, highlighted with a GOLD STAR and placed on a special list for a FULL year on the site – $39.95

Platinum Ad: Up to 500 words and 5 photos or artwork with your name, # and address, highlighted with LARGE BOLD TEXT and a flashing arrow, placed on the highest traffic area on our site for a FULL year, plus 4 week processing time or 2 **FREE** months -- $79.95

Gallery Ad: Up to 500 words and 20 photos or artwork in a fully animated slide show with up to 5 personalized words captioned on each photo, BACKGROUND MUSIC, your name, if and address, highlighted with LARGE BOLD TEXT and a flashing camera, placed on the highest traffic area of our site for a FULL year, plus 4 week processing time or 2 **FREE** months -- $99.95

We accept stamps for payment! For a **FREE** brochure/application, send us a SASE today!"

Website: prisonpenpals.com

Prison Performing Arts
3547 Olive St Ste 250
St. Louis, MO 63130

A nonprofit multi-discipline, literacy and performing arts program that serves incarcerated adults and children at St. Louis City Juvenile Detention Center, City Workhouse, City Justice Center, County Jail, Hogan Street Regional Youth Center, Northeastern Correctional Center (NECC) in Bowling Green, MO and Women's Eastern Reception, Diagnostic and Correctional Center (WERDCC) in Vandalia, MO.

Phone Number: (314) 727-5355
Website: prisonartsstl.org.

Prison Place

Started by an ex-prisoner, this website is a place for friends and families of those on the inside to communicate and support each other.

Website: prisonplace.com

Prison Profiteers

This is the third and latest book in series of Prison Legal News anthologies that examines the reality of mass imprisonment in America. Prison Profiteers is unique from other books because it exposes and discusses who profits and benefits from mass imprisonment, rather than who is harmed by it and how. This book is 323 pages, $24.95, and can be bought from Prison Legal News.

Prison Rape Elimination Act Oregon (PREA)

The DOC has an Inspector General Hotline that is toll free.

Inmate: (503) 555-1234
Public: (877) 678-4222

Prison Rape Elimination Act (PREA)
320 First St. N.W.
Washington, D.C. 20543

 Phone Number: (800) 995.6423

Prison Stamp Exchange
677 N. Milburn Ave., Ste. 160-310
Fresno, CA 93722

Get 70% face value on NEW books of Forever stamps. That's $7.70 per book. Must be NEW! No folds, bends, etc. Get 50% face value on NEW single stamps, or partial books, or books with folds, etc. You must first send a SASE requesting an order form, before sending stamps. Stamps received without an order form will be rejected and not exchanged.

Website: prisonstampexchange.com

Prison Tour Programs
3010 Fox Ave.
Kingman, AZ 86409

"Brothers and Sisters in chains,

My wife and I have a program called Prison Tour. We believe prisoners should be able to express themselves as long as it does not bring harm to others. Prison Tour is trying something new. We have created a Facebook page where we post prisoner art and poetry. We have had great success at reaching people that are interested.

If you wish to participate in this program while it's **FREE**, then your artwork (painting or drawing) and/or poetry (100 words or less) will be posted on Facebook.com/PrisonTour. Your name, number and contact info will be posted with your work.

We are not a pen pal service. If somebody decides to reach out to you, please be respectful. Any complaints will lead to your posts being deleted and Prison Tour will not work with you in the future. We ask that you send copies of your art and/or poetry or a SASE to send your work where you wish after it's been posted.

My wife and I do this at our own expense. Stamp donations are accepted to help us reach out to more prisoners around the world.

If you wish to have a 50 word or less caption posted with your art and/or poetry to explain it, describe it or just say something to your viewers, we will take the time to do that for you. It will require a donation of 5 stamps for your 50 word caption.

Prison Tour needs a logo to be used on social media. We are holding a contest. The prisoner whose drawing is chosen will be given a $50.00 reward. All drawings will be posted on our page. Prison Tour is made up of prisoners and ex-convicts only, so please be respectful with your art and/or poetry. We want to be able to help you share your prison tour with those who wish to learn more about people like us. Thank you."

Prisonology

Our Mission is to provide information to defendants, inmates and attorneys about Bureau of Prison policies in order to achieve better outcomes. To do this, we have a top team of former BOP Case Managers and US Probation Officers who use their expertise to serve those who either do not understand the process or are bogged down in it.

Our head of operations is Jack Donson who retired from the Federal Bureau of Prisons after 23 years or meritorious service as a Case Manager. He and his team know the policies and that gives you an advantage in the courtroom or even with the BOP. We have testified in federal court districts across the country on issues concerning:

- Complex Sentence Calculation
- Judicial Recommendations
- Designation
- Medical Care

- HOP Record Interpretation
- Program Eligibility
- Institutional Adjustment/Transfers
- Security Level Classification
- Public Safety Factors
- Management Variables
- Compassionate Release

Our Clients Include:

- Federal Public Defenders
- Private Attorneys
- Incarcerated Inmates Defendants

Our Services Include:

- Mitigation Strategies
- Expert Testimony
- Declarations

"I witnessed far too many people who entered prison that were underserved by well-intended attorneys who did not understand the HOP and, at worst, were preyed upon by consultants who were more interested in fees than outcomes. We wanted a solution that EVERYONE could afford, which is what we have done with Prisonology. Everyone should have the same information." – Jack Donson

Corrlinks: info@Prisonology.com
Phone: 617-858-5008
Email: info@Prisonology.com

Prison University Project
PO Box 492
San Quentin, CA 94964

They provide higher education programs to people incarcerated at San Quentin State Prison.

Phone Number: 415-455-8088
Website: www.prisonuniversityproject.org

Prison Yoga Project
PO Box 415
Bolinas, CA 94924

Two yoga manuals written especially for people in prison. A Path for Healing and Recovery offers physical practices (asana), breathing practices (pranayama) and meditation (dyhana) to improve mental, emotional and physical well-being. The book also serves as a powerful resource for anyone trying to break free of negative behavioral patterns. A

Women's Practice: Healing from the Heart offers a simple and clear guide for women, whether free or behind bars who wish to use yoga to help heal themselves from trauma, stress or addiction. Write for a **FREE** copy of either book.

Prisonworld Magazine
c/o Dawah International
PO Box 380
Powder Springs, GA 30127

facebook.com/prisonworld
dawahinc.com
prisonworldblogtalk.com
prisonworldradiohour.com
prisonworldmagazine.com

Prisoner Correspondence Project
QPIRG Concordia
C/O Concordia University
1455 de Maisonneuve O
Montreal, QC H3G 1M8

The Prisoner Correspondence Project is a collectively-run initiative based out of Montreal, Quebec. It coordinates a direct-correspondence program for gay, lesbian, transsexual, transgender, gender variant, two-spirit, intersex, bisexual and queer inmates in Canada and the United States, linking these inmates with people a part of these same communities outside of prison.

Phone Number: (514) 848 7583.

Prisoner Diabetes Handbook

Living with diabetes in prison is very difficult. Order your **FREE** copy of this handbook and start managing your diabetes and health. Order from PLN.

Prisoner Express
127 Anabel Taylor Hall Cornell University
Ithaca, NY 14853

Prisoner Express promotes rehabilitation by offering inmates information, education and the opportunity for creative self-expression in a public forum. Our semi-annual newsletter contains a description of our projects
including poetry, essay writing, art, math, history, book club and chess programs. The newsletter is full of writings and art from the participants. Send a note for your **FREE** copy.

Phone Number: 607-255-6486

Website: prisonerexpress.org

Prisoner Information Network (PIN)
980 S 700 W.
Salt Lake City, UT.

Phone Number: (801) 359-3589

Prisoner Legal Services
1540 Market St Ste 490
San Francisco, CA 94102

Legal services for prisoners.

Phone Number: (415) 255-7036

PrisonPath.com

A new and **FREE** search engine, www.PrisonPath.com. provides information for the public. The site helps users in clarifying confusion and fear of the unknown when a loved one is charged and arrested, or sentenced to Imprisonment in the United States. PrisonPath provides Information Including the ability to find a person Incarcerated, visitation rules, contact numbers, and more about every American prisons or jails. It also allows family and friends of inmates to communicate with each other on a specific page.

Prisoner Promotions
2355 Fairview Avenue #214
Roseville, MN 55113

"With our service, we connect you to the best and most popular social networking sites on the Internet today. Our plan includes a Facebook profile. Your photo and personal ad will be posted for all to see, thus allowing more people to contact you. Up to 20 other networking sites are also available to you, ranging from religion, beliefs, culture, friendship, and dating/romance. Our service allows you to have a voice and gives you the opportunity to become a part of the outside world. Site options: Craigslist Personal Ad; Lost Vault Pen Pal Profile; OK Cupid; Hot or Not; Elove Dates; Zoosk; Ourtime; Matchmaker; Jdate; Single Parent Meet; Jumpdates; Date Hookup; True Love; Six Singles; Oceans of People; Fdating; Smooch; Real Christian Singles; Black Christian Dating; Christian Fishing; Green Singles. $20.00 for 10 sites, $30.00 for 20.

Pick your 10/20 web sites; write a short bio (300 words or less); include up to 3 photos; enclose payment; send away and let the networking begin!"

For a **FREE** brochure/application, send SASE.

Comment: Never responded to specific inquiry. Sent generic forms back in SASE. - - Paul Keller, Washington

Prisoner Rights Information System of Maryland INC.
PO Box 929
Chestertown, MD 21620

Prisoners For Christ
PO Box 1530
Woodinville, WA 98072

FREE Bible correspondence course.

Prisoners Resource
17503 La Cantera Parkway, Suite 104 #415
San Antonio, TX 78257

Need a better way to stay connected? Tired of not getting any responses? Try our solutions **FREE** for 5 days. Add us on corrlinks:
info@prisonersresource.com.

Phone: 888-700-2511

Prisoner Visitation and Support
1501 Cherry Street
Philadelphia, PA 19102

PVS is a nationwide visitation that has 300 volunteers across the U.S. who visits federal and military prisoners. Their goal is to visit any federal or military prisoner who wishes to receive a visit with special priority paid to prisoners on death row, in solitary confinement, or those who are serving long sentences. The PVS volunteers visit once a month, with limited visiting services for Spanish-speaking prisoners.

Phone Number: 215-241-7117
Website: prisonervisitation.org

Prisoner/Inmate Family Service
PO Box 1852
Pismo Beach, CA 93448

This company will buy stamps, order books from online retailers, copy photos and artwork, etc., and much, much more. Send SASE for a **FREE** catalog.

Comment: This service is run by one guy named George Madison. I used him before and when I had someone email him because I thought he was taking too long, he responded that he is only one person with over 4,000 clients. I had him do some gifts for X-mas and they landed separately from each other and sporadically over the course of a week. Worse still, the gifts came as from "George Mason" and my girl thought it was some creep so she threw them in the garbage. Eventually I stopped getting mailed responses from him, and likewise when I had someone email him.so I think he gave up the game. Not recommended. - - CW Carney

Prisonnewsnetwork.us

Search this site for criminal records, warrants, inmate locations, prison headlines, gangs, news links and more.

Prisoners for Christ Outreach Ministry
PO Box 1530
Woodinville, WA 98072

They offer bible college courses. Write for more details.

Prisoners' Legal Services of New York
41 State Street, Suite M112
Albany, NY 12207

Phone Number: 518-445-6053
Website: http://plsny.org/

Prisoners' Legal Services (formerly Massachusetts Correctional Legal Services)
Ten Winthrop Square, 3d Floor
Boston, MA 02110

The mission of the Massachusetts Legal Aid Websites Project is to improve access to justice for low-income and disadvantaged persons in Massachusetts through innovative use of the web and other technologies.

Phone Number: 617-482-2773
Website: http://www.plsma.org

Prisoners' Rights Office
6 Baldwin Street, 4th Floor
Montpelier, VT 05633-3301

Phone Number: 802-828-3194

Prisoner's Rights Research Project
504 E Pennsylvania Ave
Champaign, IL 61820

Phone Number: (217) 333-0931
Website:
law.illinois.edu/faculty/profile/judithrowan

Prisoners' Rights Union
PO Box 161321
Sacramento, CA 95816

They publish self-help legal manuals based on California law, for $7.50 each. They also publish PRU News Review, quarterly; $6 per year for prisoners. Send SASE for catalog of publications and more information.

Phone Number: (916) 442-2240.

Prisoner's Self-Help Litigation Manual, 4th edition

The premiere, must-have "Bible" of prison litigation for current and aspiring Jailhouse lawyers. If you plan to litigate a prison or jail civil lawsuit, this book is a must-have. 1500 pages, $39.95, and can be bought from Prison Legal News.

Comment: "Simply the best self-help civil litigation manual on the planet! One of the cp-authors is Dan Manville. He's a former prisoner who got out and became a lawyer and teaches college students. I used this book to settle a lawsuit for $1,500 on my own federal court. Best investment I ever made. I still have my highlighted and underlined copy. TMP endorsed and recommended for every prisoner!" -- Josh Kruger, author of The Millionaire Prisoner

Prisoners with AIDS Rights Advocacy Group
P.O. Box 2161
Jonesboro, GA 30237

Provides practical and political support for prisoners with HIV/AIDS.

Professional Press
P.O. Box 4371
Chapel Hill, NC 27515

This company provides you with an opportunity to publish your book(s) at an affordable price. Send a SASE for their **FREE** brochure containing details.

Phone Number: 800-277-8960
Website: profpres.com

Project AVARY
385 Bel Marin Keys, Suite G
Novato, CA 94949

Project AVARY offers long-term support and enrichment for children and youth in the San Francisco Bay Area with a parent in prison or jail. Our program services include a summer camp, monthly outings, leadership training, and family support. Write for further details.

Phone Number: 415-382-8799
Website: projectavary.org

Project Blanket

Helps male and female prisoners with history of substance abuse make the transition from prison to the community.

Phone Number: 412-244-0329 (Pittsburgh)

Project for Older Prisoners
George Washington University Law School
2000 H Street NW
Washington, DC 20052

Law students interview and evaluate older and geriatric inmates in obtaining parole or other forms of release from incarceration. Operates in six states: LA, MD, MI, NC, VA and DC.

Phone Number: (202) 994-7001

Project Rebound
Associated Students Inc.
Cesar Chavez Student Center
1650 Holloway Avenue, T-138
San Francisco, CA 94132-1722

They support the formerly incarcerated on their journey through successful reintegration in a college setting.

Phone Number: (415) 405-0954
E-mail: projectrebound@asi.sfsu.edu

Website:
asi.sfsu.edu/asi/programs/proj_rebound/about.html

Project Return
806 4th Avenue South
Nashville, TN 37210

Phone: 615-327-9654
Email: pri@projectreturninc.org

Protecting Your Health and Safety

This book explains basic rights that prisoners have in a Jail or prison in the U.S. It deals mainly with rights related to health and safety, such as communicable diseases and abuse by prison officials; it also explains how you can enforce your rights within the facility and, if necessary, In court through litigation. This book is 325 pages, $10.00, and it can be bought from Prison Legal News.

Comment: "If you don't have the money to get Prisoner's Self-Help Litigation Manual, then this is a great starter book for convict litigators. Definitely worth $10. TMP endorsed."
- - Josh Kruger, author of The Millionaire Prisoner

Providence Books Through Bars
c/o Paper Nautilus Books
5 Angell Street
Providence, RI 02906

Requests are received for reading materials from inmates nationwide. Be sure to include mailing address with Prisoner ID# as well as subject matter preferences.

Phone Number: 401-356-0388
Website: providencebtb.org

PSI Publishing
413-B 19th St., #168
Lynden, WA 98264

They publish "The Prisoner's Guide to Survival." A comprehensive legal assistance manual for post-conviction relief and prisoners' civil rights actions. It's a 750-page paperback. It costs $49.95 for prisoners, plus $5 shipping and handling; allow 3-4 weeks for delivery.

Phone Number: (800) 557-8868.

PSSC/Parallax Press
46 Development Rd.
Fitchburg, MA 01420

Public Interest Law Firm
152 N. Third St. 3rd Floor
San Jose, CA 95112

This is a small litigation firm specializing in high-quality representation for class action and impact suits. They serve Santa Clara and San Mateo counties only. No cases re the CDC.

Phone Number: 9408) 293-5790.

Purdue University North Central at Westville Correctional Facility

Contacts:		David	Crum
Director,	Correctional	Education	Programs
Phone	Number:	(219)	785-5440

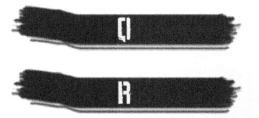

Rambles to the (Libertarian) Connection
James N. Dawson
PO Box 292
Malden, WA 99149

Debates, discussions, and diatribes on libertarianism, anarchism, religion, ethics, philosophy, and more. Write/send SASE for more information.

Randy Radic
I DO NOT RECOMMEND DOING BUSINESS WITH THIS COMPANY!

Comment: This guy is a con artist who preys on inmates. I sent him $200 to do a few emails for me; he kept the money, never again responded to me. Fuck him. - - Mike

Reaching Beyond The Walls
P.O. Box 6905
Rutland, VT 05702

Real Artist Tattoo Art Gallery

This company sells 24x30 paintings for $35. Have your people check out the website for more details.

Phone Number: (205) 545-3656
Website: kdsartworld.com.

Real Cost of Prisons Project
5 Warfield Place
Northampton, MA 01060

RCPP works to expand the organizing capacity of people and communities struggling to end mass incarceration. They'll send the comic books "Prisoners of the War on Drugs," "Prison Town," and "Prisoners of a Hard Life" to prisoners for **FREE**.

Website: realcostofprisons.org.

RedBird Books to Prisoners
PO Box 10599
Columbus, OH 43201

RedBird Books-to-Prisoners is a volunteer group providing Ohio prisoners with **FREE** reading material. Please send requests by subject.

Reentry Division Adult Probation Department City and County of San Francisco
Attn: Jennifer Scaife Director
880 Bryant Street, Room 200
San Francisco, CA 94103

The purpose of the Reentry Council of the City & County of San Francisco is to coordinate local efforts to support adults exiting San Francisco County Jail, San Francisco juvenile justice out-of-home placements, the California Department of Corrections and Rehabilitation facilities, and the United States Federal Bureau of Prison facilities.

Phone: (415) 553-1593
email reentry.council@sfgov.org
Website: http://sfreentry.com

Re-Entry Services, Philadelphia Prison Society
The Pennsylvania Prison Society
245 North Broad St.
Philadelphia, Pennsylvania 19107

The mission of the Pennsylvania Prison Society is to advocate for a humane, just and restorative correctional system, and to promote a rational approach to criminal justice issues.

Phone Number: (800) 227-2307
Website: prisonsociety.org.

Reinvestigation Project
Office of the Appellate Defender
11 Park Place, Suite 1601
New York, NY 10007

Phone: 212-402-4100

Represent Yourself in Court: How to Prepare and Try a Winning Case

Breaks down the civil trial process in easy-to-understand steps so you can effectively represent yourself in court. The authors explain what to say in court, how to say it, etc. This book is 528 pages, $39.99, and can be bought from Prison Legal News.

Resentencing Project
Center for Policy Research
2020 Pennsylvania Ave. NW, #465
Washington, DC 20006

They offer sentence reductions for assistance to federal agencies concerned with prison gang violence, homicide, and heroin trafficking, extortion, terrorism, and child exploitation. Prisoner advocacy through resentencing. Write for literature and application. (Please allow 6-8 weeks for a response).

Restore Pell Grants for Prisoners!

Prison education is on the federal legislative agenda in a way not seen since the mid-1990s. For prisoners and their supporters that provides renewed hope. It is now time to act on that hope: contact members of Congress and urge them to co-sponsor or support the REAL Act, H.R. 2521. The bill has been referred to the House Committee on Education and the Workforce, which is chaired by Rep. John Kline. The ranking Democratic member of the committee is Rep. Robert Scott. Both can be contacted at: U.S. House of Representatives, Committee on Education and the Workforce; 2182 Rayburn House Office Building; Washington, D.C. 20515.

What else can you do?
- Contact your members of Congress and let them know you support the REAL Act and ask them to support the bill, too.
- Ask friends and family to use social media to spread the word and show your support for the REAL Act.

- Ask family and friends to contact their members of congress and ask them to contact their members of Congress and ask them to co-sponsor and support the bill. They can use this link to locate them online: www.congressmerge.com/onlinedb/

"The REAL Act is about restoring education opportunities for our nation's prisoners so they will have the opportunity to reintegrate as productive members of the community post-incarceration." – Congresswoman Donna F. Edwards

HUMAN RIGHTS DEFENSE CENTER SUPPORTS PASSING THE REAL ACT!!

Revolution or RCP Publications
Box 3486, Merchandise Mart
Chicago, IL 60654

FREE bi-monthly, radical newspaper.

Comment: This paper is written from a revolutionary view point. Every time there's a police shooting these people are there protesting. They were in New York, Boston and Missouri every time the cops killed someone. It's a cool paper. -- GURU

R. Hughson

I DO NOT RECOMMEND DOING BUSINESS WITH THIS COMPANY!

Richard M. Samuels, PH.D., PLC
8776 East Shea Boulevard
Number 106-320
Scottsdale, AZ 85260

National services available for:

- "Second Chance" Eligibility Evaluation
- Comprehensive Psychological / Psychological Testing & Evaluation

Ask your attorney, friend, or family member to contact us to learn more about how our services may provide valuable assistance in your upcoming motion, hearing, or trial.

Phone: 480-661-9896
Email: expertwitnessinpsychology@gmail.com
Web: expertwitnessinpsychology.com

Rising Sun Publications
PO Box 14146
St. Paul, MN 55114

They publish the book 'Battleground: A Survival Guide for the Muslim in Prison', by Saadiqul Aqwal, which includes:

- A brutally honest work to aid practicing Muslims in navigating the challenging issues of prison life.

- Insights on how to hold onto spirituality, dignity, and observance on the inside.

- A helpful resource list for books/study materials, religious articles, civil rights, legal aid, and re-entry assistance.

Its 190 pages. Send $14.95 plus $2.75 for shipping

Robert's Company
15412 Electronic Lane #101
Huntington Beach, CA 92649

Sells "Smith's Guide to Habeas Corpus Relief," which
includes example pleadings from the initial habeas corpus petition to the final petition for a writ of certiorari. This book is 380 pages, $24.95.

Rolling Stone --LETTERS
1290 Avenue of the Americas
New York, NY 10104-0298

Letters become the property of Rolling Stone and may be edited for publication.

Rock of Ages Prison Ministry
C/O Prisoners Bible Institute
P.O. Box 2308
Cleveland, TN 37320

FREE King James Bible, correspondence course. Offers New Testament study course through the Discipleship Institute. Also available in Spanish.

Rocky Mountain Innocence Center
358 South 700 East, B235
Salt Lake City, UT 84102

Phone Number: 801-355-1888
Website: rminnocence.org

Rodriquez, Stephen G. & Associates
633 West 5th St., 26th Fl.
Los Angeles, CA 90071

Phone Number: (213) 223-2173
Website: lacriminaldefenseattorney.com.

The Safer Society Foundation
P.O. Box 340
Brandon, VT 05733-0340

"Today we view sexual abuse as a public health issue, and work to engage survivors, treatment professionals, persons with sexual behavior problems, family members, friends, policy makers, researchers and educators in creating evidence-based strategies for preventing sexual abuse, supporting those who have been abused, and managing those who have abused."

Phone Number: (802) 247-3132

Safe Streets Arts Foundation
2512 Virginia Ave. NW #58043
Washington, DC 20037

The Safe Streets Arts Foundation exhibits prisoners' art at major art fairs and festivals. In addition to selling prison art in their retail outlets, they provide the names and addresses of imprisoned artists to anyone who wishes to use their artistic service. They exhibit and sell the art of imprisoned artists, with the proceeds of art sales used for inmate art supplies and restitution requirements, if any. Prisoners receive support to use the arts to develop their self-esteem and a positive attitude vital for successful reentry.

Let me begin by thanking you for your interest in exhibiting your art with us. Our nonprofit organization accepts art created in prison for exhibit and sale at our numerous art gallery locations. But sales are rare compared to the many pieces received and most of the art is given away after a reasonable exhibition period. Simply send us your art (originals only, no copies or prints). We will prepare your art for exhibit at no cost to you. Be sure to include on the back of each piece your name and address, a description of the piece, your own background, and anything else you would like potential buyers to know about each piece. You will get 50% of whatever we receive for your art, minus any framing and/or selling expenses we incur. Please notify us of any change of address. No art is returned and if not sold is given to nonprofit organization or supporters. We do not use a contract as this letter serves as a full statement of our terms.

We are not responsible for the loss, damage or theft of your art, though we take reasonable care with it. About sculpture and crafts, we accept them but rarely show or sell these pieces. One exception is large metal or wood sculpture suitable for outdoor placement in our Prison Art Sculpture Garden. If you can create such a piece, you and your prison will get full recognition in media coverage of our Sculpture Garden. We will pay shipment for you to send the piece to us.

We have an annual art show at the Kennedy Center in Washington, DC in connection with prisoner-written productions we present there. The best art we receive is exhibited and sold there. Also, we incorporate art in a film we produce that is shown at our Kennedy Center event. The art selected for the Kennedy Center will be announced in September 2019 on the night it is exhibited or included in our movie. If you are able to have a friend or relative attend the free show and screening, you will learn the results from that person. We will send you the printed program shortly after the show if you send us a SASE at that time. The most creative art and highest quality art we receive is exhibited on our www.OutsiderArtUSA.com website. We also have an artist mentoring program and may assign an experienced artist or art collector to stay in touch with you.

Pricing of all art received is done by us. Beyond occasional sales, there are other reasons for exhibiting with us. For one, a lot of people will see your art and you could make valuable contacts. For another, you may get commissioned work from individuals who want portraits, companies that need art, or publications that desire illustrations. Our art also gets a lot of TV and press attention. If possible, please include a SASE with your art to insure a prompt reply from us. Please know that we only communicate directly with our artists when a piece is sold, in which case we will confirm with you how you would like the funds disbursed. If you send us letters inquiring about the status of your art or request photos or anything else, they will usually go unanswered.

On a related matter, Prisons Foundation (parent nonprofit organization of Safe Streets Arts Foundation) has an exciting **FREE** service for prisoners. We publish books by prisoners, including art books. We want as many books as possible, all of which we will publish. Now you have a worldwide outlet for your art on the Internet. And you don't have to send us originals which you or your family can retain for direct sale. Enclosed you will find an information sheet about this program. If you care to utilize your artistic talent to do an art book, please do so and we will publish it as submitted (if it contains original art the art will be retained for sale or giveaway by us like any other art received). You can include commentaries telling about your art, which will make fascinating reading. Include an address if you or an outside contact wants to sell the originals directly. You can also compile a book with other artists, with you (or whoever wants to coordinate it) taking credit as the book's editor. Whatever you or anyone else submits to us, we will publish (see necessary guidelines on enclosed information sheet, including that your art and other pages must be on 8.5 by 11-inch typing paper and the book must be at least 25 pages). In closing I want to thank you again for contacting us.

I look forward to hearing from you. Please know that your talent is at y valued. I am fully aware of your challenges and opportunities. Take good care of yourself.

With sincere regards, / Dennis Sobin, Director

The Foundation exhibits art by imprisoned artists, publishes books by prisoners, produces a weekly podcast ("Podcast from Prison") featuring professional actor readings of excerpts from prisoners' book, and presents prisoner-written shows at the Kennedy Center.

Phone Number: 202-393-1511
Website: safestreetsarts.org
Email: staff@safestreetsarts.org

Sagewriters
Box215
Swarthmore, PA 19081

SageWriters is a community of free and imprisoned writers, artists, musicians, filmmakers, playwrights and activists working together to give an artistic voice to movements for justice, healing, reawakening compassion in our elected officials, creating a community love ethic, supporting effective re-entry programs, ending prisons as we know them and developing community-based Houses of Healing.

Phone Number: 610-328-6101
Website: SAGEWRITERS.com.

The Salvation Army
615 Slaters Lane
Alexandra, VA 22313

They offer residential programs in some cities.

Samizdat-Socialist Prisoners Project
PO Box 1253
Fond Du Lac, WI 54936

This is a revolutionary group for prisoners that sends Marxist and radical literature as well as sells and donates the "Socialist Action" newspaper. The cost of the Socialist action is $1.

San Francisco AIDS Foundation
1035 Market St. #400
San Francisco, CA 94103

HIV/AIDS hotline at 800- 367-AIDS for CA prisoners only. Publishes "BETA," available in Spanish and English.

Phone Number: (415) 487-3000

San Francisco Bay View
Willie Ratcliff, Publisher
4917 Third St.
San Francisco, CA 94124-2309

Bay View is an independent newspaper of liberation journalism. Subscribe for $24 per year, $12 for six months, or $2 per month. Make checks payable to Bay View. You may also pay in postage stamps.

To our readers behind enemy lines: A resource list is circulating that tells you subscriptions to the Bay View are **"free** to prisoners." This is only half true. The Bay View is not funded by anyone. Subscriptions, advertising and donations are our only income. If you have no funds or stamps, your subscription request can be paid from the Prisoners Subscription Fund when donations are sufficient. Pen Pal ads are **FREE** to prisoners!

However, many who have submitted pen-pal ads are distressed not to see them in the paper. Be assured your ad is posted on our website within a month after we receive it, but because of the volume, it will take longer to appear in print.

Web Site: sfbayview.com

Comment: This is a fantastic newspaper that every prisoner should have, regardless of ethnicity or geographical location. This is the real deal. Support by subscribing or sending a donation today. - Mike

San Francisco Children of Incarcerated Parents Partnership.
P.O. Box 293
1563 Solano Ave.
Berkeley, CA 94707

2.4 million U.S. children have a parent behind bars today. The partnership formed to improve the lives of incarcerated children and to demand a "Bill of Rights" for them, downloadable from the website in English and Spanish.

San Francisco Forty Niners Limited
4949 Centennial Blvd.
Santa Clara, CA 95054

Write for **FREE** fan information on the team.

San Francisco Zen Center
c/o Jeffrey Schnieder
300 Page Street
S.F., CA 94102

This spot provides Buddhist inmates with free-world pen pals.

Comment: The key word is Buddhist. Their "gatekeeper" is Jeffrey Schnider. He's cool, but when I originally wrote he asked me to write an introduction letter, and when he got back at me he told me that I wasn't a real Buddhist so he wasn't going to hook me up, but he would write me a provide me with resources. I had to respect his gangsta. - - GURU

Sanders, Louise S
PO Box 361402
Decatur, GA 30036

They type manuscripts and papers. They also format paragraphs and chapters, edit grammar, punctuation, etc. Send SASE for **FREE** price list.

San Quentin News
1 Main St.
San Quentin, CA 94964

San Quentin News is a 16-page monthly newspaper written, edited, and produced by prisoners incarcerated at San Quentin State Prison. The SQ News encourages prisoners, staff, and others outside the institution to submit articles, poems, artwork and letters to the editor for possible inclusion. To receive a mailed copy of the SQ News, send $1.32 in postage. This process should be repeated every month for each new edition.

Please use the following criteria when submitting:

- Limit your articles to no more than 350 words.
- Know that articles will be edited for content and length.
- The newspaper is not a medium to file grievances. (For that, use the prison appeals process.) We encourage submitting articles that are newsworthy and encompass issues that will have an impact on the prison populace.
- Please do not use offensive language in your submissions.
- Poems and artwork (cartoons and drawings) are welcomed.
- Letters to the editor should be short and to the point.

Send submissions to: CSP - San Quentin; Education Dept. / SQ News; 1 Main Street; San Quentin, CA 94964

Sandra Z. Thomas
PO Box 4178
Winter Park, FL 32793

Typing services designed with special rates for the Incarcerated person. Send SASE for a **FREE** price list and more information.

Phone Number: 404-579-5563

Santa Cruz Barrios Unidos
817 Soquel Ave
Santa Cruz CA 95062

The Santa Cruz Barrios Unidos Prison Project is dedicated to providing cultural and spiritual education, support, and hope to incarcerated individuals. The Project advocates for prison policy reform and programs that reduce recidivism, support re-entry, and re-unifies families.

Phone: 831-457-8208
http://www.barriosunidos.net/prison-project.html

Save on Prison Calls

This is a discount call service. Go to their website for details.

Website: saveonprisoncalls.com.

Schatkin, Andrew Esq.
350 Jericho Turnpike
Jericho, NY 11753

This is an attorney that has 25 years' experience and specializes in prisoner rights, appeals, habeas corpus, etc. Write for details.

Phone Number: (516) 932-8120

Sec. Memps
POB 631211
Irving, TX 75063

Send $2 or 5 new stamps for their book catalog of over 1,300 books. Genres include Urban, Self Help, Exotic and more.

Second Chance Act
68 Betts St.
Winder, GA 30680

Halfway house for federal prisoners. Write for details.

Second Chance Books
14 Weaver St.
Buffalo, NY 14206-3266

"Second Chance Books is geared towards helping to give individuals who are or were incarcerated that second chance they need in life. Second Chance Books is a non-profit organization, which was founded by Abdul J. Fowler, an inmate in the Pennsylvania State Department of Corrections. The purpose of Second Chance Books is to help inmates/ex-offenders utilize their time and talents to do something constructive/productive with themselves as well as give back to their communities. Each inmate/ex-offender who becomes productive not only benefits themselves and their families, but their communities as well as society as a whole. In order for things to charge we must first make the necessary changes within ourselves. The only way for those who haven't been is for those who have been to teach them. Knowledge is the key, and like they say on G.I. Joe, 'Knowing is half the battle.'

The more inmates we help become better, the more families we can help become better. Which will in turn help better their neighborhoods, communities, and ultimately society. Not to mention the fact that it will reduce the amount of tax dollars which are going into the prison systems, and increase the amount of tax dollars for schools and educating our youth. It's a win for everyone as a whole. Therefore, I ask you to support/help us by purchasing our books and/or sending us at donation. You can do it through mail, or gofundme.com/secondchancebooks.

I ask you to please look at the big picture. In order to make a difference and change things we have to play our part and at least try. Nothing beats a try but a failure. I'm trying extremely hard, and in all honesty I seriously doubt that you'd leave me hanging because this can truly be a game changer!

For more info, please contact our Administrative Assistant Sheena Nicole "Essence" through one of the contacts below:

Phone Number: 267-601-6956 or 267-815-2349
Email: duladym.secondchancebooks@gmail.com
Twitter: @SecondChanceBks
Instagram: @SecongChanceBooks
Facebook: /SecondChanceBooks

Send SASE for our current newsletter containing news and our available books now!

Sentel, Sentel
9550 S. Eastern Ave Ste 253
Las Vegas, NV 89123

Phone Number: 702-430-9445

Cheap local federal calls. Get a local number and save up to 85% on prison calls.

The Sentencing Project
1705 DeSales Street NW 8th FL
Washington, DC 20036

The Sentencing Project is a 501(c)(3) non-profit organization which promotes reduced reliance on incarceration and increased use of more effective and humane alternatives to deal with crime. It is a nationally recognized source of criminal justice policy analysis, data, and program information. Its reports, publications, and staff are relied upon by the public, policymakers and the media.

Phone Number: 202-628-0871
Website: sentencingproject.org.

Sentinel Writing Competitions
Sentinel Poetry Movement
Unit 136
113 - 115 George Lane
South Woodford, London E18 1AB
United Kingdom

Writer's competition.

The Senza Collection
PO Box 5840
Baltimore, MD 21282

"Senza specializes in providing you several choices - -all-nude 4X6 prints in startling vivid color imagery, or non-nude 4X6 prints in startling vivid color imagery.

We have divided our catalogs into these categories: Caucasian, African-American, Hispanic, Asian, and Mixed Hotties. Each page of our catalogs has 99 gloriously seductive ladies posing just for your enjoyment. There are over 250 catalogs to collect at just $2.50 per catalog. You can order a **FREE** "99 Hotties" sample catalog by sending 2 US Forever stamps and a SASE.

For those that just cannot wait, take advantage of our introductory special -- Dirty Dozen. $19.99 gets you all of this, plus **FREE** s/h: 12 eye-popping catalogs, each with 99 pics to choose from, and 12 4X6 random prints from our Mixed Hotties selection to show off our 4X6 print quality. All for just $19.99!

Remember, you must specify nude or non-nude, as well as your institution's restrictions as to the number of prints allowed in one envelope.

Please review our policies carefully: All Senza images are sold at a flat rate of $.35 each. Anyone wishing to purchase 1000+ prints at one time will be given a flat rate of $.30 per image. We have a minimum requirement of $15, which doesn't include s/h charges.

S/H charges are as follows:
1-5 4X6 prints: $1 per envelope
6-15 4X6 prints: $1.50 per envelope
16-25 4X6 prints: $2.00 per envelope

You must notify us on the order form the amount of prints your institution will allow in each envelope. We will accept brand-new US first-class postage stamps at the rate of $5.00 per book of 20. You are required to know your institution's policies regarding what images are acceptable into your facility. There are no exceptions to this policy. Returned/rejected mail: You will have 15 business days to send us a SASE (3 stamps per 25 rejected photos) with a street address in which to mail your returned/rejected photos. After 15 days the prints will return to our inventory. All sales are final, no refunds or exchanges.

Services to Elder Prisoners, Pennsylvania Prison Society
245 North Broad Street, Suite 300
Philadelphia, PA 19107-1518

Set My Way Free Ministries, INC.
221 North Hogan St, No 141
Jacksonville, FL 32202

Not attorneys, but provide legal research, attorney searches, manuscript proofreading, and revise pro se pleadings for a fee.

Sex Abuse Treatment Alliance
P.O. Box 1022
Norman, OK 73070-1022

Phone Number: (517) 482-2085
Website: www.satasort.org

Slingshot Magazine
3124 Shattuck Avenue
Berkeley, CA 94705

Slingshot is a quarterly, independent, radical newspaper published in the East Bay since 1988 by the Slingshot Collective. Subscriptions are **FREE** to USA prisoners. Back issues are $1.

Phone Number: 510-540-0751 x3
Website: slingshot

Sinister Wisdom, INC.

P.O. Box 3252
Berkeley, CA 94703

Publishes work by lesbians only – prose, poetry, essays, graphics, and book reviews. **FREE** to women in prison.

Sisyphean Tasks, LLC
PO Box 7956
Woodbridge, VA 22195

Publishes the Book "Black American in the Desert Kingdom," $19.95 plus shipping and handling.

Skin&Ink Letters
219 Route 4 East, Suite 211
Paramus, NJ 07652

Send letters, photos, drawings, etc., to this tattoo magazine. Must include return postage if you want you shit back.

Sky Unlimited
PO Box 92704
Long Beach, CA 90809

"Tired of paying for high priced calls? We are here to help! We offer local numbers at a very low cost for those with loved ones that are not in the local area.

We are one of the cheapest phone vendors around. We compete with our competitors to get you the lowest cost for calls. If you are spending hundreds of dollars on long distance calls just to speak to a loved one far away, Sky Unlimited can help you. We're here to help you lower the cost of long distance and international calls. We have low-cost phone and minute plans as low as $9.99 per month and international calls as low as $.06 cents a minute.

How it works...

Sky Unlimited is a prepaid service. We are a third-party vendor that provides you with a prepaid calling account in which you receive unlimited minutes with one number at $19.99 per month. 1) Call or email us at Sky to set up an account and choose which plan you wish to have. 2) Provide us with the numbers your wish to call. 3) We give you a local number to the institution you are calling from. 4) We forward the calls to the number you provide.5) When you make a call to the number we provide, it will be billed as a local call. 6) You are on your way to saving! *You pay local call rates but get long distance

services. We accept Visa, Master Cards, MoneyGram or money orders.

Email: skyunlimitedllc@ymail.com
Phone: 562-386-5938

Slammer Books

I DO <u>NOT</u> RECOMMEND DOING BUSINESS WITH THIS COMPANY!

Slipstream Poetry Contest
Dept. W-1
PO Box 2071
Niagara Falls, New York 14301

Writer's competition. The annual Slipstream poetry contest offers a $1,000 prize plus 50 professionally-printed copies of your book.

Guidelines:
Send up to 40 pages of poetry: any style, format, or theme (or no theme), and a $20 check, bank draft, or money order for reading fee. Due to recent increases in the cost of mail, manuscripts will no longer be returned. Send only copies of your poems, not originals.

Smith's Guide to Chapter 7 Bankruptcy for Prisoners

Get immediate freedom from liens against offender account by filing chapter 7 bankruptcies. Includes required bankruptcy forms and detailed filing instructions. This book is $31.90 ($34.08 in CA), and can be ordered from Roberts Company and online retailers.

Smith's Guide to Executive Clemency for State and Federal Prisoners

For those who have exhausted all legal remedies or have sentences that are too long to serve, this book lays out every aspect of the clemency process. Its 288 pages, $31.90 ($34.08 in CA), and can be ordered from Roberts Company and online retailers.

Smith's Guide to Habeas Corpus

See Robert's Company

SMOOTH Fiction, c/o SMOOTH
P.O. Box 809
New York, NY 10013

Website: fiction@smoothmag.com

SMOOTH magazine accepts short fiction submissions to be published in their magazine.

SMOOTH Magazine
P.O. Box 809
New York, NY 10013

SMOOTH is an "urban-style" magazine with beautiful women and interesting articles.

SMOOTH-Talk
P.O. Box 809
New York, NY 10013

Feeling like nobody cares? Here's your chance to speak your mind and let your voice be heard – even if nobody's listening. Send your letters, photos, drawings, x-rays, etc.

SNB
2637 E Atlantic Blvd., 32495
Pompano Beach, FL 33062

"Turn your time and talent into cash!!! Illustrate books with colored pencil, simple pen and ink, or watercolor drawings. Write us."

Socialism and Democracy
411A Highland Ave., #321
Somerville, MA 02144

The Roots of Mass Incarceration in the US: Locking Up Black Dissidents and Punishing the Poor. Edited and introduced by Mumia Abu-Jamal and Johanna Fernandez. Scholars' and activists, including former and current political prisoners, explore criminalization, police terror, and the abuse of prisoners, in their political context.

Copies @ $10+ p&h ($5 in US; $10 elsewhere; no extra postage charge for larger orders).

Phone Number: 617-776-9505
Email: info@sdonline.org

Soledad Brother: The Prison Letters of George Jackson

Lucid explanation of the politics of prison by well-known prison activist. More relevant now than when it first appeared 40 years ago. This book is 339 pages, $18.95, and can be bought from Prison Legal News.

Solitary Watch
c/o James Ridgeway
PO Box 11374
Washington, DS 20008

Website: solitarywatch.com

SOON
Wilmington; Derby DE65 6BN; England

SOON contains the answers to many of life's problems such as worry, fear, and loneliness. Write or email for a **FREE** copy.

SoUnique Magazine
PO 390434
Snellville, GA 30039

This company doesn't offer a magazine, from what I gather. They offer sexy non-nude photos, a pen pal service, and a book titled 'Tales & Confessions of an Atlanta Uber Driver', by Jay-R. You can purchase the book by sending $20, or $25 in postage stamps. Send a SASE for a copy of their photo catalog. They offer good images.

They call the "pen pal company" "So Unique Females." What you'll get is a page of 41 females -- pictures. Most are decent looking. Then, you can pay $15 to write any of the females. You can pay with 60 stamps, too. You must also include 2 stamps with every letter that you send, what it looks like to me is he found some decent looking girls who are locked up, and he will middleman your letters for a one-time fee of $15, plus 2 stamps with each letter. I'm not certain, but it's what I think based on the info he sent me.

South Beach Singles, Inc
PO Box 381619
Miami, FL 33238

All photos are $1.00 each with a minimum order of 10 photos per brochure, plus a flat rate of $3.00 s/h. They offer a special -- 30 photos for $20.00. You can get 10 photos for 40 stamps (flat books only).

Brochure lists, non-nude, $2 each:

NBA Vol. 9: White, everyday women, amateurs, open logs and backshots.

NBA Vol. 10-13: Black women, strippers, amateurs, open legs, backshots. Some White girls here -- Sasha Cream, Cubana Lust (Cubana), and Amber (Vol. 12).

NBA Vol. 14-17: Mix of Black, White, action shots and adult stars.

Brochure lists, XXX, $5 each:

Tripple XXX Vol. 1: Pinky, Cherokee, Luscious Lopez, Olivia, Sky and Mason.

Triple XXX Vol. 2: Montana Fishburne, Next Door Nikki, Flower, Phoenix, Jada Isis, Angel, Kapri, more Pinky and Cherokee.

Triple XXX Vol. 3: Lacey, Misty, Mika, Kelly, Pleasure, Pinky and Cherokee.

Custom orders are 25 photos for $40 (s/h included): "I will allow you to choose from your favorite model, adult star, or celebrity of your choice. Send $40 along with your feature and I will send you 25 of the hottest photos I can find. The custom will also apply to fetishes. Also Instagram and Facebook photos you want me to find. You must have the specific Instagram or Facebook username they are using. I will not search for it. Please keep in mind this is a VIP service; you are getting photos that no one else has. Most celebs and models will NOT have action shots, but I will get you the best high-quality photos no company can match. (Sorry, no transgender.) Please allow 10 days for delivery." Karen Leblanc, CEO

Email/Corrlinks:
RD@SOUTHBEACHSINGLES.ORG
Website: southbeachsingles.org

Comment: Took 5 1/2 months to get order, and responds slow to inquiries about order, even when SASE is sent. - - Troy Shaw, Indiana

South Dakota Prisoner Support Group
PO Box 3285
Rapid City, SD 57709-3285

Their purpose is to provide support to inmates in jails and prisons and their families of those in the South Dakota prison system.

South End Press
PO Box 283132
Cambridge, MA 02238

They sell books to prisoners. Write/Send SASE for more information.

Website: southendpress.org.

Southern Poverty Law Center
400 Washington Ave.
Montgomery, AL 36104

Phone Number: (334) 956-8200
Website: http://splcenter.org.

Southland Prison News
955 Massachusetts Ave., PMB 339
Cambridge, MA 02139

This is a newsletter that covers prisoner news on East and Southern States. It's $15 per year.

Special Litigation Section
US Dept of Justice Civil Rights Division
950 Pennsylvania Ave. NE
Washington, DC 20530

They enforce federal civil rights statues regarding conditions of institutional confinement, law enforcement misconduct, and protection of institutionalized persons' religious exercise rights.

Website: usdoj.gov/crt/split

Sports Weekly
PO Box 50146
McLean, VA 22102

A sports magazine that provides stats on the NFL and MLB.

Phone Number: (800) USA-1415
Website: mysportsweekly.com.

Spring Grass Book 'Em
PO Box 71357
Pittsburgh, PA 15213

Spring Grass Book 'Em is a **FREE** books-to-prisoners program that mails books to inmates nationwide (except for PA which is served by Book 'Em same address). Request books and magazines by subject or title and or author, or just request any. No catalog is available and some books may be substituted for those requested due to scarcity Please let Spring Grass Book 'Em know of any book restrictions (or changes to any restrictions), or upon transfer to a different institution.

Phone Number: 412-251-7302
Website: springgrassbookem.org

Spanish For Prisoners
1094 DeHaven Street, Suite 100
West Conshohocken, PA 19428

This book by Ronald Bilbrey is $18.95. It's available through Infinity Publishing Book Sales.

St. Dismas Guild
PO Box 2129
Escondido, CA 92033

They offer **FREE** bible study, bibles, rosaries, pamphlets, etc.

St. Mark's School of Legal Studies
1840 Coral Way, Room 4-754
Miami, FL 33145

Become a financial mediator and earn over $185,000 a year! In its annual list of best careers, "U.S. News" and "World Report" names mediator as a top choice for 2011. Law degrees not required, no restrictions for ex-felons to practice in any state. Write for **FREE** brochure and application.

St. Patrick Friary
102 Seymore St.
Buffalo, NY 14210

Counseling provided at Attica, Wyoming, Collins, Orleans, Albion, Groveland, Gowanda, & Rochester prisons. Post release services include housing, and job training. Also assist with educational and job training opportunities.

Phone Number: (716) 856-6131

Stanford Law School
Crown Quadrangle
559 Nathan Abbott Way
Stanford, CA 94305-8610

The Stanford Three Strikes Project is the only legal organization in the country devoted to addressing excessive sentences imposed under California's Three Strikes sentencing law.

Phone: 650 723.2465

Website:www.law.stanford.edu/organizations/programs-and-centers/stanford-three-strikes-project

Starship Entertainment
2240 Robert Fulton Hwy

Peach Bottom, PA 17563

Women who write to prisoners. Send $6.00 or 1 book of stamps.

State Public Defender; San Francisco
221 Main St., 10th Fl.
San Francisco, CA 94105

This office handles capital and non-capital appeals only for indigent convicted felons. Contact Michael Hersek.

Phone Number: (415) 904-5600.

State V. Us Magazine
PO 29291
Baltimore, MD 21213

State V. Us is an online and print publication that spotlights high-profile cases; corruption in prisons, the police departments and other branches of the government; wrongful convictions; true stories of men and women in prison; and success stories of formerly incarcerated individuals. If you have a story to tell, email them, or write to the address above. They also sell advertising space if you have a product to promote.

State V. Us was nominated for the 2018 and 2019 Titan Awards for Magazine of the Year. The print magazine is high-quality, full color, and each issue is $10.99, or you can subscribe to the next 4 issues for $35.00. It comes out quarterly.

Website: StateVsUsMag.com
Facebook: StateVsUsMagazine
IG: StateVsUs
Twitter: StateVsUs
#StateVsUsMag

Comment: This is another one of my favorite magazines. It's a must-have for any prisoner. Tap in with 'em immediately if you don't wanna be lame. - - Mike

Stop Prison Profiteering!
Prison Legal News
Attn: CFPB Comments
PO Box 1151
Lake Worth, FL 33460

Take action on prison money transfer services!!

For many years, corporations that provide money transfer services in prisons and jails have profited from price gouging prisoners and their families by charging excessive fees for putting money on prisoners' institutional trust accounts.

The time to take action against these practices is now!

You can submit a complaint to the Consumer Finance Protection Bureau (CFPB) regarding your experience with prison or jail money transfer services. Please send your complaint or comments as soon as possible, addressing any of these topics:

- Excessive Fees For Money Transfer Services: Let the CFPB know what service charges are required to transfer funds, as well as any limitations on the amount that can be transferred in one transaction.
- Ancillary Fees: In addition to transaction fees, do you or your family have to pay extra (ancillary) fees to set up money transfer accounts or talk with a company customer service representative?
- Customer Service: Does the company that provides money transfer services provide a toll-free number that connects you to a live person who can assist you? Are you able to access the information you need through the company's website? Do you have any choice in which money transfer service you use?

Send us your comments by mail, and we'll file them with the CFPB for you!

Please speak from your own personal experience, and note your comments will become a public record. People with Internet access can send their comments via email tocwilkinson@prisonlegalnews.org, or submit them through our website: www.stopprisonprofiteering.org

Stop Prisoner Rape
3325 Wilshire Blvd., Ste. 340
Los Angeles, CA 90010

Seeks to end sexual violence committed against men, women, and youth in all forms of detention.

Phone Number: (510) 235-9780
Phone Number: (213) 384-1400
Website: www.spr.org

Stopmax Campaign

American Friends Service Committee
1501 Cherry St.
Philadelphia, PA 19102

Phone Number: 215-241-7000.

Stratford Career Institute
Po Box 1560
St. Albans, VT 05478

They offer correspondence courses in 52 career fields.

Phone Number: (612) 788-4197
Website: scitraining.com.

Strategic Parole Solution
PO Box 8363
Fort Worth, TX 76124

Great Tips for Prisoners to Get a Fast Parole!

If you're incarcerated and behind bars, your most compelling dream and desire is to get out and be free once again. This guide is written by a former prisoner who successfully applied these legal principles to his own situation and achieved an early parole due to his knowledge and persistence. Discover the exact way he did it! Send $15.99 (FREE shipping) to the address above.

Strawberry Dragon Zendo
1800 Robertson Blvd. #197
Los Angeles, CA 90035

Website: www.strawberrydragon.org.

Street Pixs
PO Box 302
Humble, TX 77347

"We have the sexiest, freakiest pics and stories for my incarcerated friends. It's off the chain! 100 pics for $25.00. Nude/non-nude pics. Pen pal list also available. For a **FREE** catalog, send SASE today!"

Email: streetpixll@yahoo.com
Phone: 832-286-8857

Comment: Ordered pics from them 15 months ago and never got order! Wrote 7 times and called, to no avail. RIP OFF! - - Troy Shaw, Indiana

Comment: They never responded to my inquiry and kept SASE. They still advertise in PLN. -- Paul Keller, Washington

Streetsweepers Ent.
c/o Straight Stuntin Magazine
PO 1228
New York, NY 10029

Streetsweepers Entertainment is owned and operated by hip-hop legend DJ Kay Slay. He publishes the magazine Straight Stuntin.

Comment: I fucks wit' Straight Stuntin. Mando snatch. -- Mike

Sub 0 Entertainment
POB 1222
New York, NY 10029

Sub 0 published the men's mag Phat Puffs. It's filled with non-nude photos of strippers, porn stars and girls gone wild. All magazines are $11.00 plus $7.00 shipping and handling. The mags are full-color, glossy, and 100 pages.

Website: PhatPuffsMagazine.com
Phone: 646-542-4407

Sue the Doctor and Win! Victim's Guide to Secrets of Malpractice Lawsuits

Written for victims of medical malpractice and neglect, to prepare for litigation. Note that this book addresses medical malpractice claims and issues in general, not specifically for prisoners. Its 336 pages, $39.95, and can be bought from Prison Legal News.

SummerBunnies.com
Po Box 741145
Houston, TX 77272

They sell sexy, non-nude photos. Send $3 and a SASE for their latest catalog.

Comment: Terrible. No response, even with SASE. -- Paul K.

The Sun Magazine
Attn: Molly Herboth, Circulation Manager
107 North Roberson Street
Chapel Hill, NC 27516

Independent, ad-free monthly magazine that publishes personal essays, short stories, interviews, poetry, and photographs by emerging and established artists. **FREE** subscription offered to prisoners. Also accepts submissions.

Supreme Design
PO Box 10887
Atlanta, GA 30310

Supreme Design is a publishing company operated by Supreme Understanding. Supreme Understanding is a community activist, educator, and expert on the socioeconomically and psychological struggles of oppressed people. His extensive research and life experience helped him design a system of success for even the most disadvantaged. The following books are available...

- How to Hustle and Win, Part 1: A Survival Guide for the Ghetto, by Supreme Understanding (Forward by the Real Rick Ross)

This is the book that started it all. Now an international bestseller, this book has revolutionized the way people think of "urban literature." It offers a street-based analysis of social problems, plus practical solutions that anyone can put to use. 336 pages, $14.90 (ISBN: 978-9816170-0-8)

- How to Hustle and Win, Part 2: Rap, Race, and Revolution; by Supreme Understanding (Forward by Sticamn of Dead Prez)

The controversial follow up to How to Hustle and Win digs even deeper into the problems we face, and how we can solve them. Part 1 focused on personal change, and Part 2 explores the biggest picture of changing the entire hood. 384 pages, $14.95 (ISBN: 978-9816170-9-1)

- La Brega: Como Sobrevivir En El Barrio, by Supreme Understanding

Thanks to a strong demand from Spanish-speaking countries, we translated our groundbreaking "How to Hustle and Win" into Spanish, and added new content specific to Latin America. Because this book's language is easy to follow, it can also be used to brush up on your Spanish. 336 pages, $14.95 (ISBN: 978-0981617-08-4)

- Locked Up But Not Locked Down: A Guide to Surviving the American Prison System, by

Ahmariah Jackson and IAtomic Allah (Forward by Mumia Abu Jamal)

This book covers what it's like on the inside, how to make the most out of your time, what to do once you're out, and how to stay out. Features contributions from over 50 insiders, covering city jails, state and federal prisons, women's prisons, juvenile detention, and international prisons. 288 pages, $14.95 (ISBN: 978-1935721-00-0)

- Knowledge of Self: A Collection of Wisdom on the Science of Everything in Life; edited by Sumpreme Understanding, C'BS Alife Allah, and Sunez Allah (Forward by Lord Jamar of Brand Nubian)

Who are the Five Percent? Why are they here? In this book, over 50 Five Percenters from around the world speak for themselves, providing a comprehensive introduction to the esoteric teaching of the Nation of Gods and Earths. 256 pages, $14.95 (ISBN: 978-1935721-67-3)

- The Science of Self: Man, God, and the Mathematical Language of Nature, by Supreme Understanding and C'BS Alife Allah (Forward by Dick Gregory)

How did the universe begin? Is there a pattern to everything that happens? What's the meaning of life? What does science tell us about the depths of our SELF? Who and what is God? This may be one of the deepest books you can read. 360 pages, $19.95 (ISBN: 978-1935721-67-3)

- The Hood Health Handbook, Volume 1 (Physical Health). Ed. by Supreme Understanding and C'BS Alife Allah (Forward by Dick Gregory)

Want to know why Black and Brown people are so sick? This book cover the many "unnatural causes" behind poor health, and offers hundreds of affordable and easy-to-implement solutions. 480 pages, $19.95 (ISBN: 978-1-936721-32-1)

- The Hood Health Handbook, Volume 2 (Mental Health), Ed. by Supreme Understanding and C'BS Alife Allah

This volume covers mental health, how to keep a healthy home, raising healthy children, environmental issues, and dozens of other issues, all from the same down-to-earth perspective as Volume 1. 480 pages, $19.95 (ISBN: 978-1-935721-33-8)

Sunshine Artist
4075 L.B. McLead Rd., Suite E
Orlando, FL 32811

This magazine has articles on marketing crafts and selling your art. It's $34.95 for a 1-year subscription, 12 issues per year.

Support for Kids with Incarcerated Parents, Philadelphia Prison Society

They help children with incarcerated parents build their self-esteem and cope with their parents' incarceration.

Phone Number: (215) 564-4775 x123 Contact: Ted Enoch

Support Housing and Innovative Partnerships
PO Box 8803
Boise, ID 83707

Phone Number: (208) 331-0900

SureShot Books Publishing LLC
PO Box 924
Nyack, NY 10924

"SureShot Books is a publishing company and bookstore. Our products range from law books, Bibles, urban books, self-help, sobriety, education, etc. We also have a large selection of Spanish books and magazines. Our primary objective at SureShot Books, is to assist in the process of both socializing and improving the overall education level of prison inmates, helping provide you a greater opportunity at succeeding in life. We ensure you that we clearly understand your needs and that we will fully leverage our resources to fulfill them. Please forward us any ideas that you have to help us serve you better. Send $12.95 for our current catalog."

Website: sureshotbooks.com
Email/Corrlinks: Info@sureshotbooks.com

Comment: SureShot is official. I buy ALL of my books from them. If you want good books and great service, SureShot is who you want to do business with. TCB certified! - - Mike

Surrogate Sisters

I DO <u>NOT</u> RECOMMEND DOING BUSINESS WITH THIS COPMPANY!

Suthern Cumforts
PO Box 920098
Norcross, GA 30010

"Some play the picture game... We run it! We are the ULTIMATE picture catalog!

All photos are $1.00 each, with a minimum of 10 photos per order. Shipping and handling is $2.00 per envelope needed. Please include any specific requirements when ordering. Only checks and Money Orders are accepted forms of payment for pictures. However, we will accept stamps for our catalogs, which are 5 Forever stamps for each addition. You can order from any edition at any time. All pics are 4X6, high-gloss!

Comment: I've seen several catalogs from SC. Most the pics/images they offer look like still shots from porn movies. Bad bitches, just how we like them. My penis has never once been angry at me for inspecting the catalogs of SC! Fuck with them. - Mike

Susan L. Burke
Law Offices of Susan L. Burke
1611 Park Avenue
Baltimore, MD 21217

"Please contact me if you want to join the nationwide class actions against telephone companies who have been overcharging inmates and their families for phone calls."

Website: burkepllc.com
Phone Number: (410) 733-5444

Susman, Eli
PO Box 961896
Boston, MA 02196

Write for **FREE** sample essays and book information about living congenially forever in a spirit world.

The Sutra Translation Committee of the U.S. and Canada

To request books (**FREE** of charge) from the Sutra Translation Committee, please send a message to ymba@ymba.org. Please include your mailing address in the message. They will inform you by e-mail if the books are available.

SYDA Foundation Prison Project
PO Box 99140
Emeryville, CA 94662

They will mail a correspondence course titled "In Search of Self" to prisoners for **FREE**. Their mission is to improve the state of individuals through the teaching of Siddha Yoga Meditation practices.

Email: PrisonProject@siddhayoga.org
Website: www.siddhayoga.org/SYDA-foundation/prison-project
Phone Number (510) 898-2700 ext 4113

Sylvan Clarke
PO Box 160486
Brooklyn, NY 11216-0486

Lonely? Need a partner? Looking for marriage, friendship, someone to correspond with? This is a worldwide club with members across the world waiting to hear from you. Send $1.00 U.S. or 2 IRC's for application. Join today, be a member for life!

Sylvia Rivera Law Project
147 West 24th St. 5th Floor
NY, NY 10001

Provides **FREE** legal services to transgender and gender nonconforming low-income people and people of color. Only available in NY and surrounding areas.

Phone Number: (212) 337-8550

Task Force on Prisoner Re-Entry
C/O Dept. of Public Safety and Correctional Services
Hampton Plaza, Suite 1000
300 East Joppa Rd.
Towson, MD 21286

Phone Number: (410) 585-3727

Tattoo Flash
Box 3000
Agoura Hills, CA 91376

If you have a pattern that has what it takes, Tattoo Mag would like to see it! Designs can be black and white or color, you decide, but original art only please. Every full page design pays $75, and the smaller designs pay $25. Send your drawings.

Teachers and Writers Corroborative
520 8th Ave., suite 2020
New York, NY 10018

This organization publishes a number of books on writing, which are filled with ideas and exercises. Write to request a catalog.

Website: twc.org.

Tele-pal.com

Tired of waiting on pen pals? Talk to a phone pal! Why write when you can call? We have a phone pal for you and it's more affordable than ever.

Phone Number: (719) 297-1909

Tenacious V. Law
PO Box 20388
New York, NY 10009

A zine (2-3 issues/year) of writings and art formally and currently incarcerated women. **FREE** to women (including trans women) in prison. Men in prison are asked to send 2 stamps (or $1 check or money order made out to V. Law).

Ten Men Dead

Relies on secret IRA documents and letters smuggled out from IRA political prisoners during their 1981 hunger strike at the Infamous Long Kesh prison in Belfast, where 10 men starved themselves to death. Written by David Beresford.

Texas Civil Rights Project
AUSTIN
1405 Montopolis Drive
Austin, TX 78741-3438

Phone: (512) 474-5073
tcrp.questions@gmail.com

Texas Innocence Network
University of Houston Law Center
100 Law Center
Houston, TX 77204

T.F.L.

I DO NOT RECOMMEND DOING BUSINESS WITH THIS COMPANY!

The Action Committee For Women In Prison
769 Northwestern Drive
Claremont, CA 91711

Advocates for humane treatment of incarcerated women.

Phone Number: (626)-710-7543
Website: www.acwip.net.

The Beat Within
POB 34310
San Francisco, CA 94134

Below, you'll find information/guidelines for publishing with The Beat Within we want you to be aware of. Please be sure to include your complete mailing address, including your DOC number.

We accept submissions of the following kind:

- Poems (2-4 per submission)
- Short stories (up to 3 pages)
- Original song lyrics
- Essays (up to 3 pages)
- Inspirational letters
- Stream of consciousness
- Artwork
- Excerpt of your book (select and provide 2-3 pages for a "sneak peek")

Also:

- Consider the content of your work before submitting as a large portion of our readers are minors.

- The Beat Within will not publish sexual, racist, or hateful language.

- Artwork containing any aspect of the numbers 3, 4, 13 and 14 will not be printed. If your character has 3 buttons, give him 2 or 5, 3 feathers changed to 6, etc. The Beat MUST remain neutral for our youth. Artwork containing these numbers may be subject to
- modification or not published at all.

- Write as clearly and legibly as possible, and include your name and mailing address at the bottom of your submission, or on the back for artwork.

- If published, your work becomes property of The Beat Within, but you're free to publish elsewhere.

- You'll receive recognition under your desired name. Make the name clearly known.

- There's no fee to submit.

- If published, you will receive a FREE copy of the magazine your work is in. Please be sure to include your complete mailing address, clearly.

- Publication is not guaranteed. Publication can take 1-4 months; short pieces have better chances of being published first.

- Do not plagiarize. Copying work that is not your own without quoting and referencing the writer is illegal, and we won't publish work that is not original.

Thanks. We look forward to receiving your submissions!

The Other Death Penalty Project
PO Box 1486
Lancaster, CA 93584

They provide materials to assist you and your imprisoned loved ones in your advocacy efforts to urge elected officials and others in positions of power to end life without parole sentences.

Website: info@theotherdeathpenalty.org

The Prison Mirror
 c/o Pat Pawlak
970 Pickett Street North
Bayport, MN 55003-1490

The Prison Mirror is published monthly by and for the men of the Minnesota Stillwater Correctional Facility. Subscriptions are $12. The Prison Mirror was founded in 1887 and is the oldest continuously published prison newspaper in the United States.

Phone Number: 651-779-2700

The Last Resort Innocence Project

Seton Hall University School of Law
One Newark Center
1109 Raymond Boulevard
Newark, New Jersey 07102

Phone Number: 973-642-8500

Thomas M. Cooley Innocence Project
300 S. Capitol Ave. P.O. Box 13038
Lansing, MI 48901

Phone: 517-371-5140

Thomas Merton Center
5129 Penn Avenue
Pittsburgh, PA 15224

They are people from diverse philosophies and faiths who find common ground in the nonviolent struggle to bring about a more peaceful and just world.

Phone Number: 412-361-3022
Website: www.thomasmertoncenter.org 28.

Thomson Reuter's
610 Opperman Dr.
Eagan, MN 55123

They sell books on legal topics. Write for a list.

Thousand Kites
91 Madison Avenue
Whitesburg, KY 41858

Cooperative storytelling project. Send your story to them and they will incorporate it into a performance. Ongoing Project!

Phone Number: 606-633-0108
Website: www.thousandkites.org

Thurgood Marshall School of Law Innocence Project
3100 Cleburne Street
Houston, TX 77004

Phone Number: 713-313-1139

TIC Interests
PO Box 19689
Houston, TX 77224

Tightwad Magazines
PO Box 1941
Buford, GA 30515

They have discount magazine subscriptions. Write/Send SASE for a mini catalog.

Comment: This is my favorite place to order mags from. They are super inexpensive and they accept stamps. The lady who runs it, Julie, is fast and her business is official. - - Mike

Timberwolf Litigation and Research Services, LLC
402 North Wayne Street, Suite B
Angola, Indiana 46703

"You don't have to do it alone!... Run with the pack! Attorneys, paralegals, researchers and consultants dedicated to serving your legal needs. For more info, call 1-855-712-5276 or (260) 243-5649."

Time Magazine
Time & Life Building
Rockefeller Center
New York, NY 10020

TimeZone Gifts, L.L.C.
P.O. Box 41093
Houston, TX 77241

For a **FREE** catalog with over 150 gifts ranging from $2 $12.95 (greeting cards, toys, T-shirts, stuffed animals, Jewelry and more), write them.

Timothy C. Chiang-Lin, PLLC
2155 112th Ave NE
Bellevue, WA 98004

This law office represents all individuals who suffers childhood sex abuse in Washington and Oregon.

Website:chiang-lin.com

Tim's Inmate Mail Service
3301-R Coors Rd NW #247
Albuquerque, NM 87120-1292

"Cheap in-state phone # for 1-time $50 set-up fee. Send SASE.

T.I.P. Journal
Gender Identity Center of Colorado, Inc.,
1151 S Huron St
Denver, CO 80223

Newsletter for transgender prisoners. Write for details.

Transformative Justice Law Project of Illinois
4707 North Broadway, Suite 307
Chicago, IL 60640

Provides legal services to transgender and gender non-conforming people targeted by the criminal legal system; will send resources and provides trainings to outside agencies.

Phone Number: (773) 272-1822

Transitional Housing for Georgia
Po Box 35305
Charlotte, NW 28235

Website: socialserve.com.

Tranzmission Prison Books
P.O. Box 1874
Asheville, NC 28801

Offers **FREE** books and resources. (Queer/Trans. related)

The Threepenny Review
PO Box 9131
Berkeley, CA 94709

1. At present The Threepenny Review is paying $400 per story or article, $200 per poem or Table Talk piece. This payment buys first serial rights in our print and digital editions, and the copyright then reverts to the author immediately upon publication.

2. We do not consider submissions that arrive via email. Everything must be sent either through the regular mail or via our designated online upload system (see www.threepennyreview.com). All mailed manuscripts must include an SASE; those that arrive without as SASE will not receive a reply. Mailed submissions should be sent to 'The Editor's at the above address.

3. We do not print material that has previously been published elsewhere, and we do NOT consider simultaneous submissions. We do our best to offer a quick turnaround time, so please allow us the privilege of sole consideration during that relatively brief period; writers who do not honor this request will not be published in the magazine.

4. Response time for unsolicited manuscripts ranges from one week to two months. Please do not submit more than a single story or article, or more than five poems, until you have heard back from us about your previous submission.

5. All articles should be double-spaced (except poetry, which can be single-spaced or double-spaced)! Critical articles should be about 1500 to 3000 words, stories and memoirs 4000 words or less, and poetry 100 lines or less. Exceptions are possible.

6. Critical articles that deal with books, films, theater performances, art exhibits, etc. should cite these occasions at the front of the article, using the following format:

Book Title
by Author's Name.
Publisher, Year Published, Price (cloth) (paper).

Remember that The Threepenny Review is a quarterly and national (and in some respects international publication), therefore, each 'review' should actually be an essay, broader than the specific event it covers and of interest to people who cannot see the event.

7. Writers will be consulted on all significant editing done on their articles, and will have the opportunity to proofread galleys for typographical errors.

8. It is recommended that those submitting work for the first time to The Threepenny Review take a look at a sample copy beforehand. Sample copies are available from the publisher for $12.00.

9. We do not read manuscripts in the second half of the year (July through December), so please do not submit work during those six months. Anything sent them will be discarded unread. The only two ways to submit work to us are through the mail and via our online system."

Tricycle Magazine: The Buddhist Review
1115 Broadway, Suite 1113
New York, NY 10010

Triune Arts
1804 Bedell Road RR #5
Kemptville, Ontario
Canada K0G 1J0

Educational resource for restorative justice programs; intended to raise public awareness of an alternative to the existing justice system's approach, to provide training and to encourage citizens to participate in community justice programs.

Triune Arts, a non-profit, charitable institution established in 1981, has developed award-winning educational programs on a variety of subjects including: conflict resolution, anti-bullying, restorative justice, cross-cultural communication and inter-cultural conflict, workplace violence prevention, employment training for youth, preventive intervention with preschoolers and international development.

Truman Services
PO Box 236
Baytown, TX 77522

Parole packets. Experienced paralegal. Typing for manuscripts, etc. Send SASE.

Truman State University Press
100 East Normal Avenue
Kirksville, MO 63501-4221

Reviews literary works.

Trump, President Donald
1600 Pennsylvania Ave. NW
Washington, DC 20500

Phone Number: (202) 456-1111

Turning the Tide: Journal of Anti-Racist Action
Research and Education; ARA-LA/PART
PO Box1055
Culver City, CA 90232

This covers the analysis and perspectives of the oppressed in the struggle for liberation and it's **FREE** to prisoners.

Unchained Books
PO Box 784
Fort Collins, CO 80522

Unchained Books is a small group in Fort Collins, Colorado committed to prisoner support. Our primary focus is collecting donated books and making them available **FREE** to people imprisoned in Colorado

Un-Common Law
220 4th St., Suite 201
Oakland, CA 94607

They offer prisoner rights services.

Phone Number: (510) 271-0310.

Under Lock & Key
MIM (Prisons) PO Box 40799
San Francisco, CA 94140

This is a communist-type newsletter for prisoners. It's **FREE**.

Comment: If you're a conscious prisoner and you want to be up on prison politics across the country, this is for you. These are serious comrades. Real talk. - - GURU

Union Supply Direct
Dept. 100, P.O. Box 9018
Rancho Dominguez, CA 90220

This is a package company that sells just about everything -- food, electronics, clothes, CDs, religious items and more.

Comment: In our survey, Union Supply did well with their promo items, timeliness, and did not seem to charge for missing items. They were doing well in the price category until they published their recent catalog in which they seemed to raise their prices across the table. Now they fail in the price category. They also seem to delete or substitute excessively. - - Voices.con Newsletter

Comment: Let me tell you about these grimy muthafuckas. First, last year they advertised all kinds of cheap mixtapes, so everyone rushed to order packages from them just to get new music. Then, when their packages came, nobody got any of the CDs because Union claimed that our prison doesn't allow explicit CDs. Straight bullshit! Then, in their catalog they advertise a layaway program so I had my people put a big - ass package

on layaway. They ended up paying around a hundred dollars on it, then they skipped a month. When they went to pay the remainder, Union Supply told them that the package was forfeited because they didn't pay the monthly minimum - - a detail that they don't advertise. I won't fuck wit' 'em again unless I got a stolen credit card or something. Fuck 'em! - GURU

United Consulting Services
11820 Old Drovers Way
Rockville, MD 20852

We are certified legal specialists in ALL 50 states. We understand being incarcerated is stressful. However, you may have options. Let us find those options. We assist in the following: reduction/modification, transfers, parole issues, restoration of visits, wrongfully convicted, second chance act and more. Send SASE for our brochure!

Phone: 202-417-1239

United Prison Ministries International
890 County Rd 93
P.O. Box 8
Verbena, AL 36091

Prisoners can order two at a time: What the Bible Says, The Desire of Ages, Bible Answers, Bible Questions Answered, God Still answers Prayers and Keys to Happiness.

United Shuttle

California inmate visitors' transportation services.

Phone Number: (818) 504- 0839

University Beyond Bars
PO Box 31525
Seattle, WA 98103

Website: http://universitybeyondbars.org/

University of Baltimore Innocence Project Clinic
1401 N. Charles St.
Baltimore, MD 21201

Phone Number: 410.837.4468

University of North Carolina
The Friday Center

Center for Continuation Education
Chapel Hill, NC 27599

Highly recommended college.

University of Texas Center for Actual Innocence
University of Texas School of Law
727 East Dean Keeton St.
Austin, TX 78705

Upaya Prison Outreach Project
1404 Cerro Gordo Rd.
Santa Fe, NM 87501

Upper Iowa University
External Degree Program
P.O. Box 1861
Fayette, IA 52142-1861

Highly recommended college.

Urbana-Champagne Books to Prisoners Project
PO Box 515
Urbana, IL 61803

Sends various books to state & federal prisoners in Illinois. Has large selection of novels.

Phone Number: (217) 344-8820.
Website: books2prisoners.org

Comment: "Before I started writing books, when I didn't have money, I used these guys to get all kinds of books. Especially when I was in Seg. If you're in Illinois and don't have funds to order books, write to them and request books by topic/genre. TMP endorsed!" - - Josh Kruger, author of The Millionaire Prisoner

USA TODAY
7950 Jones Branch Dr.
McLean, VA 22108

This is one of the best newspapers you can get. Subscription rates: 13 wks, $65; 26 wks, $130; 52 wks, $260.

U.S. Dept. of Justice
950 Pennsylvania Ave., NW
Washington, DC 20530

The attorney general is Eric Holder.

Phone Number: (202) 353-1555.

U.S. Small Business Association
409 3rd St, SW
Washington, DC 20416

Write for **FREE** information.

USA Song Writing Contest
2881 E. Oakland Park Blvd., Suite 414
Ft. Lauderdale, FL 33306

Song writers, write for **FREE** details.

Website: songwriting.net.

UVP
PO Box 110620
Jamaica, NY 11411-0620

"UVP is your source for non-nude photo sets of beautiful Black and Latina girls. We have exclusive photos of models, strippers, and your regular girl next door. All photos are only available in high quality 4X6 prints. All photo sets contain 10 photos of the model shown in various non-nude poses. The price for each photo set of 10 photos is $12.00 which includes **FREE** shipping. Each photo set is mailed in a separate envelope. Mall orders with checks or money orders are payable to the above company/address. If photos are being shipped to correctional facilities, please be advised we are not responsible for merchandise that is rejected by correctional institutions. Order at your own risk. In the event merchandise has to be reshipped, you will be required to pay an additional $5 s/h charge. There are no refunds. Please allow 1-3 weeks for delivery. Your friends and family can order photos for you quickly from our website."

We also offer "grab bags" of sexy random girls (sorry, you cannot pick models) at the following prices:

Set GB10 (10 photos) $12
Set GB 20 (20 photos) $20
Set GB 30 (30 photos) $28
Set GB 40 (40 photos) $36

Website: picmate.net

Comment: Fine bitches in stripper outfits. Reminds me of the hoes I was around before coming to prison. Ah... The good ol' days. - Mike

Valley Bible Fellowship
PO Box 6266
Bakersfield, CA 93217

This is a church.

Comment: They'll send you a FREE bible, Daily Bread and a correspondence course. If you send for their correspondence course they'll send you 2 stamped envelopes for each time you complete an assignment, thus paying you to participate.
- - GURU

VFC (Voice Freedom Calls)
2442 NW Market Street #612
Seattle, WA 98107

"VFC is a voice message system just like ones you have used on the outside. When you sign up, you get your own personal phone number In any US area code you choose. Friends and family call your personal number and leave voice messages and listen to voice messages from you. Inmates call their personal number and listen to messages, send messages, and place return calls to anyone that has left a message. When you send voice messages, we send a text with your phone number. It's easy for friends to tell when you have called. You use your regular prison phones to call into the system --that part cannot be avoided. But once you have called into your number, you can send multiple voice messages and place multiple return calls from a single connect -- you are not limited to calling a single person. VFC works with all major prison and Jail telecom providers: GTL, Securus, and others. VFC is available in State, County, and local jail facilities. VFC cannot be used in federal institutions. The charge for using VFC is $4.95/month, plus $2.50 per message and $1.50 per minute. These charges are in addition to what you pay the institution for making an outgoing call. Send SASE for more info, or get your own personal message number now, in less than 5 minutes by calling (603) 821-9535."

Villa Entertainment Company, Inc
14173 NW Freeway, Ste. 203
Houston, TX 77040

"Like the beautiful women on the pages of StreetSeen Magazine and the car shows we attend? Order 4X6 glossy Photos of them! $12 for 10 photos of random 4X6 glossy premium non-nude photos of car show hotties. Add $1 for each additional photo you want. Add $2 s/h for each envelope you need to have your pictures sent in. We are not responsible for rejected pictures!

product...

Car show hotties photo catalog now available. Filled with over 800 photos of the sexiest REAL girls in the car show scene. LOTS of back shots! Only $7.99 + $3 s/h! We will add 10 sexy sample photos for an extra $5!

Corrlinks: StreetSeen@ymail.com
Phone: 713-465-9599

The Vitamin Outlet
PO 2073
104 Evans Ave.
Sinking Spring, PA 19608

We provide top quality fitness systems "Sports Edge" products and other lines of vitamins and supplements at wholesale and discount prices. Serving customers worldwide since 1985, The Vitamin Outlet offers only the best 100 percent natural supplements at substantial
savings and convenient delivery. We are sure you will be especially pleased without exclusive "Sports Edge" supplement line due to its unsurpassed quality at wholesale and discount prices."

Phone: 1-800-967-1827
Email: vitaminout@aol.com

Voices.con Newsletter
PO Box 361
King City, CA 93930

The Voices.Con Newsletter is written exclusively by term-to-life prisoners, unless otherwise noted, focusing on issues of primary concern to those serving a long-tern incarceration: The newsletter is published monthly at the VoicesDotCon.org website. This information has been designed to be of potential benefit in any jurisdiction having term-to-life prisoners and is made available to any other supportive family and friends as well. No persons affiliated with the Voices.Con newsletter are lawyers. Information provided herein is not intended as a substitute for proper legal advice. All questions or comments on information contained herein should be directed to Janet@VoicesDotCon.org.

Suggested Guidelines for Submissions:

1. We have only one agenda; advocating on behalf of the term-to-life prisoner and distributing information that will further this cause, enabling the term-to-life prisoner to effectively advocate on his or her own behalf.
2. You may write an essay/article on any related subject or issue of concern to the term-to-life prisoner population.
3. We prefer that all submissions be between 250 and 500 words. Please clearly print or type all submitted material.
4. We also accept and encourage all submissions of topical artwork. Please include a SASE with any submissions of artwork or written material where a return has been requested.

Website: VoicesDotCon.org
Email: Publisher@VoicesDotCon.org

Wahida Clark Presents Publishing

134 Evergreen Place; Suite 305, Dept. DD
East Orange, NJ 07018

Wahida Clark, the Queen of "Thug Love" fiction, writes, sells, and publishes urban books.

Phone Number: (973) 678-9982
Website: wclarkpublishing.com.

WaitingPenPals.com

PO Box 24592
Fort Lauderdale, FL 33307

Send a SASE for information on their pen pal service.

Walkenhorst's

445 Ingenuity Ave
Sparks, NV 89441

This prison package company sells tons of items; food, clothing, shoes, electronics, cosmetics, CDs, and more. Write and ask for their **FREE** color catalog.

Phone Number: (800) 660-9255
Website walkenhorsts.com.

Walk In Those Shoes

c/o Kimberly Carter
POB 70092
Henrico, VA 23255

The United States is the most incarcerated country on the planet. Housed in our prisons are some people who have committed heinous crimes. Also, hundreds there are the mentally
ill; the innocent; those not yet charged; the addicted; the young and reckless; those raised in poverty by addicted parents; those whose only role models were drug dealers; those who had court appointed legal representation with a backlog of cases; those caught up in mandatory minimums; those whose parents were incarcerated before them; and those who were charged as young adults who, two and three decades later, are no longer the people they were when they entered. They've grown up and fully matured. They've changed their lives for the better, but they are serving life sentences and will never be given another chance.

We can do better. Walk In Those Shoes is about compassion and opening the door to creative solutions. While supporting creative writing and reading, we can also shed light on issues that could be improved. Acknowledging there is work to be done is the starting point for change, and giving those on the inside a platform to start the discussion not only benefits them, but also readers. Raising awareness goes hand in hand with literacy here.

It's through struggle we find our strength and although some will visit the site and get angry about the crimes represented here, it's the hope more will see past that to the potential and also gain an understanding of what can go wrong when the system doesn't work as it should.

Our Purpose...

Compassion and mercy are a great place to start repairing our prison 'system'. Walk In Those Shoes is here to promote empathy through the writing and experiences of those caught up in it.
There is an entire world behind walls and inside courtrooms that is too often misunderstood and never experienced. Things can go wrong and when they do, families pay the price, sometimes for generations.

A talented, motivated attorney is a bright light and can be an advocate. An unethical attorney can ruin countless lives during the course of a career.

A fair-minded judge can see through drama -- a courtroom is more than half drama -- and find the truth. A racist judge can ruin countless lives during a career.

A fair sentence and treatment can get a life on track. An overzealous prosecutor with no interest in truth can ruin countless lives during a career.

A prison that's designed to allow growth, through structure, rules and opportunities can give children a better version of their parents. A prison run by the 'good ole boys club', with little training and a loathing for those that reside there can ruin countless lives along with their families during their existence.

Change starts with awareness, and Walk In Those Shoes aims to encourage incarcerated writers to share their experiences while achieving literary goals.

When possible, Walk In Those Shoes will advocate for those suffering injustice.

Contact Us...

If you are currently or formerly incarcerated, are a family member of someone who is incarcerated, or care about mass incarceration in this country, we'd love to hear your thoughts.

Views From The Inside is exclusively for the writing of those in prison. Submissions most likely to be posted are those that are thought provoking and make us feel. What is most
often rejected is work that is polarizing and confrontational. Our goal is to communicate the issues in a way that lends itself to producing positive change and revealing the limitless potential behind bars.

We often post writing that helps the reader get a picture of life behind bars, everything from getting laundry done, to loneliness, to relations with staff and cell mates. Submissions
that share stories of life prior to incarceration are also considered, if they help to reflect the heart of the person who is incarcerated, or describe how they may have gotten on a path
to prison.

Please do not submit previously published material. Submissions are always accepted and cannot be returned. We consider a submission permission to edit and post. Length is very flexible, although 1,500 words or less is a typical post. Handwritten submissions are accepted.

Poetry is considered.

We also work with a handful of writers in achieving their goal of book publishing. There are always several book projects going on at one time with very limited resources, so if time is of the essence this would not be a good option.

We are building a 'library' of books written from behind bars. Write me or send me a sample of your work at the above address.

As stated above, we occasionally work with book authors of all genres in all aspects of completing their work. If you would like assistance making your story a reality, feel free to submit a chapter to the above address. We will get back to you as soon as possible if we can assist you. We hope to encourage writers to achieve their goals.

Comment: Walk In Those Shoes and Views From The Inside is ran by author Kim Carter. It's a fantastic opportunity for any author looking to get published and start getting their name out there to the folks who like to read writings from prisoners. - - Mike

Wall Periodicals
PO Box 2584
Plainfield, NJ 07060-0584

"Largest urban wholesaler in the USA."

Magazines: Don Diva, Bottles & Modelz, Bully Girl, FEDS, Assets, AS IS, Phat Puffs, Body, Hip-Hop Weekly, Urban ink, IAdore, Repect, Street Elements, UHM and many more!

Books: Dynasty series; Dipped Up; 100 Years of Lynching; Thug Lovin'; Thug Matrimony; Trust No Man; Trust No Bitch; The Cartel series; Murderville; Murda Mamas; and many, many more!

Send SASE for a **FREE** catalog. For easy ordering and more titles visit their website.

Phone Number: 718-819-1693 or 866-756-1370

Website: wallperiodicalsonline.com

Watchtower
25 Columbia Heights
Brooklyn, NY 11201

This is the Jehovah Witness Headquarters. They'll send you **FREE** biblical material.

weshippics.com
PO 280036
Houston, TX 77228

Have your family send you pics by uploading them from their cell phones to our website.

Send SASE to request any book or magazine. Best prices available!

Wesleyan Innocence Project
1515 Commerce St.
Fort Worth, TX 76102

West
PO Box 64833
St. Paul, MN 55164

They publish many legal books. Write for a full list.

Phone Number: (800) 328-9352.

West Virginia Innocence Project
West Virginia University
College of Law
P.O. Box 6130
Morgantown, WV 26506

Phone: 304-293-7249

Who Want What?
POB 18499
Philadelphia, PA 19120

Picture catalogs are full color, non-nude, double sided, and $3 each, $1 for each additional catalog. Catalogs include: Backshots 1, 2; Ebony Adult Screen Shot Queens 1, 2; Vanilla Vixens, and more. Send SASE for info.

Email: whowantwhat806@yahoo.com

Why Islam
PO Box 1054
Piscataway, NJ 08855

This is a non-profit organization that provides Islamic literature.

William L. Schmidt
Attorney at Law
P.O. Box 25001
Fresno, CA 93729

Legal services for California inmates: Appeals; Write of Habeas Corpus; Civil Rights Litigation; Catastrophic Injury/Excessive Force; Money Management; Gang Issues; Transfers.
Our clients go home, how about you?
Please submit a single page summary of your case. Due to the volume, we cannot return documents or respond to all inquiries. We are NOT a low cost or pro bono law firm, but if you want results, write us.

Email: 911civilrights@gmail.com

Windham School District
Mailing: P.O. Box 40
Physical: 804 Bldg. B, FM 2821 West
Huntsville, TX 77320

Phone: (936) 291-5300
Website: http://www.windhamschooldistrict.org

Winning Habeas Corpus and Post-Conviction Relief, 4th edition

Cases cited through 638 F.3d. Claims to be the best book for prisoners who are researching post-conviction relief and Ineffective Assistance of Counsel. Includes a virtual law library in a single book, actual case quotes; habeas procedures and prac. 2254, 2255 &rule 60(b); sixth amendment & IAC, pretrial duty to investigate; recognized defenses; over 1500 cited cases and more! This book is over 620 pages, $58.50, and available from Fast Law Publishing Associates.

Winning Writ Writers
PO Box 848
Richmond Hill, GA 31324

A writ writing team with a record of wins against the U.S. Send SASE for details and other services offered.

Phone Number: (229) 344-3838

Wire Of Hope (East Coast)
POB 7717
Jacksonville, FL 32238

Wire Of Hope (West Coast)
2000 Vassar St. #10731
Reno, NV 89510

Ready to make friends? Create a profile on Wire of Hope for only $30 a year! W0H is the newest, most modern prison pen-pal ad site, run by 2 women engaged in prison reform for years. Send SASE for **FREE** brochure!

Website: WireofHope.com

Wisconsin Innocence Project- Shaken Baby Syndrome
University of Wisconsin Madison
Attn: Lindsey Smith
975 Bascom Mall
Madison, WI 53706-1399

With Liberty for Some: 500 Years of Imprisonment in America

The best overall history of the American prison system from 1492 through the 20th Century. Well written and fact filled. A must-read for understanding how little things have changed as far as prisons go in the U.S. over hundreds of years. This book is 372 pages, $18.95, and can be bought from Prison Legal News.

Women and Prison: A Site for Resistance

The Women and Prison project is a website, installation and zine created entirely from the work and lives of America's incarcerated women.

Website: http://womenandprison.org

Women's Prison Association
110 Second Avenue
New York, NY 10003

Women's Prison Book Project
c/o Boneshaker Books
2002 23rd Ave South
Minneapolis, MN 55404

This program is for women prisoners only.

Word of Life Christian Ministry
PO Box 2164
Rockwall, TX 75087

This is a **FREE** Christian newsletter. They also send puzzles and bible verses to study.

Word Out Books
PO 2689
Eugene, OR 97402

Word Out Books, an imprint of Winding Hall Publishers, is based on a straightforward principle:

Writers deserve to be heard. We make it possible for writers of all genres, and from all backgrounds and circumstances, to become published authors.

When your book is published by Word Out Books, it is not "self-published" -- it is published by a real publishing company under the Word Out imprint.

By charging fair, transparent fees up front, Word Out Books allows authors whose works might otherwise never be published to see their books in print and made available to the world.

How It Works

Our range of services includes publishing your manuscript in book form and making it available for sale in print and e-book on Amazon and other online outlets, as well as editing and cover design services. When you submit your original manuscript by mail or email, an editor will read your manuscript and contact you with the services we offer based on your submission. Some services, such as typing a manuscript that was submitted handwritten, or scanning a typed manuscript, will be required in order for us to publish your book. Other services, such as copy editing and premium book cover design, are optional. We also offer typing, editing and book cover design as individually priced services.

Services and Fees

Required Services and Fees: In order to publish your book, we must have payment up front for all required and selected optional services. We accept installment payments, but will not begin work on your project until all payment is received.

Required services include: Publishing Service -- $335

Our Publishing Service includes the following:

1. Registering your work with the United States Copyright Office. (You keep all copyright ownership of your work. Word Out Books is granted exclusive publication rights.)
2. Book cover with text only (no images)
3. ISBN -- Every book sold commercially must have an International Standard Book Number assigned to it. Each edition and version of a book -- for examples, an e-book and a paperback edition of the same book -- must have it's own ISBN. Single ISBNs cost $125, but our publishing company buys at volume discounts to save you money. We will assign ISBNs to the print (paperback) and ebook versions of your book.
4. Formatting and setup of your book in both paperback and ebook versions.
5. Setup and management of sales on Arnazon.com, the largest bookseller in the world, and other online outlets.
6. One free copy of your book shipped to your address.
7. Marketing for your book through social media, plus outstanding customer support.

Typing or Scanning Services: Unless your manuscript is submitted via email, it will either need to be typed (if handwritten) or scanned (if submitted typed). You will need to pay either the typing or scanning per-page fees (not both):

Typing -- $2.50 per page:

We understand that not every author has access to word processing or typing equipment. Word Out Books is happy to accept handwritten manuscripts, provided they can easily be read. If we cannot read your handwriting, we may ask that you re-submit the manuscript printed by hand in block, capital letters. Please write clearly. If we can't read it, we can't publish it!

Scanning -- $1.00 per page:

All typed manuscript pages submitted as a-hard copy (not by email) will need to be scanned into our computer system. Pages should be free of any stray marks, smudges or handwritten notes as these will not scan properly. If the scanned document results in too many errors, there will be an extra $1/page charge to manually correct errors, which must be paid before publication starts.

Optional Services and Fees: The following services are optional and are charged in addition to the required fees listed above. Professional editing and an eye-catching cover will make your work much more desirable to the reading public.

Editing

All books, even works by best-selling authors published by the largest publishing houses, require editing to be marketable. You can choose which level of editing you want for your work. Editing fees are added to the per-page typing or scanning rates above.

Proofreading Edit -- $2 per submitted typed of handwritten page: Corrects basic punctuation, spelling, and capitalization errors.

Copy Edit -- $4 per submitted typed or hand-written page: In addition to basic editing, our Copy-Editing Service corrects grammar and syntax mistakes, notes inconsistencies, and provides other suggestions to improve the quality of writing. You can review our editing suggestions and accept or reject them prior to publication. We strongly urge you to consider copy editing if you plan to sell your book to the public.

Book Cover Design

Color, Text and Simple Graphic $75
Premium Full Graphic $125

Royalties

Word Out Books will set the price at which your book is sold ("list price"). Royalties are based on a percentage of the book's selling price and will vary, depending upon the length of the book, whether it is a print or ebook, and other factors. Royalties are paid quarterly. You will receive a royalty statement showing how many copies were sold and the rate at which your royalties were calculated. We will pay royalties by check to the name and address specified by you.

How To Get Started

1. Send us a copy* of your manuscript.
2. Include any additional comments, questions or information you'd like us to have.

VERY IMPORTANT: Please be sure you do not send us the only copy of your manuscript! Manuscripts cannot be returned, regardless of whether we ultimately publish them!

What We Will Do

Once we have received your manuscript, we will contact you regarding the publication services we are able to offer you and enclose a form for you to complete with the services you are requesting. Rarely, we must decline to publish a manuscript, usually because it violates one of our publication policies.

Word Out Books does not publish the following:

- Books that advocate the commission of crimes or incitement to commit crimes
- Books that could be considered libelous
- Books designed to allow a person convicted of a crime to profit from that crime
- Other books which, in our exclusive editorial judgement, violate the ethical principles of our company
- Invoicing

When we accept your manuscript for publication, we will send you an invoice requesting payment for the services you have chosen. Payment may be made by check, bank draft, or money order. We do not accept credit card payment or cash.

We will not begin work until all requested services have been paid. After publication work has begun, fees are non-refundable. If you wish to cancel publication or other services you've ordered, please contact us within 10 business days of payment, so that we can process your refund.

Please Note: If we do not receive your payment or a request for additional time for payment within 90 days of our receipt of your manuscript, we will assume the project is a no-go and will destroy the manuscript without further obligation to the author. We cannot keep unpaid manuscripts indefinitely. Again, please do not send us the only
copy of your work!

Please let us know if you have any questions regarding our services or fees. We're always happy to answer your questions. We want to help you get your word out to the world with Word Our Books!

Website: WordOutBooks.com
Email: Editor@WordOutBooks.com

Worker's Vanguard
PO Box 1377 GPO
NY, NY 10116

This is a communist newspaper.

Comment: Straight up, they real about they work. They even have a fund dedicated to class-struggle prisoners like Mumia and others and they put money on their books. This is a good publication for the conscious-minded prisoner. - - GURU

Wow Me Web Designs
PO 7879
Flint, MI 48507

Hello Everyone,
I've been getting hundreds of letters and I want to apologize if you did not get a response in a timely manner. I have been very busy and could not handle all of the orders on my own. In July, 2018 I hired two web designers and two graphic designers to help me with the heavy work load. My new employees are just as skilled as I am and I have entrusted them to produce high quality work and service on behalf of my company. I hope the following helps with any questions you have about our services. Thank you. Jazzie, at Wow Me Web Design

ONE PAGE WEBSITE -- $109.99

Our one-page websites are for businesses that just want to get their name out and are working with a small budget. Direct your clients to your website to learn more about your business, what products or services you sell, make an online donation/payment, or contact you with questions.

This package includes:

- Basic Company Logo
- Contact Information
- Payments/Donations Button
- Image Banner/Slider
- Social Media Links
- List of Services
- 3 Images

THREE PAGE WEBSITES -- $299.99

Our three-page websites will give you all the same functions as above, but we put your services and contact information on its own separate page. In addition, you get 3 blogs, 8 photos, 1 video, and add your social media feed.

This package includes:

- Basic Company Logo
- Contact Information
- 3 Blogs
- Social Media Feed Image Banner/Slider Social Media Links
- 8 Photos For Gallery Payments/Donations Button
- List of Services 6 Images
- 1 Video

The above packages are great for: Authors/Books, Stores with 3 products or less, Personal Sites, Donation Sites, Small Businesses, Consulting, Landing Page, Blogs, Informational Sites, Artist, Small Non-Profit, Marketing, Activist, Resource Site, Small Law Office, Small Medical Practices

PREMIUM WEBSITE PACKAGES -- $549.99 (Payment Plan Accepted)

Our premium websites are for non-profits and businesses with a wide range of products and services.

This package includes: (Choose Your 10 Pages)

- Home
- About
- Contact
- Payments
- Donate
- Events
- 3 Blog
- Sermons
- 7 Video Gallery
- 10 Photo Gallery
- Services
- Resources
- Testimonials
- Shop (3 Product Limit)
- Music mp3
- Informational Page
- Coupon Page

Includes Add-Ons:

- Basic Company Logo
- Contact Information
- Social Media Feed
- Image Banner/Slider
- Social Media Links
- Customer Chat Box

- List of Services
- 10 Images
- Email Capturer Box

E-COMMERCE / ONLINE STORE PACKAGES (Payment Plan Accepted)

Our full ecommerce sites start at $749.99. Get everything included in the premium package, with an addition to 35 products/pages installed and shipping and credit/debit card processing.

ADD-ONS

- Business Email Address, $12.99/year
- Extra Pages, $49.99
- Social Media Account Setup, $29.99
- Custom Logo, $79.99 Flyers, $69.99
- Banners, $69.99
- Business Cards, $39.99
- Brochure Tr-Fold, $79.99
- Online Chat Box, $79.99
- Small 3-5 Product Store, $149.99
- Email Capture Box, $59.99
- Large Posters, $79.99
- Bookmarks, $14.99
- Postcards, $69.99
- Google Business Number, $19.99
- Google Business Page Setup, $29.99
- Book Covers Basic, $69.99
- Book Covers Custom, $149.99
- Domain Names, $10.99/year
- Website Hosting, $10.99/month
- Ecommerce Website Hosting, $24.99/month (or pay by the year)
- Google Analytics -- Track your website interactions, $79.99
- Google Adsense Setup -- Make money selling ad space on your website from Google.
- Get 10,000 views on your website a month and Google will pay you $500-$800/month. $129.99/year
- Live Video or Audio Website Feed. Set up Facebook, Podcast, or YouTube. $79.99
- Social Media Management -- Monthly service. Cancel anytime. Add friends, get messages mailed or emailed to you weekly. $39.99/month

- 30 Second Advertising Commercials, $79.99

- SEO: Starting at $499/month. Request personal quote.

COMMON QUESTIONS

What is social media feed? Anything you post on social media such as Facebook will also appear on your website.

How do I make payments? Pay by check, money order, paypal, or our website.

When will I receive my login information? All login and account information will be mailed or emailed to you after payment is received in full.

Can I update my website? Yes. After your website is paid in full, you will receive instruction on how to keep it updated.

What are your update fees? If you prefer for us to keep your website updated (change wording, videos, pictures, etc.), fees range from $35-$400/month. Maintenance and Security updates are free.

How long to complete graphic work? All graphic work can take 1-3 days to complete, such as flyers, business cards, and brochures.

Can I get a picture of my site or graphic work? Yes. Please send a SASE for a color copy.

Will my website or graphic work be customized? Yes. All of our work is customized and tailored to fit the customer's vision.

What if I already have a logo? Please email your logo to contact@wowmewebdesigns.com.

What if I've already purchased a domain and/or hosting? We only use GoDaddy, but if you have a hosting or domain account, please mail or email us the company's name, web address, with your user name and password and we will build your site using that account.

Are your websites mobile ready? Yes. All our sites are mobile ready with up-to-date browser standards.

Down payment options? If your website or graphic is over $500, you may pay 50 percent down and the remaining balance after completion.

Do you print graphics? No, we are a design company, but we do have a printing company that we partner with for special orders. We offer 500 printed fliers for $30. Please send request with SASE.

When will you start my project? As soon as your payment is received. Do you do special requests? Yes. Please send request with SASE.

Can you add to our site later? Yes. You can add different plugins and extra pages at any time.
How long will my site take? Estimated completion times are 2-3 days for a 1-page site; 3-5 days for a 3-page site; 2-3 weeks for a 10-page site; 4-8 weeks for an ecommerce site.

Website: wowmewebdesigns.com
Email/Corrlinks: contact@wowmewebdesigns.com
Phone: 347-618-9116

Comment: I found my web designer on fiverr.com. A guy in Pakistan. These prices here don't sound too bad, actually, especially for being in America. If you don't have someone on the outside to find you a web guru on fiverr.com, these guys might be the way to go. Keep in mind though; these days, social media profiles will about allow you all you need to do what you probably want to do, IF you have someone to run it for you. However, a site will give you credibility that social media doesn't, if that's important to you. — Mike

WriteAPrisoner.com
PO Box 10
Edgewater, FL 32132

"We understand the loneliness incarceration can bring... There are other who understand as well. Thousands of people from all walks of life come to our website every day in search of pen pals. They are looking for friendship; they are prepared to offer support; they want to provide encouragement; and they understand the loneliness. If outside companionship could improve your quality of life while incarcerated, join WriteAPrisoner.com. We're dedicated to reducing recidivism. The first step is connecting you with those who understand.

Thousands of people who are interested in corresponding with inmates visit our site each day. Our site is easily accessed from all Internet connected devices including cell phones and is translated into 51 languages to attract overseas visitors as well. We advertise non-stop on all major search engines and receive millions of page views monthly. We've been seen on MSNBC's Lockup, Dr. Phil, CNN, Women's Entertainment, The Ney York Times, Washington Post, Boston Globe, O Magazine, and many, many more places. Place your pen-pal profile today and start making new friends!"

A one-year profile (250 words and 1 picture) is $65. You can add an additional photo or piece of artwork for $10 each. Each additional 50 words is $5. You can add a bio entry for $15 (250 words). Each additional 50 words is $5. You can pay for your profile via institutional check, money order or credit card. If you'd like to pay with postage stamps, request their Stamp Payment Guidelines/Prices first by sending them a SASE. For a **FREE** copy of their brochure with all the profile details, send SASE.

WriteAPrisoner.com Stamp Guidelines/Prices

"When we accept stamps as payment, it prohibits us from utilizing lower bulk mail rates; therefore, prices are slightly higher when paying with stamps. The prices and rules are as follows:

1. Stamps must be on sheets or rolls. No more than 10 individual stamps can be accepted.

2. Stamps must not be taped, stapled or adhered together.

3. Stamps must be an acceptable form of payment from your institution. If your institution prohibits using stamps as currency, we cannot accept them from you.

4. Only Forever stamps can be used as payment.

5. Stamps will not be accepted if they are removed from their original sheets and placed on new ones.

Profile Price List in Stamps...

Standard one-year profile: 115 Forever stamps.
Additional photo/artwork: 30 Forever stamps.
Additional words: 15 Forever stamps for each additional 50 words.
Text change: 30 Forever stamps.
Photo change: 30 Forever stamps for 1 photo.
Additional photo/artwork: 30 Forever stamps.
Additional words: 15 Forever stamps for each additional 50 words.
Standard profile renewal: 90 Forever stamps.
Blogs: 45 Forever stamps for 1 250-word blog.
Poetry: 45 Forever stamps for 250 words.

Send SASE and request 'Stamp Payment Guidelines' for further details."

Comment: "Still my favorite go-to website when I want to get some fresh pan pals. I recently used WAP in 2019-2020 and got a few college girls to write me, plus lots of cards during the C-19 pandemic. I've always been pleased with my results on WAP. After reading my book, Pan Pal Success, my friend Skylar used them and now has totaled 48 pen pal hits! Plain and simple, of you use this site and don't get any pen pals, it's because your photo sucks, or your profile sucks, or both. Write A Prisoner is legit! TMP endorsed and recommended!" - - Josh Kruger, author of The Millionaire Prisoner

Writers' Digest
4700 E. Galbraith Rd
Cincinnati, OH 45236

This magazine covers everything in regards to helping you write and or get published. It's $19.96 for a 1-year subscription, 6 issues per year. To contact Writer's Digest editorial, please e-mail: writersdigest@fwmedia.com

(Note: Due to the high volume of e-mails received, we are unable to answer all questions or requests.)

For query submissions, please e-mail: wdsubmissions@fwmedia.com;(Note: Allow 8-12 weeks for a response.)

For questions regarding Writer's Digest Competitions, contact Writer's Digest Competitions at (715) 445-4612 x13430.

For questions about our monthly Your Story Contest, please email YourStoryContest@fwmedia.com.

Phone Number: (513) 531-2222
Website: writersdigest.com.

Comment: "Every writer, especially incarcerated writers, needs a subscription to this magazine! TMP endorsed." - - Josh Kruger, author of The Millionaire Prisoner

Writer's Guild of America – East
555 West 57th St., Suite 1230
New York, NY 10019

This is an organization of professional writers and agents.

Website: wgaeast.org.

Writer's Guild of America – West
7000 West 3rd St.
Los Angeles, CA 90048

This is an organization of professional writers and agents.

Website: wga.org.

Writing to Win: The Legal Writer

Explains the writing of effective complaints, responses, briefs, motions and other legal pleadings. This book is 283 pages, $19.95, and can be bought from Prison Legal News.

Writesomeoneinprison.com; Nubian Princess Ent.
POB 37
Timmonsville, SC 29161

This is a good pen pal service. They accept stamps. Send SASE for more information.

Writetoinmates.com
5729 Main St., # 362
Springfield, OR 97478

Pen pal website.

Wrongful Conviction Clinic Indiana University School of Law
530 W. New York Street, Rm. 111
Indianapolis, IN 46202-3225

Cases Accepted: cases of actual innocence in Indiana; DNA and non- DNA cases (preference for DNA cases); will consider arson, shaken baby syndrome, and child abuse cases.

Phone Number: 317-274-5551

Wrongful Conviction Project
Office of the Ohio Public Defender
250 East Broad Street, Suite 1400
Columbus, OH 43215

Phone Number: 614-466-5394
Website: opd.ohio.gov/DP_WrongfulConviction…

The Wrongful Death Institute

The Institute conducts research on a multitude of issues within each of its departments. It performs case analysis on wrongful death and forensic science issues, and aggressively pursues issues of prison medical malpractice and negligence nationwide. The common denominator of all divisions is accountability and responsibility of those individuals who perform duties that involve the public trust. The Institute implements the team approach. All of our efforts are directed toward factually and efficiently applying investigative and scientific evidence to law.

Phone Number: (816) 941-0087

Wynword Press
P.O. Box 557
Bonners Ferry, ID 83805

They offer the book "Battling the Administration: An Inmates Guide to a Successful Lawsuit."

Phone Number: 208-267-0817

Ynot Books & More Bookstore
PO Box 574
Redan, GA 30074

This company sells urban books and magazines, as well as playing cards, stationary, and a few other things. Send SASE for flier.

Comment: This company was around a few years ago then fell off. It looks like now they're back. I've never ordered from them, but their prices are really good.

They sell urban books for only $11.00, but they have a bunch of other books, too. They'll also get you books that are not in their catalog. Write these guys and tell them to carry all the books by Mike Enemigo and The Cell Block. - - Mike

ATTENTION DIRECTORY READERS!

Be aware that running a for-prisoner business is difficult, and many people get into this line of business with good intentions, only to learn they've gotten in over their heads.

Because of this, for-prisoner companies tend to come and go rather quickly. Some may hang in there for a year or two, while others only last a couple of months. This causes the addresses in a for-prisoner resource directory, such as the one in your hands now, to expire. I cannot control this. I personally write the majority of the companies listed in this book once a year. When prisoners from around the country notify me of a company that's gone out of business, I try to make the adjustment as soon as I can. I try to update this Directory, according to the info I gather, a couple times, throughout the year.

That said, this Directory, as any other, will not remain fresh for long. In order to stay up to date on all the latest and greatest for-prisoner companies, it is recommended that you buy a copy of this Directory once a year. If you're using a Directory that's older than a year, don't be surprised when you get a lot of Return To Senders. It's not my fault. It's the nature of the come-and-go, for-prisoner business.

To show appreciation for your business and support, if you buy your Directory directly from us at The Cell Block, we will have your name/info on file. When you buy your next copy, mention this notice and we will give you 10% off. If you buy our Directory once or more a year, mention this notice and get 20% off your next Directory.

As promised, we truly are The BEST Resource Directory For Prisoners.

Sincerely,

Mike
The Cell Block

ATTENTION INMATES!

Have an experience with any of the listed companies? Good or bad, write and tell us all about it!

THE CELL BLOCK

RE: Comments/Reviews

PO Box 1025; Rancho Cordova, CA 95741

BBB
FOR PRISONERS

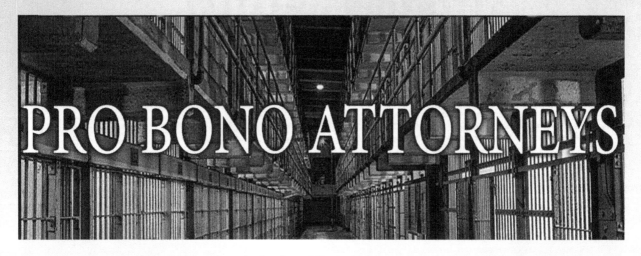

PRO BONO ATTORNEYS

Find lawyers who are willing to work "for the public good" (the meaning of *pro bono*). These law firms or organizations may be willing to work for free or for a reduced rate depending on the circumstances. Contact the closest office for more information.

Alaska Disability Law Center
3330 Arctic Blvd., Suite 103
Anchorage, AK 99501

Phone Number: (907) 565-1002

Alaska Network on Domestic Violence and Sexual Assault
130 Seward Street, #214
Juneau, AK 99801

Phone Number: (888) 520-2666

Alaska Immigration Justice Project
431 West 7th Avenue, Suite 208
Anchorage, AK 99501

Phone Number: (907) 279-2457

Alaska Pro Bono Program
P.O. Box 140191
Anchorage, AK 99514-0191

Legal Services Corporation of Alabama, Inc.
Tuscaloosa Regional Office

1351 McFarland Blvd. E, 11th Floor
Tuscaloosa, AL 35404

Phone Number: (205) 758-7503

Alabama State Bar Volunteer Lawyers Program
415 Dexter Avenue
Montgomery, AL 36104
334-269-1515

Alabama Equal Justice Initiative

122 Commerce Street
Montgomery, AL 36104

Phone Number: (334) 269-1803

Ozark Legal Services Pro Bono Project
4083 N. Shiloh Drive, Suite 3
Fayetteville, AR 72703

Phone Number: (501) 442-0600

Arkansas Volunteer Lawyers for the Elderly
2020 W 3rd Street, Suite 620
Little Rock, AR 72205

Phone Number (501) 376-9263

Legal Services of Arkansas
615 West Markham Street, Suite 200
Little Rock, AR 72201

Phone Number: (501) 376-8015

Arizona Justice for Children
P.O. Box 45500
Phoenix, AZ 85064

Phone Number: (602) 235-9300

AIDS Project Arizona
1427 N. 3rd Street
Phoenix, AZ 85004

Phone Number: (602) 253-2437

HIV/AIDS Law Project
303 E. Palm Lane
Phoenix, AZ 85004

Phone Number: (602) 258-3434

Arizona Federal Public Defender's Office
222 N Central Avenue, Suite 810
Phoenix, AZ 85004

Phone Number: (602) 379-3670

California Center for Capital Assistance
529 Castro Street
San Francisco, CA 94114

Phone Number: (415) 621-8860

Pro Bono Project
480 N. First Street
San Jose, CA 95112

Phone Number: (408) 998-5298

Bay Area Legal Aid
1735 Telegraph Avenue
Oakland, CA 94612

Phone Number: (510) 663-4755

Asian Pacific Islander Legal Outreach
1121 Mission Street
San Francisco, CA 94103

Phone Number: (415) 567-6255

Southern Colorado AIDS Project
1301 S. 8th Street
Colorado Springs, CO 80903

Phone Number: (719) 578-9092

Northwest Colorado Legal Services
P.O. Box 1904
Leadville, CO 80461
719-486-3238

Heart of the Rockies Bar Association Pro Bono Program
1604 H Street
Salida, CO 81201

Phone Number: (719) 539-4251

Colorado Office of the Public Defender
110 16th Street, Suite 800
Denver, CO 80202

Phone Number: (303) 620-4888

Connecticut Statewide Legal Services
425 Main Street, #2
Middletown, CT 06457-3371

Phone Number: (800) 453-3320

Connecticut Trial Services Unit
1 Hartford Square West
Hartford, CT 06106
203-566-5328

DELAWARE

Delaware State Bar Association Lawyer Referral Service
Wilmington, DE 19803

Phone Number: (800) 773-0606

Delaware Legal Aid Society
913 Washington Street
Wilmington, DE 19801

Phone Number: (302) 575-0660

DISTRICT OF COLUMBIA

Legal Information Help Line
Washington, DC

Phone Number: (202) 626-3499

National Association of Criminal Defense Attorneys
1627 K Street , NW, Suite 1200
Washington, DC 20006

Phone Number: (202) 872-8688 Ext: 224

American Bar Association, Death Penalty Representation Project
740 15th Street NW, Suite 1060
Washington, DC 20005-1009

Phone Number: (202) 662-1995

Domestic Violence Intake
DC Superior Court, 500 Indiana Ave., NW, Room 4235
Washington, DC 20001

Phone Number: (202) 879-0152

FLORIDA

GEORGIA

Georgia Volunteer Lawyers for the Arts
675 Ponce De Leon Ave NE
Atlanta, GA 30308

Phone Number: (404) 873-3911

Georgia Indigent Defense Council
985 Ponce de Leon Avenue
Atlanta, GA 30306

Phone Number: (404) 894-2595

Georgia Resource Center
101 Marietta Tower, Suite 3310
Atlanta, GA 30303

Phone Number: (404) 614-2014

National Association of Criminal Defense Attorneys
83 Poplar Street, NW
Atlanta, GA 30303-2122

Phone Number: (404) 688-1202

State Bar of Georgia Pro Bono Project
104 Marietta Street NW, Suite 100
Atlanta, GA 30303

Phone Number: (404) 527-8700

HAWAII

Volunteer Legal Services Hawai'i
545 Queen Street, Suite 100
Honolulu, HI 96813

Phone Number: (808) 528-7046

Legal Aid Society of Hawaii
1108 Nuuanu Avenue
Honolulu, HI 96817
808-536-4302

IOWA

Iowa Legal Aid
1111 9th Street, Suite 230
Des Moines, IA 50314

Phone Number: (800) 532-1275

Idaho Legal Aid Services
310 North 5th Street
Boise, ID 83701-0913

Phone Number: (208) 336-8980

Idaho Volunteer Lawyers Program
P.O. Box 895
Boise, ID 83701

Phone Number: (800) 221-3295

Center for Disability and Elder Law
79 W. Monroe Street
Chicago, IL 60603

Phone Number: (312) 376-1880

Cabrini Green Legal Aid Clinic
740 N. Milwaukee Ave.
Chicago, IL 60642

Phone Number: (312) 738-2452

Chicago Volunteer Legal Services
100 N. LaSalle Street, Suite 900
Chicago, IL 60602

Phone Number: (312) 332-1624

Chicago Legal Clinic
2938 E. 91st Street
Chicago, IL 60617

Phone Number: (773) 731-1762

Heartland Pro Bono Council
151 N. Delaware Street, Suite 1800
Indianapolis, IN 46204

Phone Number: (317) 614-5304

Indianapolis Legal Aid Society, Inc.
615 North Alabama Street
Indianapolis, IN 46204

Phone Number: (317) 635-9538

Community Development Law Center
1802 N. Illinois Street
Indianapolis, IN 46204

Phone Number: (317) 921-8806

Indiana Legal Services Support
151 North Delaware Street, 18th Floor
Indianapolis, IN 46204

Phone Number: (317) 631-9410

Kansas Legal Services Inc.
712 South Kansas Avenue, Suite 200
Topeka, KS 66603

Phone Number: (913) 223-2068

The Pro Bono Project
615 Baronne Street, Suite 203
New Orleans, LA 70113

Phone Number: (504) 581-4043

Legal Advocacy and Resource Center
Boston, MA

Phone Number: (800) 342-5297

Neighborhood Legal Services
170 Common Street, Suite 300
Lawrence, MA 01840

Phone Number: (978) 686-6900

Neighborhood Legal Services
37 Friend Street
Lynn, MA 01902
781-599-7730

Victim Rights Law Center
115 Broad Street, 3rd Floor
Boston, MA 02110

Phone Number: (617) 399-6720

Bar Association of Baltimore City Legal Services to the Elderly Program
111 North Calvert Street, Suite 631
Baltimore, MD 21202

Phone Number: (410) 396-1322

Civil Justice, Inc.
520 West Fayette Street
Baltimore, MD 21201

Phone Number: (410) 706-0174

Women's Law Center
305 W. Chesapeake Avenue, Suite 201
Towson, MD 21204

Phone Number: (410) 321-8761

Maryland Volunteer Lawyers Service
1 North Charles Street, Suite 222
Baltimore, MD 21201

Phone Number: (800) 510-0050

Main Equal Justice Partners
126 Sewall Street
Augusta, ME 04330

Phone Number: (866) 626-7059 (toll free)

Main Volunteer Lawyers Project
P.O. Box 547
Portland, ME 04112

Phone Number: (800) 442-4293

Michigan Legal Services
220 Bagley Avenue, Suite 900
Detroit, MI 48226

Phone Number: (313) 964-4130

Farmworker Legal Services
420 N. Fourth Avenue
Ann Arbor, MI 48104

Phone Number: (734) 665-6181

Family Law Project
Hutchins Hall, University of Michigan Law School
Ann Arbor, MI 48109

Phone Number: (734) 998-9454

Legal Services of South Central Michigan
420 N. Fourth Avenue
Ann Arbor, MI 48104

Phone Number: (734) 665-6181

Volunteer Attorney Program
314 West Superior Street, Suite 1000
Duluth, MN 55802

Phone Number: (218) 723-4005

St. Cloud Area Legal Services
830 W. St. Germain, Suite 300
St. Cloud, MN 56302

Phone Number: (888) 360-2889

Western Minnesota Legal Services
415 SW 7th Street
Willmar, MN 56201

Phone Number: (888) 360-3666

Legal Aid Society of Minneapolis

430 First Avenue North, Suite 300
Minneapolis, MN 55401-1780

Phone Number: (612) 334-5970

Legal Services of Southern Missouri
1414 East State Route 72
Rolla, MO 65402

Phone Number: (800) 999-0249

Legal Aid of Western Missouri
1125 Gran Blvd., #1900
Kansas City, MO 64106, MO 64106

Phone Number: (816) 474-6750

Legal Services of Eastern Missouri
4232 Forest Park Avenue
St Louis, MO 63108
800-444-0514

North Mississippi Rural Legal Services
5 County Road 1014
Oxford, MS 38655

Phone Number: (800) 498-1804

Mississippi Center for Justice
5 Old River Place, Suite 203
Jackson, MS 39202

Phone Number: (601) 352-2269

Mississippi Volunteer Lawyers Project
P.O. Box 2168
Jackson, MS 39225-2168

Phone Number: (800) 682-6423

Mississippi Legal Services Coalition
775 North President Street, Suite 300
Jackson, MS 39205

Phone Number: (601) 944-0765

North Mississippi Rural Legal Services
5 County Road 1014
Oxford, MS 38655

Phone Number: (800498-1804

Mississippi Center for Justice
5 Old River Place, Suite 203
Jackson, MS 39202

Phone Number: (601) 352-2269

Mississipi Volunteer Lawyers Project
P.O. Box 2168
Jackson, MS 39225-2168

Phone Number: (800) 682-6423

Mississippi Legal Services Coalition
775 North President Street, Suite 300
Jackson, MS 39205

Phone Number: (601) 944-0765

Montana Legal Services Help Line
616 Helena Avenue, Suite 100
Helena, MT 59601

Phone Number: (800) 666-6899

Montana Pro Bono Project
P.O. Box 3093
Billings, MT 59103

Phone Number: (406) 248-7113

Legal Services of Southern Piedmont
1431 Elizabeth Avenue
Charlotte, NC 28204

Phone Number: (800) 438-1254

Pisgah Legal Services
P.O. Box 2276
Asheville, NC 28802

Phone Number: (800) 489-6144

Legal Aid of North Carolina
224 South Dawson Street
Raleigh, NC 27601

Phone Number: (866) 219-5262 (toll free)

North Carolina Legal Services
224 South Dawson Street
Raleigh, NC 27611

Phone Number: (919) 856-2121

North Dakota State Bar Association LRS
515 1/2 E. Broadway
Bismarck, ND 58501-4407

Phone Number: (701) 255-1406

Legal Services of North Dakota
1025 North 3rd Street
Bismark, ND 58502-1893

Phone Number: (800) 634-5263

New Hampshire Pro Bono Referral System
112 Pleasant Street
Concord, NH 03301

Phone Number: (800) 639-5290

New Hampshire Legal Assistance
15 Green Street
Concord, NH 03301

Phone Number: (603) 225-4700

Legal Services of New Jersey
100 Metroplex Drive at Plainfield Avenue
Edison, NJ 08818

Phone Number: (888) 576-5529

Volunteer Lawyers for Justice
P.O. Box 32040
Newark, NJ 07102

Phone Number: (973) 645-1955

Legal Services Of New Jersey
100 Metroplex Drive, Plainfield Avenue, Suite 402
Edison, NJ 08818-1357

Phone Number: (908) 572-9100

Clark County Legal Services
800 S. 8th Street
Las Vegas, NV 89101

Phone Number: (702) 386-1070

Washoe Legal Services
299 South Arlington Avenue
Reno, NV 89501

Phone Number: (775) 329-2727

Volunteer Attorneys for Rural Nevadans
904 N. Nevada Street
Carson City, NV 89703

Phone Number: (866) 448-8276 (toll free)

Legal Aid Center of Southern Nevada
800 S. Eighth Street
Las Vegas, NV 89101

Phone Number: (702) 386-1070

**Albuquerque Bar Association Courthouse
Booth Lawyer Referral Service**
540 Chama Street NE
Albuquerque, NM 87108-2017

Phone Number: (505) 256-0417

State Bar of New Mexico Referral Program
P.O. Box 92860
Albuquerque, NM 87199

Phone Number: (505) 797-6066

New Mexico Legal Aid
P.O. Box 25486
Albuquerque, NM 87104

Phone Number: (505) 243-7871

The Legal Aid Society
175 Remsen Street
Brooklyn, NY 11201

Phone Number: (718) 243-6473

Kids in Need of Defense
767 Fifth Avenue
New York, NY 10153-0119

Phone Number: (646) 728-4104

Legal Services NYC
350 Broadway, 6th Floor
New York, NY 10013

Phone Number: (646) 442-3600

Urban Justice Center
123 William Street 16th Floor
New York, NY 10038

Phone Number: (646) 602-4598

Legal Aid Referral Project (Greater Columbus)
1108 City Park Avenue
Columbus, OH 43206

Phone Number: (614) 224-8374

Volunteer Lawyers Project (Greater Cincinnati)
215 E. Ninth Street, Suite 200
Cincinnati, OH 45202-2122

Phone Number: (531) 241-6800

Legal Aid Society of Cleveland -- Volunteer Lawyers Program
1223 W. Sixth Street
Cleveland, OH 44113

Phone Number: (216) 687-1900

Greater Dayton Volunteer Lawyers Project
109 N. Main Street, Suite 610
Dayton, OH 45402

Phone Number: (937) 461-3857

Tulsa Lawyers for Children, Inc.
P.O. Box 2254
Tulsa, OK 74101-2254

Phone Number: (918) 425-5858

The Senior Law Resource Center, Inc.
P.O. Box 1408
Oklahoma City, OK 73101-1408

Phone Number: (405) 528-0858

Legal Aid Services of Oklahoma, Inc.
2915 North Classen Boulevard, Suite 500
Oklahoma, OK 73106

Phone Number: (405) 557-0020

Oklahoma Alternative Resources
3015 E. Skelly Dr., Suite 385
Tulsa, OK 74105

Phone Number: (918) 742-8883

Marion-Polk Legal Aid
1655 State Street
Salem, Oregon 97301

Phone Number: (503) 581-5265

Lane County Law and Advocacy Center

376 East 11th Avenue
Eugene, Oregon 97401

Phone Number: (541) 485-1017

Center for Non-Profit Legal Services
225 W. Main Street
Medford, Oregon 97501

Phone Number: (541) 779-7291

Legal Aid Services of Oregon
921 SW Washington Street, Suite 500
Portland, Oregon 97205

Phone Number: (888) 610-8764

Neighborhood Legal Services Association
928 Penn Avenue
Pittsburgh, PA 15222-3799

Phone Number: (412) 255-6700

Lackawanna Pro Bono
321 Spruce Street
Scranton, PA 18503

Phone Number: (570)961-2715

Pennsylvania Legal Aid Network
118 Locust Street
Harrisburg, PA 17101

Phone Number: (800) 322-7572

Philadelphia VIP
42 South 15th Street, 4th Floor
Philadelphia, PA 19102

Phone Number: (215) 523-9550

Rhode Island Bar Association Volunteer Lawyer Program

115 Cedar Street
Providence, RI 02903-1082

Phone Number: (401) 421-7799

Rhode Island Legal Services
56 Pine Street, 4th Floor
Providence, RI 02903

Phone Number: (401) 274-2652

South Carolina Legal Services - Charleston
2803 Carner Avenue
Charleston, SC 29405

Phone Number: (843) 720-70441

Low Country Legal Aid, Inc.
167-A Bluffton Road
Bluffton, SC 29910

South Carolina Legal Services -- Beaufort
69 Robert Smalls Parkway, Suite 3-A
Beaufort, SC 29902

Phone Number: (843) 521-0623

South Carolina Legal Services - Columbia
2109 Bull Street
Columbia, SC 29201

Phone Number: (803) 799-9668

Second Judicial Circuit Pro Bono Project
335 N. Main Avenue
Sioux Falls, SD 57104

Phone Number: (605) 336-9230

East River Legal Services
335 North Main Avenue, Suite 300
Sioux Falls, SD 57102

Phone Number: (605) 336-9230

Nashville Pro Bono Program
300 Deaderick Street
Nashville, TN 37201

Phone Number: (615) 244-6610

Tennessee Alliance for Legal Services
50 Vantage Way, Suite 250
Nashville, TN 37228

Phone Number: (888) 395-9297

Lone Star Legal Aid
1415 Fannin Street
Houston, TX 77002

Phone Number: (800) 733-8394

Texas RioGrande Legal Aid
17 Sunny Glen
Alpine, TX 79830

Phone Number: (432) 837-1199

Legal Aid of Northwest Texas
Dallas, TX

Phone Number: (800) 529-5277

Disability Law Center
205 North 4th West
Salt Lake City, UT 84103-1125

Phone Number: (801) 363-1347

Legal Aid Society of Utah
450 South State Street
Salt Lake City, UT 84111-3101

Phone Number: (801) 238-7170

Utah Legal Services Inc.

254 West 4th Street, 2nd Floor
Salt Lake City, UT 84101

Phone Number: (801) 328-8891

Virginia Poverty Law Center
201 West Broad Street, Suite 302
Richmond, VA 23220

Phone Number: (804) 782-9430

Virginia Legal Aid Society, Inc.
513 Church Street
Lynchburg, VA 24504

Phone Number: (866) 534-5243

Southwest Virginia Legal Aid Society
227 W. Cherry Street
Marion, VA 24354

Phone Number: (800) 277-6754

Rappahannock Legal Services, Inc.
618 Kenmore Avenue, Suite 1-A
Fredericksburg, VA 22401

Phone Number: (540) 371-1105

Legal Services Law Line of Vermont Volunteer Lawyer's Project
274 North Winooski Avenue
Burlington, VT 05401

Phone Number: (802) 863-7153

Vermont Legal Aid Inc.
PO Box 1367, 12 North Street
Burlington, VT 05401

Phone Number: (802) 863-5620

Jefferson-Clallam County Pro Bono Lawyers
816 East 8th Street
Port Angeles, WA 98362

Phone Number: (360) 417-0818

Evergreen Legal Services
101 Yesler Way, Suite 300
Seattle, WA 98104

Phone Number: (206) 464-5933

Wisconsin Judicare, Inc.
300 Third Street, Suite 210
Wausau, WI 54403

Phone Number: (800) 472-1638

Legal Action of Wisconsin
230 West Wells Street, Room 800
Milwaukee, WI 53203

Phone Number: (414) 278-7722

Legal Aid of West Virginia - Charleston Office

922 Quarrier Street, 4th Floor
Charleston, WV 25301

Phone Number: (866) 255-4370

West Virginia Legal Service Plan
1003 Quarrier Street, Suite 700
Charleston, WV 25301

Phone Number: (304) 342-6814

Legal Aid of Wyoming, Inc.
211 West 19th Street, Suite 300
Cheyenne, WY 82001

Phone Number: (877) 432-9955 (toll free)

Wind River Legal Services Inc. - Southeast Wyoming Branch
1603 Capitol Avenue, Suite 405
Cheyenne, WY 82001

Phone Number: (307) 634-1566

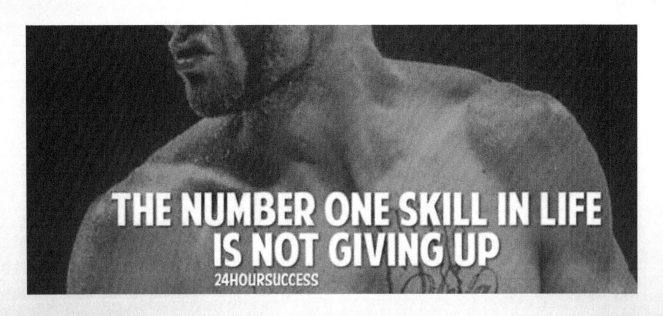

PRISON LEGAL GUIDE

The Facts You Need To Succeed In The Judicial Arena

THIS BOOK IS A "MUST HAVE" SURVIVAL TOOL THAT EVERY INMATE NEEDS! KNOW YOUR CIVIL RIGHTS AND THE PROCEDURES THAT CAN BRING YOU THE WIN!

U.S. law is complex, complicated, and always growing and changing, and many prisoners spend days on end digging through its intricacies. Pile on top of the legal code the rules and regulations of a correctional facility, and you can see how well the deck is being stacked against you. Information is the key to your survival when you have run afoul of the system (or it is running afoul of you). Whether you are an accomplished jailhouse lawyer helping newbies learn the ropes, an old head fighting bare-knuckle for your rights in the courts, or an inmate just looking to beat the latest write-up – this book has something for you. Freebird Publishers has drawn from the best legal offerings of the Lewisburg Prison Project, to put together this comprehensive guide to your legal rights. With this information in hand, you are well equipped to beat the charge or fight back against the persecution.

There are many of us out here on your side. Never give up the fight.

FREEBIRD PUBLISHERS presents

PRISON LEGAL GUIDE

Retold by MIKE ENEMIGO
Producer of The Cell Block

The Facts You Need to Succeed in the Judicial Arena

LEARN ABOUT

- Litigation
- First Amendment
- Status
- Due Process In Prison
- Cruel and Unusual Punishment
- Medical Care
- Post Conviction

Civil Action in Federal Court, Legal Research, Access Records, Federal Tort Claims Act, Injunctive Relief, Religious Rights in Prison, Speech, Visitations, Association, Rights of Pre-trial Detainees, Disciplinary Hearings, Urinalysis Drug Testing, Assault and Beatings, Conditions of Confinement, Medical Rights, Psychiatric and Disability Rights, AIDS in Prison, Post-Conviction Remedies, Detainers (Choices and Strategies), PA Megan Law, DNA Collection and Testing and more.

BOOK PUBLISHERS

Looking for a publisher to help you publish that book you worked so hard on and finally finished? Well, here's a list of some who may be interested in working with you. Remember, you always want to send a publisher a query letter asking their specific guidelines and instructions, along with a SASE, before you submit anything!

Affluent Publishing Corporation
1040 Avenues of the Americas, 24 Floor
New York, NY 10018

Contact JB Hamilton, editor
(Mainstream/Contemporary), or I. Smushkin, editor (Suspense/ Mystery).

Alondra Press, LLC
4119 Wildacres Dr.
Houston, TX 77072

Contact Pennelope Leight, Fiction editor.

Angoor Press, LLC
2734 Bruchez Parkway, Unit 103
Denver, CO 80234

Contact Carolina Maine, founder and editor.

Arkham Bridge Publishing
PO Box 2346
Everett, WA 98213

Contact James Davis, senior editor.

Arsenal Pulp Press
#101-211 East Georgia Street
Vancouver, BC V6A 126,
Canada

Contact Editorial Board.

Arte Publico Press
University of Houston

452 Collen Proformance Hall
Houston, TX 77204;2004

Contact Nicolas Kanellos. Looking for works by "Hispanics."

Backbeat Books
Hal Leonard Publishing Group
33 Plymouth St., Suite 302
Montclair, NJ 07042

Contact Mike Edison, senior editor

Bancroft Press
PO Box 65360
Baltimore, MD 21209-9945

Contact Bruce Bortz, editor and publisher.

Barricade Books, Inc.
185 Bridge Plaza N. Suite 309
Fort Lee, NJ 07024

Contact Carole Stuart, publisher.

Black Mountain Press
109 Roberts
Ashville, NC 28801

Contact James Robiningski, editor.

Black Rose Writing
PO Box 1540
Castroville, TX 78009

Contact Reagan Rothe.

Bluebridge, Imprint of United Tribes Media, Inc.
PO Box 601
New York, NY 10536

Contact Jan-Erik Guerth, publisher.

The Blumer Literary Agency
Olivia ("Liv") Blumer
350 Seventh Avenue, Suite 2003
New York, NY 10001

This is a publishing agency. Write/Send SASE for more information. Ask for submission guidelines. Specify what kind of book you are interested in submitting – fiction, non-fiction, etc.

Phone Number: 212-947-3040,
Fax 212-947-0460

Borealis Press, LTD.
8 Mohawk Crescent
Napean, ON K2H 7G6
Canada

Branden Publishing Co., Inc.
PO Box 812094
Wellesley, MA 02482

Contact Adolph Caso, editor.

Broken Jaw Press
Box 596, STN A
Frederiction NB E3B 5A6
Canada

By Light Unseen Media
PO Box 1233
Pepperell, MA 01463

Contact Inanna Arthen, owner and editor in chief.

Camino Books, Inc.
PO Box 59026
Philadelphia, PA 19102

Contact E. Jutkowitz, publisher.

Center One Publishing
PO Box 651
Kingsley, MI 49649

Contact Ann Dine, acquisitions editor; Justin Dine, publisher.

Coffee House Press

79 13th NE, Suite 110
Minneapolis, MN 55413
Contact Chris Fischbach, associate publisher.

Cricket Books
Imprint of Carus Publishing
70 E. Lake St., Suite 300
Chicago, IL 60601

Contact Submissions Editor.

Daniel & Daniel Publishers, Inc.
PO Box 2790
McKinleyville, CA 95519

Contact John Daniel, Publisher.

Daw Books, Inc.
Penguin Group (USA)
375 Hudson St.
New York, NY 10014-3658

Contact Peter Stampfel, submissions editor.

Diskus Publishing
PO Box 43
Albany, IN 47320

Contact Holly Janey, Submissions Editor.

Divertir
PO Box 232
North Salem, NH 03073

Contact Dr. Kenneth Tupper, publisher

The Ecco Press
10 E. 53rd St.
New York, NY 10022

Contact Daniel Halpern, editor-in-chief

Elohi Gadugi / The Habit of Rainy Night Press
900 NE 81st Ave., #209
Portland, OR 97213

Contact Patricia McLean, nonficton editor; Duane Poncy, fiction editor.

Faber & Faber LTD
3 Queen Square
London WC1N
3AU United Kingdom

Contact Lee Brackstone, Hannah Griffiths, and/or Angus Cargill for fiction.

Farrar, Straus & Giroux
175 Fifth Ave.
New York, NY 10010

Contact Margaret Ferguson, editorial director.

First Edition Design Publishing
5202 Old Ashwood Drive
Saratosa, FL 34233

Contact Deborah E. Gordon, executive editor.

Flying Pen Press, LLC
1660 Niagara St.
Denver, CO 80228
Contact David A. Rozansky, publisher

Gambit Publishing
1725 W. Glenlake Ave. #1W
Chicago, IL 60660

Contact Gail Glaser, editor.

Gauthier Publications, Inc.
Frog Legs Ink
PO Box 806241
Saint Clair Shores, MI 48080

Contact Elizabeth Gauthier, creative director.

Genesis Press, Inc.
PO Box 101
Columbus, MS 39701

Contact "Editor."

The Glencannon Press
PO Box 1428
El Cerrito, CA 94530

Contact Bill Harris

Grey Gecko Press
565 S. Mason Rd., Suite 154
Katy, TX 77450

Contact Hilary Comfory, editor-in-chief.

Hawk Publishing Group
7107 S. Yale Ave., #345
Tulsa, OK 74136

Contact "Editor."

Homa & Sekey Books
PO Box 103

Dumont, NJ 07628

Contact Shawn Ye, editor.

Ilium Press
2407 S. Sonora Dr.
Spokane, WA 99037-9011

Contact John Lemon, owner and editor.

Insomniac Press
520 Princess Ave.
London ON N6B 2B8
Canada

Contact Mike O'Connor, publisher; Gillian Urbankiewicz, assistant editor.

Interlink Publishing Group, Ink.
46 Crosby St.
Northampton, MA 01060

Contact Michel Moushabeck, publisher; Pam Thompson, editor.

Martin Sisters Publishing, LLC
PO Box 1749
Barbourville, KY 40906-1499

Conatct Denise Melton, publisher and editor; Melissa Newman, publisher and editor.

Mondial
203 W. 107th St., Suite 6C
New York, NY 10025

Contact Andrew Moore, editor.

Nortia Press
27525 Puerta Real, Ste. 100-467
Mission Viejo, CA 92701

Contact "Editor."

Oak Tree Press
140 E. Palmer
Taylorvolle, IL 625n8

Contact Billie Johnson, publisher; Sarah Wasson, acquisitions editor.

Obrake Books
Obrake Canada, Inc.
3401 Dufferin Street
PO Box 27538

Toronto, ON M6A 3B8
Canada

Contact Echez Godoy, acquisitions editor.

Ooligan Press
PO Box 751
Portland, OR 97207

Contact "Editor."

Outrider Press, Inc.
2036 North Winds Dr.
Dyer, IN 46311

Contact Whitney Scott, editor.

Palari Publishing
PO Box 9288
Richmond, VA 23227

Contact David Smitherman, publisher and editor.

Philomel Books
Imprint of Penguin Group, Inc. (USA)
375 Hudson St.
New York, NY 10014

Contact Michael Green, president and publisher.

Polychrome Publishing Corp.
4509 N. Francisco
Chicago, IL 60625

Contact "Editor."

Red Hen Press
PO Box 3537
Granada Hills, CA 91394

Contact Mark E. Cull, publisher and editor.

SoHo Press, Inc.
853 Broadway
New York, NY 10003

Contact Bronwen Hruska, publisher; Katie
Herman, editor; Mark Doten, editor.

Spout Press
PO Box 581067
Minneapolis, MN 55458

Contact Carrie Eidem, fiction editor.

Sunburry Press, Inc.
2200 Market Street
Camp Hill, PA 17011

Contact "Editor."

Swan Isle Press
PO Box 408790
Chicago, IL 60640

Contact "Editor."

Third World Press
c/o Tia Chucha's Centro Cultural
13197-A Gladstone Blvd.
Sylmar, CA 91342

Contact Luis Rodriguez, director.

Tightrope Books
602 Maskham Street
Toronto, ON M6G 2L8
Canada

Contact Shirarose Wilensky, editor.

To Read Aloud Publishing, Inc.
PO Box 632426
Nacogdoches, TX 75963

Contact Michael Powell, president.

Tokyo Rose Records / Chapultepec Press
4222 Chambers
Cincinnati, OH 45223

Contact David Garza.

Unlimited Publishing, LLC
PO Box 99
Nashville, IN 47448

Contact "Editor."

War Child Publishing
PO Box 4897
Culver City, CA 90231

Contact Marci Baun, editor-in-chief.

Wrod Warriors Press
930 Blackoaks Ln.
Anoka, MN 55303

Contact Gail Cerridwen, managing editor.

Zoland Books, Steerforth Press
45 Lyme Rd., Suite 208
Hanover, NH 03755

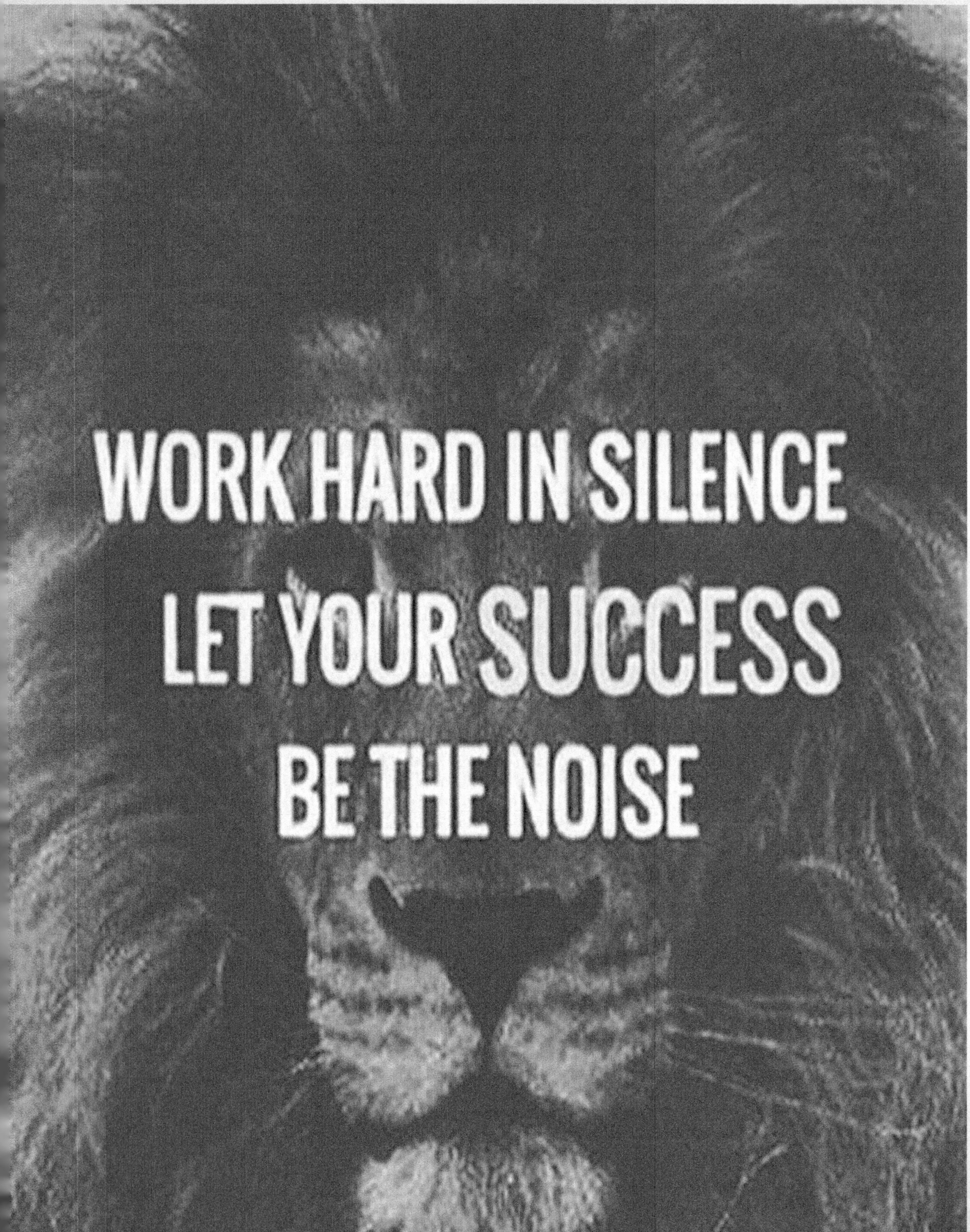
WORK HARD IN SILENCE
LET YOUR SUCCESS
BE THE NOISE

LITERARY AGENTS

Don't want to approach a publisher yourself and would rather a literary agent negotiate a deal for you? Try your luck with one of the following. As always, I suggest sending a query letter to get specific instructions before sending your entire book.

Alive Communications, Inc.
7680 Goddard Street, Suite 200
Colorado Springs, CO 80920

Contact Rick Christian. Represents fiction and nonfiction. Fiction areas: adventure, contemporary issues, crime, family saga, historical, inspirational, literary, mainstream, mystery, police, religious, satire, suspense, thriller.

Betsy Amster Literary Enterprises
6312 SW Capitol Hwy #503
Portland, OR 97239

Contact Betsy Amster. Represents fiction and nonfiction. Fiction areas: ethnic, literary, women's issues, high quality.

B.J. Robbins Literary Agency
5130 Bellaire Ave.
North Hollywood, CA 91607-2908

Contact B.J. Robbins or Amy Maldonado. Represents fiction and nonfiction. Fiction areas: crime, detective, ethnic, literary, mainstream, mystery, police, sports, suspense, thriller.

Bookends, LLC
136 Long Hill Road
Gillette, NJ 07933

Contact Kim Lionetti, Jessica Alverez, Lauren Ruth. Represents fiction and nonfiction. Fiction areas: detective, cozies, mainstream, mystery, romance, thrillers, women's.

Briar Cliff Review

3303 Rebecca St.
PO Box 2100
Sioux City, IA 51104

Write/Send SASE for more information

Browne & Miller Literary Associates
410 S. Michigan Ave., Suite 460
Chicago, IL 60605-1465

Contact Danielle Egan-Miller. Represents nonfiction books, most genres of commercial adult fiction and nonfiction, and young adult projects. Fiction areas: contemporary issues, crime, detective, erotica, ethnic, family saga, glitz, historical, inspirational, literary, mainstream, mystery, police, religious, romance, sports, suspense, thriller, paranormal.

Castiglia Literary Agency
1155 Camino Del Mar, Suite 510
Delmar, CA 92014

Contact Julie Castiglia or Winifren Golden. Represents fiction and nonfiction. Fiction areas: contemporary issues, ethnic, literary, mainstream, mystery, suspense, women's.

Concho River Review
Angelo State University, ASU Station
PO Box 10894
San Angels, TX 76909.

Reviews literary works.

Defiore & Co.

47 E. 19th Street, 3rd Floor
New York, NY 10003

Contact Lauren Gilchrist. Represents nonfiction books and novels. Fiction areas: ethnic, literary, mainstream, mystery, suspense, thriller.

Diana Finch Literary Agency
116 W. 23rd Street, Suite 500
New York, NY 10011

Contact Diana Finch. Represents nonfiction books, novels and scholarly. Fiction areas: action, adventure, ethnic, historical, literary, mainstream, police, thriller, young adult.

Dunham Literary, Inc.
156 Fifth Ave., Suite 625
New York, NY 10010-7002

Dystel & Godrich Literary Management
1 Union Square W., Suite 904
New York, NY 10003

Contact Michael Bourret or Jim McCarth. Represents nonfiction books, novels and cookbooks. Fiction areas: action, adventure, crime, detective, ethnic, family saga, gay, lesbian, literary mainstream, mystery, suspense, thriller, police.

The Evan Marshall Agency
6 Tristam Place
Pine Brook, NJ 07058-9445

Contact Evan Marshall. Fiction areas: action, adventure, erotica, ethnic, frontier, historical, horror, humor, inspirational, literary, mainstream, mystery, religious, satire, sci-fi, suspense, western, romance (contemporary, gothic, historical, regency).

Fineprint Literary Management
240 West 35th St., Suite 500
New York, NY 10001

Contact Peter Rubie. Represents nonfiction books and novels. Fiction areas: crime, detective, want, women's,

Jeany Naggar Literary Agency. Inc.
216 E. 75th Street, Suite lE
New York, NY 10021

Contact Jean Naggar. Represents nonfiction books and novels. Fiction areas: action,

adventure, crime, detective, ethnic, family saga, feminist, historical, literary, mainstream, mystery, police, psychic, supernatural, suspense, thriller.

Jodie Rhodes Literary Agency
8840 Villa La Jolla Dr., Suite 315
La Jolla, CA 92037-1957

Contact Jodie Rhodes. Represents nonfiction books and novels. Fiction areas: ethnic, family saga, historical, literary, mainstream, mystery, suspense, thriller, women's, young adult.

The Joy Harris Literary Agency, Inc.
381 Park Avenue S., Suite 428
New York, NY 10016

Contact Joy Harris. Represents nonfiction books, novels and young adult. Fiction areas: ethnic, experimental, family saga, feminist, gay, glitz, hi-Io, historical, humor, lesbian, literary, mainstream, multicultural, multimedia, mystery, regional, satire, short story collections, spiritual, suspense, translation, women's, young adult.

Loretta Barrett Books, Inc.
220 E. 23rd Street, 11th Floor
New York, NY 10010

Contact Loretta A. Barrett, Nick Mullendore and/or gabriel Davis.

Represents nonfiction books and novels. Fiction areas: contemporary, psychic, adventure, detective, ethnic, family, historical, literary, mainstream, mystery, thriller, young adult.

Lowenstein Associates, Inc.
121 W. 27th Street, Suite 601
New York, NY 10001

Contact Barbara Lowenstein. Represents nonfiction books and novels. Fiction areas: crime, detective, erotica, ethnic, fantasy, feminist, historical, literary, mainstream, mystery, police, romance, suspense, thriller, young adult.

Mendel Media Group, LLC
115 W. 30th Street, Suite 800
New York, NY 10001

Represents nonfiction books, novels, scholarly with potential for broad/popular appeal. Fiction areas: action, adventure, contemporary issues, crime, detective, erotica, ethnic, feminist, gay, glitz, historical, humor, inspirational, juvenile, lesbian, literary, mainstream, mystery, picture books, police, religious, romance, satire, sports, thriller, young adults, Jewish, etc.

Michael Larsen/Elizabeth Pomada, Literary Agents
1029 Jones Street
San Francisco, CA 94109-5023

Contact Mike Larsen and/or Elizabeth Pomada. Represents nonfiction books and novels. Fiction areas: action, adventure, contemporary issues, crime, detective, ethnic, experimental, family saga, feminist, gay, glitz, historical, humor, inspirational, lesbian, literary, mainstream, mystery, police, religious, romance, satire, suspense, chick lit.

Philip G. Spitzer Literary Agency, Inc.
50 Talmage Farm Lane
East Hampton, NY 11937

Contact Luc Hunt. Represents nonfiction books and novels. Fiction areas: crime, detective, literary, mainstream, mystery, police, sports, suspense, thriller.

Richard Henshaw Group
22 West 23rd Street, 5th Floor
New York, NY 10010

Contact Rich Henshaw. Represents nonfiction books and novels. Fiction areas: ethnic, experimental, family saga, feminist, gay, glitz, hi-lo, crime, detective, historical, humor, literary, mainstream, mystery, police, psychic, romance, satire, sci-fi, sports, supernatural, suspense, thriller.

RLR Associates, LTD
Literary Department
7 W. 51st Street
New York, NY 10019

Contact Scott Gould. Represents nonfiction books, novels, short story collections and scholarly. Fiction areas: action, adventure, cartoon, comic books, crime, detective, ethnic, experimental, family saga, feminist, gay, historical, horror, humor, lesbian, literary, mainstream, multicultural, mystery, police, satire, sports, suspense.

Robin Straus Agency, Inc.
229 E. 79th Street, Suite 5A
New York, NY 10075

Contact Ms. Robin Straus. Represents high-quality adult fiction and nonfiction, including literary and commercial fiction, narrative fiction, women's fiction, memoirs, history, bios, books on psychology, pop culture and current affairs, science, parenting and cookbooks.

Rosalie Siegel
International Literary Agency, Inc.
1 Abey Drive
Pennington, NJ 08534

Contact Rosalie Siegel. Represents nonfiction books, novels and short story collections.

Russell & Volkening
50 W. 29th Street, Suite 7E
New York, NY 10001

Contact Jessica Salky. Represents nonfiction books and novels. Fiction areas: action, adventure, crime, detective, ethnic, literary, mainstream, mystery, picture books, police, sports, suspense, thriller.

Sandra Dijkstra Literary Agency
1155 Camino Del Mar
PMB 515
Del Mar, CA 92014

Contact Sandra Dijkstra. Represents nonfiction books and novels. Fiction areas: erotica, ethnic, fantasy, juvenile, literary, mainstream, mystery, picture books, sci-fi, suspense, thriller, graphic novel.

Sanford J. Greenburger Associates, Inc.
55 Fifth Ave.
New York, NY 10003

Contact Heide Lange, Faith Hamlin and/or Dan Mandel. Represents nonfiction books and novels. Fiction areas: action, adventure, crime, detective, ethnic, family saga, feminist, gay, glitz, historical, humor, lesbian, literary, mainstream, mystery, police, psychic, regional, satire, sports, super national, suspense, thriller.

Sheree Bykofsky Associates, Inc.

PO Box 706
Brigantine, NJ 08203

Contact Sheree Bykofsky. Represents nonfiction books and novels. Fiction areas: contemporary issues, literary, mainstream, mystery, suspense.

Trident Media Group
41 Madison Ave., 36th Floor
New York, NY 10010

Contact Ellen Levine. Represents nonfiction books, novels, short story collections and juvenile. Fiction areas: crime, detective, humor, juvenile , literary, military, multicultural, mystery., police, short story collections, suspense, thriller, women's, young adult.

Veritas Literary Agency
601 Van Ness Ave., Opera Plaza, Suite E.
San Francisco, CA 94102

Contact Katherine Boyle. Represents nonfiction books and novels. Fiction areas: commercial, fantasy, literary, mystery, sci-fi, young adult.

Victoria Sanders & Associates
241 Avenue of the Americas, Suite 11 H
New York, NY 10014

Contact Victoria Sanders and/or Diane Dickenshied. Represents nonfiction books and novels. Fiction areas: action, adventure, contemporary issues, ethnic, family saga, feminist, gay, lesbian, literary, thriller.

The Wendy Weil Agency, Inc.
232 Madison Ave., Suite 1300
New York, NY 10016

Contact Wendy Weil. Represents fiction and nonfiction: literary, commercial fiction, mystery, thriller, memoir, history, current affairs, pop culture.

WM Clark Associates
186 Fifth Ave., Second Floor
New York, NY 10010

Represents nonfiction and fiction. Fiction areas: contemporary issues, ethnic, historical, literary, mainstream, southern fiction.

Writers House

21 W. 26th Street
New York, NY 10010

Contact Michael Mejias. Represents nonfiction books, novels and juvenile. Fiction areas: adventure, cartoon, contemporary issues, crime, detective, erotica, ethnic, family saga, fantasy, feminist, frontier, gay, hi 10, historical, horror, humor, juvenile, literary, mainstream, military, multicultural, mystery, new age, occult, police, psychic, regional, romance, thriller, war, young adult.

LITERARY PUBS/REVIEWS

If you are a writer/poet, you want to be published as much as possible in order to build your name. At first you may have to give it away, but there are many publications that offer to pay for your work.

Several of the following pubs/reviews offer to buy poetry and or prose. As always, before submitting anything to them, I suggest you send a query letter to specify exactly what they want. Good luck!

African American Review
Saint Louis University
Adorjan Hall 317
3800 Lindell Boulevard
St. Louis, MO 63108

As a quarterly journal, AAR promotes a lively exchange among writers and scholars in the arts and humanities who hold diverse perspectives on African American literature, art, and culture.

AGNI Magazine
Boston University
236 Bay State Road
Boston, MA 02215

Reviews literary work.

Website: agni@bu.edu

Alaska Quarterly Review
University of Alaska Anchorage
3211 Providence Drive
Anchorage, Alaska 99508

Reviews literary work.

Alligator Juniper
Prescott College
220 Grove Ave
Prescott, AZ 86301

Reviews literary work.

American Literary Review
P.O. Box 311307
University of North Texas
Denton, TX 76203-1307

Reviews literary work.

The American Scholar
1606 New Hampshire Avenue NW
Washington, D.C. 20009

Phone Number: (202) 265-3808
Website: scholar@pbk.org

The Antioch Review
P.O. Box 148
Yellow Springs, OH 45387
Reviews literary works.
Phone Number: 937-769-1365

Apalachee Review
P.O. Box 10469
Tallahassee, Florida 32302

Reviews literary works. The latest issue of Apalachee Review is available for $8.00. Back issues may be purchased for $5.00 each.

Arc Poetry Magazine
PO Box 81060
Ottawa, Ontario
Canada, K1P 1B1

Arion
621 Commonwealth Ave 4th Floor
Boston, MA 02215

A journal of humanities and the classics.

Arkansas Review
 P.O. Box 1890
State University, AR 72467.

A year's subscription (three issues) costs $20.
Make checks payable to "ASU Foundation" with
"Arkansas Review" on the memo line.

Ascent; English Dept.
Concordia College
901 Eight St.
Moorhead, MN 56562

The Awakening Review
5 Forest Hill Dr. Suite 201
Glen Ellyn, IL 60137

Reviews literary works.

Baffler
PO Box 378293
Chicago, IL 60637

The Bayou Review
One Main St.
Houston, TX 77002

Reviews literary works.

**Bellevue Literary Review NYU Dept of
Medicine**
550 First Avenue, OBV-A612
New York, New York 10016 US

Reviews literary works.

Bellingham Review
MS—9053
Western Washington University
Bellingham, WA 98225

Reviews literary works.

Bellowing Ark
PO Box 55564
Shoreline, WA 98155

Beloit Poetry Journal
PO Box 151

Farmington, ME 04938

The Bitter Oleander
4983 Tall Oaks Drive
Fayetteville, NY 13066

This is a magazine of contemporary international
poetry and short fiction.

Blackbird
Dept. of English Virginia Commonwealth
University
PO Box 843082
Richmond, VA 23284

Blue Mesa Review
MCS 03-2170
1 University of New Mexico
Dept. Of English/Hum 217
Albuquerque, NM 87131

Reviews literary works.

Boston Review
Building E 53 Room 407 MIT
Cambridge, MA 02139

Reviews literary works.

Brilliance Corners
Lycoming College
700 College Place
Williamsport, PA 17707

A journal of Jazz and Literature.

Callaloo
Dept. of English Texas A&M University
MS 4212 TAMU'
College Straton, TX 77843

Calyx
PO Box B
Corvallis, OR 97339

Capilano Review
Capilano College
2055 Purcell Way
North Vancouver, British Columbia V7J 3H5,
Canada

Reviews literary works.

The Caribbean Writer
University of Virgin Islands

RR01 Box 10,000
Kingshill
St. Croix, VI USA 00850

Carolina Quarterly
CB #3520 Greenlaw Hall
University of North Carolina
Chapel Hill, NC 27599

The Chattahoochee Review
Georgia Perimeter College
555 North Indian Creek Drive
Clarkston, GA 30021

The Chattahoochee Review is a literary journal sponsored by Georgia Perimeter College as part of The Southern Academy for Literary Arts and Scholarly Research. Reviews literary works. PAYMENT; they typically pay $50/poem and $25/page for prose. Payment for reviews, interviews, plays, and art is determined on an individual basis. All contributors receive two copies.

Chicago Review
5801 South Kenwood Avenue
Chicago, IL 60637

Guidelines for submission:
All submissions must include a self-addressed, stamped envelope with sufficient postage or International Reply Coupons for notification (or return of manuscript if desired). Address submissions to the appropriate genre editor: Poetry, Fiction, or Book Review. Simultaneous submissions are strongly discouraged. Due to the increasing volume of unsolicited submissions, the average response time is three to six months; it is especially slow during the summer.

Cimarron Review
205 Morrill Hall
Oklahoma State University
Stillwater, OK 74078

"Cimarron Review is now accepting both electronic and postal submissions. Please read these guidelines before submitting.

We accept submissions year-round in poetry, fiction and art. All postal submissions must be accompanied by an SASE. Please, regardless of whether you're submitting electronically or by the postal mail, include a cover letter with, your submission.

Please send 3-6 poems or one piece of fiction. Address all the work to the appropriate editor (fiction or poetry) and mail postal submissions to the above address.

Artists and photographers interested in having their work appear on an upcoming cover of the Cimarron Review should query by E-mail at cimarronreview@okstate.edu. If our editors are interested, we'll reply and request to see more work.

We do NOT accept the following:

• Previously published work (includes work published online).
• E-mailed submissions of any kind.

We no longer accept international reply coupons from writers living outside the United States.

We do not publish theme issues. We are interested in any strong writing of a literary variety, but are not especially partial to fiction in the modern realist tradition and poetry that engages the reader through a distinctive voice -- be it lyric, narrative, etc. When submitting fiction, please do not include a summary of your story in the cover letter. Allow the work to stand on its own. We have no set page lengths for any genre, but we seldom publish short-shots or pieces longer than 25 pages. There are, however, exceptions to every rule. Our guiding aesthetic is the quality of the work itself.

For fiction, please number each page.

When submitting electronically, poets should include all poems for submission in a single file.

We do not accept more than one story -- even if the stories are very short – in a single submission. Please send only one story at a time.

When sending postal submissions, do not staple the manuscript; paperclips are the preferred fastener. Electronic submissions should be doc, docx, pdf, or rtf files and should include your contact information in the upper left or right-hand corner of each page.

Response time varies, but we typically respond to submissions within 3-6 months, often much sooner. At times, however due to a backlog, and especially for work submitted in the summer, a response may take longer. If you have not heard from us after six months, please feel free to query by sending an E-mail to cimarronreview@okstate.edu. Please do not query before six months.

Simultaneous submissions are welcomed, but please contact us immediately through postal or E-mail (with the date and genre of your original submission) should your work be accepted elsewhere. Please also withdrawal electronically-submitted stories accepted elsewhere through the online submission manager system. Unless poets wish to withdraw all poems from a submission, they should withdraw individual poems by E-mail or postal mail only.

For publication, Cimarron Review acquires First North American Serial Rights. After publication, rights revert to the author. At this time, Cimarron Review pays its contributors two copies of the issue in which their work appears.

You may contact us through postal nail or at cimarronreview@okstate.edu. Also, please do not submit again to the Cimarron Review until you have heard back from us. We reserve the right to send multiple submissions back to the author with no response."

College Literature
West Chester University
210 East Rosedale Ave.
West Chester, PA 19382

Colorado Review
9105 Campus Delivery
Colorado State University, Dept. of English
Fort Collins, Colorado 80523-9105

Reviews literary works.

Columbia
Columbia University
2960 Broadway
New York, NY 10027

Commentary Magazine
561 7th Avenue, 16th Floor
New York, NY 10018

COMMENTARY welcomes submissions of articles or reviews for publication consideration. They should be sent via e-mail to: submissions@commentarymagazine.com

The Comstock Review
4956 St. John Drive
Syracuse, NY 13215

Reviews literary works.

Conjunctions
21 East 10th St.
New York, NY 10003

Connecticut Review
39 Woodland St.
Hartford, CT 06105

Reviews literary works.

Court Green
Columbia College Chicago, Dept of English
600 South Michigan Ave
Chicago, IL 60605

Crab Orchard Review
Dept of English Southern Illinois University
Carbondale
Faner Hall 2380, Mail code 4503
1000 Faner Dr.
Carbondale, IL 62901

Reviews literary works.

Crazyhorse
College of Charleston; Dept. of English
66 George St.
Charleston, SC 29424

Daedalus
136 Irving St Suite 100
Cambridge, MA 02138

Denver Quarterly
University of Denver; Dept. of English
2000 E Asbury
Denver, CO 80208

Descant, TCU
Box 297270
Fort Worth, TX 76129

Eclipse; A Literary Journal
1500 North Verdugo Rd
Glendale, CA 91208

This is a literary publication. Submit up to 6 poems or 1 piece of prose.

Ecotone
Dept of Creative Writing, UNCW
601 south College Rd
Wilmington, NC 28403

This is a literary publication. Submit up to 6 poems or 1 piece of prose.

Epoch; Cornell University
251 Goldwin Smith Hall
Ithaca, NY 14853

This is a literary publication, submit one manuscript only.

Esquire
300 W. 57th St. 21st Floor
New York, New York 10019

Literary publication.

Eureka Literary Magazine
Eureka College
300 East College Ave
Eureka, IL 61530

Literary publication.

Event; Douglas College
PO Box 2503
New Westminster, British Columbia V3L 5B2, Canada

This is a literary publication. Submit up to 3-8 poems or short stories with a cover letter.

Fantasy & Science Fiction
PO Box 3447
Hoboken, NJ 07030

This is a literary publication. Submit up to 25,000 words of fiction in one manuscript only. Artwork also accepted.

Faultline
University of CA, Irvine
Dept. of English and Comparative Literature
Irvine, CA 92697

This is a publication that accepts poetry, fiction, nonfiction, translations, and art.

Website: humanities.uci.edu/faultline.shing

Fiction; Mark J Mirksy, Editor
The City College of New York; Dept. of English
138th St. and Convent Ave
New York, NY 10031

This is a literary publication that only accepts fiction.

Fiction International
Harold Jaffe, Editor
San Diego State University
Dept. of English and Comparative Literature
5500 Campanile Dr.
San Diego, CA 92182

This is a Literary publication. Submit up to 3-5 poems or 4,000 words of fiction.

Fiddlehead; Campus House
11 Garland Court UNB
PO Box 4400
Fredericton, NB E3B 5A3, Canada

Field
50 N. Professor St.
Oberlin, OH 44074

This is a literary publication that only accepts poetry. No simultaneous submissions.

The First Line
PO Box 250382
Plano, TX 75025

This is a literary publication that only accepts fiction and non-fiction. However, the topic rotates, so query for current topic.

Florida Review
University of Central Florida; Dept. of English
PO Box 161346
Orlando, FL 32816

Review literary works.

Folio; Dept of Literature
The American University
Washington, DC 20016

This is a literary publication that accepts between Aug 15 – Mar 1. Submit up to 5 poems or 3,500 of prose.

Fourteen Hills
The SFSU Review; Dept. of Creative Writing
San Francisco State University
1600 Holloway Ave.
San Francisco, CA 94132

This is a literary review.

Fourth Genre; Editor
Michigan state University; Dept. of English

201 Morrill Hall
East Lansing, MI 48823

This is a literary publication that accepts between
Aug. 15 – Nov. 30.

Georgia Review
University of Georgia
Athens, GA 30602

This is a literary publication that accepts between
Aug 15- May 15.

Gettysburg Review
Gettysburg College
Gettysburg, PA 17325

This is a literary publication that accepts between,
Sept. 1 – May 31.

Grain
PO Box 67
Saskatoon, Saskatchewan
S7K 3K1, Canada

Submit up to 12 poems or 2 stories. Submissions
must be one-sided and typed.

Green Hill Literary Lantern
Truman State University; Dept. of English
Kirksville, MO 63501

Literary publication.

Greensboro Review; Jim Clark, Editor
MFA Writing Program
3302 HHRA Building; University of North
Carolina
Greensboro, NC 27401

Literary publication.

Gulf Coast
University of Houston; Dept. of English
Houston, TX 77204

Literary publication that accepts between Aug. 15
– Mar. 15.

Harper's Magazine
666 Broadway, 11th Floor
New York, NY 10012

Literary publication.

Harpur Palate

Binghamton University; Dept. of English
PO Box 6000
Binghamton, NY 13902

Literary publication.

Harvard Review
Lamont Library Harvard University
Cambridge, MA 02138

Literary publication.

Hawaii Pacific Review
Hawaii Pacific University
1060 Bishop St.
Honolulu, HI 96713

Literary publication that accepts between Sept. 1 –
Dec 31.

Hayden's Ferry Review
Arizona State University Center for Creative
Writing
C/O Virginia G. Piper
PO Box 875002
Tempe, AZ 85287

Literary publication.

The Healing Muse
Center for Bioethics & Humanities
725 Irving Ave. Suite 406
Syracuse, NY 13210

Literary publication that accepts between Sept. 1 –
May 1.

Hiram Poetry Review
PO Box 162
Hiram, OH 44234

Hotel Amerika
Columbia College English Dept.
600 S. Michigan Ave
Chicago, IL 60605

Literary publication.

Hudson Review
684 Park Ave
New York, NY 10021

Literary publication.

Hunger Mountain
Vermont College

36 College St.
Montpelier, VT 05602

Literary publication.

Idaho Review
Boise State University; Dept. of English
1910 University Dr
Boise, ID 83725

Literary publication.

Iris, UVA Women's Center
PO Box 800588
Charlottesville, VA 22908

Literary publication.

Iron Horse Literary Review
TTU Mail Stop 43091
Lubbock, TX 79409

Literary publication.

Isotope; Utah State University
3200 Old Main Hill
Logan, UT 84322

Literary publication.

Italiana Americana, University of Rhode Island
Providence Campus
80 Washington St.
Providence, RI 02903

Literary publication.

Jabberwock Reviews
Dept. of English, Drawer E
Mississippi State University
Mississippi State, MS 39762

Literary Publication that accepts between Aug. 15 – Oct. 20 and Jan15 – Mar 15.

Jewish Currents
PO Box 111
Accord, NY 12404

Literary publication.

The Journal: Ohio State University; Dept. Of English
164 West 17th Ave.
Columbus, OH 43210

Literary publication.

Karanu
English Dept.; Eastern Illinois University
Charleston, IL 61920

This is a literary publication that accepts between Sept. 1 – Feb. 15.

Kenyon Review
Finn House, Kenyon College
102 W. Wiggin St.
Gambier, OH 43022

This is a literary publication that accepts between Sept. 15 – Jan. 15.

The Laurel Review; Dept. of English
Northwest Missouri State University
800 University Dr.
Maryville, MO 64468

Literary publication.

Literal Latte
200 E. 10th St. Suite 240
New York, NY 10003

Literary publication.

The Long Story
18 Eaton St.
Lawrence, MA 01843

Literary publication that only accepts fiction.

Louisiana Literature
SLU 10792
Southern Louisiana University
Hammond, LA 70402

Literary publication.

Louisville Review
Spalding University
851 South Fourth St.
Louisville, KY 40203

Literary publication.

Malahat Review
University of Victoria
PO Box 1700, STN CSC
Victoria, British Columbia V8W 2Y2; Canada

Literary publication.

Massachusetts Review
South College, University of Massachusetts
Amherst, MA 01003

Literary publication that accepts between Oct. 1 – May 1.

Seeking experiences and suggested policy changes from Massachusetts based transgender prisoners through the "Transgender Prisoner Questionnaire." Write for a copy. Referrals to transfer specific organizations and support.

McSweeney's
849 Valencia St.
San Francisco, CA 94410

Literary publication.

Meridian, University of Virginia
PO Box 400145
Charlottesville, VA 22904

Literary publication that accepts between Aug 16 – Apr. 14.

Michigan Quarterly Review
University of Michigan 0576 Rackham Building
915 East Washington St.
Ann Harbor, MI 48109

Literary publication. Submit up to 8-12 poems or 7,000 words of prose. No simultaneous submissions.

Mid-American Review
Bowling green State University, Dept. of English
Bowling green, OH 43403

Literary publication.

Midstream
633 third Ave, 21st Floor
New York, NY 10017

Literary publication. Focuses on Jewish life and culture.

Missouri Review
357 McReynolds Hall
University of Missouri
Columbia, MO 65211

Literary publication.

Natural Bridge; Dept. Of English, University of Missouri
One University Blvd.
St. Louis, MO 63121

Literary publication that accepts between July 1 – Aug 31 and Nov. 1 - Dec. 31.

New Delta Review
Dept. of English; 15 Allen Hall
Louisiana State University
Baton Rouge, LA 70803

Literary publication that accepts between Aug. 15 – Mar. 31.

New England Review
Middlebury College
Middlebury, VT 05753

Literary publication that accepts between Sept. 1 – May. 31.

New Letter, University of Missouri
1 University House
5101 Rockhill Rd.
Kansas City, MO 64110

Literary publication that accepts between Oct. 2 – Apr. 30.

New Ohio Review; English Dept.
360 Ellis Hall
Ohio University
Athens, OH 45701

Literary publication.

New Orleans Review
PO Box 195
Loyola University
New Orleans, LA 70188

Literary publication that accepts between Aug. 15 – May 15.

The New York Quarterly
PO Box 2015
Old Chelsea station
New York, NY 10113

Literary publication that accepts poetry only. Submit up to 3-5 poems.

Nimrod International Journal
University of Tulsa

800 S. Tucker Dr.
Tulsa, OK 74104

Literary publication that accepts between Jan. 1 – Nov. 30.

Ninth Letter
University of Illinois; Dept. of English
608 S. Wright St.
Urbana, IL 61801

Literary publication that accepts between Sept. 1 – Apr. 30.

North Carolina Literary Review
Dept. of English
East Carolina University
Greenville, NC 27858

Literary publication that specializes in North Carolina stories.

North Dakota Quarterly
Merrifield Hall Room 110
276 Centennial Dr, Stop 7209
Grands Forks, ND 58202

Literary publication.

Northwest Review;The Editor, NWR
5243 University of Oregon
Eugene, OR 97403

Literary publication that accepts nonfiction only.

Notre Dame Review
840 Flanner Hall
University of Norte Dame
Notre Dame, IN 46556

Literary publication that accepts poetry and fiction only between Sept. – Nov., and Jan. – Mar.

Nylon
110 Greene St., Suite 607
New York, NY 10012

Literary publication.

Oklahoma Today
POB 1468
Oklahoma, City 73101

Literary publication.

Oxford American

201 Donaghey Ave, 107
Conway, AR 72035

Literary publication interested in stories from the South.

Painted Bride Quarterly
Drexel University Dept. Of English and Philosophy
3141 Chestnut St.
Philadelphia, PA 19104

Literary publication.

Pearl
3030 East Second St.
Long Beach, CA 90803

Literary publication that accepts between Jan – June.

Phoebe; George Mason University MSN 206
4400 University Dr.
Fairfax, VA 22030

Literary publication that accepts between Sept. 1 – Apr. 15.

The Pinch, Dept. of English
University of Memphis
Memphis, TN 38153

Literary publication.

Pleiades
University of Central Missouri
Warrensburg, MO 64093

Literary publication that accepts between Sept. 1 – Apr. 30.

Ploughshares, Emerson College
120 Boylston St.
Boston, MA 02116

Literary publication.

Poet Lore
The Writers Center
4508 Walsh St.
Bethesda, Maryland 20815

Literary publication.

Potomac Review
Montgomery College

51 Mannakee St. MT/212
Rockville, MD 20850

Literary publication that accepts between Sept. 1 –
May 1. Submit single manuscript only.

Pottersfield Portfolio
9879 Kempt Head Rd.
Ross Ferry, Nova Scotia B1X 1N3; Canada

Prairie Fire
423-100 Arthur St.
Winnipeg, Manitoba R3B 1H3; Canada

Literary publication.

Prairie Schooner
201 Andrews Hall
PO Box 880334
Lincoln, NE 68588

Literary publication that accepts between Sept. 1 –
May 1.

Prism International
University of British Columbia
Buchanan E462
1866 Main Hall
Vancouver, BC V6T 1Z1, Canada

Quarterly West
200 S. Central Campus Dr.
University of Utah
Salt Lake City, UT 84112

Literary publication that accepts between Sept. 1 –
May 1. Submit up to 3-5 poems and 1 fiction piece.

Raritan, Rutgers University
31 Mine St.
New Brunswick, NJ 08903

Literary publication that accepts fiction and essays.
Submit 1 piece.

Rattle
12411 Ventura Blvd,
Studio City, CA 91604

Literary publication.

Rattapallax
217 Thompson St., Suite 353
New York, NY 10012

Literary publication.

Redivider, Emerson College
120 Boylston St.
Boston, MA 02116

Literary publication. Submit 1 piece every 6
months.

RHINO
PO Box 591
Evanston, IL 60204

Literary publication that accepts material between
April 1 – October 1. Submit up to 3-5 poems only.

Room
PO Box 46160, Station D
Vancouver, BC V6J 5G5, Canada

Literary publication for women only.

The Saint Ann's Review
129 Pierrepont St.
Brooklyn, NY 11201

Literary publication.

Salmagundi; Skidmore College
815 North Broadway
Saratoga Springs, NY 12866

Literary publication.

Salt Hill; English Dept.
Syracuse University
Syracuse, NY 13244

Literary publication.

Santa Monica Review
1900 Pico Boulevard
Santa Monica, CA 90405

Literary publication.

Seattle Review
University of Washington
Padelford Hall
Box 354330
Seattle, WA 98195

Literary publication.

Seneca Review
Hobart & William Smith Colleges
Geneva, New York 14456

Literary publication.

Seven Days
PO Box 1164
255 south Champlain St.
Burlington, VT. 05042

Literary publication.

Sewanee Review; University of the South
735 University Ave.
Sewanee, TN 37383

Literary publication.

Shenandoah
Troubador Theater, 2nd Floor
Washington & Lee University
Lexington, VA 24450

Literary publication.

Sonora Review
Dept. of English
University of Arizona
Tucson, AZ 85721

Literary publication.
So-To-Speak
George Mason University
4400 University Dr., MSN 2C5
Fairfax, VA 22030

Literary publication.

The South Carolina Review
Center for Electronic & Digital Publishing
Clemson University, Strode Town, Room 611
Box 340522
Clemson, SC 29634

Literary publication.

South Dakota Review
University of South Dakota; Dept. of English
University Exchange
414 E. Clark St.
Vermillion, SD 57069

Literary publication.

Southeast Review, English Dept.
Florida State University
Tallahassee, FL 32311

Literary publication.

Southern Humanities Review
9088 Haley Center
Auburn University, AL 36830

Literary publication.

The Southern Review
43 Allen Hall
Louisiana State University
Baton Rouge, LA 70803

Literary publication.

Southwest Review
Southern Methodist University
307 Fondren Library West
Dallas, TX 75275

Literary publication.

Speakeasy; The loft Literary Center
1011 Washington, Ave. South; Suite 200
Minneapolis, MN 55415

Literary publication.

The Spoon River Poetry Review
4240, Dept of English; Illinois State University
Normal, IL 61790

Literary publication.

St. Anthony Messenger
1615 Republic St.
Cincinnati, OH 45210

Literary publication.

Sun
107 North Roberson St.
Chapel Hill, NC 27516

Literary publication.

Swivel
PO Box 17958
Seattle, WA 98107

Literary publication.

Sycamore Review
Purdue University; Dept of English
500 Oval Dr.

West Lafayette, IN 47907

Literary publication that accepts between Aug. 1 –
Mar. 31.

Talking River Review
Division of Literature and Languages; Lewis-Clark
State College
500 Eighth Ave.
Lewiston, ID 83501

Literary publication that accepts between Aug.1 –
Apr. 1.

Tampa Review, The University of Tampa
401 West Kennedy Blvd.
Tampa, FL 33606

Literary publication.

The Texas Review; English Dept.
Box 2146 Sam Houston State University
Huntsville, TX 77341

Literary publication.

Thema
PO Box 8747
Metairie, LA 70011

Literary publication.

Threepenny Review
PO Box 9131
Berkeley, CA 94709

Literary publication.

Tikkun
2342 Shattuck Ave., Suite 1200
Berkley, CA 94704

Literary publication.

Tin House
Po Box 10500
Portland, OR 97210

Literary publication.

Transition Magazine
104 Mt. Auburn St. 3R
Cambridge, MA 02138

Literary publication.

Turnrow; English Dept
The University of Louisiana at Monroe
700 University Ave.
Monroe, LA 71209

Literary publication.

**War, Literature & the Arts; English & Fine
Arts Dept.**
United States Air Force Academy
2354 Fairchild Dr., Suite 6045
Colorado springs, CO 80840

Literary publications.

Wascana Review
English Dept.,University of Regina
Saskatchewan S4S 0A2; Canada

Washington Square Creative Writing Program
New York University
58 W. 10th St.
New York, NY 10011

Literary publication.

Watchword
2704 Wallace St.
Berkley, CA 94702

Literary publication.

Witness
Black Mountain Institute
University of Nevada
Las Vegas, NV 89154

Literary publication that accepts between Sept. 1 –
May 1.

Xavier University
Box 110C
New Orleans, LA 70125

Literary publication.

Yale Review
PO Box 208243
New Haven, CT 06520

Literary publication.

Zahir; Sheryl Tempchin
315 South Coast HWY. 101; Suite U8
Encinitas, CA 92024

Literary publication.

Zoetrope
The Sentinel Building

916 Kearney St.
San Francisco, CA 94133

Literary publication.

SUBSCRIPTION AVAILABLE STATEVSUSMAG.COM
FOR FEATURES, AD PLACEMENT OR MORE INFO EMAIL STATEVSUSMAG@GMAIL.COM

 @STATEVSUS   @STATEVSUS   STATE VS US MAGAZINE

Freebird Publishers

Professional Self-Publishing Services

ARE YOU AN AUTHOR IN NEED OF PUBLISHING SERVICES? THAN WE ARE THE COMPANY FOR YOU!

OUR COMPANY

At Freebird Publishers we will guide you from your handwritten pages to publication. Are you an author in need of publishing services, then we are the company for you.

RATES OF SERVICE

Every writer requires personalized service. For these reasons Freebird Publishers offers an a la carte service menu. Our clients are not forced into high priced packages, with us, you can purchase exactly what you need. We have various levels of services to fit every budget.

FAQ's

We have listed some of the most commonly asked questions about the basic procedures and processes involved in book publishing. Our comprehensive informational publishing package is available to you, order yours today.

Self-Publishing Package Order Form

Name:_____ Registration No:_____

Facility Full Name :_____

Address :_____ City:_____ State:_____ Zip:_____

SEND 8 FCS STAMPS TO: FREEBIRD PUBLISHERS, BOX 541, ATTN: BOOK PROJECT DEPT., NORTH DIGHTON , MA 02764

We Service All Your Outside Needs With Inside Knowledge

BOOK REVIEWS

Reviewer: Josh Kruger, Author of The Millionaire Prisoner: Special TCB Edition

BOOK: Pretty Girls Love Bad Boys: The Prisoner's Guide To Getting Girls, by Mike Enemigo & King Guru

Rating: 5 Stars

Most prisoners think they are good at MACn (Master At Communication). They think they know how to get girls. But how come they don't get mail, commissary, or visits from women? Probably because they haven't read and applied the wisdom in *Pretty Girls Love Bad Boys.*

Mike Enemigo and King Guru have hit a home run with this book. I wrote *Pen Pal Success*, and I thought I knew everything there was about getting girls. But then I read this book and realized I didn't know the half of it.

Not only will this book teach you how to get pen pals, but how to bump a female in your immediate vicinity. Included are sample bios, letters, poems, songs, and jokes that you can use in your MACn. The real strength in this book is how they break down the different types of women, and the techniques and points of conquest you need to close the deal with each. There are eight separate chapters with different types of women profiled. That alone makes this book worth buying and studying! There's a chapter with numerous questions you can ask to get your conversations started. There's a chapter on "Phone Game," including phone sex. There's a "Shy Girl's Guide," "Sex Myths," and 117 Secrets to Keep Women Infatuated with You!" Included in the back of the book is a resource guide with addresses of companies that can help you get girls.

This book is a must-have for any prisoner who is serious about getting and keeping girls while inside. Highly Recommended!

BOOK: The Art & Power of Letter Writing for Prisoners: Deluxe Edition

Rating: 5 Stars

Malcolm X, Nelson Mandella, Martin Luther King, George Jackson, Voltaire, Casanova, and Tupac Shakur. What do all these people have in common? All of them were in prison at some time in their life, and all of them wrote letters from their cell to the outside world that are now famous. Perhaps the most famous prison letters are those written by Apostle Paul, which are in the Bible!

No matter what you're trying to accomplish from prison, it will most likely take a letter to get it done. If you need something from the prison mailroom, the county court clerk, an attorney, your counselor, or a business, you'll most likely have to write a letter to obtain it. Wouldn't it be nice to have a book on hand with these types of letters to use as a format? Well, lifer Mike Enemigo has put together such a book in *The Art & Power of Letter Writing for Prisoners: Deluxe Edition: A Complete Guide to Writing High-Quality Formal (Business) & Informal (Personal) Letters.* Inside this 145-page book you'll find sample letters for every occasion. From sample love letters to sales letters to an idea protection letter, it's all included here. There's a basic punctuation guide included in case you get stuck and don't know the correct way to write it. There are over 50 sample letters included to assist you in whatever you're trying to do from your prison cell. Every prisoner should own a copy of this book!

BOOK: The Ladies Who Love Prisoners: Secrets Exposed!, by Mike Enemigo

Rating: 5 Stars

This Special Report has been formulated into a 64-page book. Inside its pages is an interview with Sheila Isenberg, author of *Women Who Love Men Who Kill*, and she reveals the psychology behind why women love prisoners. Other chapters in this Special Report are "Why Are Women Drawn To Men Behind Bars?," "Dating a Prisoner," "The Women Who Love Prisoners," "Love Behind Bars," and a chapter composed by a woman who fell in love with an inmate. This Special Report is laced with quotes and explanations from psychologists and experts on "Hybristophilia," which is the recognized psychiatric condition in which a person -- usually a woman -- experiences strong sexual desires for a man known for crimes that society considers repulsive. There's also a special chapter on the cases of women who have fallen for some of the more notorious criminals in the American penal system. This Special Report gives you a huge advantage because it details the psychology behind women who fall in love with prisoners. And as most of you already know: Capture the mind and the body will follow.

This book can help you do just that.

BOOK: The Prison Manual: The Complete Guide to Surviving the American Prison System, by Mike Enemigo (300 pages, 8"x 10")

Rating: 5 Stars

When I started doing time 26+ years ago, there was no book that showed a prisoner how to successfully navigate the prison system. Thankfully, now there is.

Lifer and CEO of The Cell Block, Mike Enemigo, has put together a much-needed to me. Every prisoner should read this book, especially newbies. Chapter 1 starts of with "Use Your Time Wisely." Other chapters include: "Letter Writing Like a Pro," "Pen Pal Websites: The Secrets," and "Surviving a Celly." There are special chapters for juveniles, women, and the federal prison system. One of the best chapters is "Chess: The Strategies." It teaches you how to play the treacherous "game" of prison, and the mental and physical tactics you need in order to win.

If your prison system offers parole, then you should study the many chapters on how to successfully get parole, and what to do when you actually do. The wisdom in this book comes from prisoners who have, or are, successfully making the best out of their prison experience. I have written five books for American prisoners, and I still was able to learn from this book. I highly recommend this book. If you have a loved one just starting out on their prison journey, then this is a book you should give them as a gift. It will pay the best interest on your money.

Josh Kruger is an incarcerated author who's written several books. His book The Millionaire Prisoner is available now from The Cell Block. Josh is currently working on many more books in The Millionaire Prisoner series that will be published by The Cell Block shortly.

Attention Inmates: Our new website is active! Have your family and friends log on now to order our books at a discounted price!

MIKE ENEMIGO PRESENTS...
THE CELL BLOCK
BOOKSHOP

THE CELL BLOCK; PO BOX 1025; RANCHO CORDOVA, CA 95741

The Cell Block is an independent multimedia company with the objective of accurately conveying the prison/street experience and culture, with the credibility and honesty that only one who has lived it can deliver, through literature and other arts, and entertain and enlighten while doing so.

Represent and support the company that represents and supports *you*.
Represent and support the TCB movement!

ORDER ALL BOOKS NOW ON thecellblock.net

To order, simply write what you want clearly on a piece of paper and send with proper payment via institutional check, money order, or NEW books of Forever Stamps. All books are also on Amazon!

THE MILLIONAIRE PRISONER
SPECIAL 2-in-1 EDITION

Why wait until you get out of prison to achieve your dreams? Here's a blueprint that you can use to become successful!

The Millionaire Prisoner is your complete reference to overcoming any obstacles in prison. You won't be able to put it down! With this book you will discover the secrets to:

Making money from your cell!
Obtain FREE money for correspondence courses!
Become an expert on any topic!
Develop the habits of the rich!
Network with celebrities!
Set up your own website!
Market your products, ideas and services!
Successfully use prison pen pal websites!
How to get FREE pen pals!

All of this and much, much more! This book has enabled thousands of prisoners to succeed and it will show you the way also!

PRICE: $24.99 + $7 S/H

THE MILLIONAIRE PRISONER
PART 1

Wish you could make real money from your cell? Tired of waiting around for someone else to take care of the request? Want to learn how to do it yourself? Then *The Millionaire Prisoner: Part 1* is especially for you! It will show you how to overcome any obstacles in prison. You won't be able to put it down!

With this book you'll discover the secrets to:

- Get pen-pals you won't have to pay for;
- Form the proper attitude and mindset;
- Successfully market your products and services;
- Get FREE money for college that you don't have to pay back;

PRICE: $16.95, $5 S/H

THE MILLIONAIRE PRISONER
PART 2

Wish you could make real money from your cell? Tired of waiting around for someone else to take care of the request? Want to learn how to do it yourself? Then The Millionaire Prisoner: Part 2 is especially for you! It will show you how to overcome any obstacles in prison. You won't be able to put it down!

With this book you'll discover the secrets to:

- Deliver quality products and services that keep them coming back;
- Setting goals and proper preparation with less mistakes;
- Getting started right now from your prison cell;
- Two ways that you could use to make thousands of dollars;
- Standing on the shoulders of giants by copying what they do;
- Keep your passion for life even behind bars.

All of this and much, much more!

PRICE: $16.95, $5 S/H

THE MILLIONAIRE PRISONER 3
SUCCESS UNIVERSITY

Why wait until you get out of prison to achieve your dreams? Here's a new-look blueprint that you can use to be successful!

The Millionaire Prisoner 3 contains advanced strategies to overcoming any obstacle in prison. You won't be able to put it down!

With this book you will discover the secrets to:

• Make money from arts and crafts while inside;
• How to find and get free money for your dreams;
• Mastering your time to become a cellpreneur;
• Successfully build your network while growing your network;
• Attract good luck to your life;
• Stock trading strategies to utilize;
• How to publish for profit from prison;
• Using free sources to get publicity;
• Walk on clouds by using video.

All of this and much, much more!

The TMP program has enabled thousands of prisoners to succeed and it will show you the way also!

PRICE: $16.95 + $5 S/H

BLACK DYNASTY
ENEMY OF MY FAMILY

After their parents are murdered in cold blood, the Black siblings are left to fend for themselves in the unforgiving streets. But when the oldest brother, Lorenzo, is introduced to his deceased father's drug connection, he is given the opportunity of a lifetime to put his family back on top.

However, as their empire grows, so does their knowledge as to who was really behind the murders of their parents. And this leaves the Black siblings with a very big decision to make; one that, with a single wrong move, can destroy everything they've worked so hard to build, and even cost them life itself...

Witness the beginning of a new dynasty – the Black Dynasty – as publishing boss Mike Enemigo and Street-Lit legend Kwame "Dutch" Teague team up with Assa Reigns, one of the hottest urban fiction writers in the game, to bring you this new twisted tale of money, betrayal, and murder....

PRICE: $15.00 + $5 S/H

DEVILS & DEMONS

When Talton leaves the West Coast to set up shop in Florida he meets the female version of himself: A drug dealing murderess with psychological issues. A whirlwind of sex, money and murder inevitably ensues and Talton finds himself on the run from the law with nowhere to turn to. When his team from home finds out he's in trouble, they get on a plane heading south...

PRICE: $15.00 + $5 S/H

DEVILS & DEMONS PART 2

The Game is bitter-sweet for Talton, aka Gangsta. The same West Coast Clique who came to his aid ended up putting bullets into the chest of the woman he had fallen in love with. After leaving his ride or die in a puddle of her own blood, Talton finds himself on a flight back to Oak Park, the neighborhood where it all started...

The is the second installment of the Devils & Demons series. Once again, publishing boss Mike Enemigo and street-lit legend and screenwriter Kwame "Dutch" Teague have collaborated with The Cell Block's very own hitmaker, King Guru, to bring you this urban saga that promises to have you turning pages till your fingers bleed!

PRICE: $15.00 + $5 S/H

DEVILS & DEMONS PART 3

Talton is on the road to retribution for the murder of the love of his life. Dante and his crew of killers are on a path of no return. This urban classic is based on real-life West Coast underworld politics. See what happens when a group of YG's find themselves in the midst of real underworld demons...

This is the third installment of the Devils & Demons series. Once again, publishing boss Mike Enemigo and street-lit legend and screenwriter Kwame "Dutch" Teague have collaborated with The Cell Block's very own hitmaker, King Guru, to bring you this urban saga that promises to have you turning pages till your fingers bleed!

PRICE: $15.00 + $5 S/H

DEVILS & DEMONS PART 4

After waking up from a coma, Alize has locked herself away from the rest of the world. When her sister Brittany and their friend finally take her on a girl's night out, she meets Luck – a drug dealing womanizer.

Things get complicated when the Columbian sisters who were with B.A. when he killed Mike in the first book of this series slide into the picture; it triggers a psychotic breakdown in the murderess known as Ze. Follow your favorite Devil as she explodes in her unpredictable actions of rage!

PRICE: $15.00 + $5 S/H

PIMPOLOGY
THE 7 ISMS OF THE GAME

It's been said that if you knew better you'd do better. So, in the spirit of dropping jewels upon the rare few who truly want to know how to win, this collection of exclusive Game has been compiled. And though a lot of so-called players claim to know how the Pimp Game is supposed to go, none have revealed the real... Until now!

As a cross-country practitioner of professional paper chasm' activities, Manny Fresh has become one of the best players in the Game of makin' somethin' out of nothin'. The extensive experience he's gathered along the way is the foundation of this raw, uncut collection of instructions that will make anyone a master of the Game!

Pimpology will captivate you with Pimp Principles and Player Perspectives from start to finish. Packed with proof of the truth and testimonial stories that show how to apply this timeless philosophy, the mind-blowing information contained in these pages are sure to change the life of anyone who reads, remembers, and replaces what they think they know, with what they'll learn from The 7 Isms of the Game!

PRICE: $16.95, $5 S/H

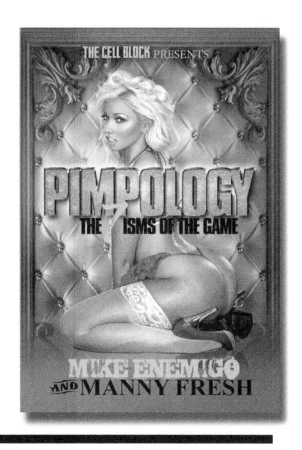

A.O.B.

Growing up in the Bay Area, Manny Fresh the Best had a front-row seat to some of the coldest players to ever do it. And you already know, A.O.B. is the name of the Game! So When Manny Fresh slides through Stockton one day and sees Rosa, a stupid-bad Mexican chick with a whole lotta 'talent' behind her walking down the street tryna get some money, he knew immediately what he had to do: Put it In My Pocket!

From none to one to some, Manny Fresh begins to build his team, gettin' money from city to city and state to state. But as his success grows, an abundance of haters and suckas are not far behind, waiting for an opportunity to knock him down. Treachery seeps into the Game, threatening to poison what he's built, but will Manny crumble under the forces determined to crush him? Or, will he overcome them and take he and his team to the top?

PRICE: $15.00, $5 S/H

THE CEO MANUAL: HOW TO START YOUR OWN BUSINESS WHEN YOU GET OUT OF PRISON!

This new book will teach you the simplest way to start your own business when you get out of prison. Includes: Start-up Steps! The Secrets to Pulling Money from Investors! How to Manage People Effectively! How To Legally Protect Your Assets from "Them"! Hundreds of resources to get you started, including a list of "loan friendly" banks!

PRICE: $16.95 + $5 S/H

GET OUT, GET RICH: HOW TO GET PAID LEGALLY WHEN YOU GET OUT OF PRISON!

Many of you are incarcerated for a money-motivated crime. But with today's tech & opportunities, not only is the crime-for-money risk/reward ratio not strategically wise, it's not even necessary. You can earn much more money by partaking in anyone of the easy, legal hustles explained in this book, regardless of your record. Help yourself earn an honest income so you can not only make a lot of money, but say good-bye to penitentiary chances and prison forever! (Note: Many things in this book can even be done from inside prison.)

PRICE: $16.95 + $5 S/H

BMF

BMF – the Black Mafia Family – was a drug organization headed by brothers Demetrius "Big Meech" Flenory and Terry "Southwest T" Flenory. Rising up from the shadows of Detroit's underbelly, they created a cross-country cocaine network, becoming two of the wealthiest, most dangerously sophisticated drug traffickers the United States has ever seen. With an estimated networth of $270 million, they cloaked their ill-gotten gains with legal business endeavors like exotic car dealerships, and infiltrated the hip-hop industry in a way that's never been done before, aligning themselves with megastars like Sean "Diddy" Combs, Jeezy, Nelly, and Fabolous.

Nevertheless, through wiretaps, cross-country collaborations and shady investigation tactics, the DEA ultimately indicted BMF, crumbling the brothers' empire...

PRICE: $18.99 + $5 S/H

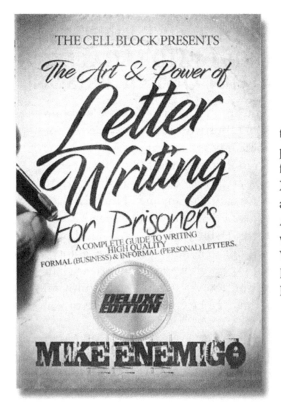

THE ART & POWER OF LETTER WRITING FOR PRISONERS: DELUXE EDITION

When locked inside a prison cell, being able to write well is one of the most powerful skills you can have. Some of the most famous and powerful men in the world are known for letters they've written from inside their prison cells, such as: Martin Luther King; Malcolm X; Nelson Mandella; George Jackson; and perhaps the most famous and powerful of all, Apostle Paul, who's letters are in the Bible! The Art and Power of Letter Writting for Prisoners will show you how to write high-quality personal and business letters. Includes: How to Write Letters Like A Pro! Pen Pal Website Secrets and Strategies! Letter Templates! Over 50 Sample Letters (Love, Legal, Personal, Business, and more)! And a Punctuation Guide!

PRICE: $16.95 + $5 S/H

RAW LAW FOR PRISONERS

TIRED OF FEELING POWERLESS BECAUSE UNSCRUPULOUS GUARDS HAVE VIOLATED YOUR RIGHTS WITHOUT FEAR OF CONSEQUENCE? THEN THIS BOOK IS FOR YOU!

Raw Law For Prisoners is a clear and concise guide for prisoners and their advocates to understanding civil rights laws guaranteed to prisoners under the US Constitution, and how to successfully file a lawsuit when those rights have been violated! From initial complaint to trial, this book will take you through the entire process, step by step, in simple, easy-to-understand terms. Also included are several examples where prisoners have sued prison officials successfully, resulting in changes of unjust rules and regulations and recourse for rights violations, oftentimes resulting in rewards of thousands, even millions of dollars in damages!

If you feel your rights have been violated, don't lash out at guards, which is usually ineffective and only makes matters worse. Instead, defend yourself successfully by using the legal system, and getting the power of the courts on your side!

PRICE: $15.00 + $5 S/H

GET OUT, STAY OUT!

This book should be in the hands of everyone in a prison cell. It reveals a challenging but clear course for overcoming the obstacles that stand between prisoners and their freedom. For those behind bars, one goal outshines all others: GETTING OUT! After being released, that goal then shifts to STAYING OUT! This book will help prisoners do both. It has been masterfully constructed into five parts that will help prisoners maximize focus while they strive to accomplish whichever goal is at hand.

Part One: Get Out! Preparing For Board Hearings breaks down the process step by step. **Part Two:** Understanding Recidivism explains the forces that make recidivist prisoners repeat the same cycle over and over -they themselves are often baffled at their situation. **Part Three:** The Change Process provides prisoners with proven strategies to a positive life change. **Part Four:** Stay Out! Preparing for Release covers obvious survival issues like money, employment, housing, and transportation. **Part Five:** Social Security and Other Benefits covers benefits that are available to prisoners reentering society. It focuses on what these benefits offer, which ones they qualify for, and how they can get those benefits.

PRICE: $16.95 + $5 S/H

HOW TO HUSTLE AND WIN: SEX, MONEY, MURDER

How To Hu$tle and Win: Sex, Money, Murder Edition is the grittiest, underground self-help manual for the 21st century street entrepreneur in print. Never has there been such a book written for today's gangsters, goons and go-getters. This self-help handbook is an absolute must-have for anyone who is actively connected to the streets.

PRICE: $15.00 + $5 S/H

THEE ENEMY OF THE STATE (SPECIAL EDITION)

Experience the inspirational journey of a kid who was introduced to the art of rapping in 1993, struggled between his dream of becoming a professional rapper and the reality of the streets, and was finally offered a recording deal in 1999, only to be arrested minutes later and eventually sentenced to life in prison for murder... However, despite his harsh reality, he dedicated himself to hip-hop once again, and with resilience and determination, he sets out to prove he may just be one of the dopest rhyme writers/spitters ever .... At this point, it becomes deeper than rap .... Welcome to a preview of the greatest story you never heard.

PRICE: $9.99 + $4 S/H

THE BEST RESOURCE DIRECTORY FOR PRISONERS

This book has over 1,450 resources for prisoners! Includes: Pen-Pal Companies! Non-Nude Photo Sellers! Free Books and Other Publications! Legal Assistance! Prisoner Advocates! Prisoner Assistants! Correspondence Education! Money-Making Opportunities! Resources for Prison Writers, Poets, Artists, and much, much more! Anything you can think of doing from your prison cell, this book contains the resources to do it!

PRICE: $17.95 + $5 S/H

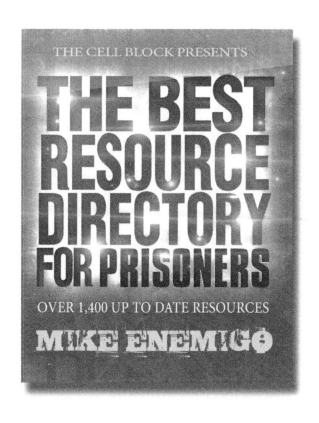

THE PRISON MANUAL

This is your all-in-one book on how to not only survive the rough terrain of the American prison system, but use it to your advantage so you can THRIVE from it! How to Use Your Prison Time to YOUR Advantage; How to Write Letters that Will Give You Maximum Effectiveness; Workout and Physical Health Secrets that Will Keep You as FIT as Possible; The Psychological impact of incarceration and How to Maintain Your MAXIMUM Level of Mental Health; Prison Art Techniques; Fulfilling Food Recipes; Parole Preparation Strategies and much, MUCH more!

PRICE: $24.99 + $7 S/H

MONEY IZ THE MOTIVE

Like most kids growing up in the hood, Kano has a dream of going from rags to riches. But when his plan to get fast money by robbing the local "mom and pop" shop goes wrong, he quickly finds himself sentenced to serious prison time. Follow Kano as he is schooled to the ways of the game by some of the most respected OGs who ever did it; then is set free and given the resources to put his schooling into action and build the ultimate hood empire...

PRICE: $12.00 + $4 S/H

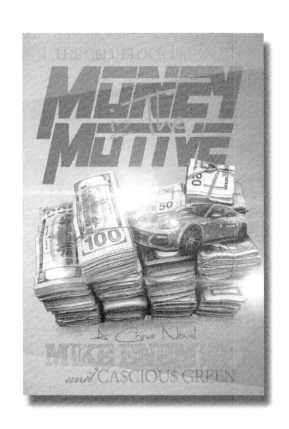

MONEY IZ THE MOTIVE 2

After the murder of a narcotics agent. Kano is forced to shut down his D&C crew and leave Dayton, OH. With no one left to turn to, he calls Candy's West Coast Cuban connection who agrees to relocate him and a few of his goons to the 'City of Kings" -- Sacramento, CA, aka Mackramento, Killafornia! Once there, Kano is offered a new set of money-making opportunities and he takes his operation to a whole new level. It doesn't take long, however, for Kano to learn the game is grimy no matter where you go, as he soon experiences a fury of jealousy, hate, deception and greed. In a game where loyalty is scarce and one never truly knows who is friend and who is foe, Kano is faced with the ultimate life or death decisions. Of course, one should expect nothing less when...Money iz the Motive.

PRICE: $12.00 + $4 S/H

MOB$TAR MONEY

After Trey's mother is sent to prison for 75 years to life, he and his little brother are moved from their home in Sacramento, California, to his grandmother's house in Stockton, California where he is forced to find his way in life and become a man on his own in the city's grimy streets. One day, on his way home from the local corner store, Trey has a rough encounter with the neighborhood bully. Luckily, that's when Tyson, a member of the MOBTAR, a local "get money" gang comes to his aid. The two kids quickly become friends, and it doesn't take long before Trey is embraced into the notorious MOB$TAR money gang, which opens the door to an adventure full of sex, money, murder and mayhem that will change his life forever... You will never guess how this story ends!

PRICE: $12.00 + $4 S/H

BLOCK MONEY

Beast, a young thug from the grimy streets of central Stockton, California lives The Block; breathes The Block; and has committed himself to bleed The Block for all it's worth until his very last breath. Then, one day, he meets Nadia; a stripper at the local club who piques his curiosity with her beauty, quick-witted intellect and rider qualities. The problem? She has a man -- Esco -- a local kingpin with money and power. It doesn't take long, however, before a devious plot is hatched to pull off a heist worth an indeterminable amount of money. Following the acts of treachery, deception and betrayal are twists and turns and a bloody war that will leave you speechless!

PRICE: $12.00 + $4 S/H

CONSPIRACY THEORY

Kokain is an upcoming rapper trying to make a name for himself in the Sacramento, CA underground scene - home of rap stars Brother Lynch Hung, C-Bo, and Mozzy - and Nicki is his girlfriend .... One night, in October, Nicki's brother, along with her brother's best friend, go to rob a house of its $100,000 marijuana crop. It goes wrong; shots are fired and a man is killed .... Later, as investigators begin closing in on Nicki's brother and his friend, they, along with the help of a few others, create a way to make Kokain take the fall .... The conspiracy begins.

PRICE: $12.00 + $4 S/H

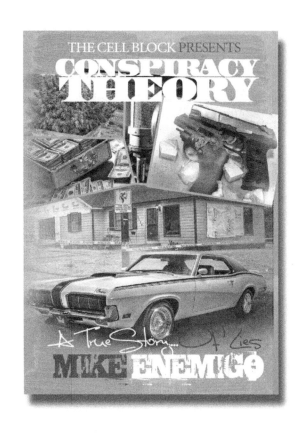

HOOD MILLIONAIRE
HOW TO HUSTLE & WIN LEGALLY

Hustlin' is a way of life in the hood. We all have money motivated ambitions, not only because we gotta eat, but because status is oftentimes determined by ones' own salary. To achieve what we consider financial success, we often invest our efforts into illicit activities -- we take penitentiary chances. This leads to a life in and out of prison, sometimes death -- both of which are counterproductive to gettin' money. But there's a solution to this, and I have it Hood Millionaire: How to Hustle & Win Legally is the official hustler's handbook for block bleeders and go-getters to learn how to hustle and win legally in their quest for wealth and prosperity. Produced by self-made millionaire prisoner Mike Enemigo and self-made hood millionaire Sav Hustle, this book will give you the secrets to success. You will get the closely guarded game on subjects like The 20 Secret Habits of Self-Made Millionaires; How to Make a Fortune Selling Real Estate...That You Don't Own!; How to Fatten Your Pockets Using Amazon; How to Sell Water to a Whale; How to How to Start Your Own Independent Rap Label in Just 9 Steps. You will learn How One Hustler Made 20 Million Dollars, and You Can, Too; and How a Teen Averages $2,800 a Month From a Little-Known Secret. All of this and much, much more! Stop taking UNNECESSARY changes. Increase your odds of success today by learning what it is "they" don't want YOU to know and start gettin' REAL money. Join the movement and become the next self-made millionaire in your hood!

PRICE: $16.95 + $5 S/H

CEO MANUAL:
START A BUSINESS, BE A BOSS

This new book will teach you the simplest way to start your own business when you get out of prison. Includes. Start-up Steps! The Secrets to Pulling Money from Investors! How to Manage People Effectively! How To Legally Protect Your Assets from "Them"! Hundreds of resources to get you started, including a list of "loan friendly" banks! **(ALSO PUBLISHED AS THE CEO MANUAL)**

PRICE: $16.95 + $5 S/H

THE MONEY MANUAL:
UNDERGROUND CASH SECRETS EXPOSED!

Becoming a millionaire is equal parts what you make, and what you don't spend -- AKA save. All Millionaires and Billionaires have mastered the art of not only making money, but keeping the money they make (remember Donald Trump's tax maneuvers?), as well as establishing credit so that they are loaned money by banks and trusted with money from investors: AKA OPM -- other people's money. And did you know there are millionaires and billionaires just waiting to GIVE money away? It's true! These are all very-little known secrets "they" don't want YOU to know about, but that I'm exposing in my new book!

Be enlightened and change your financial future TODAY!

PRICE: $16.95 + $5 S/H

LOYALTY AND BETRAYAL DELUXE EDITION

Chunky was an associate of and soldier for the notorious Mexican Mafia -- La Eme. That is, of course, until he was betrayed by those he was most loyal to. Then he vowed to become their worst enemy. Though they've attempted to kill him numerous times, he still to this day is running around making a mockery of their organization.

Loyalty & Betrayal: Special Deluxe Edition contains the original Loyalty & Betrayal book that started it all; "The Lost Chapters", which is the prequel to the original book; the brand-new release of Loyalty & Betrayal part 2; and an exclusive, never-before published interview of Armando "Chunky" Ibarra detailing what life has been like since the release of the highly controversial Loyalty & Betrayal story. You will never guess how this story ends. You do NOT want to miss this...

PRICE: $19.99+ $5 S/H

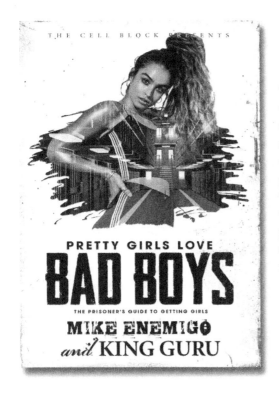

PRETTY GIRLS LOVE BAD BOYS: A PRISONER'S GUIDE TO GETTING GIRLS!

Tired of the same, boring, cliché pen pal books that don't tell you what you really need to know? If so, this book is for you! Anything you need to know on the art of long and short distance seduction is included within these pages! Not only does it give you the science of attracting pen pals from websites, it also includes psychological profiles and instructions on how to seduce any woman you set your sights on! Includes interviews of women who have fallen in love with prisoners, bios for pen pal ads, pre-written love letters, romantic poems, love-song lyrics, jokes and much, much more! This book is the ultimate guide – a must-have for any prisoner who refuses to let prison walls affect

PRICE: $16.95 + $5 S/H

THE MOB

PaperBoy is a Bay Area boss who has invested blood, sweat, and years into building The Mob-- a network of Bay Area street legends, block bleeders, and underground rappers who collaborate nationwide in the interest of pushing a multi-million dollar criminal enterprise of sex, drugs, and murder.

Based on actual events, little has been known about PaperBoy, the mastermind behind The Mob, and intricate details of its operation, until now.

Follow this story to learn about some of the Bay Area underworld's most glamorous figures and famous events...

PRICE: $16.99 + $5 S/H

THE LADIES WHO LOVE PRISONERS
SECRETS EXPOSED!

New special report reveals the secrets of real women who have fallen in love with prisoners, regardless of crime, sentences, or location. This inforamiton will give you a huge advantage in getting girls from prison.

PRICE: $12.00, $2 S/H

OJ'S LIFE BEHIND BARS

In 1994, Heisman Trophy winner and NFL superstar OJ Simpson was arrested for the brutal murder of his ex-wife Nicole Brown-Simpson and her friend Ron Goldman. In 1995, after the "trial of the century," he was acquitted of both murders, though most of the world believes he did it.

In 2007 OJ was again arrested, but this time in Las Vegas, for armed robbery and kidnapping. On October 3, 2008 he was found guilty sentenced to 33 years and was sent to Lovelock Correctional Facility, in Lovelock, Nevada. There he met inmate-author Vernon Nelson. Vernon was granted a true, insider's perspective into the mind and life of one of the country's most notorious men; one that has never provided…until now.

This is the story of their friendship, conversations, confessions, loyalty, and betrayal…

PRICE: $15.00 + $4 S/H

In 2010, after flirting with the idea for two years, Mike Enemigo started writing his first book. In 2014, he officially launched his publishing company, The Cell Block, with the release of five books. Of course, with no mentor(s), how-to guide, or any real resources, he was met with failure after failure as he tried to navigate the treacherous goal of publishing his books from his prison cell. However, he was determined to make it. He was determined to figure it out and would not quit.

Today, he is America's #1 incarcerated author and jailhouse publisher, with over 30 books published, and many more on the way. He makes more money per month than many people in the free world (including writers and publishers), is known all over the world, and has received praise from the big dogs, such as New York Times Bestselling author JaQuavis Coleman, Street Lit pioneer Dutch, and Jailhouse Publishing legend Seth Ferranti.

In Mike's new book, Jailhouse Publishing for Money, Power, and Fame, he breaks down all is jailhouse publishing secrets and strategies, so you can do all he's done, but without the trials and tribulations he had to go through…

PRICE $ 24.99 + $7 S/H

HOW TO WRITE URBAN BOOKS FOR MONEY & FAME: PRISONER EDITION

Inside this book you will learn the true story of how Mike Enemigo and King Guru have received money and fame from inside their prison cells by writing urban books; the secrets to writing hood classics so you, too, can be caked up and famous; proper punctuation using hood examples; and resources you can use to achieve your money motivated ambitions! If you're a prisoner who wants to write urban novels for money and fame, this must-have manual will give you all the game!

PRICE: $16.95 + $5 S/H

LOST ANGELS

David Rodrigo was a child who belonged to no world; rejected for his mixed heritage by most of his family and raised by an outcast uncle in the mean streets of East L.A. Chance cast him into a far darker and more devious pit of intrigue that stretched from the barest gutters to the halls of power in the great city. Now, to survive the clash of lethal forces arrayed about him, and to protect those he loves, he has only two allies; his quick wits, and the flashing blade that earned young David the street name, Viper.

PRICE: $15.00 + $5 S/H

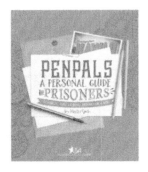

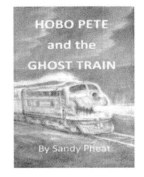

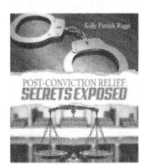

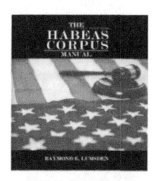

CRIME COMICS

CONFESSIONS OF A COLLEGE KINGPIN by Seth Ferranti
A kid from the suburbs descends into a haze of drugs on an LSD fueled mission to become a cash millionaire. But as his dream edges closer to reality, he instead becomes an unlikely poster boy for America's expanding War on Drugs.

SUPREME TEAM by Seth Ferranti
At the dawn of crack and hip-hop, the Supreme Team towered above their contemporaries- the players, pimps and dope boys in Jamaica Queens, New York. With their hip-hop flavor, the team dominated the drug game like none before and their exploits reverberated in rap's lyrical lore.

LUCKY by Christian Cipollini
The Roaring Twenties ...
Among the ensemble cast of soon-to-be crime kingpins ... arose one of the most prolific, mythologized, misunderstood, vilified and at times - idolized. His name was Salvatore Lucania, and in 1929, a near-death experience altered his physical appearance, produced outrageous misinformation, but most of all - cemented his status as the most infamous, influential, and polarizing organized crime figure in the annals of America's darker history.

VERDICT by Kwame Teague
In what's been billed "The Trial of the Century," James Bernard a.k.a Dutch, gangster extraordinaire, finds himself embroiled in a courtroom battle of epic proportions. With his former criminal cohorts testifying against him and spilling it all, his outlaw past becomes headline fodder.

ORDER DIRECT: Gorilla Convict, LLC/1019 Williott Rd./St. Peters, MO 63376

$5.00 per Comic. Shipping and Handling: $2.99 for the first Comic and $2.25 for each additional Comic.

Postal tracking $1.00 per order. Not responsible for orders without tracking number. Money orders only. All sales final.

KITE
SUBSCRIBE NOW
TO STAY CONNECTED WITH THE STREET CULTURE

Issues
Provided
Bi-monthly

FREE
SHIPPING

SAVE by Subscribing to the next
3 issues for $24.99
6 issues (1 Year) for $49.99

_____   _____
First Name   Last Name

_____
ID Number

_____
Address

_____   _____ _____
City   State   Zip

Send Disbursement to: **KITE Magazine**
P.O. BOX 100971
Brooklyn NY 11210

KiteMagazineCulture.com

SUBSCRIBE NOW

THE EYES & EARS OF THE STREETS

STREET MONEY

Volume 2 Issue 1.9

AY STREETZ AKA
T H O T
KING
SPEAKS TO SMM

EXCLUSIVE
INTERVIEW WITH
STREET-LIT LEGEND
KING KWAME TEAGUE
AKA DUTCH

MUSIC VIDEO
GONE WRONG

SMM DIVA
C O U R T N E Y
GOODZ

SAMARI MAHNYE'
DROPS
MULAA SZN

NEW HEAT IN THE STREET
INDUSTRY SPOTLIGHT

BOBBY DOLLA
FUNK SWAY
I.W.T
PRODDA
SAMARI MAHNYE'

PLUS!
BIGG DAWGG
IS READY FOR
THE INDUSTRY

Behind The Wall

We started the Behind The Wall section of our magazine because we wanted to give a voice to the men and women in prison.

YES! Street Money Magazine

Order Today

☐ Current Issue $5 + $2 shipping

☐ 3 Issues $15 + $2 shipping

☐ 6 Issues $30 + $2 shipping

Name: _____

Shipping Address: _____

Address _____

Email _____

Phone: _____

Mail payments to: Street Money Magazine P.O. Box 441 Troutman NC 28166

Order Street Money Magazine online @ streetmoneymagazine.com

Payment Type:

☐ Cash

☐ Check

BEHIND THE WALL

"I don't......play the radio"

BRANDON RUSSELL

Before I got released, about 60 days ago, I seen brothers leaving and coming right back to prison. I knew that I wanted to do something different, something positive and constructive when I got released, but seeing brothers come right back after only being out a few weeks, or a few days, really discouraged me. Doubt, the biggest enemy of man, crept in. I was Kendrick Lamar in "Black Boy Fly." I felt the odds were stacked against me. I felt like, if all these dudes aren't making it, then what makes me think that I'll make it

Now when I sit back and reflect on it all, I don't even know what I was worried about. Right before I set down to write this, I was finishing up a book order for two inmates, complete strangers, which I now "sponsor" since I've been released. Not only did I touch down and do *everything* I said I was going to do, I reached back to be a light to others still journeying through probably the darkest hours of their lives.

A few people were skeptical reading letters I sent them from prison, and who wouldn't be? Most people have memories of me living a very reckless, unconstructive life. I had to put it down, you feel me? I had to make believers out of people who rightfully doubted me. Seven of my comrades died while I was incarcerated. I feel like I pay homage to them by straightening up, so I don't fall to the same forces that took them under.

In prison, when someone says that they, or so and so, "don't play the radio," it means they don't play any games, with them hands or that knife; they put it down; they "move the ethers," make things happen.

My family supported me to the best of their ability when I got released. But naturally, I felt I had to do for myself, too...by all legitimate means. I hit the ground running...literally. I got out and walked my ass off. I was broke, so I got a monthly bus pass through a reentry program called Vera Pathways. With the bus passes, and a bicycle my grandfather would later buy for me, I put my pride aside and began to plant the seeds for my legitimate empire. I got my license back, after studying for the written test and having to take the driving part all over again. I got a job, a library card, food stamps, and a gym member-ship with the YMCA. I started a blog site with my big brother, giving advice and guidance to young men (www.myuncierussell.com). I spend quality time with my son. I enrolled in college. But most importantly, I'm documenting all of this. Be on the lookout for 5 Years, 4 Months...And Some Change.

I had to become hard to take these steps. I had to become a man to be under the pressure with a sober mind, no drugs or alcohol. I had to expose myself to the elements, walking two miles to the bus stop in the middle of winter, in freezing rain. I had to develop tough skin. I didn't play any games. I moved the ethers. I made things happen. Reader, can you hear that? Aunty, big bruh, grandma, can you all hear that? I can't hear it either, cause ain't nothing there. The radio isn't on...because I don't play it. Peace.

SEND ARTICLES'S & PHOTO'S TO
BEHINDTHEWALL@STREETMONEYMAGAZINE.COM
OR P.O. BOX #441 TROUTMAN, NORTH CAROLINA 28166

- **Packages starting at $799**
- **Non-Packaged Items starting at $50**
- **ISBN#**
- **Manuscript**
- **Masters**
- **Edits**
- **POD**
- **Barcodes**
- **Distribution**
- **Bookclub Submission**
- **And More**

For a quote or submission please email us alltitlespd@gmail.com

FREE & LOW-COST MAGAZINES

Dear Readers,

I've compiled a list of magazines that that you *should* be able to get for **FREE**, or close to it (there is no guarantee with this. Often it works, sometimes it doesn't). As a prisoner, receiving **FREE** or almost **FREE** magazines can benefit you tremendously. As prison budgets are being slashed left and right, we must find ways to educate ourselves. And magazines that cover specific subjects are treasure troves of information regarding whatever it is they specialize in. For example, if you're interested in opening a restaurant when you get out of prison, ordering SANTE would be a wise decision because that's what that magazine is all about.

Another reason this is a valuable resource is because, if you ever end up in the hole, you're gonna need some reading material. Sometimes it's hard to get books, but if you get magazines sent to you through the mail, you're likely to get them.

People; whenever you write a company asking for something, whether it's magazines or something else in this book, represent yourself properly. Don't send them a dirty, crumpled up piece of paper saying, "Send me a free copy." These companies exist to do BUSINESS, not entertain bored, sloppy inmates looking for free shit -- what most people probably automatically assume when they see the prison envelope. And don't write no long-ass request using big-ass words, tryna sound smarter than you really are, either. You'll look stupid. If you have a typewriter, certainly type your request. If you don't have a typewriter, and no one you know does, be sure to write your request nice and neat.

Now, here's the secret to this. Magazines are always looking for two things: More subscribers, and more writers/contributors. If these magazines believe you may fall into one or both of these groups, you're more likely to get what you're asking for.

Here's an example of how your request letter should look:

Wilberto Bellardo,
POB 1902
Tehachapi, CA 93581

SANTE

160 Benmost Ave., Ste 92
3rd Floor West Wing
Bennington, VT 05200

Date: January 1, 2020
Re: Consumer Promotions

Dear SANTE:

I love your magazine. Is it possible you could send
me a complimentary or promotional copy to the
address above, as well as your writer's guidelines? It
would be very much appreciated.

Truly,

Wilberto

ABA JOURNAL
c/o American Bar Association
321 N. Clark St., 20th FL
Chicago, IL 60654

Free. Covers the legal profession.

AD ASTRA
c/o National Space Society
1155 15th St. NW, Ste. 500
Washington, DC 20005

Send 9x12 SASE. Covers the international space
programs.

ADIRONDACK LIFE
Box 410
Route 9N
Jay, NY 12941

Send $3 and 9x12 SASE. Covers history and
activities of Adirondack region.

AFRICAN AMERICAN CAREER WORLD
c/o Equal Opportunity Publication, Inc.
445 Broad Hollow Rd., Ste. 425
Melville, NY 11747

Free. Focused on African American students and
professionals.

AKRON LIFE
c/o Baker Media Group
1653 Merriman Rd., Ste. 116
Akron, OH 44313

Free. Covers Summit, Stark, Portage and Medina
counties in OH.

ALABAMA LIVING
c/o Alabama Rural Electric Association
340 Technacenter Dr.
Montgomery, AL 36117

Free. Covers topics of interest for Alabamians.

ALBERTA VIEWS
c/o Alberta Views, Ltd.
320 23rd Ave SW, Ste. 208
Calgary, Alberta T2S OJ2
Canada

Free. Covers Alberta, Canada culture.

AMBASSADOR MAGAZINE
c/o National Italian American Foundation
1860 19th St. NW
Washington, DC 20009

Free. Covers Italian American history and culture.

AMERICAN CHEERLEADER
c/o Macfadden Performing Arts Media, LLC
110 William St., 23rd FL.
NY, NY 10038

Send $2.95. Covers school, college, and competitive
cheerleading.

AMERICAN MOTORCYCLIST
c/o American Motorcyclist Association
13515 Yarmouth Dr.
Pickerton, OH 43147

Send $1.50. For enthusiastic motorcyclists.

THE AMERICAN SALESMAN
c/o National Research Bureau
320 Valley St.
Burlington, IA 52601

Free. Covers sales and marketing.

AMERICAN STYLE MAGAZINE
c/o The Rosen Group
3000 Chestnut Ave., Ste. 300
Baltimore, MD 21211

Send $3. Covers arts, crafts, travel and interior
design.

ANN ARBOR OBSERVOR
c/o Ann Arbor Observer Co.
2390 Winewood
Ann Arbor, MI 48103

Send 12.5x15 SASE and $3 postage. Covers Ann
Arbor, MI.

ANTIQUEWEEK
c/o MidCountry Media
27 N. Jefferson St.
POB 90
Knightstown, IN 46148

Free. Covers antiques and collectables.

THE APPRAISERS STANDARD
c/o New England Appraisers Association
6973 Crestridge Dr.
Memphis, TN 38119

Send 9x12 SASE and $1 postage. Covers appraisals of antiques, art, jewelry, coins, stamps and real estate.

ARIZONA FOOTHILLS MAGAZINE
8132 N. 87th Pl
Scottsdale, AZ 85258

Send #10 SASE. Covers Arizona Lifestyle.

ARIZONA WILDLIFE VIEWS
5000 W. Carefree Hwy.
Phoenix, AZ 85086

Free. Covers AZ wildlife.

ARMY MAGAZINE
C/o Assn. of the U.S. Army
2425 Wilson Blvd.
Arlington, VA 22201

Send 9x12 SASE and $1 postage. Focused on military interests.

ART & ACTIVITIES
c/o publishers Development Corp.
12345 World Trade Dr.
San Diego, CA 92128

Send 9x12 SASE and 8 FCS. Covers Art Education.

ART JEWELRY MAGAZINE
c/o Kalmbach Publishing
21027 Crossroads Circle
Waukesha, WI 53186

Send request. Info for jewelry makers.

THE ARTILLERYMAN
c/o Historical Publications, Inc.
234 Monarch Hill Rd.
Tunbridge, VT 05077

Send 9x12 SASE and 4 FCS. antique artillery, fortifications and crew served weapons.

ART MATERIALS RETAILER
c/o Fahy-Williams Publishing, Inc.
171 Reed St.
POB 1080
Geneva, NY 14456

Free. Covers art material.

ARTS NEW
31 Mamroneck Ave.
White Plains, NY 10601

Free. Covers arts and entertainment in Westchester County, NY.

ARTS PERSPECTIVE MAGAZINE
c/o Shared Vision Publishing
POB 3042
Durango, CO 81302

Free. Covers art.

ART TIMES
POB 730
Mount Marion, NY 12456

Send 9x12 SASE and 6 FCS. Covers the arts.

ASTRONOMY MAGAZINE
c/o Kalmbach Publishing
21027 Crossroads Circle
Waukesha, WI 53186

Send request. Covers the science of astronomy.

ATLANTIC BUSINESS MAGAZINE
c/o Communications Ten, Ltd.
POB 2356 Station C
St. Johns, NL A1C 6E7
Canada

Free. Covers business in Atlantic Canada.

AUTHORSHIP
c/o National Writers Assn.
10940 S. Parker Rd. #508
Parker, CO 80134

Send 8.5x11 SASE. Covers article writing.

BARTENDER MAGAZINE
C/o Foley Publishing
POB 158

Liberty Corner, NJ 07938

Send 9x12 SASE and 4 FCS. Covers liquor and bartending.

BASSMASTER MAGAZINE
c/o B.A.S.S. Publications
1170 Celebration Blvd., Suite 200
Celebration, FL 32830

Free sample. Covers large mouth, small mouth, and spotted bass.

BREAD STYLE
c/o Kalmbach Publishing
21027 Crossroads Circle
Waukesha, WI 53186

Send request. Covers quick jewelry projects in today's hottest fashion and colors.

THE BEAR DELUXE MAGAZINE
c/o Orlo
810 SE Belmont, Studio 5
Portland, OR 97214

Send $3. Covers fictional essays, poetry and more.

BIBLE ADVOCATE
c/o Bible Advocate Church of God (7th Day)
POB 33677
Denver, CO 80233

Send SASE and 3 FCS. Covers religion.

BIRDING WORLD
c/o Sea Lawn
Coast Road Cley Next the Sea
Holt Norfolk NR25 7RZ
United Kingdom

Free. Covers birds and birdwatchers.

B'NAI B'RTH MAGAZINE
2020 K. St. NW, 7th FL
Washington, DC 20006

Send $2. Covers Jewish Communities in North America and Israel.

BOOK DEALERS WORLD
c/o North America Bookdealers Exchange
POB 606

Cottage Grove, OR 97424

Send $3. Covers writing, self-publishing and marketing books by mail.

BOULEVARD
c/o Opojaz, Inc.
6614 Clayton Rd.
Box 325
Richmond Heights, MO 63117

Send SASE. Features fictional poetry and essays.

BOW & ARROW HUNTING
C/o Beckett Media, LLC
22840 Savi Ranch Prkwy,Suite 200
Yorba Linda, CA 92887

Free. Covers bow-hunting.

BOWHUNTER
c/o Intermedia Outdoors
6385 Flank Dr., Suite 800
Harrisburg, PA 17112

Send 8.5x11 SASE and $2. Covers hunting big and small game with bow and arrow.

BRAND PACKAGING
c/o BNP Media
2401 W. Big Beaver Rd., Suite 700
Troy, MI 28084

Free. Covers how packaging can be a marketing tool.

BUTTON
POB 77
Westminster, MA 01473

Send $2.50. Lit mag for poetry, fiction and gracious living.

CALIFORNIA LAWYER
c/o Daily Journal Corp.
44 Montgomery St., Ste. 250
San Francisco, CA 94104

Send #10 SASE. Law related articles.

CANADIAN DIMENSION
2E-91 Albert St.
Winnipeg, Manitoba R3B 1G5
Canada

Send $2. Covers politics and world issues from a socialist perspective.

CANADIAN SCREENWRITERS
c/o Writers Guild of Canada 366 Adelaide St. W,
Suite 401
Toronto, Ontario MV5 1R9
Canada

Free. Covers Canadian screenwriting.

CAR AND DRIVER MAGAZINE
1585 Eisenhower Place
Ann Arbor, MI 48108

Send REQ. Covers new automobiles.

CARLSBAD MAGAZINE
Wheelhouse Media
POB 2089
Carlsbad, CA 91408

Send $2.31. Covers people, places, events and arts in Carlsbad, CA.

CATHOLIC DIGEST
POB 6015
New London, CT 06320

Free. Covers aspects of the Catholic church.

CELEBRATE LIFE MAGAZINE
c/o American Life League
POB 1350
Stafford, VA 22555

Send 9x12 SASE and 4 FCS. Covers educational articles and human interest.

CHICAGO MAGAZINE
435 N. Michigan Ave., Suite 1100
Chicago, IL 60611

Send $3. Covers Chicago.

CHRISTIAN COMMUNICATOR
9118 W. Elmwood Dr., Suite 1G
Niles, IL 60714

Send SASE and 5 FCS. Covers Christian writing and speaking.

CHRISTIAN BOOK DISTRIBUTORS
POB 7000
Peabody, MA 01961

Send REQ. Covers Christian books.

CHURCH & STATE
1301 K. St. NW, Suite 805E
Washington, DC20005

Send 9x12 SASE and 3 FCS. Covers religious liberty and church/state relations.

CITY LIMITS
c/o Community Service Society of NY
105 R 22nd St., FL 3
NY, NY 10010

Send $2.95. Covers urban politics and policy in New York City.

COLORADO BIZ
6160 Syracuse Way #300
Greenwood Village, CO 80111

Send SASE and $2.95. Covers people, issues and trends statewide.

COLORADO HOMES & LIFESTYLES
c/o Network Communications, Inc.
1780 S. Bellaire St., Suite 505
Denver, CO 80222

Send #10 SASE. Covers beautiful homes, landscapes and architecture.

COMMERCE & INSUSTRY
c/o Mercury Publications, Ltd.
1740 Wellington Ave.
Winnipeg, Manitoba R3H OE8
Canada

Free. Covers business and industrial sectors.

CONSCIENCE
c/o Catholics for Choice
1436 U St. NW, Suite 301
Washington, DC 20009

Send 9x12 SASE and $1.85 postage. Religious magazine.

COUNTRY WOMAN

c/o Reiman Publications
5400 S. 60th St.
Greendale, WI 53129
Free. For contemporary rural women of all ages and backgrounds in the US and Canada.

COUNTY
c/o Texas Association of Counties
1210 San Antonio St.
Austin, TX 78701

Send 8.5x11 SASE and 3 FCS. Covers county and state government in TX.

CQ AMATEUR RADIO
c/o CQ Communications, Inc.
25 Newbridge Rd.
Hicksville, NY 11801

Free. Covers amateur radio.

CRAIN'S DETROIT BUSINESS
c/o Crain Communications, Inc.
1155 Gratiot
Detroit, MI 48207

Send $1.50. Covering business in Detroit metro.

CREDIT UNION MANAGEMENT
c/o Credit Union Executive Society
5510 Research Park Dr.
Madison, WI 53711

Free. Covers credit union, banking trends, HR and marketing issues.

DAC NEWS
c/o Detroit Athletic Club
241 Madison Ave.
Detroit, MI 48226

Free. For Detroit Athletic Club members.

DECA DIMENSIONS
1908 Association Dr.
Reston, VA 20191

Free. Covers marketing, business, and career training.

DEER & DEER HUNTING
c/o F&W Media, Inc.
700 E. State St. Iowa, WI 54990

Send 9x12 SASE. Covers white tail deer.

DELAWARE TODAY
3301 Lancaster Ave., Suite 5C
Wilmington, DE 19805

Send $2.95. Covers people, places and issues of DE.

DETAILS
c/o Details, Customer Service Dept.
POB 37686
Boone, IA 50037

Send REQ. Styles and trends for the modern man.

DIGGER
c/o Oregon Association of nurseries
29751 SW Town Center Loop W.
Wilsonville, OR 97070

Free. Covers nursery and greenhouse industry.

DIGITAL PHOTO MAGAZINE
c/o Digital Photo
POB 37857
Boone, IA 50037

Send REQ. Covers digital photos.

DISCOVER MAGAZINE
c/o Kalmbach Publishing
21027 Crossroads Circle
Waukesha, WI 53186

Send REQ. Covers science, medicine, technology and the world around us.

DOG SPOTS MAGAZINE
c/o Cher Car Kennel
4215 S. Lowell Rd.
St. Johns, MI 48879

Free. Covers working dogs.

THE EAST BAY MONTHLY
c/o The Berkeley Monthly, Inc.
1305 Franklin St., Suite 501
Oakland, CA 94612

Send $3. Covers San Francisco.

ESQUIRE

300 W. 57th St.
NY, NY 10019

Send REQ. Covers the latest news, politics and more.

ESSENCE
135 W 50th St.
NY, NY 10020

Send $3.25. Covers today's black woman.

EXOTIC MAGAZINE
c/o X Publishing, Inc.
818 SW 3rd Ave., Suite 1324
Portland, OR 97204

Send 9x12 SASE and 5 FCS. Covers adult entertainment and sexuality.

EXPERIENCE LIFE
2145 Ford Pkwy, Suite 302
St. Paul, MN 55116

Send REQ. Covers health and fitness and related topics.

FCA MAGAZINE
c/o Fellowship of Christian Athletes
8701 Leeds Rd.
Kansas City, MO 64129

Send 9x12 SASE and 3 FCS. Covers religious matters.

THE FEDERAL CREDIT UNION
c/o N.A.F.C.U.
3138 10th St. N.
Arlington, VA 22201

Send 10x13 SASE and 5 FCS. Published by the National Association of Credit Unions.

FINGERHUT
POB 500
Saint Cloud, MN 56372

Free. General merchandise and gifts.

FREELANCE MARKET NEWS
c/o Writers Bureau Ltd.
8-10 Dutton St.
Manchester, M3 ILE
England

Free. Covers freelance writers.

FREELANCE WRITERS REPORT
c/o CNW Publishing, Inc.
45 Main St., P03 A
North Stratford, NH 03590

Send SASE and 2 FCS. Covers freelance writing.

FREEMAN: IDEAS ON LIBERTY
30 S. Broadway
Irvington-on-Hudson, NY 10533

Send 8.5x11 SASE and 4 FCS. For laymen and fairly advanced student of liberty.

FUNNY TIMES
c/o Funny Times, Inc.
POB 18530
Cleveland Heights, OH 44118

Send 9x12 SASE and 3 FCS. Covers humor.

FUR-FISH-GAME
2878 E. Main St.
Columbus, OH 43209

Send 9x12 SASE and $1. For outdoorsmen of all ages.

GAME DEVELOPER
c/o United Business Media
303 Second St., South Tower, 9th FL
San Francisco, CA 94107

Free. Computer game development.

GAME & FISH
POB 420235
Palm Coast, FL 32142

Send $3.50 and 9x12 SASE. They publish 28 different mags on fishing and hunting.

GARGOYLE
c/o Paycock Press
3819 N. 13th St.
Arlington, VA 22201

Send SASE. For writers.

GAY & LESBIAN REVIEW

POB 180300
Boston, MA 02118

Free. Covering gay and lesbian history, culture and politics.

GEORGIA MAGAZINE
c/o Georgia Electric Membership Corp.
POB 1707
Tucker, GA 30085

Send $2. For and about Georgians.

GOOD OLD DAYS
c/o Annie's
306 E. Parr Rd
Berne, IN 46711

Send $2. First person nostalgia.

GROUP MAGAZINE
c/o Simply Youth Ministry
1515 Cascade Ave.
Loveland, CO 80535

Send 9x12 SASE and 3 FCS. Christian mag for young people.

GUIDE
55 W. Oak Ridge Dr.
Hagerstown, MD 21740

Send 6x9 SASE. For Christian youth, 10-14.

GUN DIGEST THE MAGAZINE
c/o F+W Media
700 E. State St.
Iowa, WI 54990

Free. Covers guns.

HADASSAH MAGAZINE
50 W. 58th St.
NY, NY 10019

Send 9x12 SASE. Covers Jewish issues.

HISPANIC BUSINESS
c/o Hispanic Business, Inc.
5358 Hollister Ave., Suite 204
Santa Barbara, CA 93111

Free. Covers Hispanic business.

HISPANIC CAREER WORLD
c/o Equal Opportunity Publications, Inc.
445 Broad Hollow Rd., Suite 425
Melville, NY 11747

Free. Aimed at Hispanic students and professionals.

THE HOLLINS CRITIC
POB 9538
Hollins University
Roanoke, VA 24020

Send $3. Covers poetry.

HOME FURNISHING RETAILER
c/o NHFA
3910 Tinsley Dr., Suite 101
High Point, NC 27265

Send REQ and 5 FCS.

HOOT
1413 Academy Ln.
Elkins Park, PA 19027

Send $2. Covers writing and is designed with original art and photography.

HOUSTON PRESS
2603 La Branch St.
Houston, TX 77004

Send REQ and $3. Covers news and arts of interest to Houston.

INCENTIVE
c/o Northstar Travel Media, LLC
100 Lighting Way
Secaucus, NJ 07094

Send 9x12 SASE. Covers sales promotion and employee motivation.

INGRAMS
c/o Show-Me Publishing
POB 411356
Kansas City, MO 64141

Free. Covers KC business and economic development.

ITALIAN AMERICA

219 E. St. NE,
Washington, DC 20002

Free. Covers timely info about OSIA.

JOURNAL OF COURT REPORTING
c/o National Court Report Association
8224 Old Courthouse Rd.
Vienna, VA 22180

Free. Covers court reporting.

JOURNAL PLUS MAGAZINE
654 Osos St.
San Luis Obispo, CA 93401

Send SASE and $2. Journal is strictly for central
coast of California.

KC MAGAZINE
7101 College Blvd., Suite 400
Overland Park, KS 66210

Send 8.5x11 SASE. Covers life in KC, Kansas.

KHABAR
c/o Khabar, Inc.
3790 Holcomb Bridge Rd., Suite 101
Norcoss, GA 30092

Free. Covers Asian-Indian community in and around
GA.

KING ARTHUR FLOUR
c/o The Bakers Catalogue
58 Billings Farm Rd.
White River JCT, VT 05001

KIWANI'S
c/o Kiwanis International
3636 Woodview Trace
Indianapolis, IN 46268

Send 9x12 SASE and 5 FCS. For business and
professional people.

THE LANE REPORT
c/o Lane Communications Group
201 E. Main St., 14th FL
Lexington, KY 40507

Free. Covers statewide business.

LATINA
c/o Latina Media Ventures
120 Broadway, 34th FL
NY, NY 10271

Send REQ. Covers Latina American issues.

LEADERSHIP JOURNAL
c/o Christianity Today Intl
465 Gunderson Dr.
Carol Stream, IL 60188

Free. In support of pastors and church leaders.

LIFE EXTENSION
c/o Life Extension Northeast Fulfillment
150 Fieldcrest Ave.
Edison, NJ 08837

Send REQ. Covers men's health.

THE LIVING CHURCH
c/o Living Church Foundation
POB 514036
Milwaukee, WI 53203

Free. Covers articles of interest to members of the
Episcopal Church.

LL&A MAGAZINE
c/o Media Diversified, Inc.
96 Karma Rd.
Markham, Ontario, L3R 4Y3
Canada

Free. Covers the travel business and accessory
market.

THE LOOKOUT
c/o Standard Publishing
8805 Governors Hill Dr., Suite 400
Cincinnati, OH 45249

Send $1. For Christian adults with emphasis on
spiritual growth and family.

LUCKY
POB 37650
Boone, IA 50037

Send REQ. Covers women's fashion.

MAINLINE TODAY

c/o Today Media, Inc.
4699 West Chester Pike
Newton Square, PA 19073

Free. Covers PA's mail line and western suburbs.

MARLIN
POB 8500
Winter Park, FL 32790

Send SASE. Covers the sport of big game fishing.

MEMPHIS DOWNTOWNER MAGAZINE
c/o Downtown Publications, Inc.
408 S. Front St., Suite 109
Memphis, TN 38103

Free. Features positive aspects with a Memphis tie-in.

MERCER BUSINESS MAGAZINE
2550 Kuser Rd.
Trenton, NJ 08691

Send #10 SASE. Covers business related topics.

MICHIGAN OUT-OF-DOORS
POB 30235
Lansing, MI 30235

Send $3.50. Focused on Michigan hunting and fishing.

MOUNTAIN REVIEW
c/o MCCX Education Dept., Mike Napier
Newspaper Sup
POB 2000
Wartburg, TN 37887

Free. Morgan County Correctional publication.

THE MUSIC & SOUND RETAILER
c/o Testa Communications
25 Willowdale Ave.
Port Washington, NY 11050

Send #10 SASE. Covers music instruments.

MUSKY HUNTER MAGAZINE
POB 340
7978 Hwy. 70 E. St.
Germain, WI 54558

Send 9x12 SASE and $2.79. Covers musky fishing.

MUZZLE BLASTS
POB 67
Friendship, IN 47021

Free. Covers guns.

MY BUSINESS MAGAZINE
c/o Imagination Publishing
600 W. Fulton St., 6th FL
Chicago, IL 60661

Free. Covers small business.

MY DAILY VISITOR
c/o Our Sunday Visitor, Inc.
200 Noll Plaza
Huntington, IN 46750

Send #10 SASE and 3 FCS. Scripture meditations based on the day's Catholic mass.

NASH NEWS
c/o Nash Corr. Institution ATTN: Zollie Boone
POB 600
Nashville, NC 27856

Free. By and about prisoners.

NATIONAL
c/o Canadian Bar Assn.
500-865 Carling Ave.
Ottawa, Ontario K1S 5S8
Canada

Free. Covers practice trends and developments in the law.

OUTDOOR NW
10002 Aurora Ave. N. #36
Seattle, WA 98133

Send $3. Covers outdoor recreation in the Pacific Northwest.

OUTREACH MAGAZINE
2231 Faraday Way, Suite 120
Carlsbad, CA 92008

Free. Covers outreach in Christianity.

PACIFIC COAST BUSINESS TIMES

14 E. Carrillo St., Ste. A
Santa Barbara, CA 93101

Free. Financial news for Santa Barbara, Ventura and San Luis Obispo counties.

PENNSYLVANIA
c/o Pennsylvania Magazine Co.
POB 755
Camp Hill, PA 17001

Free. Covers people, places, events and history in PA.

THE PENNSYLVANIA LAWYER
c/o Pennsylvania Bar Assn.
100 South St.
POB 186
Harrisburg, PA 17108

Send $2. For legal professionals and members of the PV Bar Association.

PET AGE
c/o Journal Multimedia
220 Davidson Ave, Ste. 302
Somerset, NJ 08873

Free. Covers pet supplies for the pet industry.

PITTSBURG MAGAZINE
c/o Weisner Media Washington's Landing
600 Waterfront Dr., Ste. 100
Pittsburg, PA 15222

Send. $2. covering the Pittsburg metro area.

POLICE & SECURITY NEWS
c/o Days Communication
1208 Juniper St.
Quakertown, PA 18951

Send 10x13 SASE and $2.53 postage. Covers public law enforcement and homeland security.

POPULAR COMMUNICATIONS
c/o CQ Communication
25 Newbridge Rd.
Hicksville, NY 11801

Free. Covers the radio communications hobby.

POWER BOATING CANADA
1121 Invicta Dr., Unit 2
Oakville, Ontario L6H 2R2
Canada

Free. Covers recreational power boating.

POWER & MOTOR YACHT
10 Bokum Rd.
Essex, CT 06426

Send REQ. Covers powerboats 24 ft. and larger.

POZ
c/o CDM Publishing, LLC
462 Seventh Ave., 19th FL
NY, NY 10018

Free. For people impacted by HIV and AIDS.

PRAIRIE BUSINESS
c/o GFFC Company
808 Third Ave. #400
Fargo, ND 58103

Free. Covers business on the Northern Plains

PRISM MAGAZINE
c/o Evangelical for Social Action
POB 367
Wayne, PA 19087

Send $3. Covers Christianity and social justice.

PROFIT
c/o Rogers Media
1 Mt. Pleasant Rd., 11th FL
Toronto, Ontario M4Y 2Y5
Canada

Send 9x12 SASE and 844 postage. Covers small and medium business.

THE PUBLIC LAWYER
c/o ABA, Gov and Public Sector
Lawyer Division
321 N. Clark St., MS 19.1
Chicago, IL 60610

Free. Covers government attorneys and the legal issues that pertain to them.

PURPOSE
1582 Falcon

Hillsboro, KS 67063

Send 9x12 SASE and $2. Focused on Christian discipleship.

QUAKER LIFE
c/o Friends United Meeting
101 Quaker Hill Dr.
Richmond, IN 47374

Free. Covers Christian news and inspirational issues.

RACK MAGAZINE
c/o Buckmaster Ltd.
10350 US HWY 80 E.
Montgomery, AL 36117

Free. Covers big hunting.

REDBOOK
POB 6093
Harlan, IA 51593

Send REQ. Covers fashion, antiaging and more.

REUNIONS MAGAZINE
POB 11727
Milwaukee, WI 53211

Send #10 SASE. Cover reunions -- all aspects and types.

RIDER MAGAZINE
1227 Flynn Rd., Suite 304
Camarillo, CA 93010

Send $2.95. Covers motorcycling.

ROAD RACER X
c/o Filter Publications
122 Vista Del Rio Dr.
Morgantown, WV 26508

Send #10 SASE. Covers motorcycle road racing.

ROCHESTER BUSINESS JOURNAL
45 E. Ave., Suite 500
Rochester, NY 14604

Free. Covers local business.

RTOHQ: THE MAGAZINE
1504 Robin Hood Trail

Austin, TX 78703

Free. Covers the rent-to-own industry.

RUSSIAN LIFE
c/o RIS Publications
POB 567
Montpelier, VT 05601

Send 9x12 SASE and 6 FCS. Covers Russian culture, history and business.

SACRAMENTO NEWS & REVIEW
c/o Chico Community Publishing
1124 Del Paso Blvd.
Sacramento, CA 95815

Send 50₵. Covers alternative news and entertainment in Sacramento, CA.

SACRAMENTO PARENT
c/o Family Publishing, Inc.
457 Grass Valley Hwy., Ste. 5
Auburn, CA 95603

Free. Covers parenting in the Sacramento, CA area.

SALT WATER SPORTSMAN
c/o Bonnier Corporation
460 N. Orlando Ave., Ste. 200
Winter Park, FL 32789

Send #10 SASE. Covers saltwater sport fishing.

SAN QUENTIN NEWS
c/o San Quentin Edu. Dept.
1 Main St.
San Quentin, CA 94964

Send $1.61 in FCS. Publication for, about, and by prisoners.

SAVANNAH MAGAZINE
c/o Morris Publishing Group
POB 1088
Savannah, GA 31402

Free. Covers homes and entertainment in Savannah, GA.

SCREEN PRINTING
c/o ST Media Group, Intl.
11262 Cornell Park Dr.

Cincinnati, OH 45242

Free. For the screen-printing industry.

SEATTLE WEEKLY
307 Third Ave. 5, 2nd FL
Seattle, WA 98104

Send $3. Covers art, politics, food, business and book with local interest.

THE SECRET PLACE
c/o American Baptist Home Mission Societies
POB 851
Valley Forge, PA 19482

Send 6x9 SASE. Covers Christian daily devotion.

SHOPPER MARKETING
c/o Path to Purchase Institute
8550 W. Bryn Mawr Ave., Suite 200
Chicago, IL 60631

Free. Covers advertising and the shopper marketing industry.

SHEPERD EXPRESS
c/o The Brooklyn Company, Inc.
207 E. Buffalo St., Suite 410
Milwaukee, WI 53202

Send $3. Covers news and entertainment with a progressive news edge.

SIGN BUILDER ILLUSTRATED
c/o Simmons Boardman Publishing
55 Broad St, 26th FL
NY, NY 10004

Free. Covers sign and graphic industry.

SKYDIVING
1665 Lexington Ave., Suite 102
Deland, FL 32724

Send $2. For skydivers, worldwide dealers and equipment manufacturers.

SNOWEST MAGAZINE
c/o Harris Publishing 360 B. St.
Idaho Falls, ID 83402

Free. Covers snowmobiling.

SPORT FISHING
c/o Bonnier Corporation
460 N Orlando Ave., Ste. 200
Winter Park, FL 32789

Send #10 SASE. Covers saltwater fish and fisheries.

THE STATE JOURNAL
c/o World Now
POB 11848
Charleston, WV 25339

Send #10 SASE. Provides stories to the business community in WV.

SUPER LAWYERS
c/o Thomason Reuters
610 Opperman Dr.
Eagan, MN 55123

Free. Covers law and politics.

TELEVISTA
304 Indian Trace #238
Weston, FL 33326

Free. Written in Spanish and covers Hispanic entertainment.

TOASTMASTER
c/o Toastmaster International
POB 9052
Mission Viejo, CA 92690

Send 9x12 SASE and 4 FCS. Covers public speaking, leadership and club concerns.

HOCKY MAGAZINE
c/o Touchpoint Sports
1775 Bob Johnson Dr.
Colorado Springs, CO 80906

Free. Covers amateur hockey in the U.S.

USA PHILATELIC
c/o Stamp Fulfillment Services
POB 7247
Philadelphia, PA 19101

Send REQ. Covers stamp collecting and ordering.

VIBRANT LIFE
c/o Review & Harold Publishing Association
55 W Oak Ridge Dr.
Hagerstown, MD 21740

Send $1. Covering health for Christians.

VFW MAGAZINE
c/o Veterans of Foreign Wars of the US
406 W. 34th St.
Kansas City, MO 64111

Send 9x12 SASE and 5 FCS. Covers veteran affairs, military history and current events.

VINEYARD & WINERY MANAGEMENT
POB 14459
Santa Rosa, CA 95402

Free. Aimed at professional grape growers, winemakers and winery sales.

VM+SD
c/o ST Media Group Intl.
11262 Cornell Park Dr.
Cincinnati, OH 45242

Free. Covers retail store design, store planning and visual merchandise.

WEST BRANCH
c/o Stadler Center of Poetry Bucknell University
Lewisburg, PA 17837

Send $3. Literary magazine.

WHAT'S HERS/WHAT'S HIS MAGAZINE
c/o What! Publishers, Inc.

108-93 Lombard Ave.
Winnipeg, Manitoba R3B 3B1
Canada

Send 9x12 SASE w/ Canadian or International postage. Covers teen issues and pop culture.

WHOLE LIFE TIMES
c/o Whole Life Media, LLC
23705 Vanowen St. #306
West Hills, CA 91307

Send $3. Holistic living.

WINDSPEAKERS
c/o Aboriginal Multi-media Society of Alberta
13245-146 St.
Edmonton, Alberta, T51, 4SL
Canada

Free. Covers native issues.

WOMEN IN BUSINESS
c/o American Business Women's Association
11050 Rose Ave., Suite 200
Overland Park, KS 66211

Send 9x12 SASE and 4 FCS. Covers issues affecting working women.

THE WRITER'S CHRONICLE
c/o Assn. of Writers & Writing Program
George Mason University
Carty House MS 1E3
Fairfax, VA 22030

Free. Covers the art and craft of writing.

THE MILLIONAIRE PRISONER PEN PAL ATTRACTION SYSTEM

By Josh Kruger

Most prisoners use pen pal websites when trying to get pen pals. You may be one of those who have? I used them for years. We all know what typically happens. One of the comrades in our cellhouse uses a pen pal website and gets a couple of hits. He brags about it and gets other prisoners to sign up for the same service (which he gets "credit" for). So, we go on said site and get a hit or two. Not the success we really wanted, right? There has to be a better way. There is. If you want better results, let me show you how to get them.

My name is Josh Kruger, I'm a lifer in Illinois, and the author of several books, including *The Millionaire Prisoner*. Also *Pen Pal Success*. You may have read them? I wrote *Pen Pal Success* in 2015 based on my 20+ years inside the pen pal game. But when I wrote it I had not yet used Facebook. (I've been down since 1999, well before Mr. Zuckerberg started Facebook.) What I've found since then is that by using a combination of social media with a prison pen pal sire produces the best results. Especially when it comes to your money.

I know that a lot of your still got stimulus check money burning holes in your pocket that you want to blow. Some of you want to use it to go online and find the girl of your dreams. Nothing wrong with that. But first, I want to show you how to make any money you spend in the pen pal game go farther with the best results. You can do that with The Millionaire Prisoner Pen Pal Attraction System.

What's this system? It's a process that works time after time to deliver pen pal hits to your tablet or mailbox. It allows you to get these hits with minimal effort on your part with the least amount of money spent. Here's how I came up with this system.

After my twin brother got out of the fed joint he helped me set up a Facebook page. I wrote short posts for it and was able to reconnect with friends that I went to school with and hadn't seen in years. Some of them didn't even know I was doing life in prison! One of them thought I was living in California, LOL.

One day I wrote a post about a cat I saw sunning himself on a rock in my prison yard. Immediately, all the women who were friends on my page liked it. Then I got contacted by Nikki. She was a girl who lived in my old neighborhood. We started talking. She started visiting me every week, putting money on my books, and accepting my calls. Then I started talking to another girl who was friends with my sister growing up.

We talked on the phone every day and had weekly video visits. I was doing so good that some of the prison guards who worked the visiting room asked me what my secret was. The truth? Facebook helped me get to the top of the prison pel pal world.

Because of my success with Facebook I started noticing a lot of companies that were using social media websites to help get us pen pals. I wanted to test out their services and it was then that I had my revelation. I used CagedKingdom.net to post my pen pal profile on Facebook. They charged me $7.00 for a post guaranteed to reach at least 200 people. (It actually went to 213 people and I got 13 hits.) I got a couple of new pen pals from that post so it was worth it. But what if we took that strategy to a whole new level? To understand why this is so powerful, let me show you the truth behind "hit" counters.

A few years ago, I paid $50.00 for a profile on WriteAPrisoner.com. Because they showed me the hit counter, I know my profile was seen by 1,304 people in six months. Do you think those views were hits? No, those were just people viewing my profile. Out of those 1,304 views I got seven responses. That's a .005% response rate. Not good. Using typical advertising metrics, I should at least get a .01% response rate to be considered a success. Online ads guru Perry Marshall says a 20% click through rate (CTR) is good.

My Caged Kingdom promotion on Facebook got 13 engagements on 213 people. That's .06%! So, what do I get if I took $50.00 and used targeted Facebook posts to women?

According to the fantastic book, *Ultimate Guide to Facebook Advertising*, I could reach at least 41,000 people, and up to 110,000 people on that $50.00, depending on my targeted metrics. Using WriteAPrisoner's metrics I would have to spend $1,572 to reach 41,000 people. (41,000 - 1,304 = 31.44 x $50.00 = $1,572.) Using my Caged Kingdom result, how many engagements could I expect to get off those 41,000 people? 2,460! (41,000 x .06% = 2,460!) The real key to this strategy would be that any Facebook promo that you did should be targeted to specific women (or men) of a certain age, location, demographic, etc. That target demographic is where you find your pen pal avatar.

Your Pen Pal Avatar

Who is your perfect pen pal? What magazines do they read? What TV shows do they watch? What beliefs do they have? What fetishes do they have? What hobbies do they have? What websites do they visit? You ask these questions so you can target your perfect pen pals online. You'll get more hits for your money this way. For instance, here's my perfect pen pal avatar:

"My best pen pal is a single, lonely woman, 30+, college graduate, who reads *Inc*, *Entrepreneur*, and *Prison Legal News* (or believes in prisoner's rights). She watches Love After Lockup, Shark Tank, The Profit, and ABC's For Life."

Write out you own pen pal avatar profile like above. That way you know who you're looking for in the first place!

How would you find this perfect pen pal? By using Facebook and other social media sites. You could do searches for them using search metrics you listed in your pen pal avatar.

Go on Facebook and join all the prison pen pal groups. Search for "people who like *Prison Legal News*." Or "Love After Lockup." Or "The Cell Block." Do a Google search for "prison pen pal forums." And "prison rights forums." This is how you find websites and network opportunities you've never heard of.

"If you have less money in the bank than you have followers on Instagram, you need to get a new group of friends." - Billionaire P.A.

Setting Up the System

Once you find these groups and websites, you should start posting on them and networking. One way is to ask a simple thought-provoking question. Then, after they answer, you ask them: "How did you come to that conclusion?" I had a cellmate who used to do this on phone calls to the party line. After getting the girls on the line involved in a discussion, he would send them to his online pen pal page. He came up numerous times like that. You can do the same in prison pen pal and prisoner rights forums.

Now I know what you're probably thinking. That you don't have the ability to post regularly on Facebook, Instagram, or Twitter. Because of that, I've developed a system how to attract your perfect pen pal. (Remember: you have to know who your perfect pen pal avatar is before you can successfully implement this tactic.)

This is my Millionaire Prisoner Pen Pal Attraction System:

Step 1: Set up a prison pen pal website profile. You need one on a website that allows your first contact email to be sent to you by mail. I've used both PenACon and WriteAPrisoner. I prefer PenACon because I can pay $65.00 and have a lifetime profile instead of $40.00 a year.

Step 2: After your pen pal profile is set up, go on a Facebook and set up a profile page, if you don't already have one. Then link your Facebook profile page with your prison pen pal page.

Step 3: Do Facebook posts and then "Boost" it to your targeted pen pal avatar demographic. Or do Facebook ads target to the same audience. Done right you're bound to get hundreds of hits. Here's how to do a system post right.

Come up with a question that you can write a post for. Try to think of something relevant to the present time and yourself. Here's how I do mine:

Does "Love After Lockup" hurt lifers?

Most of us inside think so. Why? Because there are no lifers on the show. Some women who watch it are overlooking us. They want a short-timer who'll come home and be their prince charming. Nothing wrong with that. Btu lifers need love too. And if given a chance, we might be better?

Yes, I'm a lifer. And in my book *Pen Pal Success* I show prisoners how to get pen pals. When I wrote that book there was no "Love After Lockup" TV show. So, I'm serious. What's the woman's side of the debate? What does a lifer have to do to find his dream girl? I'd love to hear your thoughts. Maybe I'll put you in my next book?

You can learn more by clicking on the link below:
freejoshkruger@gmail.com

Notice at the end I used my email address. If you want pen pals, use your pen pal profile link. If you use your email address, make sure you have an auto response set up that directs them to your pen pal profile anyway. The whole key to this tactic is that their responses are automatically sent to you.

After you write these types of posts, boost them on Facebook to women you "choose through targeting." My maximum budget would be $20.00 for five days (or $4.00 a day). Just to test it out. I'd target only United States and United Kingdom women, ages 28-50, with all the interests in my pen pal avatar. After that first week I'd check my results and see what I needed to tweak. I'd keep testing new metrics until I got all the pen pals I wanted or needed.

You're probably wonder how this system actually works? I can tell you that my friend Brian Rooney at Prison Social Network reported great success with it. He said he had 38 pen pals at one time when he was inside. One of his clients uses this exact strategy on his site to get over 3,000 views a week. Out of those views Brian reports a 10% response rate. He couldn't figure out why they are still using it. We all know why.

You can never have enough pen pals, right? For more about my results, be sure to read my book, *The Millionaire Prisoner 4: Pen Pal Mastery* (coming soon from The Cell Block). I will go more in-depth about this system in that book.

For more about getting pen pals and women in general, be sure to check out *Pretty Girls Love Bad Boys* by Mike Enemigo and King Guru. They are fellow pen pal gurus who get it right. And for more about writing top-notch letters, be sure to read Mike Enemigo's book, *The Art & Power of Letter Writing for Prisoners Deluxe Edition*. Lastly, if you liked what I shared here, you'll love my books, *The Millionaire Prisoner*, parts 1, 2, and 3 (all published by The Cell Block).

Always remember that it only takes one "yes" to change your life. But you'll never get that one yes unless you try. So, get out of your comfort zone. Write those letters. Set up your profiles. Send emails. Build your network. Do whatever it takes. You can start by having your family and friends like thecellblock.net content online!

A Case for Relapse Prevention for Prisoners
By Charles Howard Hottinger Jr.

As with anything in life, preparation and planning is the key to success. It is vital to self-empowerment, and is a mechanism to reduce the rate of recidivism in the ex-offender population. The California Department of Corrections and Rehabilitation (CDCR), specifically the board of prison hearings (BPH), has taken notice of the importance in relapse prevention planning. Every prisoner who comes before the BPH is required to prevent a comprehensive "Relapse Prevention Plan"; one that addresses warning signs and triggers for maladaptive or problematic behaviors and demonstrates ways of successfully managing them in the community. What is a "Relapse Prevention Plan" exactly? How does one compose it?

Many California prisoners have fallen victim to the BPH's expectations in providing a comprehensive Relapse Prevention Plan, and subsequently have been faced with years of denials in obtaining a parole date. The BPH simply places the expectations on the prisoner without any instruction as to what a comprehensive Relapse Prevention Plan encompasses. This has left many prisoners ill-prepared or deficient in the plan they present to the BPH. First, prisoners must understand why the BPH is asking for this document. The reason is simple: a comprehensive Relapse Prevention Plan is a fortified plan for preventing a return to substance abuse before the prisoner is triggered to use again while on parole. The key is to plan ahead. The BPH wants to see that prisoners are prepared; that they have given real thought to how they are going to navigate parole and keep sobriety intact. If a prisoner's sobriety is constantly challenged, the regular obstacles of parole will be impossible to deal with; hence, the need for a Relapse Prevention Plan.

During my research and learning process, I couldn't find anything directed a specifically addressing the issues of how to create a "relapse prevention plan." It took years of attending Narcotics and Alcoholics Anonymous, reading addiction literature and trying to understand my own reasons for using chemical substances before I began to understand what the word "comprehensive" meant as it relates to relapse prevention planning. The word "comprehensive" means "covering all the possibilities completely." When I began to understand addiction and relapse factors in such a broad term I was able to translate that insight into the development of my own personal relapse prevention plan, and subsequently a book titled A Guide to Relapse Prevention for Prisoners. I gained the awareness that success is a moving target that, in an ever-changing world, my life must actively be managed in a way that generates the high-quality results I desire. The benefits of a comprehensive Relapse Prevention Plan meant I had the proper stepping stones in life to remain abstinent. It inspired me with the goal of sharing what managing life is like when you have a consciously designed strategy that looks at maladaptive or problematic behaviors and shows you what life can be like when you effectively minimize or eliminate those problems. Understanding why something happens is helpful, but being able to predict that something is going to happen gives me more options. When I tried to stop using in the past, I tried to do it with self-control. I believed I was strong enough to do it on my own. It did not help because I failed to address any of the real issues that made me feel the need to start using drugs and, furthermore, those issues that triggered me to use drugs. The self-control method became a temporary band-aid to my addiction problem and only lasted a limited amount of time before my addiction would take control again. I remember feeling frustrated many times, and I thought I was a failure who would hopelessly use drugs to cope for the rest of my life. Everything changed, however, the moment I created my Relapse Prevention Plan and held it in my hands for the first time. For once, I felt like I had power over my addiction, and that I was in control of my life rather than out of control.

The information presented in A Guide to Relapse Prevention for Prisoners is a must-have for any prisoner, in any state, who wants the same control in their life and over their addiction. It is for any prisoner who finds themselves confronted with being the best candidate for parole before a Parole Board, and who believes in giving themselves every opportunity to succeed while on parole. Every prisoner will learn to identify and address issues that have caused them to become addicted, and move them towards responsibility and accountability by guiding the prisoner through the process of preparing and quality and comprehensive Relapse Prevention Plan.

With a Relapse Prevention in place, every prisoner will find themselves on a path to successfully re-enter into mainstream society where they can reunite with family and become productive citizens.

Author Charles Howard Hottinger Jr is a life-term prisoner and former addict who has dedicated his life to helping other prisoners change their way of thinking and remain abstinent.

To order "A Guide To Relapse Prevention for Prisoners" send $15.00 plus $5 for s/h to: The Cell Block; PO Box 1025; Rancho Cordova, CA 95741

ORDER NOW!

FREE MONEY

Need money for a lawyer, to publish your book, buy art supplies or any other legit project you have going on? Crowdfunding presents opportunities for prisoners!

Kickstarter and other crowdfunding websites provide an interesting option for prisoners with imagination and originality to explore career-expanding opportunities, raise money and gain access to a commodity often in short supply behind bars -- hope.

Basically, crowdfunding involves developing online campaigns for specific projects, charitable causes or services, or to develop certain products. People who want to support a campaign can donate funds, from as little as $1 to as much as they want. Hundreds, thousands or even tens of thousands of people may join together to support and fund a campaign, and once a project achieves its target funding amount the money is paid to the campaign organizer so they can make the project a reality.

Kickstarter, founded in 2009, is a popular crowdfunding site that specializes in entrepreneurial campaigns with an artistic focus, while other sites like GoFundMe, IndieGoGo, Fundly and RocketHub are more flexible. Some sites allow campaigns for legal defense expenses, bail money and prison ministries. Almost all of these services charge fees ranging from around 4 to 9 percent of the money collected during the campaign; some are all-or-nothing, meaning the entire amount of the project must be funded or the campaign is cancelled. Donors retain no equity interest in the funded projects but usually receive recognition or incentives for their contributions.

Modest crowdfunding projects that have been started by or on behalf of prisoners have included a $5,700 campaign to produce "Amazing Grace" by women in a New York prison, $582 to finance a creative writing class at the Garner Correctional Institution in Connecticut and a project to collect art supplies for incarcerated students. Individual prisoners have used crowdfunding to raise money to prove their innocence or to make bond. The success of such campaigns often depends on the ability to tap in to a large network of potential funders who might be interested in the project.

Since March 2014, the Cook County Jail has run a 10-week culinary program involving a small group of prisoners to help them learn marketable skills and obtain jobs in the food service industry upon their release. Chef Bruno Abate, an Italian native who runs the program, called "Recipe for Change," became inspired after learning about an award-winning bakery at the Due Palazzi prison in Padua, Italy. In May 2015, Abate wanted to take the culinary program to the next level.

"When you know how to make pizza well, you can find a job anywhere," he said. Abate joined forces with prominent businessman Ronald Gidwitz to buy a pizza oven for the program. They raised almost $5,000 through an IndieGoGo campaign and another $11,000 through Gadwitz's personal network, and were able to buy a top-of-the-line oven. They hope to eventually bake and sell pizzas to hungry customers outside the jail.

Innocence projects and prisoners' rights organizations have used crowdfunding for a variety of causes, too. The Human Rights Defense Center, PLN's parent non-profit organization, launched a successful campaign through IndieGoGo that raised around $15,000 for the Prison Ecology Project to fight toxic prisons.

Claudia Whitman with CURE's National Death Raw Assistance Network raised $2,600 through IndieGoGo to help fund a wrongful conviction investigation on behalf of Michigan prisoner Lacino Hamilton.

Many prisons and jails have institutional rules that make crowdfunding projects difficult if not impossible. Some have regulations that prevent prisoners from receiving funds from other prisoners, parolees or individuals not related to them. Others prohibit prisoners from having checking or savings accounts, and deduct expenses for the cost of incarceration from money placed in their prison trust accounts. Therefore, crowdfunding campaigns for prisoners and prison-related projects are usually organized and run by friends, family members of other contacts outside of prison.

While many prisoners have an entrepreneurial spirit, it generally goes unrewarded; creative outlets such as writing books, producing songs and creating artwork are not only discouraged but sometimes purposely impeded by corrections officials. Such Limitations, often justified by rote references to "institutional security," but in reality implemented by unimaginative and sometimes hostile guards and prison administrators, do little to assist with prisoners' rehabilitation.

The global economy is a digital economy that is ruled by computers, smart phones and Internet-savvy businesses, which are anathema to prison and jail officials who largely operate in the analog era. Although prisoners are increasingly being allowed to use secure, monitored email systems, such as Corrlinks in federal prisons, the vast majority do not have access to the Internet -- even though computer and online skills are a perquisite for most living wage jobs in the non-prison economy.

Projects such as those funded by Kickstarter and similar sites would be a welcome alternative to many prisoners, who would be encouraged to think in a positive, creative and thoughtful manner about how to successfully pursue funding campaigns for their projects, products and services -- a skill that would serve them well after they are released. Such endeavors should be encouraged, and prisoners with initiative should be given the resources and opportunities to either succeed or fail based upon their own originality, ideas and drive. Instead of fearing change our nation's corrections system needs to embrace it, taking advantage of all the Internet has to offer instead of viewing technology as an inherent threat. By devoting resources to online education, job training and business opportunities, including crowdfunding campaigns -- all available with a few keystrokes at often minimal cost -- prisoners could spend their time engaging in worthwhile and positive projects to help them prepare for their eventual release.

Sources: Derek Gilina for PLN, kickstarter.com, forbes.com, notimpossiblenow.com, rebelnews.com, dnainfo.com

Only MIKE ENEMIGO and THE CELL BLOCK provide certified game...

BEFORE!

AFTER!

BEFORE!

AFTER!

Don't be a schmuck, order these books now!

PRI$ONER $UCCE$$ $TORY!

Popular New Snack Born Behind Bars

In 2009, Seth Sundberg was sentenced to five years for a fraudulent $5 million tax refund. The former pro basketball player had managed a California mortgage office and went from a comfortable living in the real estate industry to earning $5.25 a month in a prison kitchen. While working in that position, Sundberg noticed a label on a box of frozen chicken that said "Not for Human Consumption."

That discovery led him to swear off prison poultry forever. He began to look for nutritious, protein-rich foods in the commissary to supplement the subpar institutional meals. He developed a recipe with another prisoner using trail mix, oatmeal, peanut butter and honey that merged to form a tasty, satisfying granola bar. Soon Sundberg and his partner were making about $200 a month selling the bars to other prisoners.

Upon his release, Sundberg sought help from a nonprofit whose motto is "transform your hustle." Defy Ventures offered him mentorship, business training and a small amount of funding; a year later, Sundberg launched a company called Prison Bars.

Prison Bars now uses organic, non-GMO and gluten-free ingredients in its "criminally delicious" snacks. The company markets and distributes the bars online and in the San Francisco area; it currently employees six people -- four of them formerly incarcerated. Sundberg is planning to expand into ten other cities with representatives who have left prison and face an adversarial job market. Prison Bars has also partnered with the grocery store chain Bi-Rite, which will start carrying the granola bars in September 2016.

"Everyone's made mistakes, and everyone's been given a second chance at some point," Sundberg said. "My vision was to see if people incarnated about this topic, to start having conversations that raise awareness. You never know what kind of ripple effect that can cause." According to the Prison Bars website (www.prison-bars.com), "Each purchase of criminally delicious Prison Bars supports our movement to provide redemption and second chances, reduce recidivism, and raise awareness of America's prison issues."

As a huge supporter of one turning his negative into a positive, cellpreneurship/entrepreneurship, and learning how to hustle and win legally, I respect what Mr. Sundberg has managed to accomplish and I find it inspiring. Not only did he create something that allowed him to make a few bucks while in prison, but he was able to take it to the next level when he was released from prison and turn it into an entire business. And it all started from an idea he had when doing something as common as working in the prison's kitchen! Many of you are creative. Keep your eyes and mind open at all times. Mr. Sundberg's accomplishment is the epitome of one turning his negative into a positive, what I often refer to as "pimping your time." You, too, can do it! ! Mike

SOCIAL NETWORKING
Start and Manage Your Social Media Site Today!

ITEM #016 - Print Facebook Friend list pages!
Color $ 1.50 per page / Black and White $1.00 per page (plus tax; shipping and handling) Have your entire Facebook friend list printed in color or black/white and mailed directly to you. Users of this service must first add info@inmatephotoprovider.com to your corrlinks.com account. An email must be sent providing the Facebook Username, Password, and if the order preference is color or black and white. Once I.P.P. is able to login; the total pages will be counted and an email will be provided detailing the total cost of the order. I.P.P. will not print any pages until payment has been received in full. It takes 2 to 3 business days for print receipts, based on institution location.

Photo Prints: Once the I.P.P. email address has been added to the corrlinks.com account and an email has been provided detailing the Username and password to access the Facebook page, photos of family/friends from your page and/or from photo album folders can be printed. In order to print photos nom photo albums, provide the individual s first/last name and/or the photo album name to print from. Include the total number of copies of each photo. All orders will be processed at the standard 4x6 size, price and shipping rate listed on the I.P .P. order form. Orders will be received within 2 to 3 business days, dependent on institution location. All Local or State inmates who do not have email access are required to physically write I.P.P. all appropriate information, listed above, in order to take advantage of this service.

ITEM #017 - Set-up a Dating/Social Networking page................... $15 per account (Flat Fee)
I.P.P. will set up a dating/social networking page on the most popular sites around. Examples include websites such as Facebook, Tagg, Instagram, POF (plenty of fish) or any FREE site. Provide I.P.P. with site(s) and your bio and photo(s) will be uploaded to the site(s). To take advantage of this service you must-first add info@inmatephotoprovider.com to your corrlinks.com account. Afterwards, mail I.P.P. (1) profile page photo, (3) additional pictures to have added to your page during the set-up phase and a typed or neatly handwritten Bio of up to 200 words. If a general profile description page is provided, I.P.P. will update the information within the space provided on each page. Accounts will be created within 24-hours
once payment is received in full. Please allow 2 to 3 business days for receipt of your profile page information, dependent on institution location. An email with the username and password will be provided. In addition, a copy of profile pages with original photos will be provided by mail. All Local and State inmates who do not have email access contact I.P.P. by mail in order to get connected to an online world of male/female singles.

ITEM #018 - Add and Upload Photos to all social media pages $7.50 (Flat Fee)
Email I.P.P. your user name and password or physically mail in your requests in order to take advantage of this service. (10-photo limit)

ITEM #019 - Social Media Monitoring Service (prices vary)
Accounts/pages must be previously created and ACTIVE in order for I.P.P. to manage/monitor each of the accounts. Four (4) monitoring options are offered at this time. With each option, provide the actual website(s) address, email user name and account password. Once I.P.P. is able to gain access and payment is received in full the monitoring service will begin. Socialmedia@inmatephotoprovider.com must be added directly to an inmates corrlinks email account. All State and Local inmates without email accounts can write I.P.P. at the company address to take advantage of this monitoring service.

*GENERAL SERVICE PACKAGE: $21 per month!
From Monday-Sunday I.P.P. will monitor one (1) social media page. Tax and S/H is included. What better way to spend $.70 a day for 30 days? Quality service is guaranteed and $21 is all you pay! No 24/7 monitoring however messages will be received daily. Send UNLIMITED inbox messages to friends/family daily. Receive all responses sent from your friends/family daily. (No maximum number of messages) Print received friend's photos. (Use regular photo; copying rates.) Create new photo albums and upload additional .photos.to social media website page(s). (Use the regular advertised rate.) NO WALLPOST are allowed with this package. NO FRIEND search requests are allowed with this package. Friend list color print outs are not included with this package. Friend photos are not included with this package.

BASIC SERVICE FEES: Less than $35 per month!

For only $1.15 a day (30 day timeframe), I.P.P. will monitor one (1) social media page from Monday- Sunday. *Total price of $34.45, Tax and S/H included in total pricing.

- Receive around the clock page monitoring ALL DAY.
- Send unlimited inbox messages to friends/family daily.
- Receive inbox messages from friends/family daily.
- Search up to three (3) people per week. Full name, city and state MUST be provided.
- Update page status/wallpost once per week.

GOLD SERVICE FEES: Less than $60 per month!

30 days of quality guaranteed 24/7 service of one (1) social media page at only $1.86 a day! (Total price of $55.75. All fees included.)

- Receive one (1) color copy of the account's friends. (Mailed to address provided. Will not email.)
- Update page status/wall post daily.
- Send unlimited inbox messages to friends/family daily.
- Receive inbox messages from friends/family daily.
- Search up to five (5) people per week. Full name, city and state MUST be provided.

PLATINUM SERVICE FEES: Approximately $100 for a three (3) month package!

90 days of uninterrupted service for $109.00 (all fees included). Only $1.22 a day for three (3) months to have I.P.P. manage/monitor up to three (3) social media pages of your choice 24/7, seven days a week. Quality Service GUARANTEED!

- Receive one (1) color copy of your friend list from each website page.
- Receive messages 24/7, seven days a week as received on ALL SITES.
- Receive weekly wallpost responses and pictures of senders in the mail.
- Upload ten (10) new photos to each page per month.
- Send unlimited inbox messages to friends/family on all sites.
- Receive daily messages from all sites daily.
- Update page status/wallpost daily on all sites.
- Search up to ten (10) people a week. Full name, city and state MUST be provided.
- Change page profile pictures for FREE as desired.

EXCLUSIVE VIP SERVICE FEES: $163 for a six (6) month package!

For $.90 a day (6 month timeframe) I.P.P. will maintain, manage and monitor up to five (5) social media pages 24/7 for seven (7) days a week. That's 180 days of service for $162.25 with all fees included! Quality Service GUARANTEED!

- Receive one (1) color copy of your friend list once every two (2) months (ALL sites).
- Receive messages 24/7, seven (7) days a week as received on ALL sites.
- Print up to three (3) 4x6 size friend photos per month. Additional photo copies at standard rates.
- Upload fifteen (15) new photos to each page per month.
- Create new photo albums as desired.
- Send unlimited inbox messages to friends/family on all sites.
- Receive daily messages from all sites daily.
- Update page status/wall post daily on all sites.
- Search up to fifteen (15) people a week. Full name, city and state MUST be provided.
- Update bio, page profile information and change page profile pictures once a month.

Mail All Payments To: Institutional Checks ; IPP Company
P.O. Box 2451
Forrest City AR, 72336

For Faster Service Send Money Gram Payments To:
Richardett Edwards
Email address:.Jonese531@yahoo.comj
P.O. Box 2451
Forrest City, AR 72336

When sending payment always click yes when it ask about the address you are sending funds to. Due to you sending funds to an unlisted street address your system will ask you if you're sure you would like to proceed. Clicks and we will load your account and start your service.

234

PACKAGETRUST

POWERED BY DON DIVA

Full Color Photos of Sexy Woman

Complete Head to toe shots real photo processing in stock and ready to ship.

NO NUDITY. $1 PER PHOTO

Accepted in most facilities

Photo Duplication

$1.00 — 4 x 6 print

$5.00 — 5 x 7 print

$10.00 — 8 x 10 print

People Search

$5.00

Are you looking for a Person or information on a business? We can do the research for you.

- Full Name
- Aliases
- Address
- Age & DOB
- Aliases
- Phone Number
- Relatives
- Address History
- Social Network
- Email Address
- Property Owned
- Relatives
- Employer
- Education

Background Search

$40.00

Need a background check on someone? We will search criminal records in 43 states.

Internet Research

$20.00 per hour

We will provide you with thorough research from credible and relevant sources.
We will research any subject you request and send you print outs of all information found

---

Order form:

Inmate Name: _____

Inmate #: _____

Address _____

City: _____ State _____ Zip _____

[ ] Please send me a complete 4/color catalog of model photos send $7.00.

Send Money Order or Institution Check ONLY! to:

Package Trust

370 W. Pleasantview Avenue Ste #303
Hackensack, NJ 07601
p. 347.815.3229
e. packagetrust@dondivamag.com

Please allow 2-3 weeks to process your order

* Please label all photos clearly

* Photo specialist will provide minor color correction as a courtesy only

* Oddly sized photos will need to be resized at company discretion

USE ADDITIONAL PAPER IF NEEDED
NO ORDER FORM NECESSARY

Photo Duplication

Photo 1

____ 8 x 10 ($10 each) = _____
(Qty)   (Total)

____ 8 x 10 ($10 each) = _____
(Qty)   (Total)

____ 5 x 7 ($5 each) = _____
(Qty)   (Total)

____ 5 x 7 ($5 each) = _____
(Qty)   (Total)

____ 4 x 6 ($1 each) = _____
(Qty)   (Total)

____ 4 x 6 ($1 each) = _____
(Qty)   (Total)

NOTE

Please be sure any photo you purchase will be allowed in your facility. Packagetrust is not responsible for any photos that are rejected by any institution for any reason. We will not reship orders rejected by any institution.

ORDER ANY BOOK OR MAGAZINE

Order our brochure to find out how to order any book or magazine you are looking for- including vintage and out-of-print.

SEND $7.00 FOR A FULL COLOR CATALOG OF SERVICES AND OVER 500 AVAILABLE SEXY PHOTOS .

Get Social!

Finally... real Social Media for inmates and a forum for their loved ones.

Sign up for your own Blog Page!

More than a penpal service- Inmates and their loved ones can post photos, messages, updates and blogs as well as showcase their poetry, novels, and artwork.

Inmate New Profile

Standard One Year Profile: $50

Blog (Must have an active profile) $10

* inmate doesn't need internet access

TO SIGN UP, VISIT DONDIVAMAG.COM OR ORDER OUR CATALOG FOR SIGN UP INSTRUCTIONS.

If you would like a return response from Packagetrust, you **MUST** include a **SASE** (self addressed stamped envelope.)

PEN A CON

Penacon is owned and operated by Freebird Publishers, your trusted inmate service provider.

Penacon.com dedicated to assisting the imprisoned community find connections of friendship and romance around the world. Your profile will be listed on our user-friendly website. We make sure your profile is seen at the highest visibility rate available by driving traffic to our site by consistent advertising and networking. We know how important it is to have your ad seen by as many people as possible in order to bring you the best service possible. Pen pals can now email their first message through penacon.com! We print and send these messages with return addresses if you get one. We value your business and process profiles promptly.

To receive your informational package and application send two stamps to:

PEN A CON

Box 533
North Dighton, MA 02764
Penacon@freebirdpublishers.com
Corrlinks: diane@freebirdpublishers.com
JPay: diane@freebirdpublishers.com

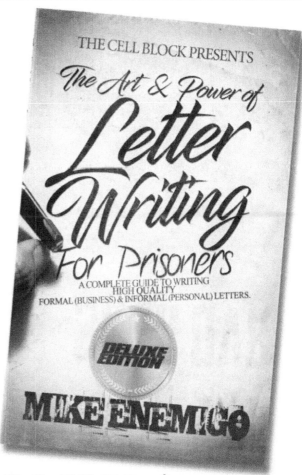

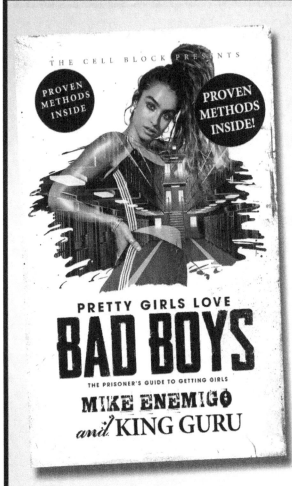

Postage Rates 2022

- First Class Letters (1 oz.) rates .55
  - Each additional ounce will cost an extra .15
- First Class Flats/Large Envelopes (1 oz.) rates 1.00
  - Each additional ounce will cost an extra .15
- Postcard rates $0.36
- First-Class Letters International - 1 oz. $1.20
- Regular Flat Rate Envelope $7.95
- Legal Flat Rate Envelope $8.25

Postage Stamp Conversion
55¢ @ 80% = 44¢
55¢ @ 75% = 41¢
55¢ @ 70% = 39¢
55¢ @ 65% = 36¢

NAME: _____

STREET: _____

CITY: _____

ZIP: _____

PHONE: _____

EMAIL: _____

WEBSITE: _____

NAME: _____

STREET: _____

CITY: _____

ZIP: _____

PHONE: _____

EMAIL: _____

WEBSITE: _____

NAME: _____

STREET: _____

CITY: _____

ZIP: _____

PHONE: _____

EMAIL: _____

WEBSITE: _____

NAME: _____

STREET: _____

CITY: _____

ZIP: _____

PHONE: _____

EMAIL: _____

WEBSITE: _____

NAME: _____

STREET: _____

CITY: _____

ZIP: _____

PHONE: _____

EMAIL: _____

WEBSITE: _____

NAME: _____

STREET: _____

CITY: _____

ZIP: _____

PHONE: _____

EMAIL: _____

WEBSITE: _____

NAME: _____

STREET: _____

CITY: _____

ZIP: _____

PHONE: _____

EMAIL: _____

WEBSITE: _____

NAME: _____

STREET: _____

CITY: _____

ZIP: _____

PHONE: _____

EMAIL: _____

WEBSITE: _____

NAME: _____

STREET: _____

CITY: _____

ZIP: _____

PHONE: _____

EMAIL: _____

WEBSITE: _____

NAME: _____

STREET: _____

CITY: _____

ZIP: _____

PHONE: _____

EMAIL: _____

WEBSITE: _____

NAME: _____

STREET: _____

CITY: _____

ZIP: _____

PHONE: _____

EMAIL: _____

WEBSITE: _____

NAME: _____

STREET: _____

CITY: _____

ZIP: _____

PHONE: _____

EMAIL: _____

WEBSITE: _____

NAME: _____
STREET: _____
CITY: _____
ZIP: _____
PHONE: _____
EMAIL: _____
WEBSITE: _____

NAME: _____
STREET: _____
CITY: _____
ZIP: _____
PHONE: _____
EMAIL: _____
WEBSITE: _____

NAME: _____
STREET: _____
CITY: _____
ZIP: _____
PHONE: _____
EMAIL: _____
WEBSITE: _____

NAME: _____
STREET: _____
CITY: _____
ZIP: _____
PHONE: _____
EMAIL: _____
WEBSITE: _____

NAME: _____
STREET: _____
CITY: _____
ZIP: _____
PHONE: _____
EMAIL: _____
WEBSITE: _____

NAME: _____
STREET: _____
CITY: _____
ZIP: _____
PHONE: _____
EMAIL: _____
WEBSITE: _____

NAME: _____
STREET: _____
CITY: _____
ZIP: _____
PHONE: _____
EMAIL: _____
WEBSITE: _____

NAME: _____
STREET: _____
CITY: _____
ZIP: _____
PHONE: _____
EMAIL: _____
WEBSITE: _____

NAME: _____
STREET: _____
CITY: _____
ZIP: _____
PHONE: _____
EMAIL: _____
WEBSITE: _____

NAME: _____
STREET: _____
CITY: _____
ZIP: _____
PHONE: _____
EMAIL: _____
WEBSITE: _____

NAME: _____
STREET: _____
CITY: _____
ZIP: _____
PHONE: _____
EMAIL: _____
WEBSITE: _____

NAME: _____
STREET: _____
CITY: _____
ZIP: _____
PHONE: _____
EMAIL: _____
WEBSITE: _____

NAME:	NAME:
STREET:	STREET:
CITY:	CITY:
ZIP:	ZIP:
PHONE:	PHONE:
EMAIL:	EMAIL:
WEBSITE:	WEBSITE:
NAME:	NAME:
STREET:	STREET:
CITY:	CITY:
ZIP:	ZIP:
PHONE:	PHONE:
EMAIL:	EMAIL:
WEBSITE:	WEBSITE:
NAME:	NAME:
STREET:	STREET:
CITY:	CITY:
ZIP:	ZIP:
PHONE:	PHONE:
EMAIL:	EMAIL:
WEBSITE:	WEBSITE:
NAME:	NAME:
STREET:	STREET:
CITY:	CITY:
ZIP:	ZIP:
PHONE:	PHONE:
EMAIL:	EMAIL:
WEBSITE:	WEBSITE:
NAME:	NAME:
STREET:	STREET:
CITY:	CITY:
ZIP:	ZIP:
PHONE:	PHONE:
EMAIL:	EMAIL:
WEBSITE:	WEBSITE:
NAME:	NAME:
STREET:	STREET:
CITY:	CITY:
ZIP:	ZIP:
PHONE:	PHONE:
EMAIL:	EMAIL:
WEBSITE:	WEBSITE:

NAME: _____	NAME: _____
STREET: _____	STREET: _____
CITY: _____	CITY: _____
ZIP: _____	ZIP: _____
PHONE: _____	PHONE: _____
EMAIL: _____	EMAIL: _____
WEBSITE: _____	WEBSITE: _____

NAME: _____	NAME: _____
STREET: _____	STREET: _____
CITY: _____	CITY: _____
ZIP: _____	ZIP: _____
PHONE: _____	PHONE: _____
EMAIL: _____	EMAIL: _____
WEBSITE: _____	WEBSITE: _____

NAME: _____	NAME: _____
STREET: _____	STREET: _____
CITY: _____	CITY: _____
ZIP: _____	ZIP: _____
PHONE: _____	PHONE: _____
EMAIL: _____	EMAIL: _____
WEBSITE: _____	WEBSITE: _____

NAME: _____	NAME: _____
STREET: _____	STREET: _____
CITY: _____	CITY: _____
ZIP: _____	ZIP: _____
PHONE: _____	PHONE: _____
EMAIL: _____	EMAIL: _____
WEBSITE: _____	WEBSITE: _____

NAME: _____	NAME: _____
STREET: _____	STREET: _____
CITY: _____	CITY: _____
ZIP: _____	ZIP: _____
PHONE: _____	PHONE: _____
EMAIL: _____	EMAIL: _____
WEBSITE: _____	WEBSITE: _____

NAME: _____	NAME: _____
STREET: _____	STREET: _____
CITY: _____	CITY: _____
ZIP: _____	ZIP: _____
PHONE: _____	PHONE: _____
EMAIL: _____	EMAIL: _____
WEBSITE: _____	WEBSITE: _____

NAME: _____   NAME: _____

STREET: _____   STREET: _____

CITY: _____   CITY: _____

ZIP: _____   ZIP: _____

PHONE: _____   PHONE: _____

EMAIL: _____   EMAIL: _____

WEBSITE: _____   WEBSITE: _____

NAME: _____   NAME: _____

STREET: _____   STREET: _____

CITY: _____   CITY: _____

ZIP: _____   ZIP: _____

PHONE: _____   PHONE: _____

EMAIL: _____   EMAIL: _____

WEBSITE: _____   WEBSITE: _____

NAME: _____   NAME: _____

STREET: _____   STREET: _____

CITY: _____   CITY: _____

ZIP: _____   ZIP: _____

PHONE: _____   PHONE: _____

EMAIL: _____   EMAIL: _____

WEBSITE: _____   WEBSITE: _____

NAME: _____   NAME: _____

STREET: _____   STREET: _____

CITY: _____   CITY: _____

ZIP: _____   ZIP: _____

PHONE: _____   PHONE: _____

EMAIL: _____   EMAIL: _____

WEBSITE: _____   WEBSITE: _____

NAME: _____   NAME: _____

STREET: _____   STREET: _____

CITY: _____   CITY: _____

ZIP: _____   ZIP: _____

PHONE: _____   PHONE: _____

EMAIL: _____   EMAIL: _____

WEBSITE: _____   WEBSITE: _____

NAME: _____   NAME: _____

STREET: _____   STREET: _____

CITY: _____   CITY: _____

ZIP: _____   ZIP: _____

PHONE: _____   PHONE: _____

EMAIL: _____   EMAIL: _____

WEBSITE: _____   WEBSITE: _____

NAME: _____

STREET: _____

CITY: _____

ZIP: _____

PHONE: _____

EMAIL: _____

WEBSITE: _____

NAME: _____

STREET: _____

CITY: _____

ZIP: _____

PHONE: _____

EMAIL: _____

WEBSITE: _____

NAME: _____

STREET: _____

CITY: _____

ZIP: _____

PHONE: _____

EMAIL: _____

WEBSITE: _____

NAME: _____

STREET: _____

CITY: _____

ZIP: _____

PHONE: _____

EMAIL: _____

WEBSITE: _____

NAME: _____

STREET: _____

CITY: _____

ZIP: _____

PHONE: _____

EMAIL: _____

WEBSITE: _____

NAME: _____

STREET: _____

CITY: _____

ZIP: _____

PHONE: _____

EMAIL: _____

WEBSITE: _____

NAME: _____

STREET: _____

CITY: _____

ZIP: _____

PHONE: _____

EMAIL: _____

WEBSITE: _____

NAME: _____

STREET: _____

CITY: _____

ZIP: _____

PHONE: _____

EMAIL: _____

WEBSITE: _____

NAME: _____

STREET: _____

CITY: _____

ZIP: _____

PHONE: _____

EMAIL: _____

WEBSITE: _____

NAME: _____

STREET: _____

CITY: _____

ZIP: _____

PHONE: _____

EMAIL: _____

WEBSITE: _____

NAME: _____

STREET: _____

CITY: _____

ZIP: _____

PHONE: _____

EMAIL: _____

WEBSITE: _____

NAME: _____

STREET: _____

CITY: _____

ZIP: _____

PHONE: _____

EMAIL: _____

WEBSITE: _____

MIKE ENEMIGO PRESENTS

THE CELL BLOCK

as seen on/in

HUFFPOST

US RAP, THE #1 SOURCE FOR US RAP, US RAP NEWS, & US RAP RADIO!

DONDIVAGL🌐BAL

KITE

Prison Legal News
Dedicated to Protecting Human Rights

GORILLA CONVICT
THE MOST POTENT VOICE OF THE STREETS.

Hood Illustrated
Dedicated To That Hip-Hop Grind

THE SACRAMENTO BEE

≡ **THIZZLER** 🔍

SACRAMENTO RAP
SACRAMENTO RAP NEWS STRAIGHT FROM THE SOURCE!!!

STRAIGHT STUNTIN

IMM
INTERNATIONAL MUSIC MAGAZINE

GETMYBUZZUP

and more!

CORRLINKS / magdepotorders@gmail.com

WE ARE ALSO THE OWNER OF THE SHYGIRL MAGAZINE BRAND

$5.95 +$2.00 s/h paperbound booklet.

If you know how to draw but want to level up, this booklet walks you through the methods any pro needs to know. But with a twist: The techniques and illustrations are done with the limited resources and supplies available to maximum-security prisoners.

Provides contact info for companies and organizations interested in buying, selling, or marketing prisoner art.

Make check or money order payable to:
Wynword Press, P.O. Box 557, Bonners Ferry, ID 83805

$5.95 +$2.00 s/h paperbound booklet.

In addition to being a spelling and grammar manual, this booklet contains practical editing methods, and instruction about logic and argument. This booklet is a desk reference for busy prisoner writers who need a quick reminder, not a textbook English course.

Provides contact info for companies and organizations interested in publishing prisoner books, short stories, and poetry.

BORN GREEDY ENTERTAINMENT

MAGAZINES

ISSUE #1
$9.99

ISSUE #2
$9.99

ISSUE #3
$9.99

ISSUE #4
$9.99

ISSUE #5
$9.99

BOOKS

$10

$6

COMING SOON

COMING SOON

+ $3.99 S&H FOR 1 MAGAZINE/BOOK
+ $6.99 S&H FOR 2 OR MORE

SEND ORDERS ALONG WITH CHECK/MONEY ORDERS TO:
BORN GREEDY ENTERTAINMENT
2 ORCHARD HILL CIRCLE SUITE D
HIGHLAND, NY 12528
WWW.BGEMAGAZINE.COM

2022 Calendar

January
S	M	T	W	T	F	S
						1
2	3	4	5	6	7	8
9	10	11	12	13	14	15
16	17	18	19	20	21	22
23	24	25	26	27	28	29
30	31					

February
S	M	T	W	T	F	S
		1	2	3	4	5
6	7	8	9	10	11	12
13	14	15	16	17	18	19
20	21	22	23	24	25	26
27	28					

March
S	M	T	W	T	F	S
		1	2	3	4	5
6	7	8	9	10	11	12
13	14	15	16	17	18	19
20	21	22	23	24	25	26
27	28	29	30	31		

April
S	M	T	W	T	F	S
					1	2
3	4	5	6	7	8	9
10	11	12	13	14	15	16
17	18	19	20	21	22	23
24	25	26	27	28	29	30

May
S	M	T	W	T	F	S
1	2	3	4	5	6	7
8	9	10	11	12	13	14
15	16	17	18	19	20	21
22	23	24	25	26	27	28
29	30	31				

June
S	M	T	W	T	F	S
			1	2	3	4
5	6	7	8	9	10	11
12	13	14	15	16	17	18
19	20	21	22	23	24	25
26	27	28	29	30		

July
S	M	T	W	T	F	S
					1	2
3	4	5	6	7	8	9
10	11	12	13	14	15	16
17	18	19	20	21	22	23
24	25	26	27	28	29	30
31						

August
S	M	T	W	T	F	S
	1	2	3	4	5	6
7	8	9	10	11	12	13
14	15	16	17	18	19	20
21	22	23	24	25	26	27
28	29	30	31			

September
S	M	T	W	T	F	S
				1	2	3
4	5	6	7	8	9	10
11	12	13	14	15	16	17
18	19	20	21	22	23	24
25	26	27	28	29	30	

October
S	M	T	W	T	F	S
						1
2	3	4	5	6	7	8
9	10	11	12	13	14	15
16	17	18	19	20	21	22
23	24	25	26	27	28	29
30	31					

November
S	M	T	W	T	F	S
		1	2	3	4	5
6	7	8	9	10	11	12
13	14	15	16	17	18	19
20	21	22	23	24	25	26
27	28	29	30			

December
S	M	T	W	T	F	S
				1	2	3
4	5	6	7	8	9	10
11	12	13	14	15	16	17
18	19	20	21	22	23	24
25	26	27	28	29	30	31

2023 Calendar

January

S	M	T	W	T	F	S
1	2	3	4	5	6	7
8	9	10	11	12	13	14
15	16	17	18	19	20	21
22	23	24	25	26	27	28
29	30	31				

February

S	M	T	W	T	F	S
			1	2	3	4
5	6	7	8	9	10	11
12	13	14	15	16	17	18
19	20	21	22	23	24	25
26	27	28				

March

S	M	T	W	T	F	S
			1	2	3	4
5	6	7	8	9	10	11
12	13	14	15	16	17	18
19	20	21	22	23	24	25
26	27	28	29	30	31	

April

S	M	T	W	T	F	S
						1
2	3	4	5	6	7	8
9	10	11	12	13	14	15
16	17	18	19	20	21	22
23	24	25	26	27	28	29
30						

May

S	M	T	W	T	F	S
	1	2	3	4	5	6
7	8	9	10	11	12	13
14	15	16	17	18	19	20
21	22	23	24	25	26	27
28	29	30	31			

June

S	M	T	W	T	F	S
				1	2	3
4	5	6	7	8	9	10
11	12	13	14	15	16	17
18	19	20	21	22	23	24
25	26	27	28	29	30	

July

S	M	T	W	T	F	S
						1
2	3	4	5	6	7	8
9	10	11	12	13	14	15
16	17	18	19	20	21	22
23	24	25	26	27	28	29
30	31					

August

S	M	T	W	T	F	S
		1	2	3	4	5
6	7	8	9	10	11	12
13	14	15	16	17	18	19
20	21	22	23	24	25	26
27	28	29	30	31		

September

S	M	T	W	T	F	S
					1	2
3	4	5	6	7	8	9
10	11	12	13	14	15	16
17	18	19	20	21	22	23
24	25	26	27	28	29	30

October

S	M	T	W	T	F	S
1	2	3	4	5	6	7
8	9	10	11	12	13	14
15	16	17	18	19	20	21
22	23	24	25	26	27	28
29	30	31				

November

S	M	T	W	T	F	S
			1	2	3	4
5	6	7	8	9	10	11
12	13	14	15	16	17	18
19	20	21	22	23	24	25
26	27	28	29	30		

December

S	M	T	W	T	F	S
					1	2
3	4	5	6	7	8	9
10	11	12	13	14	15	16
17	18	19	20	21	22	23
24	25	26	27	28	29	30
31						

ATTENTION!

PRISON RIOT RADIO

INDUSTRY REPS WANT TO HEAR YOU!

WE WILL UPLOAD YOUR FREESTYLES TO OUR
WEBSITE FREE FOR TOP INDUSTRY EXECS TO HEAR.

PICK UP THE PHONE AND BECOME A STAR!

WE WILL RECORD YOU ON THE PHONE!!!
ALL RAW FREESTYLES WILL BE RECORDED FREE
IF YOU NEED A RECORDING AND A BEAT.
THE PRICES ARE BELOW...

SONGS! SPOKEN WORD! POD CASTS AND INTERVIEWS!

LEARN THE GAME AND HOW TO
GET YOUR MONEY

$25	PER RECORDING
$150	FOR 8 RECORDINGS
$30	PER BEAT
$10	FOR COVER ART

FOR MORE INFORMATION, SEND MATERIAL
OR TO SETUP A PHONE RECORDING SESSION
EMAIL: PRISONRIOTRADIO@GMAIL.COM
OR JAYRENE@PRISONRIOTRADIO.COM

KEIKO 'O.G. KAYKO' THOMAS

presents...

PENITENTIARY RICH

Penitentiary Rich is a publishing and multimedia company that is dedicated to helping inmates worldwide share their content with the world by exclusively promoting authors and artists that are incarcerated.

At Penitentiary Rich, we give inmates all around the world the resources to showcase their talents or to be heard while striving to offer the highest royalty rates and sign on bonus options for special contracts. Our Company is founded on the knowledhe and understanding of how difficult it can be to make moves from the cell and how to overcome these challenges to still succeed. It is our duty to assist and support you on your path to succeed from behind that wall. Our main goals and Penitentiary Rich are to inspire, educate, uplift, motivate, and help you on your path to financial freedom. Please note that we do not offer packages that charge the creator up front.

Penitentiary Rich is not only a brand but a state of mind. The one who has the soul of a winner, spirit of a hustler, and motivation to become something greater is already 'Penitentiary Rich'.

Please let others know that time is money!!!

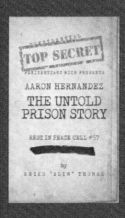

AVAILABLE NOW
penitentiaryrich.com or Amazon

Welcome to the Penitentiary Rich family!

We are accepting all complete manuscripts, short stories, artwork, poetry, and scriptwriting. (Please do not send originials.)

Penitentiary Rich LLC
PO BOX 860037
Plano, Tx 75086

 PenitentiaryRichPublishing

 @PenitentiaryRich

www.penitentiaryrich.com

INMATE LINK MAGAZINE

A NEW Magazine thats designed specifically for those incarcerated. We are an urban entertainment / penpal magazine. There is nothing like it.

We are seeking short story writers and artists to publish works. We will pay for content as well. Want to be featured in upcoming publications? SIMPLE. Send for and fill out applications and submission forms.

Our goal is to entertain as well as get you seen by as many pen pals as possible. We offer the latest celebrity gossip, entertainment, models, and more. Prisoner cover stories, do you want you story heard?

Reach out join the family and subscribe.

We accept all submissions and applicants.

All creators are WANTED let's grow together.

Send in a request for an application to the following:

Penitentiary Rich, LLC

Attention:Inmate Link Magazine

PO BOX 860037

Plano, TX 75086

PENITENTIARY RICH

MIKE ENEMIGO

Mike Enemigo is the new prison/street art sensation who has written and published several books. He is inspired by emotion: hope, pain, dreams and nightmares. He physically lives somewhere in a California prison cell where he works relentlessly creating his next piece. His mind and soul are elsewhere; seeing, studying, learning and draw-ing inspiration to tear down suppressive walls and inspire the culture by pushing artistic boundaries.

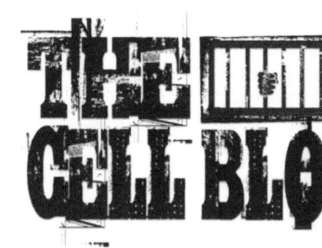

PRAISE FOR

"Besides extreme determination, what makes Mike so successful is that he understands publishing is a business. He's not just a writer/author, he's an entrepreneur. And that's taking him from the cell block to the bank!" – Wahida Clark, Publishing Mogul and 4-time New York Times Best Selling Author

"Mike Enemigo is the truth. An emerging writer who plies his trade inside the belly of the beast. A convict author of epic proportions, reaching out to the world with his pen as he fights an unjust system." – Seth Ferranti, writer/producer of *White Boy* (STARZ)

"My man Mike represents the west coast like a literary OG! I respect his grind and pen game! Look out for The Cell Block!" – Dutch

"Mike Enemigo's work is raw, authentic, and powerful. It's made all the more remarkable by the fact that Mike's books are written from inside a California prison. His work gives hope to incarcerated writers everywhere struggling to get their voices heard. " – Kevin Deutsch, Award-winning True Crime Writer, Author of *'Pill City: How Two Honor Roll Students Foiled the Feds and Built a Drug Empire.'*

"This author has a unique voice and his versatile pen is refreshing. Mike has my stamp of approval." – JaQuavis Coleman, New York Times Best Seller, Co-Author of 'The Cartel.'

"[Mike Enemigo is] proof that success is still possible after incarceration." – The Huffington Post.

"Mike has taken his negative situation [prison] and turned it into a positive by writing about his experiences and publishing over twenty books from his prison cell. A perfect example of the hustle we represent at Street Money Magazine." – Street Money Magazine.

"Mike is the only one nailing down this street lit authentically. Salute to brudda brudda." Snubbz Zilla, CA Mozzy.

"Mike Enemigo is the Big Meech of Street Lit." PaperBoy, Leader of The MOB.

"Read Mike Enemigo. He lays courses of words down like a master mason lays bricks, tight and bold. It's no wonder he's one of America's most published prisoners." George Kayer; Author, Editor, and Founder of Inmate Shopper.

"Mike Enemigo is the blueprint – a great motivation for guys like me with a lot of time. " – Big Chris, Author of East Side or Die Chronicles.

"I've read three books [by Mike Enemigo and The Cell Block]. Very well written with a true interpretation of what prison and street life is like. Certainly, going to buy more books. How to Hustle and Win: Sex, Money, Murder Edition is very interesting." -- NASA, thizzler.com

"I'm in prison in Tennessee. I'm a huge fan and receive knowledge and wisdom from your teachings. Upon receiving my order, I'll be spending more!" -- J. Johnson, Prisoner.

"Thank you for all you do to help make life easier for us prisoners. Your books and reports are money well spent!" -- F. Hendricks, CA Prisoner.

"I purchased your Resource book about a year ago and sent out for many of the resources listed. Thank you! Btw, I've gotten a lot of help!" -- J. Coffman, Coffee Creek Prisoner.

THE MIKE ENEMIGO STORY: HOW ONE PRISONER IS CHANGING THE GAME, ONE BOOK AT A TIME

By Seth Ferranti

"If a person has done even a couple of years in prison and possess even the most basic means to obtain literature, there is a 99 percent chance that they've heard about Mike Enemigo and The Cell Block," says Damaneh Abdolah, who plans to produce a podcast and documentary on Mike's book *Conspiracy Theory*. But, make no mistake about it, things were not always this way. "Getting to this point has been a very long and arduous process," says Mike about his journey to becoming America's #1 incarcerated author. "Everything I've done, I've done from inside my prison cell. No Internet, computer, phone, text, e-mail or other fancy, helpful devices. Just a few pennies for a budget, and a bunch of ink pens, paper, stamps, envelopes, coffee, adversity, failures, determination, dedication, resilience, creativity and hard work. Oh, and a lot of time. In fact, several years."

See, Mike's plan was never to write books, it was to rap. He started rapping back in 1993. Unfortunately, he got caught up in the streets, was arrested in February of 1999, and in 2002 was sentenced to Life Without the Possibility of Parole – LWOP, as it's called – for a 1998 murder. Despite this, in 2004, after he'd been incarcerated for about 5 years, he decided he was going to do what he had to do to record his vocals, even if he had to do it over the prison phone, have his songs produced in the style of mixtapes, and distribute them independently – " maybe have my folks slang 'em out the trunk, put 'em in some local stores, etc. – nothin' too fancy." And though he hoped to make a few bucks, he didn't expect to get rich and famous and become a huge rap star: "My primary objectives were to break my story out of prison, give my brain something to focus on other than my confinement, and at least make the money back I'd spent producing the records," he says.

He contacted some people he knew from the streets who were in the rap game and got the ball rolling. But though progress was made, things moved extremely slow. "Being that my resources were very limited, it took a long time to get the simplest of things done." And by the time he'd accomplish one thing, the music game would change and make what he'd just gotten done less significant. In addition to that, as the years went on, people bought music less and less, due to things like file sharing and illegal downloading, and artists had to start depending more and more on things like live performances to make money; something he obviously couldn't do from his prison cell. With that, the

270

hope of making any profit got smaller and smaller. However, "I didn't want to give up because I figured I could create my own little lane, and I'd use my music to promote it, feel me? I'd give my music away by way of downloads to promote myself, then I'd make my money off of something else that couldn't be illegally downloaded or need to be performed live: maybe I'd learn to draw really well, become a 'famous' prison artist and sell my artwork, start a T-shirt line, or maybe even ghostwrite rhymes – something like that."

He continued on, but so did the problems. In addition to the rapid game changes, coming up on a recorder (something prisoners are not allowed), then recording his vocals and smuggling them out, was a near-impossible task (though he did manage to record and get the vocals to over 100 songs to the streets). And if that wasn't enough, he began having problems with unreliable industry people and producers who didn't put his music together the way he wanted, being that he wasn't able to be present during his studio sessions. In the end, "It got to be too costly for me to do it myself, with my resources, or lack thereof, and I had to pull the plug because it was just to economically foolish to continue," he explains. So, though it was tough, Mike shut everything down; even to the point of distancing himself from most of the world. "I had to strategize and figure out what my next move was going to be." He began to research. He began to study. He began to learn, and he began to plot...

Welcome to...The Cell Block

In 2010, while in the hole, Mike decided it was time to redirect his efforts from that of the rap game to the book game. He'd been flirting with the idea for nearly two years already, so when he was given his property in the hole, he made sure to grab the *English Grammar for Dummies* book he'd bought for this very reason – so he could tighten up his grammar game. "I was always creative 'cause I'd been writin' raps. But writin' raps and writin' books is a whole different game. I knew if I was gonna do this, I needed to learn to write properly, and I had to master it," he says. "So I began studying *English Grammar for Dummies*, while also working on my first book, which was *Surviving Prison*." (This book wouldn't be published until 2018.) Eventually Mike got out of the hole, where he was able to buy a typewriter and other supplies, and he began typing the books he'd written by hand, as well as figuring out how he was going to publish them, under the new publishing company he was building, The Cell Block, which he planned to run just like a record label.

"When first trying to figure out how I was going to publish my books, I had no idea what I was gonna do," he says. "My people were taking the Directory [*The BEST Resource Directory for Prisoners*] to Kinkos, trying to have it printed up. I think it cost us around $17 to have one copy printed and bound with one of those plastic strips. And with the leading directory at the time priced at $18, there was no way we were going to be able to sell ours at a profit," he explains. "But one thing I knew for sure, I wasn't gonna quit or give up. So I kept reading everything I could find, and eventually I saw something about CreateSpace. This was a game-changer for me."

Mike launched The Cell Block officially in 2014 with five books – *The BEST Resource Directory For Prisoners*, *The Art & Power of Letter Writing for Prisoners*, *Thee Enemy of the State* and *Conspiracy Theory*, all of which he wrote; and *Loyalty & Betrayal*, a book he did with Armando Ibarra – with a promise of many more to come. And, though things did not go exactly as he hoped (what else is new, right?) in 2014, he learned a lot and built upon his team. In January 2015 he dropped four more books – *BASic Fundamentals of The Game*, by Mac B.A.$.; *Lost Angels*, a book he did with Alex Valentine; and *Money iz the Motive*, a book he did with TCB author Ca$ciou$ Green, plus the revision of his *Directory*.

He continued on, and in 2016 dropped seven books: *How to Hustle & Win; Sex, Money, Murder Edition*, and *Underworld Zilla*, with TCB author King Guru; *Money iz the Motive 2*, *MOBSTAR Money* and *Block Money*, with TCB author Ca$ciou$ Green; *The Millionaire Prisoner: Special TCB Edition*, with incarcerated author Josh Kruger; and *A Guide to Relapse Prevention For Prisoners*, with inmate Charles Hottinger. In 2017 he dropped the newest edition of *The Best Resource Directory for Prisoners*, and *Kitty Kat*, a non-nude adult entertainment resource book he did with Freebird Publishers.

In 2018 he dropped several more books: *Surviving Prison: The Secrets to Surviving the Most Treacherous and Notorious Prisons in America!*; *The Art & Power of Letter Writing for Prisoners, Deluxe Edition; and* the revised edition of *The Best Resource Directory for Prisoners*. He dropped *Pretty Girls Love Bad Boys: An Inmate's Guide to Getting Girls* and *How to Write Urban Books for Money & Fame* with TCB author King Guru. He dropped *Get Out, Get Rich: How To Get Paid Legally When You Get Out of Prison!* (also titled *Hood Millionaire: How to Hustle & Win Legally*); *The CEO Manual: How to Start Your Own Business When You Get Out of Prison!* (also titled *CEO Manual: Start a Business, Be a Boss!); and Money Manual: Underground Cash Secrets Exposed*, all with self-made hood millionaire Sav Hu$tle; and he dropped *Prison Legal Guide* with Freebird Publisher. He also completely revamped his website, thecellblock.net.

In 2019, the hustle didn't stop, or even slow down. He tapped in with Wahida Clark, the Official Queen of Street Lit and worked a distribution deal for TCB books *Underworld Zilla*; *How to Hustle & Win: Sex, Money, Murder Edition*;

and *Money iz the Motive: Special 2-in-1 Edition.* Then he dropped *The Prison Manual: The Complete Guide to Surviving the American Prison System* and *The Ladies Who Love Prisoners,* both of which he wrote; *Loyalty & Betrayal: Special Deluxe Edition*; *OJ's Life Behind Bars: The Real Story*, a book he did with incarcerated author Vernon Nelson; *Get Out, Stay Out: The Secrets To Getting Out of Prison Early, and Staying Out For Good!* with Shane Bowen; and *Raw Law For Prisoners: Your Rights And How To SUE When They Are Violated!* with TCB author King Guru. He also dropped two e-shorts: *The Mob*, with author PaperBoy; and *Angel* with incarcerated author Tre Cunningham.

As you can see, the hard work, determination, and perseverance has paid off. When asked about his drive: "I've always been a hustler. Above all else, that's what I am – a hustler. My desire's always been to get the bag [money]. Before, I put a lot of effort and drive into negative things – thuggin', basically. So, the things I was doin' to get the bag was, essentially, just getting me further into debt, you feel me? I knew I had to transform my hustle if I wanted to truly be successful, and this writing thing is a major part of that. I also knew that if I put the same drive and energy into this as I did the gimy shit I was doin', I'd win.

"So, I went from dope dealer to hope dealer. I dreamed of slangin' birds, but now I'm achieving my dreams slangin' words, you feel me? I'm shippin' boxes of books like I wanted to ship bricks. And not only am I completely legit, I'm making more money now than I ever did with my grimy endeavors.

"I found my lane – my frequency. I want to be the best, and I'm willing to do whatever it takes to ensure that happens."

Not only has Mike been making noise inside prison, the streets are taking notice, too. He's received praise from bestselling authors like JaQuavis Coleman and Kevin Deutsch, and he and/or The Cell Block have been featured in magazines like *Straight Stuntin*, *Kite*, *State V. Us*, *Street Money*, *Prison Legal News*, and others, and on websites like The Huffington Post, Gorilla Convict, Thizzler, Rap Bay, Hood Illustrated, and many more. "I promise you I'm just gettin' started," he says.

What's next? Well, more books, of course. "For years prisoners have written me, asking how to go about doing what I do in regards to publishing books, so I wrote a book on jailhouse publishing that I'ma drop sometime this year [2020]. The book contains everything I've learned over the last ten years the hard and expensive way. I have several more books in the works, including audio books, something I plan to take to the next level. I also have some things in the works with the big homie, Dutch, the OG of the street lit game. I have a bunch of projects going on right now that I'm excited about." But something he's especially proud of? "I launched a new blog on my website where me and other TCB writers provide raw, uncensored news, entertainment and resources on the topics of prison and street-culture. It's connected to all social medias, as well as book platforms like Amazon, Goodreads, etc. It's a game-changer. I'm building The Cell Block's own digital platform so we're not at the mercy of anyone else. This is going to increase our power and presence dramatically. Everyone needs to tap in to our website, thecellblock.net, and follow us on all social medias."

And when asked about the possibility of getting out of prison? "Laws are changing in my favor. In addition to that, I'm not sittin' around waitin' on somebody to just let me out. I'm taking aggressive, proactive measures to earn my freedom. I have a 5-year plan and a 10-year plan. I'd say I'll be out in about eight. It took me a minute to understand how all this works, but if one wants to get out bad enough, and is willing to do what it takes, it can be done. At least in California. And though I'm not certain, probably most everywhere else, too. The secret is to identify what it is you need to do, then do double that."

And Mike's been inspiring prisoners all over the country, as evident by the mass amounts of letters he gets, thanking him for what he's done. "I'm in prison in Tennessee. I'm a huge fan and receive knowledge and wisdom from your teachings," writes one prisoner. "Thank you for all you do to make life easier for us prisoners," writes another, from California. "I have bought every book that you've published and I encourage you to keep serving it like you're doing," says prisoner Ethan McKinney. And Jorge Cabrera from Oregon says, "I have to say, I've been incarcerated for 20-plus years, and this is the first time I've invested money into something that's profitable." Literally, the list goes on and on.

"I'm proud of all that's been accomplished," says Mike. "Not only have the years of hard work paid off for me and the TCB team, I'm proving that, despite our situation, we can still achieve success if we're willing to do what it takes.

"I'm very grateful to the prisoners who've been rockin' with us. It's because of them – their loyalty – that we've been able to get to where we're at. You can be the dopest writer in the world, but if the people don't fuck with you, you ain't ever gonna get anywhere. Fortunately, for me, the people fuck with me. They understand I'm talkin' their language, and for that, they embrace me."

And when asked what kind of advice he'd share to other prisoners? "Stay positive and motivated. When you live inside a box, you must learn to think outside of one. Be creative. Confinement can cause a man to tap into the deepest parts of the mind. Take advantage of that, be dedicated and determined, and you'll be surprised at what you can pull off. This is proof. My story is a testament that you must never give up. You're first idea is rarely your best one, and the road to success is not a straight shot.

"Now get to work and hustle hard."

Indeed.

274

DON DIVA magazine

Raw & Uncut

 ISSUE 14
 ISSUE 15
 ISSUE 19
 ISSUE 21
 ISSUE 22
 ISSUE 23
 ISSUE 24
 ISSUE 25
 ISSUE 26

 ISSUE 27
 ISSUE 28
 ISSUE 29
 ISSUE 30
 ISSUE 31
 ISSUE 32
 ISSUE 33
 ISSUE 34
 ISSUE 35

 ISSUE 36
 ISSUE 37
 ISSUE 38
 ISSUE 39
 ISSUE 40
 ISSUE 41
 ISSUE 42
 ISSUE 43
 ISSUE 44

 ISSUE 45
 ISSUE 46
 ISSUE 47
 ISSUE 48
 ISSUE 49
 ISSUE 50
 ISSUE 51
 ISSUE 52
 ISSUE 53

ORDER TODAY

Visit dondivamag.com to order with a credit card

Name: _____

Inmate #: _____ (inmate # required)

Address: _____

Apt: _____

City/State/Zip: _____

Email: _____ (status updates will only be emailed)

No subscription form necessary. If subscribing from any correctional institution and you would like an order form, order confirmation or status, please include a Self Addressed Stamped Envelope with your payment or correspondence or log on to dondivamag.com

[ ] Issue #7
[ ] Issue #8
[ ] Issue #14
[ ] Issue #15
[ ] Issue #18
[ ] Issue #19
[ ] Issue #21
[ ] Issue #22
[ ] Issue #23
[ ] Issue #24
[ ] Issue #25
[ ] Issue #26
[ ] Issue #27
[ ] Issue #28
[ ] Issue #29
[ ] Issue #31
[ ] Issue #32
[ ] Issue #33
[ ] Issue #34
[ ] Issue #37
[ ] Issue #38
[ ] Issue #39

[ ] Issue #40
[ ] Issue #41
[ ] Issue #42
[ ] Issue #43
[ ] Issue #44
[ ] Issue #45
[ ] Issue #46
[ ] Issue #48
[ ] Issue #49
[ ] Issue #50
[ ] Issue #51
[ ] Issue #52
[ ] Issue #54
[ ] Issue #55
[ ] Issue #56
[ ] Issue #57
[ ] Issue #58
[ ] Issue #59
[ ] Issue # 60
[ ] Issue # 61
[ ] Issue # 62
[ ] Issue #63

Cover Price is $7.99. Allow 12 to 16 weeks for your first issue of your subscription to arrive.
Your yearly subscription will begin with the next available issue and continue for one year. (4 issues per year). Back Issues will arrive within 10 to 14 days from the time your order reaches our offices. Address changes must be received before subscriptions are mailed or there will be a reshipping charge of $3.50 per issue. Rejected issues by any jail/prison will require a reshipment fee of $3.50 to resend to an alternate address. Don Diva is not liable for any orders not delivered to an inmate. NOT RETURNED FOR ANY REASON.

IF YOU NEED THE STATUS OF YOUR ORDER, PLEASE EMAIL:
CUSTOMERSERVICE@DONDIVAMAGAZINE.COM

ONLY ISSUES AVAILABLE FOR INMATES

11, 12, 13, 17 18, 19 22, 23, 24, 25, 26, 27, 28, 34, 44, 49, 55, 56, 59, 62, 63

We will randomly replace any issues ordered that are unavailable for inmate purchase.

Send Money Order or Institution Check ONLY (No Personal Checks) to:

Don Diva Magazine
603 W. 115th Street, #313
New York NY 10025

Don't Forget Shipping and Handling. $3.95 for 1 or 2 Back Issues. $2.00 each additional back issue.

Kim Kardashian West: Sex Symbol. Reality TV Star. Business Mogul. Prison Reform Advocate. Attorney?

By Mike Enemigo

Most of us first noticed Kim Kardashian -- now Kim Kardashian West -- when she was hanging around Paris Hilton. Who was this beautiful girl with, as she described it, a "big, fat ass"? She certainly got our attention, and if you were a prisoner, like myself, you likely had a picture of her "big, fat ass" on your wall for, well, "inspiration."

From there she "broke the Internet," before the term "break the Internet" was even a thing, when a sex tape of her and R&B singer Ray J was "leaked." This video increased Kim's popularity to "Superstar" status. And though haters began to bash Kim, saying, like Paris, she's only "famous for being famous," and she's "talentless," she proved to be a savvy businesswoman, using her platform to "put on" her entire family with one of the most popular TV shows of all time, *Keeping Up with the Kardashians*. This new, TV platform further boosted Kim's status, as well as those of her sisters', all of whom are drop-dead gorgeous, into moguls; her youngest sister, Kylie Jenner, has even become a billionaire. All of the sisters now run their own, independent empires, and the Kardashian-Jenner dynasty is one of the most famous and powerful in the world.

But despite Kim's seduction of the world and large real estate ownership in the hearts and minds of millions, it's the latest efforts that the "talentless" Kim has embarked upon that's not only impressed some of her haters (though there are still plenty of those), but has earned her a new-found respect: her work in prison reform; her defense of defenseless prisoners; and her relentless efforts to make a difference -- including taking on the enormous amount of work necessary to become a lawyer. "There's obviously time where I'm overwhelmed and stressed and feel like I have a lot on my plate," she admits. "My kids know that I'm in school just like they are. It's 20 hours a week, so it is a lot of my time."

Surprised? You shouldn't be. See, Kim has had an interest in criminal law since she was a little girl. Don't forget who her father is: Robert Kardashian; an attorney who was part of the Johnny Cochran-led "Dream Team" who won OJ Simpson an acquittal for the murders of ex-wife Nicole Brown Simpson and her friend Ron Goldman.

But Kim's father wasn't her only inspiration. During the OJ trial, when Kim was around 14, she became extremely close with Cochran protégé (who was also part of the Dream Team), attorney Shawn Holley. By the time OJ's case was over and he'd been acquitted, Kim saw Holley as a cross between a role model and a relative. "Oh my gosh," Kim remembers thinking, "I just want to be like her." And it was only two years later, when Kim was 16, that she reached out to Holley for the first time for legal assistance. Kim and Holley were out to dinner in Santa Monica when Kim, who'd learned that a friend had been arrested at Urban Outfitters for shoplifting, asked Holley if she could help in any way. To make a long story short, Kim's friend was out in just a matter of hours.

Ever since, Kim has entrusted Holley with some of her most sensitive legal matters –like contracts, protective orders, nondisclosure agreements, and the like. Over the years, Kim and Holley have maintained their close relationship; Holley is one Kim often calls for advice, or even just to vent, and she -- Holley -- is a regular at Kardashian family gatherings.

According to Holley, Kim has tracked criminal justice issues for decades, so it wasn't surprising when, in October of 2017, Kim sent her a link of a video that had gone viral about a 62-year-old prisoner named Alice Marie Johnson, who was 24 years in on a life sentence for a first-time, nonviolent drug offense. "This is so unfair," Kim texted. "Is there anything we can do about it?" Though Holley wanted to help, she wasn't sure what could be done.

After thinking about it, she came to the opinion that their only shot would be to get a Presidential pardon, but Trump was in the White House, and "he didn't seem like the person who would be for this."

After all, Jennifer Turner, human rights researcher at the American Civil Liberties Union appealed for clemency for Johnson when Obama was in office, and despite granting 1,927 petitions, he denied hers. "I was shocked," Turner says. "Her case was a slam dunk." So when President Trump was elected on his "law and order" platform, Turner "feared that might be the end of hope for her."

The odds did not look good to Holley, who doesn't do a lot of federal criminal work because "it seems so incredibly unfair, so stacked against the defense," that she finds it "too depressing." However, Kim asked for her help and she promised Kim she'd try to figure something out. And, one strength of Holley's, in addition to tenacity, is when knowing when to ask for help, so she knew she needed clemency experts on the team, ASAP. "I said to Kim, 'We have to retain some of these people.' And she said, 'How much?'" Kim wired the funds to Holley immediately, without hesitation.

Holley connected with Turner; Amy Povah, founder of the CAN-DO Foundation; and Brittany K. Barnett, cofounder of the Buried Alive Project, which, among other things, focuses on dismantling Life Without Parole (LWOP) handed down by federal drug law (Barnett has known Johnson for years). According to Turner, "If it were any other President, Kim Kardashian's advocacy might not make much of a difference"; meaning, since Trump loves celebrities, they might just have a chance.

Holley contacted Johnson and told her the good news -- "that a very famous woman" wanted to help her. "Of course, I told her I was interested," Johnson says. Afterwards, Johnson had her children Google Holley to see who her clients are, and Johnson's daughter is the one who figured out it was probably Kim Kardashian.

While the attorneys went to work, Kim reached out to Ivanka Trump, with whom she is loosely acquainted. Ivanka then put Kim in touch with her husband, Jared Kushner, who has an interest in criminal justice reform, as his father served time for tax evasion and other crimes.

The women began making hopeful progress, but by January 2018, things seemed to fizzle out a bit. The women weren't sure what to do. They didn't want to "annoy" the White House, but they needed to do something. They decided they should "whisper" in the ear of the administration, careful not to offend those who could make their cause a success.

However, in 2018, something much louder than a whisper transpired, getting the attention they needed: Kim's husband, Kanye West, got on Twitter and declared his support for Trump, which caused a social media firestorm, but also gained the attention, and favor, of the President. Within weeks the White House set a date for Kim's visit.

With Holley along, the May meeting started off with small talk about Kim's sister Khloe, who'd appeared on Trump's Celebrity Apprentice. It then went to Trump asking how Kim and Holley met. Holley wasn't excited to announce the connection being OJ Simpson, but luckily, it turned out Trump had also known OJ way back when, so no judgment was passed. Then it was time for business. Kim began explaining her case, and when it was time, like a dynamic duo tag team or sorts, Holley took over. Moments later, Trump delivered his verdict: "I think we should let her out." It was Johnson's sixty-third birthday.

Perhaps hardly unable to believe what she'd heard, Holley pushed Trump to make an announcement that day to solidify the verdict. After all, it would be a great PR move for Trump. However, the ladies wouldn't be that lucky. Kushner, though, assured them everything had went well. He even invited Kim and Holley over for dinner so they could begin to plot a path forward. "They are lovely people," says Holley. "Engaged, engaging, interested in us, interested in the world."

A week later, while Holley was in court on another matter, she received a text from Kim: "Call me. I just heard from the White House." Trump had signed the paperwork: Johnson would be free in hours.

Holley got Kim, Turner and Barnett on the phone and the team contacted Johnson. "You don't know?" Kim said. "Know what?" Johnson asked. "You're going home," Kim told her. When word began to spread about what Kim had done, as usual, the haters began to criticize her, questioning her qualification and motives. But what they don't know is, Kim's not just putting her face on the work and taking all the credit, she's intimately involved. Kim participated in routine calls between Holley and Johnson, and would even clear her very busy schedule to do so if she had to. And when momentum would seem to fizzle, she'd send delicate e-mails to Kushner. She even spent the week between Christmas and New Years of 2017 in near-constant communication with Turner and Barnett because the White House needed court documents.

"Kim is not a criminal justice reform expert," Barnett explains. "She doesn't claim to be. But you don't need to be an expert to know that it's wrong to sentence people like Alice to spend the rest of their lives in prison."

The success of the experience with Johnson really inspired and motivated Kim. She had an epiphany of sorts: she wanted to get further involved in prison reform, and not only that, she wanted to become a lawyer. When asked if she felt criminal justice reform was her "calling," she said, "I do, I really do," adding: "I don't see how I could just say no to someone that really needs help if I know that I can help them."

Kim decided to start a 4-year apprenticeship with a law firm in San Francisco where she's being mentored by attorneys Jessica Jackson and Erin Haney, who are part of #cut50, a bipartisan criminal reform initiative cofounded by Jackson and CNN commentator Van Jones. Kim plans to take the bar in 2022.

Despite not being an actual attorney just yet, it has not stopped Kim from continuing to lend her efforts and influence in advocating for prisoners. In July of 2018, right after the success of Johnson, Kim advocated for female prisoners in California to help create a program for them after jail. She also tweeted then-Governor Brown to sign a bill to increase female safety around male guards, which he did the following month.

In the first few months of 2019, Kim quietly helped fund and 90 Days of Freedom Campaign, led by a team of kick-ass women lawyers who have helped free 17 first-time nonviolent offenders. "Kim Kardashian has been instrumental in funding the legal fees for vital attorney representation, transportation for newly freed prisoners so they have a ride home to their families and reentry costs related to our clients' smooth transition back into society," says lawyer MiAngel Cody, founder of the Decarceration Collective. "She has supported 17 prisoners' release from prison and their longing decarceration."

Also, in March of 2019, Kim met with California Governor Gavin Newsom and tweeted that she supports his efforts to end the death penalty in California. Newsom signed the order, granting reprieve for more than 730 condemned prisoners for as long as he is governor.

In May 2019, Kim helped negotiate the release of Jeffrey Stringer, a low-level drug offender who'd already served 20 years. She posted, "We did it again! Had the best call w/this lovely family & my attorney @msbkb who just won the release for their loved one Jeffrey in Miami!" Two months later, in July, Kim helped with the release of Monolu Stewart at District of Columbia Correctional Treatment Facility, who'd served 22 years for a murder he committed when he was 17. Kim wrote the judge a letter and the judge reduced Stewart's sentence to time served with 5 years parole.

In January of 2020 Kim tweeted the trailer of her project *Kim Kardashian West: The Justice Project*. The tweet says, "The official trailer for my new documentary is here! Criminal justice reform is something that's so important to me, and I can wait to share these stories with all of you." In the trailer, Kim says, "There is a mass-incarceration problem in the United States," as she looked somberly into the camera. "I went into this knowing nothing, and then my heart completely opened up."

The Justice Project focuses on four prisoners -- Monolu Stewart, Dawn Jackson, Alexis Martin, and David Sheppard -- whose cases Kim and her legal team have taken on. The documentary shows Kim being visibly moved by the prisoners recounting their stories of landing behind bars. Kim talks to their families and friends, lobbies public officials, and consults with their attorneys as well as her own. "Once you hear the circumstances that led them to make those decisions, your heart would completely open up," Kim says. "I hope that this is a step to opening up people's hearts and minds. And then hopefully they can help with changing some actual laws that really do have to be changed."

When asked why she's doing all of this, Kim says, "I just felt like I wanted to be able to fight for people who have paid their dues to society." She continues: "I just felt like the system could be so different, and I wanted to fight to fix it, and if I knew more, I could do more."

How does she decide who to help? "Every case that I choose is really personal to me and a lot of times it's from a letter that I receive from someone that's inside that just really touches my heart and something that moves me," she explains. And as far as the haters, she's not worried about them: "It can be exhausting, frustrating, but I know that we can make a difference, and so all the criticism in the world will not deter me from what I want to do." She adds: "I'm very used to criticism and nothing really fazes me. I'm one of those not-human souls that can really deal with it. However, I really genuinely just stay focused on cases and people and am extremely compassionate."

Recently, Kim took the "Baby Bar," so called because it's a one-day exam in reference to her first year in law school. "I aced a test recently," she said. "There's so much behind the scenes that has never been publicized...I literally do this every single day and spend time away from my work, everything else, my family, because once you get so deep into the system...you just can't give up."

Kim explains one of the most rewarding things about all of this: "I love seeing the choices that they [the released prisoners] make in the exciting projects that they're working on outside."

As a man who's been incarcerated since February 23, 1999, sentenced to LWOP for a 1998
murder, when I was 19, I can tell you that what Kim is doing, the work she's doing, is nothing new. There are countless "faceless" advocates and organization that work tirelessly for, oftentimes pennies, but are unable to get the attention necessary to make as much progress as needed. This is where, among other things, Kim has been such a huge blessing. She has brought a new and much-needed light to these issues.

And, though I absolutely believe she is investing an enormous amount of work and money personally, rather than just being the "face" and taking credit for publicity, as some of her haters would suggest, I can assure you, we wouldn't care anyway. All we care about is the progress, the end results, and she's getting them; just ask Alice Marie Johnson, or one of the other many former prisoners whose lives she's changed. In addition, Kim has made being a prison reform advocate cool. She's going to make being an attorney cool. Obviously, we all know being an attorney is a great job to have, a great profession to be in, one where you can be very successful, but now it's going to be more than that. It's going to be cool. Nobody can bring the cool factor to something like Kim can. Girls will now not only aspire to be an IG model, reality TV star, singer or actor like most the famous people they idolize; they will now aspire to be an attorney, like Kim. Kim has given a much-needed jolt of energy to an issue that, in turn, has given a much-needed jolt of hope to many hopeless men and women, especially those who have been improperly sentenced, either due to unfair laws, or because we were sentenced based on a crime committed while lacking development, before we were able to make proper decisions, due to our youth. For this, and I think I'm qualified to speak on behalf of all of us longtime prisoners, we are grateful.

GET YOUR COPY NOW
THIS PUBLICATION CONTAINS ABSOLUTELY NO NUDITY

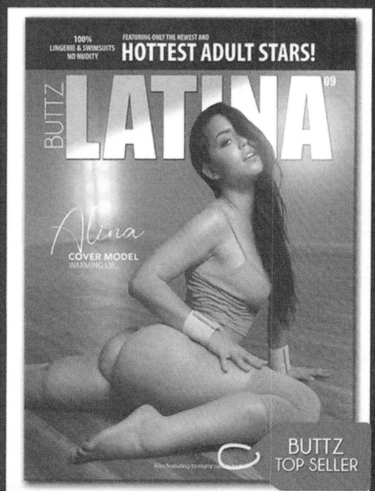

YOUR OPINION MATTERS!

The BEST Resource Directory For Prisoners begins and ends with YOU, THE PRISONER, which is why we would like to hear YOUR feedback! Please answer these questions, cut the page out and return it back to us. If you don't want to cut the page out, just write the answers on a blank sheet of paper!

Name? _____

State? _____

How old are you?

_____

What is your nationality?

_____

What kind of music do you like?

_____

What are your favorite books?

_____

How/where did you first hear about us?

_____

How many people other than you read your Directory copy?

_____

Do you want more graphics and pictures to liven up the book? If so, what?

_____

Would you like to see prison artwork?

_____

Would you like us to include prison recipes?

_____

Would you like puzzles and other games?

_____

What subjects would you like to see more of?

_____

What do you like best about our Directory?

_____

Is there anything you don't like about our Directory?

_____

Do you buy any other Directories? If so, which ones?

_____

If you buy other Directories, what do you like about them, and what don't you like?

_____

Do you want more "entertainment" articles?

_____

Anything else?

_____

Our Directory is made for YOU. Our objective is to provide you with the BEST Directory possible! Please tell us HOW you want us to do that. Your voice is HEARD! **Please send your opinion to: TCB, POB 1025, Rancho Cordova, CA 95741**

THE CELL BLOCK
PO BOX 1025
RANCHO CORDOVA, CA 95741

PHONE # 1-888-950-8253

BOOK TITLES	QTY	UNIT PRICE	S/H	TOTAL
THE BEST RESOURCE DIRECTORY FOR PRISONERS		$ 17.95	$5.00	
JAILHOUSE PUBLISHING: FOR MONEY, POWER & FAME		$ 24.99	$7.00	
THE MILLIONAIRE PRISONER PART 1		$ 16.95	$5.00	
THE MILLIONAIRE PRISONER PART 2		$ 16.95	$5.00	
THE MILLIONAIRE PRISONER PART 3 SUCCESS UNIVERSITY		$ 16.95	$5.00	
THE MILLIONAIRE PRISONER: SPECIAL 2-in-1 EDITION		$ 24.99	$7.00	
THE PRISON MANUAL		$ 24.99	$7.00	
BMF		$ 18.99	$5.00	
ART & POWER OF LETTER WRITING FOR PRISONERS DELUXE EDITION		$ 16.95	$5.00	
ART & POWER OF LETTER WRITING FOR PRISONERS		$ 9.99	$4.00	
A GUIDE TO RELAPSE PREVENTION FOR PRISONERS		$ 15.00	$5.00	
CONSPIRACY THEORY		$ 12.00	$4.00	
LOYALTY & BETRAYAL DELUXE EDITION		$ 19.99	$7.00	
LOYALTY & BETRAYAL		$ 12.00	$4.00	
MONEY IZ THE MOTIVE		$ 12.00	$4.00	
MONEY IZ THE MOTIVE 2		$ 12.00	$4.00	
MONEY IZ MOTIVE 2-IN-1 (SPECIAL EDITION)		$ 19.99	$7.00	
BASIC FUNDAMENTALS OF THE GAME		$ 12.00	$4.00	
BLOCK MONEY		$ 12.00	$4.00	
DEVILS & DEMONS PT 1		$ 15.00	$5.00	
DEVILS & DEMONS PT 2		$ 15.00	$5.00	
DEVILS & DEMONS PT 3		$ 15.00	$5.00	
DEVILS & DEMONS PT 4		$ 15.00	$5.00	
MOBSTAR MONEY		$ 12.00	$4.00	
LOST ANGELS		$ 15.00	$5.00	
THEE ENEMY OF THE STATE		$ 9.99	$4.00	
HOW TO HUSTLE & WIN: Sex, Money, Murder Edition		$ 15.00	$5.00	
GET OUT, GET RICH (Also released as Hood Millionaire)		$ 16.95	$5.00	
THE CEO MANUAL (Also released as CEO Manual)		$ 16.95	$5.00	
HOOD MILLIONAIRE: How To Hustle & Win Legally (Also released as Get Out, Get Rich)		$ 16.95	$5.00	
CEO MANUAL: Start A Business, Be A Boss (Also released as The CEO Manual)		$ 16.95	$5.00	
THE MONEY MANUAL: Underground Cash Secrets Exposed!		$ 16.95	$5.00	
HOW TO WRITE URBAN BOOKS FOR MONEY & FAME		$ 16.95	$5.00	
PRETTY GIRLS LOVE BAD BOYS: An Inmate's Guide to Getting Girls		$ 16.95	$5.00	
THE LADIES WHO LOVE PRISONERS		$ 12.00	$4.00	
RAW LAW: Your Rights, & How to SUE When They Are Violated!		$ 15.00	$5.00	
BLACK DYNASTY		$ 15.00	$5.00	
PIMPOLOGY: 7 ISMS OF THE GAME		$ 16.95	$5.00	
A.O.B.		$ 15.00	$5.00	
GET OUT, STAY OUT		$ 16.95	$5.00	
THE MOB (Urban Short)		$ 7.99	$4.00	
OJ'S LIFE BEHIND BARS		$ 15.00	$5.00	
PRISON LEGAL GUIDE		$ 24.99	$7.00	
PRISON HEALTH HANDBOOK		$ 19.99	$7.00	
KITTY KAT NON NUDE ADULT ENTERTAINMENT		$ 24.99	$7.00	
SUBTOTAL				
THANKS FOR YOUR BUSINESS TOTAL				